LAND
OF THE LIVING

LAND
OF THE LIVING

A Theology of the Last Things

By

REV. JAMES T. O'CONNOR

Foreword by
JOHN CARDINAL O'CONNOR

CATHOLIC BOOK PUBLISHING CO.
NEW YORK

NIHIL OBSTAT: Francis J. McAree, S.T.D.
    Censor Librorum
IMPRIMATUR: ✠ Patrick J. Sheridan, D.D.
    Vicar General, Archdiocese of New York

(T-174)

1 2 3 4 5 6 7 8 9 10 11 12 13 14 15

TABLE OF CONTENTS

5

6   Contents

FOREWORD

NO reader of this latest work from the hand of Monsignor James O'Connor will ever again be able to dismiss out of hand Marc Connolly's hit show of 1930, *Green Pastures*. On the contrary, readers will find new delight in the Twenty-third Psalm and will find themselves hoping that the psalm is at least potentially eschatological. "Fresh and green are the pastures where he gives me repose. Near restful waters he leads me, to revive my drooping spirit." Except that our spirits will surely not droop in heaven, it's nice to envision a future life of tranquillity beside a lovely lake in a beautiful green valley. I can do that quite enjoyably since reading Monsignor O'Connor's book, which raises fascinating possibilities of an afterlife for the world we know, and not merely for our own bodies and souls.

Such a treatment of the enduring potential of the glory of the universe comes as no surprise from an author who can readily find in Gerard Manley Hopkins' "The Wreck of the Deutschland" an illustration of the "Father of lights" (James 1:17), "leading out all the stars, calling them by name" (Isaiah 40:26), while "the morning stars sing together" (Job 38:7)!

The passage from "The Wreck of the Deutschland" is typical, mystical Hopkins and I suspect that many readers will envy Monsignor O'Connor's being so at ease with it.

> *I kiss my hand*
> *To the stars, lovely-asunder*
> *Starlight, wafting him out of it; and*
> *Glow, glory in thunder;*
> *Kiss my hand to the dappled-with-damson west;*
> *Since, tho' he is under the world's splendour and wonder,*
> *His mystery must be instressed, stressed;*
> *For I greet him the days I meet him, and bless when I*
> *understand.*

Monsignor O'Connor is equally at ease in passing from Sacred Scripture to theology, to philosophy, to literature, in at least a half-dozen languages. Yet he is never condescending. He takes the reader for granted, speaks to him pleasantly and amiably, while offering him an extraordinary study in scholarliness. As he called almost casually upon such modern American authors as Flannery O'Connor in his beautiful work on the Eucharist, *The Hidden Manna,* so he calls in this current work on English authors C.S. Lewis and Robert Browning, and Irish poet Joseph Mary Plunkett and popes and theologians and artists without affectation and always purposefully.

Throughout, Monsignor O'Connor keeps the focus on a basic question: What is, or rather, what constitutes the beatific vision, or "face-to-face union with God"? Are the anticipations of heaven of a St. Therésè of Lisieux, for all of her being a Carmelite, identical with those of her "big" St. Teresa predecessor, of Avila? How would St. John of the Cross read Monsignor O'Connor's discussion about death in Christ or the "hidden face" in terms of his own dark night of the soul and of the senses?

If memory serves me, many years ago Leon Bloy began his *The Woman Who Was Poor* with a drunk on the steps of a church raving, "This place stinks of God." It struck me then, as it strikes me now, that Bloy's sense of the pervading presence of the divine was infinitely more powerful than the "odor of sanctity" in which so many Saints were once said to have died. It is this kind of powerful imagery of the divine penetration of the universe that gives Monsignor O'Connor's work a special authenticity. In the same Bloy novel, the anguish experienced by dumb animals during the cruxifixion gives an extraordinary sense of both the intended harmony of all things in the universe and the centrality and indispensability of Christ to that harmony. As I read Monsignor O'Connor's speculation on the translation of the here-and-now universe into an enduring, if transformed, state of being, I cannot but think of that anguish of the dumb animals resurrected into the joy of the One with whose agony and death they identified. If, indeed, all things were made "through Him," and if He is the same, yesterday, today and forever, then should it be out of the question that all things will somehow endure?

Monsignor O'Connor, however, would be quick, I suspect, to reject anything like Origen's "apocatastasis." There *is* a heaven, whether it includes a glorification of the world as we know it, or not. But there *is* also a hell. And there will be a final battle and a coming of the Lord and a judgment. There is evil, there is sin. The "law" of St. Paul to the Romans is very much at war within us. One can find nothing in this book to suggest that "all things return to God" automatically, despite their own will to the contrary played out in a lifetime of choosing evil in this world.

It is hard for me not to write more, for this work is hypnotic and entrancing. Monsignor O'Connor not only quotes others with remarkable insight; he himself is becoming with each of his works remarkably quotable. It is with such quotability that he concludes his robust vision of the last things. "Let it be remembered, finally, that eating—if there be such in the life to come—will always be a reminder of Him Who feeds us with Himself. For the finest food of the new creation will be that which is our best food now."

I like that so much more than I like to hear heaven defined simply as "a state of being."

✠ John Cardinal O'Connor

PREFACE

ALTHOUGH it deals explicitly with death and the life that follows it, this book is essentially about friendship: the everlasting friendship of the Elect with God and His Christ and among one another. However, friendship is more than just the theme of the work; it is the cause of its publication.

It was a friend, Fr. Michael Morin of the Diocese of Lincoln, Nebraska, who, in a long, late-night discussion about heaven, gave me the inspiration to attempt a work on the life that God has prepared for us. The book falls far short, I know, of all we spoke of that night, but I hope he recognizes some of our ideas in it. It is another friend—whom I've known since I was a child praying before his image in my home parish dedicated to him—Augustine of Hippo, who says most of what is worthwhile in the completed work. I trust I've been faithful to his understanding of what God has revealed.

In addition to these two, other friends deserve special thanks: Patricia Brozon who has a knack for finding those many unknown but wonderful books that delight and enrich the mind; Msgr. George Kelly, a friend always ready to help and encourage and who has now celebrated his seventy-fifth birthday and years of dedication to the Church; Fr. John Quinn of the Dunwoodie faculty with his ability to remind one of—and help find—a forgotten Patristic text; Mr. Anthony Buono of Catholic Book Pub. Co. for his generous editorial assistance. I am deeply indebted to these and many others. Particular thanks is due to the Cardinal Archbishop of New York, John J. O'Connor, not just for graciously writing the Foreword, but for all that I learn from his preaching and writing and for being an overly generous "cheering section."

In one way or another, I came to know all the persons mentioned above—with the obvious exception—while living and teaching at St. Joseph's Seminary, Dunwoodie. That institution, with its great tradition, will soon celebrate the hundredth anniversary of its dedication. In gratitude for all that Dunwoodie stands for, I dedicate this book to the Seminary's patron who, in his spirit of fidelity and love for Christ and Mary, has preserved and watched over us. It is also fitting, I think, that a book on the life to come should be dedicated to him who is Patron of the Universal Church and of a happy death.

I

WHAT EYE HAS NOT SEEN, GOD HAS REVEALED BY HIS SPIRIT

For I know that my Redeemer lives,
and at the end He shall stand upon the dust;. . .
and from my flesh I shall see God.
I myself shall see Him;
my own eyes will look upon Him, and not another.
My innermost self is consumed with desire (Jb 19:25-27; *New Vulgate*).[1]

TODAY there are significant numbers who would not share afflicted Job's certitude. Many of us live in a society so empiricist that even the imagination is overloaded, gorged into saturated sleep. As a result, talk of what is as unlikely as seeing God in the flesh tends to be dismissed as chimerical or merely pious (*read* unreal) opinion. Even among Christians there are those who, like St. Thomas when Jesus spoke of His coming departure, would say, "Lord, we do not know where You are going, or the way." Others, in the midst of pain or the loss of a loved one, follow Tennyson in his questioning, unable to arrive, as he ultimately did, at an answer capable of giving assurance.

Are God and Nature then at strife,
That Nature lends such evil dreams?
So careful of the type she seems,
So careless of the single life.

"So careful of the type?" but no.
From scarped cliff and quarried stone
She cries, "A thousand types are gone;
I care for nothing, all shall go.

---

[1] The translation of the Hebrew for these verses is very difficult, yielding differences in the various versions.

"Thou makest thine appeal to me.
I bring to life, I bring to death;
The spirit does but mean the breath;
I know no more." And he, shall he,

Man, her last work, who seemed so fair,
Such splendid purpose in his eyes,
Who rolled the psalm to wintry skies,
Who built him fanes of fruitless prayer,

Who trusted God was love indeed
And love Creation's final law—
Tho Nature, red in tooth and claw
With ravin, shrieked against his creed—

Who loved, who suffered countless ills,
Who battled for the True, the Just,
Be blown about the desert dust,
Or sealed within the iron hills?[2]

Truly even many whose faith is resolute rather habitually consider the unseen that awaits us after death the inevitable but surely non-preferable alternative to the present situation. Such grudging acquiescence comes about—at least in part—because of the way that the life to come is too frequently depicted in theology and in sermons. What follows death, so it seems to many, is the enjoyment of the "Beatific Vision," an intuition that totally occupies those who have been saved. While never put so baldly, the impression is often conveyed that the future is a type of contemplative repose that absorbs all activity and renders everything else superfluous. At the end, admittedly, one will have a body, but a body that is hardly material in any usual sense of the word. Furthermore, it is to be one that cannot have sex, nor eat, nor play, nor work, nor create anything new. The only proper occupation of the risen life will be "prayer," a "heavenly liturgy," often conceived in terms equivalent to what we experience now as suitable forms for such activities.

For the somewhat better informed, there is indeed a realization that there will be a new earth as well as a new heaven. However, what either of these will be like, and whether their exis-

---

[2] Tennyson, *In Memoriam.*

tence will make any significant difference for those absorbed in worshiping God are questions rarely raised and less often acknowledged. "The more common understanding of the concept of beatific vision easily creates the impression that, at least in the Scholastic understanding and in that of the Magisterium, the joy of heaven is totally unrelated to the world."[3] Properly qualified (as its author does qualify it) there is truth in that statement. Much of the time, for many of us, the life to come appears to be an endless rainy day at the beach, which of course cannot be openly admitted because that would be to insult God.

This and similar images of what follows death are possible because the relationship between our present life and the one to come has long suffered from the type of dichotomy that has existed in the theological considerations about the relationship between "the Jesus of history and the Christ of faith." The Son of Man has been treated at times as though He and the Christ were different entities, having but the most tenuous connections. The Church has had to defend the fact that the Jesus of history is in all truth the Christ of faith, the same individual though now risen in glory. In similar fashion, there has frequently occurred a disjunctive treatment of the relationship between nature and grace, between our daily (real) life and our "spiritual" life. They are envisioned as realities that exist "side by side"; or superimposed, the one on the other, or "transformed," the one into the other. In respect to our own topic, the notion that what is to come may well be the perfected version of this present life is not infrequently considered naive. In fact, it is a fear of appearing simplistic or even materialistic in one's faith that has caused the nearly total disappearance from theological writings of many questions about the life to come that were once given extensive treatment.

There are, it must be admitted, philosophical and theological positions that militate against a realistic view of what awaits us. Some effort must be made to understand such positions, even if not everyone is called upon to master the arguments that refute them. For most of us it is enough to possess the faith while avoiding the "intricacies" that defend it. As Augustine wrote:

---

[3] Zachary Hayes, *Visions of a Future*, p. 199.

"The one who knows how to defend the truths of the faith is better educated, not more faithful. Another may not have the facility, the time or the education to defend the faith, but has nonetheless the faith itself."[4] It is an important truth. Nevertheless, we must remember that our faith operates in a context of preexisting personal, societal and theological conditions that can do much to shape—or even distort—what we believe. Augustine was well aware of this and often called the attention of his people to such factors in order to protect what had been handed down to them. For that same reason we must consider briefly those influences that currently fashion the way some people view the afterlife. And, to do that, we must review quickly the development of what is called Eschatology.

Eschatology

The word is a Greek derivative that means precisely what we have traditionally described in English as a study of the "last things." This was the tract of theology that covered what the Tradition, the Bible and Church teaching had to say about death, judgment, purgatory, the resurrection of the dead, eternal life, heaven, hell and the Beatific Vision. Given such a range of subjects, both the Greek derivative and its English counterpart are somewhat unfortunate terms. They readily give the impression that one is treating of the last chapter, that beyond which there is no more, the very end. From one perspective such indeed is the case because part of what is involved here is the end of life in the present phase of history. There is, however, much more life and history to come. Unlike the Greek and English, the Latin title for this section of theology was *de novissimis*. This can be translated "the last things," but it is not quite the same as saying *de ultimis* (the final things) and can more literally be read as "the newest things." This latter is a more "open-ended" approach to this theological tract.

The Romance languages, in their own ordinary references to this part of theology, still speak of "that which is farther on" (the French *au delà* or the Spanish *más allá*, for example). In other words, Latin and the Romance languages indicate that we are

---

[4] Augustine, *Sermon 240, 1: PL* 38, 1131.

dealing here with "what's down the road," as might be said colloquially. Now this seems a more positive way of approaching the matter than does speaking of "last" things. We will attempt to follow their example, knowing through faith that what appears final is in fact not the end nor the beginning of the end, but an endless beginning. For the moment we will speak of eschatology only for the purpose of surveying selective modern developments relevant to the Christian doctrine about the life to come.

In 1892, the Protestant scholar Johannes Weiss published a work that dealt with the preaching of Jesus concerning the Kingdom of God. In it he presented ideas about the Lord's teaching that have been influential in one form or another until our own day. In some circles his theories have even been accredited a form of dogmatic certitude. According to Weiss, Jesus came as a proclaimer of the last times, a man who preached the *imminent* coming of the Kingdom of God. The arrival of this kingdom was not a spiritual or interior mystery, but was to come about by a visible, divine intervention in human history. In short, according to Weiss, Jesus preached that the world was about to end. Alfred Loisy, in 1902, accepted the basic insights of Weiss and incorporated them into his musings on the development of Christian belief and the appearance of the Church.

A further contribution to the subject of eschatology—not unrelated to the thought of Weiss—was made in 1913 by Albert Schweitzer in his *The Quest of the Historical Jesus*. He sought to locate the preaching and teaching of Jesus within the apocalyptic atmosphere of first century Judea. By this he meant the following: because of Roman domination, the Jews lived in an oppressed society. For some of them, relief and consolation was found by interpreting human history in a setting that envisioned God and the forces allied with Him as about to overthrow the existing powers and establish a kingdom of universal well-being.[5]

---

[5] Cf. A. Feuillet, "Eschatologism" in *Sacramentum Mundi*, for a good historical survey and critique of the various positions of theologians on the eschatological teaching of Jesus. E. Schillebeeckx, *Jesus*, pp. 119ff, also studies the apocalyptic background of the teaching of Jesus. It should be noted, however, that he, like some others, does not sufficiently emphasize the connection between apocalyptic literature and the prophetic literature of Israel's prophets.

The insights of Weiss and Schweitzer were taken up by the theologians Barth, Bultmann and Dibelius, all of whom, however, attempted to reinterpret the future about which Jesus spoke. These men, in different ways and at different times (Barth in his earlier writings, Bultmann consistently), understood the futurist language of the New Testament *symbolically*. This was true especially with Bultmann who "demythologized" the language that spoke of the future by reformulating it in existentialist categories, that is, he took the Biblical references to the future and applied them to the present. He and the others reread the words of Jesus and the New Testament that spoke of what lay ahead in a linear perspective of history, and interpreted them as being either a form of a "realized eschatology" (i.e., a "future" that has already happened by becoming present in the person of Jesus) or a call here and now to repentance. In this latter case, talk about the "future" was fundamentally a preaching device intended to move the hearer to make a decision for God. With either of these approaches, the future as "something down the road" is of no real interest for its own sake; it has value only because of its power to illuminate or move one to action in the present. Of Bultmann's views on this matter, Joseph Ratzinger comments:

> Bultmann's formalistic eschatology of decision was able to exercise the fascination it did because it united deep spirituality and complete freedom from the world with a continuing acceptance of secular rationality. However, in the process it robbed faith of all content and cut off the question of the meaning of the world and its history in mid-sentence.[6]

In more recent years this tendency to "neutralize" the futurist language of the New Testament has been combated by Wolfhart Pannenberg and Jürgen Moltmann. In his *Theology of Hope*—a work flawed in various ways by the author's own reading of Christian theology and Christian theologians (especially his inadequate misunderstanding of Augustine[7])—Moltmann

---

[6] Joseph Ratzinger, *Eschatology: Death and Eternal Life*, p. 57.

[7] Cf. Moltmann, *Theology of Hope*, pp. 62-64, which simplifies Augustinian "mysticism," emphasizing its early "Platonic" elements and neglecting the lively realism of the Saint who consistently corrected the excessive "spiritualist" elements in Platonic thought by his own deepening awareness of the message of Revelation.

criticized the theologies of Barth and Bultmann. The writings of these men, said Moltmann, de-historicized the Christian message.

> In the second edition of his *Romerbrief*, Karl Barth in 1921 makes the programmatic announcement: "If Christianity be not altogether and unreservedly eschatology, there remains in it no relationship whatever to Christ." Yet what is the meaning of "eschatology" here? It is not history, moving silently and interminably onwards, that brings a crisis upon man's eschatological hopes of the future, as Albert Schweitzer said, but on the contrary it is now the *eschaton*, breaking transcendentally into history, that brings all human history to its final crisis. This, however, makes the *eschaton* into a transcendental eternity, the transcendental meaning of all ages, equally near to all the ages of history and equally far from all of them. Whether eternity was understood in transcendental terms, as in Barth . . . or whether the *eschaton* was understood in existentialist terms, as in Bultmann, . . . men became the victims of a transcendental eschatology which once again obscured rather than developed the discovery of early Christian eschatology.[8]

If we understand him correctly, what Moltmann is saying is that Barth and Bultmann abandoned a linear view of history that looked forward to God's final manifestation and replaced Christianity's references to a definite future with a notion that substituted the "transcendent" for the future. In this way, what was *above* us or around us and not what is *ahead of* us became the significant factor in eschatological thinking. Moltmann himself argued for what can be called "modified *futurist eschatology.*" By this he was attempting to say that the future, i.e., what is truly going to happen in time to come, indeed the absolute future itself, has been revealed ahead of time (*proleptically*) in the resurrection of Jesus.

The centrality that Moltmann gave to Christ's resurrection has not directly served to revitalize the theology of "what's down the road." Instead, the recognition of the paramount significance of the resurrection—as well as influences that came from Ernst Bloch and other Marxist writers—helped Moltmann and others to use his view of eschatology as a foundation for a Christian critique of the political-social order. Christian faith and hope

---

[8] Jürgen Moltmann, *Theology of Hope*, pp. 39-40.

in a real, historical future thus became the stimulus for a theology of social commitment.[9] This line of thinking produced, in turn, the so-called theologies of Politics and of Revolution, both of them popular in the 1960's and 1970's. The positive insights from those movements were subsequently incorporated into the writings of those theologians associated with the various "theologies of liberation" arising in and out of Latin America.

What has happened to Moltmann's efforts to "return" a future to Christian theology is not unprecedented. There is no doubt that futurist eschatology (i.e., one that speaks of an actual future in linear time) and apocalyptic writing have traditionally served as the basis for a social critique. This becomes clear when one considers the history and influence of the various human "Utopias." Contemporary with the prophets Malachi (c. 460 B.C.) and Joel (c. 400-358 B.C), Plato published his *Republic,* his version of the ideal society. In it he touched upon many of the concerns that would spring up over and over again in the course of Western history: the function and duties of the State; the relationship between the sexes; slavery and discrimination; the proper economic system; procreation; the arts and media vis-à-vis society; the right to information versus censorship; the relation of religion to the State, and so forth.

In 1516 Thomas More produced the work that has given its name to a literary genre, the *Utopia.* Subsequently the works of Plato and More begot their like. Some notable works of the Utopian genre were *Christianopolis* by the Lutheran Johann Andrea in 1619; *The City of the Sun* by T. Campanella, O.P. in 1623; *The New Atlantis* by Francis Bacon in 1627; *A Modern Utopia* by H. G. Wells in 1905, and later the works of George Orwell. In our own time some of the writing that falls into the category of science fiction is in fact a mutated form of Utopian composition.

As is evident from the inclusion of Orwell in the list of Utopians, not all the futurist projections were depicting an ideal society. Some were admonitory; they spoke of what should be avoided.

---

[9] Cf. Moltmann's work, *Religion, Revolution and the Future.*

The value of Utopian publications is not insignificant. They portray something that is better than present conditions (or, in the case of the admonitory opus, something that is worse) and thus encourage the reader to take a critical stance toward the present. Such a discriminating perspective should then enable us either to work for what is better or to avoid foreseen dangers and their consequences. Such Utopian writing is not—as some would dismissively claim—necessarily a form of "daydreaming." Its dangers, as well as its positive functions, were authoritatively indicated by Pope Paul VI in his letter *Octogesima Adveniens*.

> . . . we are witnessing the rebirth of what it is agreed to call "utopias." These claim to resolve the political problem of modern societies better than the ideologies. It would be dangerous to disregard this. The appeal to a utopia is often a convenient excuse for those who wish to escape from concrete tasks in order to take refuge in an imaginary world. To live in a hypothetical future is a facile alibi for rejecting immediate responsibilities. But it must clearly be recognized that this kind of criticism of existing society often provokes that forward-looking imagination both to perceive in the present the disregarded possibility hidden within it and to direct itself towards a fresh future; it thus sustains social dynamism by the confidence that it gives to the inventive powers of the human mind and heart; and, if it refuses no overture, it can also meet the Christian appeal.[10]

What is being noted by the Pope is similar to what Robert Browning voiced in his line: "Ah, but a man's reach should exceed his grasp,/Or what's a heaven for?"[11] In such a perspective, heaven exists to make us stretch and, in that exercise, achieve something that we otherwise would not have even considered attainable. In this sense indeed the work of social critique espoused by Moltmann and others, theologians and non-theologians, has been significant. It can also remind us that how one views the end of our current phase of history is obviously going to influence the present, as well as how one strives to build the future.

[10] Paul VI, *Octogesima Adveniens* (May 1971), 37; text from O'Brien and Shannon, *Renewing the Earth* (New York: Doubleday Image, 1977), p. 371.

[11] Browning, *Andrea Del Sarto*.

Given the value in Utopian paradigms, there is, neverthe-less, from a Christian viewpoint, an inherent danger in such models. The idealized conceptions of the future—whatever their admitted importance in serving as a means to evaluate present social conditions—can lead one to forget the *ultimate* future of this world and its inhabitants and concentrate all efforts toward the achievement of full happiness in the present eon. This danger comes about because of a transposition of values which makes what is intrinsically relative (earthly existence in the present age) into an absolute. The Marxist experiment is an obvious ex-ample. One need not agree with all the positions in his article to see the truth of what Karl Rahner observed:

> Christianity . . . has great significance for intramundane soci-ety and its goals. By its hope for an absolute future, Christianity defends man against the temptation of engaging in the justified intramundane efforts for the future with *such* energy that every generation is always sacrificed in favour of the next, so that the future becomes a Moloch before whom the man existing at present is butchered for the sake of some man who is never real and always still to come.[12]

Less obvious than the totalitarian aberrations, but equally
✳ dangerous, is the temptation of Western capitalism to construct an idealized earth grounded in consumerism and pleasure. The intimate link between the Marxist view and that of Capitalist consumerism has been pointed out by Pope John Paul II in his encyclical *On Human Work (Laborem Exercens).* The Pope indi-cates that the origins of the evils in both systems come from what
✳ he calls "the error of economism, that of considering human labor solely according to its economic purpose."[13]

> This fundamental error of thought can and must be called an error of materialism, in that economism directly or indirectly includes a conviction of the primacy and superiority of the ma-terial, and directly or indirectly places the spiritual and the per-sonal (man's activity, moral values and such matters) in a posi-tion of subordination to material reality. This is still not *theoretical materialism* in the full sense of the term, but it is

---

[12] Rahner, "Marxist Utopia and the Christian Future of Man," *Theological In-vestigations,* vol. 6, pp. 65-66.

[13] "Economism" is a word the Pope apparently borrowed from Heinrich Pesch, S.J.; cf. "Heinrich Pesch S.J.—A Reminder" by Rupert J. Ederer in *Social Justice Review,* July-August 1990, p. 148.

certainly *practical materialism*, a materialism judged capable of satisfying man's needs, not so much on the grounds of premises derived from materialist theory, as on the grounds of a particular way of evaluating things, and so on the grounds of a certain hierarchy of goods based on the greater immediate attractiveness of what is material.[14]

One could extend the Holy Father's critique so as to speak of a hierarchy of goods based not only on what is immediately attractive materially but also on what appears useful or opportune or pleasurable. To the extent that such a view of reality dominates life, the Christian mysteries that speak of the perduring force of original sin, the Cross and Resurrection, and of a life that perdures beyond physical death are either overlooked or have no practical consequences. It forgets the flat assertion of Jesus that heaven and earth will pass away but not His teaching. Consequently the utopian paradigms, instead of remaining important tools for the reformation and improvement of social conditions, become implicitly a model whose immediate realization is looked for and ardently sought, and one in which the value of the individual person and human liberty, as well as personal moral responsibility, are often considered to be—at least temporarily—expendable.

The dangers latent in the use of utopian models should not blind us to the fact that they are—at their best—flawed reproductions of a reality. Worth realizing, as well, is the truth that "Utopia" is not simply an idealized representation of what the future will be like. In a way, it is a memory of *what has been*, the Paradise, Eden, in which God placed the first humans. Already in the Old Testament, the idea of the original condition of things was held up as a rule by which to judge the misery of the present (cf. Jl 2:3 and Is 51:3). As we shall see, the opening chapters of Genesis continued to be employed, in Christian tradition, as a sign of what the definitive future (and thus all "Utopias") would be like. The world's beginning was viewed as anticipating the end, and in this way was a prod for human striving and change. The end, of course, is the life of unending fulfillment and peace that God has prepared for those who love Him. When Truth is known, we shall see that it is the faith in such a future that

---

[14] John Paul II, *On Human Work* (Boston: St. Paul Editions, 1981), p. 32.

gives the semblance of credibility to the Utopian models and that the human heart almost instinctively responds to when the picture of a better life is set before it. What we desire we will pursue, as long as there is the conviction that it is realizable, even if with great difficulty. Human desires are, as we know, practically unlimited, but radically they can be summarized as the reaching out for uninterrupted happiness. As such, it is eternal life itself or the longing for it that is the horizon of all other desires. This is so even when the desire for eternal life is not explicit or is denied. On the other hand, when the conviction exists that such a possibility is realizable, then one is capable of working for the future—even the immediate one—with a better will. Indeed "a cheerful confidence in things to come"[15] works greatly to enhance the present. Likewise every present effort toward something better, for a happiness longer-lasting, for a world more just, for a life more care-free, stimulates—at least implicitly—a desire for the everlastingly perfect, the desire that undergirds the others and moves to action. In short it is the City of God and what it offers that serves as the final cause for the city of man's efforts to raise itself to what is better.[16]

Hope

Desires for an everlasting future—especially when that future is only partially known—of course, are ineffective unless accompanied by hope. Now hope—in a partial and limited definition—is the conviction that something more, something better can be attained. As such, hope can be a weapon used to surmount the apparently hopeless. When all the forces of the enemy seemed destined for triumph and the weary army of Alfred of England doomed to destruction, the Mother of God appeared to the king with foreboding words, and an invitation.

---

[15] Wordsworth, *The Prelude*, bk. 1, line 67 (58).
[16] The Magisterium of the Church has explicitly taught the connection between our heavenly hopes and our hopes for a better world here and now. Cf. *Gaudium et Spes*, 39; Cong. for Doctrine of the Faith, *Instruction on Christian Freedom and Liberation*, ch. 3, part V, nos. 58-60 (Boston: St. Paul Editions), pp. 35-37.

I tell you naught for your comfort,
Yea, naught for your desire,
Save that the sky grows darker yet
And the sea rises higher.

Night shall be thrice night over you,
And heaven an iron cope.
Do you have joy without a cause,
Yea, faith without a hope?[17]

What Mary suggested to the King was hope against hope, which, of course, is really an invitation to have the virtue of hope as distinguished from *hopeful feelings.* St. Thomas Aquinas can help us understand the difference. He tells us that hope is an activity that is concerned with some future good that is difficult to accomplish but that we are capable of achieving relying on the help of God (*Summa Theol.*, IIa, IIae, q. 17, a. 1). Hope is, therefore, an "act of reliance," a placing of oneself in the hand of God with the assurance that His hold cannot slip. In such a case, our confidence is so well placed, says Thomas, that we are able to speak of a certitude (*ibid.*, q. 18, a. 4). By this he does not mean that we can be certain that we will attain eternal happiness. Apart from a special revelation to us by God such certitude is not possible. The Council of Trent teaches:

> No persons, as long as they are in this life, should be so presumptuous about the hidden mystery of divine predestination that it would be certain that they were among the number of the Elect, as if it were true that, once justified, they are no longer able to sin or, if they sin, they can be assured of repentance. For, except by special revelation, those whom God has chosen for Himself cannot be known (*DS* 1540; cf. *DS* 1565-1566).

Thus, when St. Thomas speaks about the "certitude of hope," he means that we can be certain that God will not fail us. The Lord is true to His promises. Even if we are unfaithful, He remains faithful so that we can be confident His all-powerful support is always there if we but make use of it. Presumption, of course, enters when we become convinced that, of our own ef-

---

[17] G. K. Chesterton, *The Ballad of the White Horse.*

forts, we can turn to use it only and whenever we want. Matthias
Scheeben expresses all this vividly when he writes:

> Even our natural frailty, even the evil disposition of our will
> which precedes grace, is paralyzed by grace as far as its oper-
> ation is concerned, so that it cannot detain us on the road along
> which God wishes to lead us, if only we do not barricade our-
> selves against grace. And grace possesses this unfailing, invin-
> cible, and all-conquering power and efficacy even if it does not
> actually bring about the complete transformation of the will.
> For it places in the will so strong an impulse toward good that
> the previous disposition can no longer hinder the conversion of
> the will, and endures only to the extent that the will withdraws
> from the influence of grace. But when the will is converted, the
> conversion or actual turning toward good is an effect of that
> supernatural power of grace which the will receives and per-
> mits to work in itself. In short, the antecedent will of God so
> powerfully moves us toward our end through prevenient grace,
> which is given to everyone, that all the barriers set up in its
> path, whether they come from outside or from our nature or
> even from the will itself, are virtually overcome and eliminated,
> and are no longer insuperable obstacles, if we really wish to
> consent to grace.[18]

Because it is confident reliance on the help that God offers to
obtain everlasting happiness, hope is said to *touch* God Himself;
it rests on Him. Indeed, He works within us to produce such confidence, a confidence that resides in the will, not primarily in the
feelings. For that very reason those gifted with this trust are capable of voluntary acts of hope even when the feelings counsel despair. Such inward assurance is evoked by the working of the
Spirit of God.

> The Spirit is not only light and fire, He is also strength; He is the
> spiritual unction that invigorates those who struggle on earth,
> the strength of the Most High, the Gift of the omnipotent right
> hand of the Father. If we wish to consecrate ourselves to Him,
> it is not enough that we never take our eyes off His light and
> that our heart be always open to the holy effusions of His love:
> it is necessary also that our arm receive the support of His most
> strong arm, that, like the spouse of the Canticles, we come out

---

[18] Scheeben, *The Mysteries of Christianity*, p. 710.

of the desert of our need by the luminous path of faith, unraptured by the delights of charity and supported on the arm of the Beloved, the arm of hope.[19]

It is this reliance on the strength of God that enables the Psalmist to say:

> The Lord is my light and my salvation; whom do I fear? The Lord is my life's refuge; of whom am I afraid? . . . Though an army encamp against me, my heart does not fear; though war be waged against me, even then do I trust. . . . I believe I shall enjoy the Lord's goodness in the land of the living (Ps 27).

That hope we are speaking of is a theological virtue, which is to say that it comes from, is grounded in and is directed toward God Who is Himself our future, as St. Augustine so often said. Furthermore, it is this theological hope that gives rise to what is called *human hope*, that natural confidence that the world is capable of improvement by the application of the rational powers of our race; that things can be made better and that we have the aptitude to make them so. For that reason Christian hope is not "otherworldly" in the sense that it forgets this earth, but only in the sense that it tends to draw this present world toward its maturity. This is the teaching of the Church as expressed in the Second Vatican Council.

> Constituted Lord by His resurrection, Christ, to Whom all power in heaven and earth has been given, already works in human hearts through the power of His Spirit. He not only stirs up a desire for the age to come but, by that very fact, animates those generous desires—and purifies and strengthens them— by which the human family strives to make its life more human, even subjecting the whole earth to this purpose. However, the gifts of the Spirit are diverse: while He calls some to give clear testimony to the desire for a heavenly dwelling and preserve that desire alive in the human family, He calls others to dedicate themselves to the earthly service of the human race, preparing by this ministry the material for the heavenly kingdom (*Gaudium et Spes*, 38).

---

[19] Martinez. *The Sanctifier*, p. 60.

The preservation among our race of a living desire for the heavenly dwelling, and the service to the present earth that follows upon the maintenance of such a desire, has been threatened by tendencies that continue to bear the stamp of the Bultmannian approach, at least to the extent that they prefer to stand silent or agnostic about the actual future prepared for us by God. We live in an age wherein almost any concrete definition of *what is hoped for* has disappeared. Whereas First Corinthians 2:9 ("What eye has not seen, and ear has not heard, and what has not entered the human heart, what God has prepared for those who love him") was once the standard text with which to begin a discourse on the life to come, it is now often employed to prove that it is impossible to know what lies ahead because it is beyond imagination. A fine Christian theologian once wrote:

> Men have pondered the mystery of their own death and wondered about the unknown. All the clinical information about death at our disposal only makes this mystery more profound and this wonder more haunting. The Christian view of death is not intended to supplement this clinical information with additional data about the human constitution. It is intended to give men the faith to live in courage and to die in dignity, knowing very little about the undiscovered country except that, by the grace of his cross, our Lord Jesus Christ has changed the shape of death. That is all we can know, that is all we need to know.[20]

All the lack of clarity—as well as lack of attractiveness—about the life to come cannot be traced, of course, to modern theology. It is important to note that, from early Christian times, there has been a certain tension between various ways of understanding what lies ahead of us. We may take as an example the nature of the resurrected body. Typical of what we will call a *realistic* view of this body is the theology of Irenaeus of Lyons and Tertullian.[21] The great theologian Origen, on the other hand, heavily influenced by Plato and the philosophical school associated with that name, held a decidedly *spiritualistic* view of the resurrected body. Indeed, some have thought that, for Origen, the body itself would ultimately disappear. Jean Daniélou wrote:

---

[20] Jaroslav Pelikan, *The Shape of Death*, p. 123.
[21] Cf. Chapter III: "My Flesh Will Rest in Hope," pp. 99-156, for texts from Irenaeus and Tertullian.

Being in the body is a punishment, but in Origen's view punishments are also means of recovery. Bodiliness, then, is a consequence of the Fall. One day it will come to an end and then there will be an *apocatastasis*, a return to a purely spiritual state. The resurrection is not therefore denied, but it will be only a stage on the way back to pure spirit: the glorious body is an intermediate degree between the terrestrial, animal body and the state that pure spirits are in.[22]

Not all would agree with Daniélou's understanding of what Origen taught.[23] However, even so valiant a defender of Origen as Urs von Balthasar must say, "Assuredly, Origenism is not 'Spiritualism.' The body maintains its rights; the world is not pantheistically cursed. But under the tendency to bring together human-spirit and God-Spirit into the infinite, the material pole of creation inevitably suffered devaluation."[24] Henri Crouzel, recognized expert on Origen and his theology, writes:

According to [Origen's] *Commentary on Matthew* the conception of the resurrection underlying the Sadducean objection [in Mt. 22:29-33] is that each will be raised to a life like today's. Relations with other human beings will continue as in the past, husband to wife, father to son, brother to brother. Now the Creator only makes what is useful. That is the postulate that governs Origen's reply. In the world of becoming there are generation and corruption; so there are sexual relations, procreation, relations of parents to children, brothers to brothers. But all that was then necessary will not be necessary in the world to come. To suppose with the Sadducees that there is sexual life there, is to re-establish in the new world all the realities of this one, necessarily accompanied by their woes. With an implacable logic, but one that is carried too far, Origen reaches the point of ruling out in the world to come the permanence of those relationships, including those of family, which have marked our life in this lower world. . . .[25]

---

[22] Jean Daniélou, *Origen* (New York: Sheed and Ward, Inc., 1955), p. 218. The notion of a progressive "spiritualization" may be found, if I understand him correctly, in Peter Kreeft's work *Every Thing You Ever Wanted To Know about Heaven But Never Dreamed of Asking*. Cf. pp. 55-56, 94-97.

[23] Cf., for example, *The Resurrection of the Body*, by H. Cornelis, O.P., p. 165, note 68. Henri Crouzel also holds that Origen held for resurrected existence in the body, albeit a very "spiritualized" body (*Origen*, pp. 251-252).

[24] Hans Urs von Balthasar, *Origen: Spirit and Fire*, p. 19.

[25] Henri Crouzel, *Origen*, p. 252.

As far as familial relations are concerned, the Church's faith and prayer life reject the position of the great Alexandrian doctor. This is also the case with other views of Origen on the life to come. Specifics aside, it is surely correct to say that "Origen's emphasis on the changed and adapted character of the risen body gives his eschatology, in any case, a very different tone from that of the second century apologists for the resurrection."[26]

As tendencies, the *spiritualist* and the *realist* viewpoints have persisted. As will be seen below when we discuss the particulars about the life ahead, a marked shift toward the "spiritualistic" perspective took place at the end of the twelfth or the beginning of the thirteenth century. It is possible, as some have claimed, that the ascendancy of the "spiritualist" viewpoint at that time may have come about as a reaction to the Moslem views about heaven.[27] Some part of the shift may also have been due to a reaction against the revival in the eleventh and twelfth centuries of forms of *millenarianism,* the ancient view about a thousand year reign of the Lord on the earth before the Last Judgment. These factors, together with the systematization of the doctrines of the Last Things as shaped by the genius of St. Thomas, by the publication of the Constitution *Benedictus Deus* in 1336, and by the decrees of the Councils of Florence and Trent on Purgatory, brought it about that the teaching of Catholic theologians on the realities of the life to come showed no fundamental development and aroused little controversy until our own century. They had become fixed in a moderately "spiritualist" and fundamentally static conception of what follows our death to this world.

---

[26] Brian E. Daley, "The Ripening of Salvation: Hope for Resurrection in the Early Church," *Communio,* vol. 17, no. 1 (Spring 1990), p. 36. Daley's study is a very good one, although one would have to object to his remark that Augustine's view of the last things "resembles that of Gregory [of Nyssa] in many respects" (p. 43). While correcting Origen in some respects, Gregory (as Daley recognizes) is well within the "spiritualist" lines of interpretation espoused by the Alexandrian. Augustine, as we shall see, is, in most specifics, to be reckoned among the "realists" such as Irenaeus and Tertullian.

[27] Cf., for example, McDannell and Lang, *Heaven: A History,* pp. 92, 140, 153.

Mediterranean Realism

The purpose of this book is to demonstrate that a trust in God's provision for the future is not "all we can know" or "all we need to know." We must be able to say more than that, and indeed we are able to say more. Christ Himself and many Christian theologians and writers through the centuries have said more. The assertion of a future beyond this life, accepted as a truth, cannot therefore be left as a "formal statement." By this I mean that it cannot be treated as a truth that has little, if any, real *content*, at least in the sense of concreteness. True as it is to say that what we hope for still remains veiled to an extent, we must also confess, with the author of the Letter to the Hebrews, that hope enters beyond the veil (cf. Heb 6:19). Already, in the person of Christ the Lord, that veil has been penetrated by our humanity.[28] In Him and through Him, and by His teaching, we can discern specifics beyond the veil.

Thus, in thinking about the life to come, we have to restore what might be called a "Mediterranean realism" to our theological considerations. This means that, when speaking of the life to come, we must deal again with particulars and not abstractions, and we must do so based on a love for the material creation, for life on this earth, and for the human body as works of God, and that recognizes them as predestined, by that same God, to endure everlastingly. With the exception of the Greeks and others afflicted by some aspects of Platonic speculation, such realism marks the outlook of the Mediterranean peoples, especially the Jews—above all in their apocalyptic writings—as well as of the great theologians of Western North Africa.

It is a North African who, I think, best and most systematically expresses this Mediterranean realism about the life to come. He is Augustine of Hippo Regius who, having overcome the enticements of a "spiritualizing" Manichaeism and then, through a progressive deepening of his appreciation of what was revealed in Christ, having purged himself of Platonic idealism, came to embody a balanced but vigorous understanding of creation and its vocation to an everlasting life with God. In my estimation, he is more capable than any other in helping to restore

---

[28] Cf. Aquinas, *Summa Theol.*, IIa, IIae, q. 17, a. 2, ad 1.

to theology such a realism. In this regard—but with insight far
more sure—he can assume for us the role for which Virgil and
Beatrice are justly renowned. Although his own thought on the
last things underwent development, we shall generally not attempt to trace that progress, being content to follow him in his
mature formulations on the subjects involved, especially as they
are found in his great work, *City of God.*

The Meaning of Eschatological Statements

The lack of concreteness in many theological treatises on
the life to come occurs, I believe, because, not infrequently,
theologians have accepted as axiomatic the theorem that Biblical
language about the future is *merely* symbolic, figurative, or
metaphorical. This inadequate perception is found in too much
of the writing about the *hermeneutics* or meaning of eschatological statements. On this topic, viz., the *meaning* of statements
about the future, the late German theologian Karl Rahner wrote
extensively. Since his thought is still influential in this area,[29] we
must consider briefly some of his ideas on this matter, and the
following remarks in his *Foundations of Christian Faith* are a
suitable starting point.

> In view of the mode in which eschatological statements are
> made in the Old and New Testaments, a Christian is always
> tempted to read and to interpret the eschatological statements
> of Christianity as anticipatory, eyewitness accounts of a future
> which is still outstanding. This gets him almost inevitably into
> problems and difficulties with regard to the credibility of es-
> chatological statements as he understands them, difficulties
> which objectively are quite avoidable. The Old and New Testa-
> ments as well as the doctrine of the church do say a great deal
> about the future, about what is one day going to be, about
> death, about purgatory, about heaven, about hell, about the re-
> turn of Christ, about a new heaven and a new earth, about the
> last days, and about the signs by which the coming and the re-
> turn of Christ can be recognized. Christian eschatology speaks
> about man's future by making statements about the futurity
> and the future of man in all of his dimensions.[30]

---

[29] Cf., for example, Zachary Hayes, *Visions of a Future*, pp. 90-91.
[30] Rahner, *Foundations of Christian Faith*, pp. 431-432.

The declaration that the Bible as well as the Church does in fact tell us a "great deal" about the future is a positive assertion and it is true. It may not be improper to point out, however, that our authority for affirming that truth is higher than any declaration by Karl Rahner. The Bible indicates to us that God has revealed much about this, telling His covenanted people what He has planned for them. As the Lord says through Isaiah, "At the beginning I foretell the outcome; in advance, things not yet done. I say that my plan shall stand. I accomplish my every purpose" (Is 46:10). "For the vision still has its time, presses on to fulfillment, and will not disappoint; if it delays, wait for it, it will surely come, it will not be late" (Hab 2:3). Indeed, all too frequently overlooked is the verse of Scripture that immediately follows the often quoted passage in First Corinthians 2:9. The entire passage reads:

> "What eye has not seen, and ear has not heard, and what has not entered the human heart, what God has prepared for those who love him," this God has revealed to us through the Spirit (1 Cor 2:9-10).

Now in fact, both Isaiah, whom Paul is quoting (cf. Is 64:4), and Paul himself are, in context, speaking primarily of the present blessings that God has prepared for those who love Him. Neither man is thinking only or even in the first place of the future blessings. Nevertheless, the point in both cases is true. What is naturally unknowable, because it lies completely in God's providence, has been revealed to us. This is the truth that Rahner is reaffirming by his statement. However, when it comes to specifying not *that* something is said, but *what* is said, he is less forthcoming. The Jesuit theologian lays down a principle clearly intended to avoid what he considers the "difficulties" involved in thinking of the statements of God's revelation as "anticipatory, eyewitness accounts of a future which is still outstanding." His principle states that it is necessary to distinguish between the content of a statement and the form in which it is expressed.

> In any case he [the Christian] may interpret the eschatological statements in the New Testament in the light of our hermeneutical principle, and hence may distinguish between the content of a statement and its mode of expression, between the non-

perceptual content which is really meant and its conceptual model.[31]

The distinction between content and mode of expression, between what is being said and the way that it is said, is a theological commonplace in our day. In itself such a distinction appears to be perfectly sound. It may also, however, be somewhat simplistic inasmuch as it seems to imply that it is *easy* to separate the content of a statement from the linguistic, philosophic, theological and historical factors that affect the "mode of expression" or "conceptual model" in which the content is expressed.[32] In fact, it is not easy to do so, and when it is done it is not infrequently to the detriment of the content. Proper safeguards for the employment of the distinction must be made in the treatments of fundamental theology, and an examination of them cannot detain us here. What is of concern to us is the way the distinction is used when applied to the teaching of the Bible and the Church about death and what follows it. The following are, I think, representative examples of how the distinction is utilized.

. . . it is clear that Revelation . . . does not provide us with a description of the future, a "futurology," but rather a knowledge of the future such as is able to clarify our present.[33]

---

[31] Rahner, *Foundations of Christian Faith*, p. 443. Cf., also, his article "The Hermeneutics of Eschatological Statements" (*Theological Studies*, vol. IV, pp. 323ff).

[32] The distinction has a foundation in Vatican II in number 62 of *Gaudium et Spes*, which was elaborated upon in the Declaration *Mysterium Ecclesiae* of 1973. The International Theological Commission has come to recognize the difficulties involved in a simplistic presentation of this distinction. In a document approved in October 1989, entitled "On the Interpretation of Dogmas," the Commission writes: "Nevertheless, no clear-cut separation can be made between the content and form of the statement. The symbolic system of language is not mere external apparel, but to a certain extent the incarnation of a truth. This is the case, against the background of the incarnation of the eternal Word, especially with regard to the proclamation of faith by the Church. Of its nature, that proclamation takes concrete form by way of articulation and thus as a real, symbolic expression of the content of faith contains and makes present what it designates. Therefore the images and concepts (employed in that proclamation) are not arbitrarily interchangeable" (*Origins*, vol. 20, no. 1 [May 17, 1990], p. 12). Cardinal Ratzinger has also expressed reservations about the manner in which the distinction is used by some. Cf. Bovone, Ratzinger, et al., *Mysterium Filii Dei*, pp. 11, 21-22.

[33] Jean-Hervé Nicolas in *Synthèse dogmatique*, p. 619.

From a cognitive viewpoint, hoping for a better future is quite different from knowing the reality of the present condition of the world. In a sense, hope points beyond our power of exact knowledge. Therefore the primal levels of the language of hope are characteristically the language of image, picture, and metaphor rather than the language of precise definition. If this is true of the language of human hope in general, it is even more the case with respect to religious hope in a future offered to the human race by God. If God is ultimately an incomprehensible mystery never to be comprehended by the human mind, then the final relation between humanity and that incomprehensible divine mystery remains fundamentally unknown to us in history. Revelation assures us that God does, indeed, hold such a relation open to us, and that it is in this relation that humanity will ultimately find its salvation and fulfillment. But revelation does not give any precise definition of that relation. On the other hand, it does employ a wide range of images, similes, and metaphors that point toward the fullness of being and meaning that we hope for together with the rest of humanity, a fullness that can be found only in relation to God. This language is suggestive and evocative rather than descriptive in a literal sense. It holds open to us the sense of a future, both personal and collective, that transcends any of the day-to-day futures from which we live in our every-day existence; for it is a future promised by God and can be measured by no norm but that of God's infinitely generous love.[34]

The tenor of such assertions, I think, is to hold out before us an *amorphous future,* one that can never be accurately portrayed. In some cases, as in the last quotation above, the future is practically identified with God Himself and thus becomes as unknowable as He is. Even outstanding theologians, in an effort to avoid a naive realism, make statements that tend toward a less than realistic view of the life to come.

The Assumption [of Mary] cannot mean, of course, that some bones and corpuscles of blood are forever preserved somewhere. It means something much more important and profound. To wit: that what continues to exist is not just a part of a human being—the part which we call the soul and which is separated out from the whole—while so much else is annihilated. It means rather that God knows and loves the entire person which we now are. The immortal is that which is now growing and developing in our present life. The immortal is that

---

[34] Zachary Hayes, *Visions of a Future,* pp. 93-94.

which is developing in this body of ours wherein we hope and rejoice, feel sadness, and move forward through time; that which is developing *now* in our present life, among and by means of the things of this world. It is this 'whole man,' as he has existed and lived and suffered in this world, that will one day be transformed by God in eternity and be eternal in God himself.[35]

The difficulty with such a statement is not found in what is affirmed, but in what is denied. Is the resurrection of the body— in addition to all the true and wonderful things said about it—not also to include "bones and corpuscles of blood"? The idea that such graphic descriptions are either false or idle speculation is not new. As we have seen, Origen long ago tended to a very radical spiritualizing notion of the life to come. Nor has he ever been without disciples in this matter. In the sixteenth century, Cardinal Cajetan, commenting on St. Thomas, concluded:

Therefore, joining philosophy to theology it must be said that it seems that blood pertains to the necessity of the human body according to animal life because it is the ultimate food: it does not pertain to the necessity of the spiritual human body such as the Body of Christ was in the Resurrection. Thus, when it is said [by Aquinas] that "All that died rose, if it is a perfect resurrection" must be understood about all that is necessary for the human body in its spiritual state or life and not about all that is necessary for the human body in its animal state or life.[36]

Aquinas' own principle is comprehensive: "Whatever pertains to the nature of the human body was complete in the Body of the Risen Christ."[37] What Cajetan was doing, as he himself recognized, was qualifying St. Thomas, and, by doing so, leaving

---

[35] Joseph Ratzinger in "The Assumption of Mary," in *Dogma and Preaching,* pp. 116-117.

[36] Cajetan, Commentary on III, q. 54, a. 3 in Leonine edition of the *Opera Omnia* of Aquinas, vol. 11, p. 512. The Latin reads: *Iugendo ergo philosophiam theologiae, dicendum videtur quod sanguis pertinet ad necessitatem humani corporis secundum vitam animalem, quia est ultimum alimentum: et non pertinet ad necessitatem humani corporis spiritualis, quale fuit corpus Christi in resurrectione. Et secundum hoc, cum dicitur,* totum quod per mortem cecidit, resurrexit, si perfecta est resurrectio, *intelligendum est de toto quod est de necessitate corporis humani in statu seu vita spirituali: et non de toto necessario ad corpus humanum in statu seu vita animali.*

[37] *Summa Theol.,* III, q. 54, a. 3 c.

open the possibility that the resurrected body did not have blood and such like constituents because those would not be needed in the resurrected life.

A danger in all such spiritualizing tendencies—proper as they are in their efforts to avoid a grossly materialistic view of the life ahead of us—is that they deprive the imagination and the conceptualizing intellect of any object upon which to focus and nourish themselves. This deprivation ultimately influences the will. Since the intellect has nothing concrete to offer the will as a motive for action, the volitional faculty will lack motivation sufficient to move it toward the future. As a result, it will be directed even more naturally toward what is immediate and tangible. Likewise, the virtue of hope is attenuated since it is given as a goal something that can only be indistinctly apprehended. This impoverishment of the imagination, intellect and ultimately of the will itself becomes, in its own way, a subtle form of Gnosticism. It calls into doubt the value of the specific, the concrete and the material, thus running counter to the Biblical tradition that depicts the future in attractive material as well as spiritual images.

Principles for a Proper Understanding of Church Teaching

To counteract a lack of concreteness about the realities that follow upon death and thereby to provide sustenance for imagination, intellect and will, we must attempt to be more specific than is currently the practice in dealing with what lies before us. To achieve this aim, some relevant truths need to be recalled.

1. We are dealing here with truths of faith, verities therefore that involve mystery. Consequently, a certain lack of clarity should be expected. Such obscurity *will be due not to the lack of concreteness in the truths themselves but to the weakness of our intellects.* In this regard, St. Thomas teaches a most important point when he notes: "God is the most knowable reality."

Since anything is knowable to the extent that it actually is, then God, Who is pure actuality with no mixture of potentiality, is supremely knowable in Himself.[38] However nothing prevents that which is more certain in itself from being less certain as far as we are concerned because of the weakness of our intellect, which reacts to the most evident things of nature as an owl reacts to the sunlight. Therefore, the doubt that occurs to some people in respect to the articles of faith happens not because of any lack of certitude in the reality itself but because of the weakness of the human intellect. Nevertheless, the minimum knowledge that is able to be had about the highest things is preferable to the most certain knowledge that can be had about unimportant things.[39]

The lack of clarity we experience in our present knowledge of God is due then to the infirmity of our own intellects, not to any lack of definition on His part, to any "vagueness" in Him. Likewise with the other mysteries of our faith. It is not because their truth lacks concreteness or definition but because we are limited in our abilities to perceive the truth.

Something more, however, needs to be said of this present lack of clarity in apprehending the truths of faith. It is this: Our human intellects, weak as they are, do not find all the revealed realities equally difficult to understand. Just as there is what the Second Vatican Council calls a "hierarchy of truths" in the sense that some are more important than others both in themselves and as far as concerns us, so too there may be said to be a hierarchy of truths in respect to their intelligibility. This should be evident from the fact that there are some things revealed that can be naturally known (e.g., the very existence of God); others totally surpass natural ability (e.g., the Trinity). Then there is an "in-between" category that applies to truths that are not as shrouded in darkness as the mystery of the Trinity, but not as evident as those that can also be known by the proper use of human reason. In this middle area, there are some truths that we are able to correlate more readily with what we naturally know through experience and intellection. As such they are more intelligible to us.

---

[38] *Summa Theol.*, I, q. 12, a. 1 c.
[39] *Summa Theol.*, I, q. 1, a. 5, ad 1.

2. In the matter at hand, part of what will constitute the life to come is more readily knowable than other revealed truths. This greater ability to be understood comes, as we have said, from the fact that we can make better correlation with what we do already know. To clarify what all this means, we must look briefly at the theme of *knowledge by analogy.*

To use an analogy is to make a comparison. The purpose of the comparison is either to teach what is new or to deepen our understanding of something we already know. The Lord Himself was the Master at doing this, as His many comparisons and parables indicate. Frequently He used nature to throw light on something not easily grasped in itself. At times He used one revealed truth to illumine another (cf., for example, his resort to Exodus 3:15 to help the Sadducees understand the resurrection or His employment of the Genesis account of the creation of man and woman to support what He was teaching about divorce). This latter use of comparison came to be called the *analogy of faith,* the utilization of one revealed truth to shed light on another or even to lead to a new insight. Since He used such comparisons to elucidate the mysteries of the Kingdom, the Church has followed His example and employs the same technique. This form of comparison, the analogy of faith, was specifically recommended to exegetes and theologians by the Second Vatican Council when it taught:

> Since Sacred Scripture should be read and interpreted in the same Spirit by Whom it was written, then in order to search out correctly the meaning of the scriptural texts one must no less diligently attend to the content and unity of the whole of Scripture, taking into account the living Tradition of the entire Church and the analogy of faith (*Dei Verbum,* 12).

The Council itself gave an example of this analogy of faith when, in its *Constitution on the Church,* it drew a comparison between the union of the divine and human natures in Christ and the union of spiritual and earthly elements in the Church.

> ... the earthly Church and the Church endowed with heavenly goods must not be considered to be two realities; rather they form one complex reality that possesses a divine and human element. Therefore, by no weak analogy is the Church com-

pared to the mystery of the Incarnate Word. For as the nature assumed by the divine Word, inseparably united to Him, serves as a living organ of salvation, so, in a similar way, does the social fabric of the Church serve the Spirit of Christ (*Lumen Gentium*, 8).

Now there are times when the comparison or analogy is rooted in some kind of intrinsic nexus between the things being compared. This connection may even be casual in the sense that one of the realities is actually produced or generated by the other and carries in itself the stamp or likeness of its cause.

 All these forms of comparison must be employed when we reflect upon death and what comes after it. In some cases the simile will be between what we do or can know naturally and what we do not or cannot know. Some examples may help at this point. There is, for instance, surely a great element of natural (as well as supernatural) mystery about death. Nonetheless, we do have some experience of the thing we know as death and are able to use what we know to deduce other probable information. We have some idea of transformative change; we witness such changes regularly. Thus, we can make the comparison between such alteration and what will occur to us after death. St. Paul does this to great effect in First Corinthians 15. In other cases, when we wish to shed light on the obscurities of the life to come, we must use the analogy of faith, allowing one doctrine to help us understand another.

Before looking briefly at those revealed truths to which, by the analogy of faith, we can have recourse in order to shed light on death and what follows it, let us return to something we said earlier about not all that is revealed being equally obscure. If we accept that as being the case, then we may also say that the analogies used will also be more or less illustrative. When we use analogy to help us understand God, for example, we are reminded forcibly by the great theologians of the Church that the comparison will limp badly. God is more *unlike* what we say about Him than He is like the comparison we make. Thus, His goodness and justice and mercy and love are more unlike these qualities as we know them than they are like them. This is so because He infinitely surpasses all things natural and thus all our comparisons. We know better what He is not than what He is.

This weakness in our use of analogy when applied to the mystery of God is, unfortunately, often taken as a universal law and applied equally to all the revealed mysteries. If this were valid, our use of analogy would limp in every case and the mystery we sought to comprehend would, like God, be more unlike than like our comparison. This, however, is not true—at least in respect to the mysteries that are not God Himself. There is, as said above, a *hierarchy of intelligibility* among the revealed truths. Some are, as far as we are concerned, more understandable than others because they are more *like* things we already know. Since this is so, we must use analogy analogously, i.e., we must realize that we are not applying it in the same way in all cases. In some cases the comparison offered by analogy will be of greater service than in others. Realizing this will help us avoid hyperbolic statements that are in fact not accurate. For example: to speak or write of "the complete 'otherness' of the body after the resurrection"[40] is to exaggerate and open the way to misunderstanding.

When I was a student in the seminary, a fine teacher was accustomed to saying frequently that the life to come would be *totaliter aliter* (completely different) from what we expect. I realize now that this was hyperbole. The relationship between this life and the life to come is indeed like the relationship between the Jesus of history and the Christ of faith when this latter term is properly understood. In both cases one is speaking of the *continuation* of what began here, an extension in perfected and intensified conditions. There truly will be great differences between this life and the next, but not the ones we often think. In the life to come there will be immortality, freedom from sickness and concupiscence and many other such things. These are real differences, dissimilarities between the now and the then. Nonetheless, there are other things that will be more like than unlike, at least if we are to believe the Scriptures and the teaching of the Church. What is like and what unlike we hope to be able to indicate as we go along.

---

[40] Christoph Schonborn, "Resurrection of the Flesh," *Communio*, vol. 17, no. 1 (Spring 1990), p. 20. It is the phrase, not the theology, that is the problem here. Schonborn is in fact presenting in his article a strong defense of the resurrection of the flesh.

Before continuing, however, we must at least mention those revealed mysteries that can help us, by way of the analogy, in our investigations of what lies before us. Some of the more important ones are:

(1) *The value of creation.* Under the impulse of the Spirit, the author of Genesis tells us that the Lord God was pleased with the work of His hands. He passed on it the judgment of goodness.

> God is the cause of things through His intellect and will, just as an artist is of his artistic works. An artist works through the idea conceived in his intellect and through the love for something as found in his will. So also God the Father has effected creation through His Idea, which is the Son, and through His love, which is the Holy Spirit.[41]

In this way, and like any artist, the Architect finds Himself reflected, however dimly, in what He crafts. The very goodness of the creation comes about because it mirrors its Creator. Typical of His generosity, God has made a gift of His own goodness so that it belongs intrinsically to the created effects. Moreover, the Goodness to be reflected is so vast—indeed it is infinite—that no work could suffice to express it. Thus God has made many creatures and made them diverse so that what is lacking in one may be complemented by another. How many and how various the works of this Artist are, we humans do not yet comprehend. God's "imagination" is astoundingly fertile. Just think of what varieties one can call to mind between the amoeba and the elephant, the hummingbird and the vulture, the clam and the whale. If we dwell long enough on them, we realize that some part of the whole is breathtaking in beauty, some is commonplace, some is grotesque, some terrifying. What kind of a mind could dream it all up? An intellect madder than Van Gogh's was thought to be, more bizarre than Blake's, an eye for color as different as Gauguin's, yet a perspective more idyllic than Monet's, more ordered than Mozart's.

God's imagination is like that of some children before the advent of television, wildly and endlessly constructive. Its conceptions move from the fascinating to the frightening, from a

---

[41] Aquinas, *Summa Theol.*, I, q. 45, a. 6 c.

sunset over the Palisades to a praying mantis devouring her mate. We cannot understand, only recognize and worship. And that imagination does not weary with time as does ours. Now imagination is not the proper word, of course. God has no imagination as such, but the riches of His being are so great that our imaginations—from elegiac delight to nightmare—could not begin to conjure up all that flows from His creative decision. Even the visible universe is so vast that we have not properly begun to fathom either its beauty or its variety. Indeed there seems to be so much of it that one could call Him wanton in the way He disperses being.

God, moreover, conserves what He has made and has preserved it through billions of years, even while varying it through numerous permutations. What is more: there are indications in what He has revealed of Himself that His intention is to preserve in some fashion and everlastingly *all* that He has made. As we shall see, this is what the Biblical doctrine of the new heavens and new earth mean, even when taken in a minimal sense. This determination to preserve makes sense. It is in harmony with what we know of His own inner consistency, and, above all, with the fact that He Himself has become part of what He has created.

(2) *The Incarnation.* God's own Idea, in which He has known the variety of ways in which He could image Himself in what He has produced, has become part of the material and spiritual creation. The Word became flesh and has lived among us. For the Christian it is a matter of faith that, having taken to Himself human nature composed of matter and spirit, God will never again lay them aside, shirking them off, as it were, much as some creatures leave aside a chrysalis. The wholly spiritual, transcendent God has loved the creation in such a way as to wed it everlastingly to Himself. This fact is of unique importance for the future that awaits all creation beyond the dissolution suffered by everything that has material components. As Pope John Paul II has written:

> The incarnation of God the Son signifies the taking up into unity with God not only of human nature, but in this human nature, in a sense, of everything that is "flesh": the whole of humanity, the entire visible and material world. The incarnation, then, also has a cosmic significance, a cosmic dimension. The

"firstborn of all creation," becoming incarnate in the individual humanity of Christ, unites himself in some way with the entire reality of man, which is also "flesh"—and in this reality with all "flesh," with the whole of creation.[42]

In this perspective, Jesus of Nazareth becomes the key that opens for us the hidden ways of the future not only of the human race but of the universe as well. He is also, as Teilhard de Chardin wrote, the goal and purpose of universal evolution.

The Incarnation is a renewal and a restoration of all the forces and powers of the universe; Christ is the instrument, the centre, the end of all animate and material Creation; by Him all things are created, sanctified, made alive. This is the constant and customary teaching of St. John and St. Paul (the most 'cosmic' of the sacred writers), the teaching conveyed by the most solemn sentences of the Liturgy . . . but which we repeat, and which future generations will repeat to the end, though they cannot master or measure its mysterious and profound significance: it is bound up with the comprehension of the Universe. . . .

Since the time when Jesus was born, when He finished growing and died and rose again, *everything has continued to move because Christ has not yet completed His own forming.* He has not yet gathered in to Himself the last folds of the Garment of flesh and love which His disciples are making for Him. *The mystical Christ has not yet attained His full growth.* In the pursuance of this engendering is situated the ultimate spring of all created activity. . . . Christ is the Fulfillment even of the natural evolution of beings.[43]

Even should the thesis of evolution be inadequate or inaccurate, what Teilhard says is true in the sense of the central role of the Incarnate God in the past, present and future of this universe and of our race (among others?) in it.

(3) *The Resurrection of Christ.* Having come in the flesh of our race, God also underwent the diminishing experience we call death. This death of Life must also serve us in understanding the nature of death and its power. However, Life conquered death in the very flesh and human soul that He has taken as His own in

---

[42] John Paul II, *Dominum et Vivificantem*, no. 50 (Boston: St. Paul Editions).
[43] Teilhard de Chardin, "The End of the Species," *The Future of Man*, pp. 304-305.

order to die. In doing this He has begun, for flesh and soul, for the matter of which flesh is composed, and for the universal elements that produced, nurtured, sustained and became part of that flesh, a new and definitive form of existence. He has, moreover, associated with Himself in this new material life the Woman who is His human mother. In them both, as the new Adam and new Eve, the future Paradise has already begun to exist. What we know of them in their resurrected state, through Revelation and the teaching of the Church, must also be allowed to shape our understanding of the future.

(4) *The Eucharist.* Not only has Christ risen in the flesh, thereby giving us some idea of the future that awaits our flesh, but He has also, through the Sacrament of the Eucharist, made that flesh present to us in such a way that it becomes our food, and assimilates our mortal flesh to His resurrected flesh. The Mystery of Faith has also long anticipated what modern physics points out to us with ever greater detail, even while deepening the natural mystery, viz., the capabilities inherent in matter. In the Eucharist God changes the material reality of bread and wine into the material reality of the flesh and blood of Christ. He does this even while leaving intact the appearances of the matter of the bread and wine. The pliability of matter in the hands of the Potter has always been evident to those who believe in the doctrine of the Eucharist.

However, modern physics—now far advanced from a simplistic view of matter that saw it composed of readily definable "particles" or atoms—has also become progressively aware of the potentialities of matter. We can now envision its convertibility with energy, its "invisibility," its capacity to manifest properties previously unsuspected. Such advances in the physical sciences are themselves not irrelevant to the Christian belief that speaks of resurrected matter, a material human body with special properties, and a material universe restored and even more perfectly material.

It is not just in giving us indications of matter's capacities to be transformed that the Eucharist scatters some of our darkness in respect to the life to come. As sacrament and sacrifice, the Eucharist celebrates death because of humanity's triumph over

death. It is also the point of contact between this age and the
world to come since, beneath the appearances of bread and wine,
the beginning of the future world, the resurrected Christ, touches
this present age as well as touching those who receive Him. Finally, as Viaticum, it is the Eucharist that assures safe passage
through the clouds of death to that world which needs no sun because the Lamb Himself is its light.

(5) *The Biblical imagery.* In a particular manner, we must
pay more docile attention to what the Bible, in its imagery, tells
us of death and what follows it. By *docile* attention we want to indicate that one must not feel at liberty simply to recognize a Biblical statement for what it is (e.g., a comparison, or symbol or
image) and then dismiss it as if it were *no more than* imagery.
We must be teachable enough to recognize that even images convey to us something real. As St. Paul says: "At present I know
partially" (1 Cor 13:12). The Biblical imagery about the life to
come is not that type of analogy according to which the reality is
totally different from the comparison. Vatican II enunciates this
truth when it says the growth of the Body of Christ here on earth
"is already able to offer some foreshadowing of the new age"
(*Gaudium et Spes*, 39). In like fashion, the Congregation for the
Doctrine of the Faith has noted:

> Moreover, when dealing with the human condition after death,
> in a particular manner there must be avoided representations,
> that rest solely on the invention or decision of the mind; im-
> moderation in this regard is often the cause of difficulties. . . .
> However, reverence must be paid to the images whose use is
> found in Scripture. It is necessary to perceive their profound
> meaning and to remove every danger of weakening them too
> much because this often renders meaningless the realities that
> are indicated by the images.[44]

Thus, if we are to restore definition and concreteness to our
hope we must not hesitate to deal honestly with the images and
symbols used in the Bible, even to "reverence" them as the Congregation for the Faith suggests.

(6) *The arguments from fittingness and beauty.* Theology
has long employed what is called the argument *ex convenientia,*

---

[44] *Letter to the Heads of the Episcopal Conferences on Certain Questions of
Eschatology*, SCDF, May 17, 1979: *AAS*, 71, p. 942.

which is a consideration of the suitability of what God has done or how He has acted in a particular case. This argument from fittingness has been most fruitfully employed when used properly. When it is applied in conjunction with the mysteries already mentioned, and with what we can garner from natural analogy and comparison, the consideration of "what is fitting" can guide us well in any discussion of what our future may be like. Moreover, along with Augustine, the argument from fittingness can be made more comprehensive. North Africa's great teacher varied the argument somewhat by adding the argument from beauty. Speaking of the life to come he coined a dictum that can serve as a key to many of the reflections that follow. "Take away corruption," says Augustine, "and add what you want."[45] This principle—for principle it is with Augustine—may be said to be Augustine's own *via pulchritudinis,* the theological argument from beauty. The phrase *via pulchritudinis* was used by Paul VI in his talk to the Fourteenth Marian Congress in May of 1975.[46] Speaking then of ways to renew Marian devotion in the Church, the Pope said that one way was that of scholarly research and writing; another was the *via pulchritudinis,* the way of beauty, that is, by considering and being attracted to the beauty of Mary.

For Augustine, God Himself was the Beauty—so ancient, yet ever new—Who created all beautiful things in the universe and intended to preserve them because they are beautiful. It is this intention to preserve things *because of their loveliness* that sets Augustine's theology of everlasting life so markedly apart from those Fathers of the Church and theologians who, like Origen and Cajetan, employ a principle of utility or functionality in their consideration of what will remain in the future.

The Danger of Rash Speculation

The question of rash speculation must be faced before closing this introductory chapter. It must be confronted if for no other reason than the fact that outstanding theologians have

---

[45] Augustine, *Sermon 242 (147),* 4: *PL* 38, 1140.
[46] Paul VI, "Talk to the Fourteenth Marian Congress" in *TPS,* vol. 20, nos. 3 and 4, pp. 199-203.

judged as rash much of the speculation of the kind we are about to undertake. Henri de Lubac, one of the truly great thinkers of our age, writes about those who have too realistic a view of the state of eternal life:

> They forget about St. Augustine's efforts to drive home to the worldly mind the fact that its longing to eat and drink is the longing of a sick man, which holds it back from the joy which is God, and his warning against rash curiosity where the state of the resurrected body is concerned.[47]

As evidence for Augustine's position, de Lubac cites Augustine's Sermon 255, 5 and 7 (not, as a mistaken footnote indicates, Sermon 253, 5, 7) and the *City of God*, book 22, ch. 21. Sermon 255 we will return to later.[48] As for Augustine's warning against "rash curiosity," de Lubac quotes the text from the *City of God* thus: "I fear that any word about what and how great the spiritual grace of that body might be could be rash, since it has not come within our experience. . . ."[49] De Lubac, however, does not cite the sentence that immediately follows those words. Augustine continues: "Nevertheless, because we cannot keep silent about the joy of our hope, because of the praise due to God and because it was from the depths of a heart burning with love that it was said, 'Lord, I love the beauty of Your house,' we will conjecture, with His help and to the best of our ability, from the gifts that He abundantly gives both good and bad in this miserable life, how great will be the blessings in the life to come, which, of course, not having experienced, we are not able to speak of worthily."[50]

---

[47] Henri de Lubac, *Splendor of the Church*, pp. 71-72.

[48] Cf. below, Chapter VI: "The City of Compact Unity," pp. 287-288.

[49] " . . . *quae sit autem, et quam magna spiritualis corporis gratia, quoniam non dum venit in experimentum, vereor ne temerarium sit omne quod de illa profertur eloquium.* . . ."

[50] Augustine, *City of God*, bk. 22, ch. 21: CSEL 40, 2, pp. 634-635. The *CSEL* text does not differ from the *PL* cited by De Lubac. The Latin reads: "*Verum tamen quia spei nostrae gaudium propter Dei laudem non est tacendum de intimis ardentis sancti amoris medullis dictum est 'Domine, dilexi decorem domus tuae,' de donis eius, quae in hac aerumnosissima vita bonis malisque largitur, ipse adiuvante coniciamus, ut possumus, quantum sit illud, quod nondum experti utique digne eloqui non valemus.*"

Thus, Augustine recognizes the dangers in speculation about the life to come. He also, however, recognizes its utility, and notes as well that, by the use of analogy (comparing the "gifts that He abundantly gives . . . in this miserable life" with what is to come), one may be able to speak of the subject, even if not as well as one should. What he says in another context is also pertinent.

> When questions are raised about these things and each one, as ability permits, conjectures an answer, then one's abilities are not uselessly employed as long as the discussion is balanced and one avoids the error of thinking that what is not known is known.[51]

Nor does Augustine fail to mention the reason why such speculation is valuable. Its purpose, he says, is to stimulate hope and especially *desire* for what lies before us.

> The entire life of a good Christian is holy desire. What you desire you do not yet see: but by desiring you are made capacious so that when it comes you may be filled up with what you see. By delaying [the fulfillment of our desires] God enlarges our desire; enlarging our desire He enlarges our soul; enlarging our soul He enlarges our capacity. . . . Such then is our life, that we may be exercised though desiring.[52]

> Let [the Christian's] footsteps not hesitate, nor eyes blink, but rather proceed with the tendency that comes of faith in order to arrive at that which eye has not yet seen, nor ear heard, nor the human heart conceived. It is believed before it is seen so that the one who has believed will not be confused when it comes. Therefore, let the Christian go forward, walking in hope, hoping for what is not yet possessed, believing what is not yet seen, loving what is not yet embraced. Indeed the exercise of our soul in faith, hope and charity makes one suitable to grasp what is to come.[53]

By such exercise, our speculations concerning the future that God has prepared for our race, founded on the teaching of Jesus and His Church, can become a "gift that consecrates the joy"[54] in the sense that they make possible our present joys by

---

[51] Augustine, *Enchiridion*, XV (59): CCSL 46, p. 81.
[52] Augustine, *In Epistolam Primam Ioannis*, Tract. 4: PL 35, 2008-2009.
[53] Augustine, *Sermon 4*, 1: CCSL 41, p. 20.
[54] Wordsworth, *The Prelude*, bk. I, line 40 (32).

serving as a permanent backdrop against which those joys are
played out, and even enriching their meaning. Indeed if we are
capable of recognizing joy here and partaking of it as a token of
things to come, then in a certain sense we will never be totally
"surprised by joy," but, recognizing it, we too, "impatient as the
Wind," will turn "to share the transport."[55] That turning will be
toward our brothers and sisters, but above all to the One Whose
hands hold our future. To Him in prayer:

> In our transient life, O Lord, we sense your quiet eternity.
> Things begin and have their time and end. At the break of day
> we can already feel how it will sink into evening. In all happi-
> ness is felt the coming sorrow. We build a house and do our
> work and know that it must all end. But you, O Lord, live and
> no transience touches you. . . . You, Jesus Christ, came—and
> brought us news of what "no eye has seen, no ear has heard, no
> human heart conceived." . . . Let my longing . . . never die in my
> heart, so that in the changes of life I may keep my sense of what
> alone gives shape and purpose to all life. Let my spirit be
> touched by the breath of your eternity, so that I may do my tem-
> poral work rightly and may in due time carry it over into your
> eternal kingdom. Amen.[56]

The Land of the Living

Interpreting verse thirteen of Psalm 27 it was common for
early Christian writers to read it in a deeper sense than what
may have been in the mind of the human author who wrote it.
The Psalmist expresses the confidence that he shall see the good
things of the Lord in the land of the living. For him, perhaps, this
meant life in this present age. Others would interpret it as a reference to what is to come. Thus Cassiodorus wrote:

> "I believe that I shall see the bounty of the Lord in the land of
> the living. Wait for the Lord." The Psalmist promises himself
> that he shall see the bounty of the Lord in the land of the living,
> that is, in the future life where the good things are everlasting.
> And that land is correctly said to be the land of the living be-
> cause this is the land of the dying.[57]

---

[55] Wordsworth, op. cit., I, p. 863.
[56] Romano Guardini, Prayers from Theology, pp. 61-62.
[57] Cassiodorus, Expositio in Psalterium: In Ps 26: PL 70, 192.

And Augustine says:

> He [the Psalmist] returns to his one request after these [present] dangers, these labors, after the difficulties from those who persecute and torment him; he returns to it burning, gasping and laboring but firm and certain of the One Who upholds him, of the One Who helps him, of the One Who leads him, of the One Who rules over him. . . . He says, "I believe that I shall see the bounty of the Lord in the land of the living." O sweet, immortal, incomparable, everlasting and unchangeable bounty of the Lord! And when will I see you, O bounty of the Lord? I believe that I will see you, but not in the land of the dying. "I believe that I shall see the bounty of the Lord in the land of the living." Let the Lord snatch me from the land of the dying, that Lord Who, for my sake, deigned to take on Himself the land of the dying and to die at the hands of those who die. Let Him snatch me from the land of the dying.[58]

It is this land of the living that will arouse our hopes and stimulate our desires. It is the contours of this land of the living that must serve as the magnet that attracts both us and our world to what God plans to be their future. Before considering that land and its wonders, however, we must look at what is associated with it or prepares for it: death, judgment, hell, the in-between time, and the like. All these, however, are very secondary concerns compared with that which is central: the everlasting life of the Blessed with God and with each other in a restored universe. For that is our hope and the hope of the world.

> Do you [Lord Jesus], speaking through my lips, pronounce over this earthly travail your twofold efficacious word: the word without which all that our wisdom and our experience have built up must totter and crumble—the word through which all our most far-reaching speculations and our encounter with the universe are come together into a unity. Over every living thing which is to spring up, to grow, to flower, to ripen during this day say again the words: This is my Body. And over every death-force which waits in readiness to corrode, to wither, to cut down, speak again your commanding words which express the supreme mystery of faith: This is my Blood.[59]

---

[58] Augustine, *Ennarr. in Ps 26*, Sermon 2, 22: CCSL 38, p. 167.
[59] Teilhard de Chardin, *Hymn of the Universe*, p. 23.

II

THE VEIL THAT COVERS
ALL PEOPLES

. . . we die, my Friend,
Nor we alone, but that which each man loved
And prized in his peculiar nook of earth
Dies with him, or is changed; and very soon
Even of the good is no memorial left.[1]

IT is probably a function of the truly philosophic or religious mind to reflect at least at times on the propinquity of death. Long before and since the *"Heu fugaces, Postume, Postume, labuntur anni,"* of Horace,[2] the swift passage of life and the inevitability of death have been themes for poets, philosophers and theologians.

John Henry Newman, with his great powers of language, dwelt upon the topic this way.

Man rises to fall: he tends to dissolution from the moment he begins to be; he lives on, indeed, in his children, he lives on in his name, he lives not on in his own person. He is, as regards the manifestations of his nature here below, as a bubble that breaks, and as water poured out upon the earth. He was young, he is old, he is never young again. . . .

Such is man in his own nature, and such, too, is he in his works. The noblest efforts of his genius, the conquests he has made, the doctrines he has originated, the nations he has civilized, the states he has created, they outlive himself, they

---

[1] Wordsworth, *The Excursion,* bk. 1, line 470, *The Poems,* vol. 2, p. 53.
[2] Horace, *Odes,* bk. 2, XIV. *Heu fugaces, Postume, Postume,// labuntur anni, nec pietas moram// rugis et instanti senectae// adferat indomitaeque morti.//* Alas, O Friend whose day has passed,/ The years so swiftly glide away; /And upright life cannot restrain/ The lines of age and puissant death.

outlive him by many centuries, but they tend to an end, and that end is dissolution. Powers of the world, sovereignties, dynasties, sooner or later come to nought; they have their fatal hour.

The Roman conqueror shed tears over Carthage, for in the destruction of the rival city he discerned too truly an augury of the fall of Rome; and at length, with the weight and the responsibilities, the crimes and the glories, of centuries upon centuries, the Imperial City fell.

Thus man and all his works are mortal; they die, and they have no power of renovation.[3]

Our age could add to Newman's catalog of all that moves to its allotted end. We can already discern the coming death of that race which has peopled much of what we call the "West"; when, in order to sustain a transitory ease, we transgress by mechanical sterility and abortion the injunction to grow. Thus, races die or kill themselves.

However, it is not just individual men and women, or their works and accomplishments, their societies and nations and civilizations that tend to dissolution and do dissolve in this "valley of tears." More extensive yet, if modern astrophysics is correct, is the phenomenon of decay. It is the universe itself, this cosmos of which we know so much and yet so little, that expands, by the law of entropy, to its fatal hour, or, as others would have it, expands only to contract again and begin over, being destroyed even in its refashioning.[4]

---

[3] John Henry Newman, "The Second Spring," *Sermons Preached on Various Occasions* (London: Longmans, Green, and Co., 1900), pp. 165-167. The famous sermon was preached in 1852. Whether its title is drawn from the 1850 edition of Wordsworth's *Prelude* is a matter of conjecture. Wordsworth wrote: "Yet every thing was wanting that might give// Courage to them who looked for good by light// Of rational Experience, for the shoots// and hopeful blossoms of a second spring" (*The Prelude*, bk. 11, line 6).

[4] Stephen Hawking, with his "no boundary" proposal on the nature of the universe, would seem to expound an infinite expansion-contraction theory. Cf. Chapter 8 and pp. 150-151 of his *A Brief History of Time*. This view presupposes that matter has always existed, which view he thinks raises questions about a Creator (cf. *ibid.*, p. 141). He is apparently unaware that, from a *philosophical* viewpoint, Aquinas too thought one had to deal with the possibility that matter always existed, but did not see this as a difficulty in demonstrating philosophically the need of a Creator. Whether Hawking would accept Aquinas' demonstration is another question.

The notion of universal disintegration, of course, by its nature does not concern most of us greatly. It is—if scientific calculations be true and if we ignore the warning that it will come as quickly as a thief in the night—a long way off, and thus a cataclysm of no personal concern to us. And what is true of our general indifference to the fate of the universe is too frequently the case in respect to reflections upon our own fate. We can all pass remarks, it is true, on the "Hubble Law" of astrophysics, applying it to ourselves. That theorem states that the farther away in the universe matter is from its origins the greater is its velocity. And so for us: the farther we are away from our origins the faster things seem to go, time apparently passing more quickly with age. As often as we mouth that truth, it is probably nonetheless accurate to say that most of us, most of the time, steer clear of any recognition beyond the merely notional of our own inevitable hour.

We live in a society that cosmeticizes the dead so that, with a kind of macabre courtesy, we can stand beside their coffins to comment on how good they look. Such idle comments intend no real flattery to the deceased, but are part of the charade that keeps the ugliness of death at least once removed from ourselves. As Pascal noted, "Being unable to cure death . . . men have decided, in order to be happy, not to think about such things."[5] The unwillingness to face this enemy is augmented, of course, by the uncertainty and fear about what, if anything, follows it. With the prince of Denmark it is easy to deliberate:

> . . . who would fardels bear,
> To grunt and sweat under a weary life,
> But that the dread of something after death,
> The undiscover'd country, from whose bourn
> No traveller returns, puzzles the will,
> And makes us rather bear those ills we have,
> Than fly to others that we know not of?[6]

[5] Pascal, *Pensées*, no. 133, p. 66.
[6] Shakespeare, *Hamlet*, act 3, scene 1.

This fear and avoidance of death and the "undiscovered country" beyond it are surely not universal. What is inevitable for all will intrude itself whether we like it or not, especially upon the reflective mind. Indeed as has been wisely said,

> The more the individual is conscious of his personality, the more natural is it for death, not the concept but the reality, his own inescapably impending death, to seem to him a destructive event, something not only frightening but also and above all senseless, an insult and a scandal.[7]

Now, when we speak of death, we must include all that is allied to it, those gruesome companions described so well by Virgil.

Vestibulum ante ipsum *primisque in faucibus Orci//* *Luctus et ultrices posuere* *cubilia Curae,// pallentesque* *habitant Morbi, tristisque* *Senectus,// et Metus, et* *malesuada Fames, ac turpis* *Egestas,// terribiles visu* *formae, Letumque Labosque,//* *tum consanguineus Leti Sopor,* *et mala mentis//Gaudia,* *mortiferumque adverso in* *limine Bellum// ferreique* *Eumenidum thalami, et* *Discordia demens// vipereum* *crinem vittis innexa cruentis.* (Aeneid, VI, 273-281)	*Before the door of death, at* *the very jaws of the underworld,* *grief and tormenting cares* *have placed their beds.* *Pale disease dwells there,* *along with forlorn old age,* *and fear and that hunger* *which counsels evil.* *There, too, shameful poverty,* *as well as forms terrible* *to look at: destruction and toil,* *sleep the relative of death,* *and evil delights of the mind.* *On the other side of the entrance* *is war, the death-bringer,* *and the iron chambers of the furies,* *as well as insane discord,* *its hair bound with bloody,* *snake-like ribbons.*

One could add political torture, boredom and many others. In the midst of all the grandeur and beauty of life, we realize that so much of it is, for ourselves and others, a taste of the "bread of adversity and the water of affliction" (Is 30:20—NIV

---

[7] J. Pieper, *Death and Immortality*, p. 75.

translation). As a result, at least by some, death is confronted if only in an attempt to make sense out of it, or put it in perspective or even soften its contours.

Various Solutions to the Questions Raised by Death

An ancient answer to the question about the meaning of life and death is the theory of reincarnation. It is, in its popularity at least, a theorem of the East and of Hinduism, newly taken up and advocated by sections of the "New Age" movement in the de-Christianized culture of modern Western society. Long ago, though, before the victory of Christianity, it was known in the West. Indeed, the idea, in one of its forms, was explained by Anchises to Aeneas as they traveled through Hades.

Ergo exercentur poenis, veterumque malorum/ supplicia expenunt. Aliae panduntur inanis/ suspensae ad ventos, aliis sub gurgite vasto/ infectum eluitur scelus aut exuritur igni./ Quisque suos patimur Manis. Exinde per amplum/ mittimur Elysium, et pauci laeta arva tenemus,/ donec longa dies perfecto temporis orbe/ concretam exemit labem, purumque relinquit/ aetherium sensum atque aurai simplicis ignem;/ has omnis, ubi mille rotam volvere per annos,/ Lethaeum ad fluvium deus evocat agmine magno,/ scilicet immemores supera ut convexa revisant/ rursus, et incipiant in corpora velle reverti.

Thus [the souls of the dead] are refined by punishments and suffer the torments due their old evils. Some are stretched out, suspended useless to the winds; others have their infectious crimes either washed out in a vast torrent or burned out by fire. Each of us suffers his own way in the underworld. Then we are sent through wide Elysium and a few possess the joyous fields until many days in a completed cycle of time take away the ingrained stain and leave a pure heavenly awareness and a fire of unalloyed light. When they have spent a thousand years, God calls all these, in a great line, to the river Lethe so that, former things forgotten, they may visit the earth again and begin to wish a return to their bodies.
(Aeneid, VI, 739-751)

To all this Aeneas has no comment, although the remarks made previous to his father's explanation may be said to express the reaction of many to such a view: do these unfortunates have such a dire desire for the world's light *(Quae lucis miseris tam dira cupido)*? Augustine, citing Aeneas' question, writes against reincarnation calling it a "groundless" idea.[8] For the believing Catholic, the error of this view has been rejected in our own day by the Second Vatican Council. Citing Hebrews 9:27, which alludes to the only course of our earthly life,[9] the *Constitution on the Church*, in number 48, reminds us of the definitive importance of our present existence.

Another stance adopted when confronted by death is that of a tranquil courage in the face of the inevitable.

> .... *When thoughts*
> *Of the last bitter hour come like a blight*
> *Over thy spirit, and sad images*
> *Of the stern agony, and shroud, and pall,*
> *And breathless darkness, and the narrow house,*
> *Make thee to shudder, and grow sick at heart;—*
> *Go forth, under the open sky, and list*
> *To Nature's teachings, while from all around—*
> *Earth and her waters, and the depths of air—*
> *Comes a still voice—Yet a few days, and thee*
> *The all-beholding sun shall see no more*
> *In all his course; nor yet in the cold ground,*
> *Where thy pale form was laid, with many tears,*
> *Nor in the embrace of ocean, shall exist*
> *Thy image. Earth, that nourished thee, shall claim*
> *Thy growth, to be resolved to earth again,*
> *And, lost each human trace, surrendering up*
> *Thine individual being, shalt thou go*
> *To mix for ever with the elements,*
> *To be a brother to the insensible rock*
> *And to the sluggish clod, which the rude swain*
> *Turns with his share, and treads upon. The oak*
> *Shall send his roots abroad, and pierce thy mould.*

---

[8] Augustine, *City of God*, bk. 14, ch. 5; cf. *Sermon 241, 5.*
[9] On the significance of the text as teaching against reincarnation, cf. the official commentary on *Lumen Gentium*, 48 in *Acta*, vol. 3, part 8, p. 143. Reliable Christian treatments on reincarnation are rare in the English language. One such, however, is Robillard's *Reincarnation: Illusion or Reality?*

Yet not to thine eternal resting-place
Shalt thou retire alone, nor couldst thou wish
Couch more magnificent. Thou shalt lie down
With patriarchs of the infant world—with kings,
The powerful of the earth—the wise, the good,
Fair forms, and hoary seers of ages past,
All in one mighty sepulchre. The hills
Rock-ribbed and ancient as the sun,—the vales
Stretching in pensive quietness between;
The venerable woods—rivers that move
In majesty, and the complaining brooks
That make the meadows green; and, poured round all,
Old Ocean's gray and melancholy waste,—
Are but the solemn decorations all
Of the great tomb of man. The golden sun,
The planets, all the infinite host of heaven,
Are shining on the sad abodes of death,
Through the still lapse of ages. All that tread
The globe are but a handful to the tribes
That slumber in its bosom.—Take the wings
Of morning, pierce the Barcan wilderness,
Or lose thyself in the contiguous woods
Where rolls the Oregon, and hears no sound,
Save his own dashings—yet the dead are there:
And millions in those solitudes, since first
The flight of years began, have laid them down
In their last sleep—the dead reign there alone.
So shalt thou rest, and what if thou withdraw
In silence from the living, and no friend
Take note of thy departure? All that breathe
Will share thy destiny. The gay will laugh
When thou art gone, the solemn brood of care
Plod on, and each one as before will chase
His favorite phantom; yet all these shall leave
Their mirth and their employments, and shall come
And make their bed with thee. As the long train
Of ages glide away, the sons of men,
The youth in life's green spring, and he who goes
In the full strength of years, matron and maid,
The speechless babe, and the gray-headed man—
Shall one by one be gathered to thy side,
By those, who in their turn shall follow them.

So live, that when thy summons comes to join
The innumerable caravan, which moves
To that mysterious realm, where each shall take
His chamber in the silent halls of death,
Thou go not, like the quarry-slave at night,

Scourged to his dungeon, but, sustained and soothed,
By an unfaltering trust, approach thy grave,
Like one who wraps the drapery of his couch
About him, and lies down to pleasant dreams.[10]

William Cullen Bryant's famous poem is meant to be a consolation for those who fear the fated final struggle. It is Socratic in tone, a philosophic attitude that we would now call a Stoic approach to death. It counsels a resigned peace far different from what was experienced by the Jewish Carpenter with His bloody sweat and anguished prayer. As such it may teach us to face the unavoidable with an equanimity made possible by a certain lack of realism.

The descriptive phrases, found in *Thanatopsis* and commonly, about earth as sepulcher are reminiscent of another great poetic masterpiece, the Book of Job.

Why did I not perish at birth, come forth from the womb and expire? . . . For then I should have lain down and been tranquil; had I slept, I should then have been at rest with kings and counselors of the earth who built where now there are ruins or with princes who had gold and filled their houses with silver (Jb 3:11-14).

A stoic approach to death has never been sufficient for all. And so, in face of ultimate dissolution, others will say: make the most of here and now.

Some for the Glories of This World, and some
Sigh for the Prophet's Paradise to come—
Ah, take the Cash and let the Credit go,
Nor heed the rumble of a distant Drum.[11]

As agnostic and cynical as the view is, it is still a step removed from those who find no meaning whatsoever in life, even if that meaning be the shallow one of present gratification.

---

[10] William Cullen Bryant, *Thanatopsis*, in Oscar Williams, *Palgrave's Golden Treasury*, pp. 347-348.

[11] Edward Fitzgerald, *The Rubaiyat of Omar Khayyam*, p. 338 of Oscar Williams' edition of Palgrave's *The Golden Treasury*.

Life's but a walking shadow, a poor player
That struts and frets his hour upon the stage
And then is heard no more: it is a tale
Told by an idiot, full of sound and fury,
Signifying nothing.[12]

Those words, of course, were uttered by a man whose crimes had earlier led him to admit that he had given his soul, that "eternal jewel, to the common enemy of man," the devil. Ultimately, rather than cope with that prospect, Macbeth denied all meaning to life.

To such cynicism and despair, another voice, with poetic imagery still more powerful, responds:

Remember your Creator . . . before the silver cord is snapped and the golden bowl is broken, and the pitcher is shattered at the spring, and the broken pulley falls into the well, and the dust returns to the earth as it once was, and the life breath returns to God who gave it (Eccl 12:1, 6-7).

The author of Ecclesiastes, of course, had himself no full answer to the vanity of a life that ends in the emptiness of death. Nonetheless, the Old Testament did already contain a good part of what God intended to reveal about the enigma of death.

The Bible on Death

After the Lord God had made humans to live, breathing into them the spirit of life (cf. Gn 2:7), He placed them in a Paradise. In the whole of creation, they were meant to be such

As, more than anything we know, instinct
With godhead, and, by reason and by will,
Acknowledging dependency sublime.[13]

Dependency sublime, however, Adam and Eve did not consider it. They longed for independence. The Life-Giver warned them: "From that tree you shall not eat; the moment you eat from it you are surely doomed to die" (Gn 2:17). In disobedience they ate and incurred the consequence. "By the sweat of your face

---

[12] Shakespeare, *Macbeth,* act V, scene V.
[13] Wordsworth, *The Prelude,* bk. VIII, lines 638-640 (492-494).

shall you get bread to eat, until you return to the ground, from which you were taken; for you are dirt, and to dirt you shall return" (Gn 3:19). In this way, the very description of human origins contains as well the theme of human destiny: death. This death is the result of sin, something from which the human creation would have been immune if Adam and Eve had not turned away from the Source of life and entered into a "covenant with death" (cf. Is 28:18). It is traditional and correct to say that death has a "penal" character; it is a punishment for the disobedience of sin. For all that, it is a punishment self-inflicted, the inevitable consequence of that sinful aversion from Life, which is God Himself. The Lord did not "add" death as something over and above the sin in order to punish it. Death flowed and flows surely and irreversibly from sin itself. It is the flower that blooms from the tree of sin.

In the Genesis account, God is like the parent who says to the very young child, "If you put your hand on the flame, you will be burned." The parent is not the one who does the burning. It is a warning; the "punishment" follows the disobedient act about which one has been forewarned. So with God. The "you are surely doomed to die" is a consequence of separating oneself from God. Thus, the Potter's "you are dirt, and to dirt you shall return" is a declaration of what He has permitted to happen, and what originates from the nature of things: to turn one's back on Life is to die; to slip from the Potter's hand is to break. Sin is always such a turning and fall. Even when one only chooses directly the "turning toward" something else that is contrary to God's good order, one must turn from God to achieve it. In the case of Adam and Eve and the death that entered the human world because of their decision, God permitted it. Indeed it becomes not merely a consequence but also a punishment that He, the Physician, would use medicinally. He knew already, of course, that He would do what is proper to Him: use an evil to achieve a good greater than would have otherwise been the case.

The connection between sin and death expresses itself in other ways in the Old Testament. It is seen in the fact that death was named as the penalty for so many of the sins that violated the Covenant. Onan's death, for example, follows his refusal to plant life (Gn 38:8-10). Subsequently the Book of Leviticus legislates death for numerous sins against the Covenant that brings light and life (cf. Lv 20:2, 9-12; 24:16; etc). Faithfulness to the Covenant is rewarded; infidelity has terrible consequences: "wasting and fever to dim the eyes and sap the life" (Lv 26:16).

In continuity with such Old Testament sources, St. Paul, his understanding perfected by the mystery of Christ, made his own commentary on the relation between sin and death, between what is ours from Adam and what is offered now in Christ.

> Therefore, just as through one person sin entered the world, and through sin, death, and thus death came to all, inasmuch as all sinned. . . . The gift is not like the result of the one person's sinning. For after one sin there was the judgment that brought condemnation; but the gift, after many transgressions, brought acquittal. For if, by the transgression of one person, death came to reign through that one, how much more will those who receive the abundance of grace and of the gift of justification come to reign in life through the one person Jesus Christ. In conclusion, just as through one transgression condemnation came upon all, so through one righteous act acquittal and life came to all. For just as through the disobedience of one person the many were made sinners, so through the obedience of the one the many will be made righteous (Rom 5:12-19).

This Pauline text has always had a special place in the theological discussions of Original Sin. Because of the ancient Latin translation (it would read in English: "Therefore, just as sin entered the world through one man, *in whom all sinned,* and death through sin . . ."), verse twelve was often used as a "proof text" for the doctrine of inherited sin, which sees all of us as having sinned in the father of the race.[14] In this sense Romans 5:12 was frequently cited by Augustine. In his steps, numerous Church councils appealed to the verse when teaching on Original Sin, although they refrained from defining the meaning of the verse itself. In fact, it is not the one verse but the sense of the whole section that makes clear the teaching that Paul himself summarizes in verse eighteen: ". . . just as through one transgression condemnation came upon all, so through one righteous act

---

[14] The famous *"in quo omnes peccaverunt"* has been changed in the New Vulgate to read *"eo quod omnes peccaverunt,"* thus bringing it into conformity with most modern vernacular translations.

acquittal and life came to all." According to the Apostle of the Gentiles, what came with condemnation was death, which is, first of all, separation from God and consequently physical death. Paul teaches the same thing in lapidary form in First Corinthians 15:21-22: "Just as in Adam all die, so too in Christ shall all be brought to life."

The Biblical understanding of death is probably well summed up in the Book of Wisdom where we read: "God did not make death nor does He rejoice in the perdition of the living; . . . the wicked summoned it by their deeds and words; thinking it to be a friend, they fell upon it and pledged themselves to it. . . . For God created man for incorruptibility and made him the image of his own likeness; however by the envy of the Devil death entered the world; they experience death who belong to it" (Wis 1:13, 16; 2:24 from the *New Vulgate).*

Even in earlier days of our own century the beautiful and moving account in Genesis, read in the Pauline perspective, was able to do what theology should do: raise profound questions and propose answers about life and its meaning, death, its origin and significance, the nature and consequences of sin, etc. Subsequently, however, many exegetes and theologians began to read Genesis in a new fashion, and changed their perspectives on the lessons the Book intended to convey. Often enough, treatments of Genesis 1—3 became exercises in what was essentially literary analysis, semantics and vague symbolism. Many, following R. Bultmann, called the Biblical account of origins a special form of "myth," using that word in so novel a sense that they were constantly obliged to explain that it was not the same as a fairy tale, an impression they never succeeded in erasing from the general mind. Some such development should probably have been expected. A rationalism that was almost totally lacking in self-criticism, evolutionism and the naive theological theories such as Modernism that it encouraged, these and more had challenged the traditional understandings of the Biblical account. Advances in the physical sciences beyond a simplistic Darwinism continued the challenge well into the twentieth century.

By the mid-1950's, studies in anthropology had arrived at the stage where human or humanoid specimens such as "Javaman" and "Peking man" appeared to give strong support to a polygenistic (even polyphyletic) origin for the human race. Humans, so it seemed, had appeared almost simultaneously over widely separated areas of the planet. Death had existed in the animal kingdom before the appearance of the species *homo*. Humans themselves derived from forms that died and were thus bound to die themselves. As a result of such a picture, death was seen as a natural and inevitable occurrence of the evolutionary process and not as a result of some primordial disobedience. Even Karl Rahner, who had defended monogenism (the view that the entire race originated in a single couple) as a demonstrable philosophic truth in the celebrated essay that he wrote in the early 1950's, soon abandoned that view.[15]

The state of natural sciences being such, many Christians, theologians included, replaced a naively literalistic reading of Genesis with a naively symbolic one. Adam and Eve became representative figures for primitive groups of humans; the snake became the symbol of evil in general; the consequences of their disobedience an etiology suited for the primitive mind, and other similar reasoning.

Unfortunately, having adopted some variation of the above positions or concordant ones, and having espoused them—at least in part—because of the state of research in the natural sciences, theologians and Christian catechists rested content. The warnings of Pius XII, Paul VI and John Paul II that polygenism, a dubious hypothesis at best,[16] was not to be accepted were generally explained away. The attempt by John Paul II to reinvigorate a theological reading of Genesis (probably the most concerted such effort since the work of Augustine) by showing the profundity of the thought contained in the passages (like the writings of Plato and Aristotle, the Genesis account is

---

[15] Cf. K. Rahner, "Theological Reflections on Monogenism," *Theological Investigations,* vol. 1, pp. 229ff; "The Sin of Adam," *Theological Investigations,* vol. 11, pp. 247ff; "Evolution and Original Sin," *Concilium,* vol. 3 (1967), pp. 33ff.

[16] Cf. for Pius XII, *DS* 3897; for Paul VI, *AAS,* 58 (1966), p. 654 *(TPS,* vol. 11, no. 3, pp. 229-235); for John Paul II, "Catechesis of October 1, 1986," *L'Osservatore Romano,* English edition of Oct. 6, 1986, p. 1 *(Insegnamenti,* IX, 2, pp. 760-761). The popes are commenting in part on the teaching of Trent (cf. *DS* 1513, which teaches that the first sin is "one in origin and transmitted by propagation not by imitation").

"primitive" only in the sense of being old, not in the sense of being shallow) has not yet been sufficiently appreciated. Even the vast changes and discoveries in the fields of anthropology and genetics have so far appeared to make little impression on the "theology" created for Genesis by the theologians of the sixties and seventies who were relying on a scientific state of affairs that was current in the late fifties and sixties. At the present time science has discarded much of the evolutionary picture presupposed by the Christian exegetes of Genesis in the 1960's and 1970's (and 1980's as well). Some of the natural sciences now seem to point to the monophyletic origin of the human race, in one very narrow area of our planet (East Africa), and perhaps even to the presence of a common female ancestor for all humans now inhabiting earth.[17]

One offshoot of the "naturalistic" approach to human origins was the conclusion that death for humans was "natural," at least

---

[17] *National Geographic* has reported on the "Eve" theory this way:

"Molecular biologists at the University of California, Berkeley, expert at unraveling the genetic codes found in human cells, applied their arcane skills to the puzzle of modern man. They collected tissue specimens from the placentas of 147 woman of different racial backgrounds. They concentrated their analysis on the DNA, or genetic code, of a part of the human cell called the mitochondrion, which is inherited only from the mother. . . . They deduced an African 'Eve,' the ancestor of every living person, who lived some 200,000 years ago. Her descendants, they theorized, carried her DNA to the rest of the world" (vol. 174, no 4, Oct. 1988, p. 460).

Along with Alan Wilson and Mark Stoneking, one of the scientists involved in the original research, Rebecca Cann, reported the results in her article "The Search of Eve" for *The Sciences* of Sept./Oct. 1987. An independent study by a Stanford University team under Luigi Luca Cavalli-Sforza arrived at similar results in 1988.

None of these studies, it should be noted, are speaking directly of a monogenetic origin of humans. All they are explicitly saying is that all current humans inherit some of the genetic makeup of one woman whose female descendants through intermarriage passed on the mitochondrial DNA inherited from her. Nonetheless, given the nature of the studies, the *possibility* arises for the first time in modern scientific research that the race is descended from one woman. In this way another supposed barrier to the teaching on monogenism may be disappearing. One must be cautious, however, and not repeat the mistakes of earlier theologians by adopting as certain tentative scientific evidence. All the evidence is not in. The genetic conclusions of Wilson, Cann and others have been disputed, especially by some paleoanthropologists. Cf. James Shreeve, "Argument over a Woman," *Discover*, August 1990, pp. 52ff. For a balanced reporting of the current state of the matter, cf. Michael H. Brown, *The Search for Eve* (New York: Harper and Row, 1990).

in its primary, physical sense. In his article "Death" in *Sacramentum Mundi*, Karl Rahner more or less sums up the thesis proposed in his work, *On the Theology of Death*. He writes:

> Death is a consequence of original sin. This does not of course mean that if there were no original or personal sin man would have continued in perpetuity his biological life in time, or that before "Adam" there was no death in the animal kingdom. Even without sin man would have ended his biological, historical life in space and time, and would have entered into his definitive condition before God by means of a free act engaging his whole life. Death as we know it now, as part of man's constitution subject to the concupiscence, in darkness, weakness and obscurity regarding its actual nature, is a consequence of sin.

Such statements were quite regularly understood as meaning that not death itself, but *only* "death as we know it" was the result of the original turn from the Author of life. Such an interpretation found a friendly hearing among other theologians[18] and is even *similar* to the thought of St. Thomas who wrote: "The necessity of dying comes partly from human nature and partly from sin."[19]

However, Thomas' teaching is distinguished from that which sees only "death as we know it" as being the result of sin. For he also wrote:

> God, to Whom every nature is subject, in the very creation of mankind, supplied for the defect of nature and, by the gift of original justice, gave the body a certain incorruptibility.[20] . . . if we consider the nature of the body, death is natural; if we consider the nature of the soul and the disposition supernaturally given the body in the beginning for the sake of the soul, death is *per accidens* and contrary to nature, since it is natural for the body to be united with the soul.[21]

Hans Urs von Balthasar beautifully expressed the Thomistic conclusions when he wrote:

> As a creature, man is finite. But because God gave him the power of submitting his spirit to the grace of mission and of let-

---

[18] Cf. for example, Michael Schmaus, *Dogma II* (New York: Sheed and Ward, Inc., 1971), pp. 160, 167-168.

[19] Aquinas, *In Sent.*, d. 3, 16, 1, 1.

[20] Aquinas, *Summa Theol.*, Ia, IIae, q. 85, a. 6 c. Cf. I, q. 97, a. 1.

[21] Aquinas, *Compendium*, cap. 152, *Opera Omnia*, XLII, p. 139.

ting his body be enveloped by his spirit, his finiteness was open to God. Once he had freed himself from God, however, and had made a goal of what should have been a means, his finiteness appeared openly in all its nakedness. Earthly life, when it is no longer hidden in eternal life, becomes hopelessly immured in its own finiteness. The wall that encloses it is *death*. Through sin death came into the world (Rom 5:12), and through death, anxiety about the flame of life in this world, imperiled as it is from within and without. For death is not just the sudden ending of life. It is also the corroding illness, the aging, the blunting of one's powers, the weariness, the disgust with boredom and barrenness, with the transitoriness and hopelessness of earthly life. Because of man, all nature is affected by this decay. The abundance of paradise has been exhausted.[22]

The Magisterium of the Church has always taught and continues to teach that death is a consequence of and punishment for sin. Vatican Council II, in a memorable paragraph, summarizes previous teaching when it gives the following reflection on death, even as it offers the Christian hope for deliverance from so great an evil.

Confronted with death, the enigma of the human condition especially manifests itself. Not only is our race tormented by pain and by the progressive dissolution of the body, but even more by the fear of perpetual extinction. However, humanity rightly judges with the instinct of the heart when it shuns and rejects total ruin and the definitive disappearance of one's own person. The seed of eternity that each bears within, and that is not able to be reduced to matter alone, rises up against death. All the endeavors of technical skill, though extremely useful, are not able to soothe human anxiety: for longevity, biologically prolonged, is not able to satisfy our desire for a further life that is inevitably present in our hearts.

While the imagination fails when confronted with death, the Church, nevertheless, taught by divine revelation, affirms that humanity was created by God for a happy end beyond the limits of earthly misery. Furthermore, Christian faith teaches that bodily death, from which mankind would have been removed if it had not sinned,[23] will be conquered when the race, ruined by its own fault, will be restored to salvation by the al-

---

[22] Von Balthasar, *The Christian State of Life*, p. 103.
[23] The Church's earlier pronouncements on death are all in accord with this statement: death comes from sin. Cf. *DS* 222, 239, 371, 372, 1511-1512; Paul VI to Symposium on Original Sin, *TPS*, vol. 11, no. 3, pp. 229-235.

mighty and merciful Savior. For God has called and still calls humanity so that it may adhere to Him with the fullness of human nature in a perpetual communion of incorruptible divine life. Christ won this victory, freeing us from death through His death and rising to life. Therefore to every thoughtful person, faith, presented with solid argumentation, offers a response to anxiety about one's future destiny; at the same time faith offers the power to be in communion, in Christ, with our loved ones who have already been taken by death, giving the hope that they have found true life with God *(Gaudium et Spes,* 18).

In this statement, the Council speaks of "bodily death," not simply of aspects of "death as we know it." It is death itself that Vatican II and the whole of Tradition see as being the result of sin.

Along with the tendency to see bodily death as "natural" with only its accompanying miseries as being the consequences of sin, there has developed a theological view that extols certain "positive" facets of death. Rahner wrote:

The end of the human being as a spiritual person is an active immanent consummation, an act of self-completion, a life-synthesizing self-affirmation, an achievement of a person's total self-possession, a creation of himself, the fulfillment of his personal reality.[24]

The language is so exuberant that, Lorelei-like, it beguiles one. For Rahner and other Christian theologians, such a view of death can be had, of course, only because of and in Christ. Jesus has, they say, transformed death itself.

... it is in death, and in death alone, that man enters into an open, unrestricted relationship to the world as a whole. Only in death will man be integrated ... into the world as a whole, through his own total reality achieved in his life and in his death.... Applying this hypothesis of the metaphysical anthropology of death to the death of Christ, we must say that through Christ's death, his spiritual reality, which he possessed from the beginning, enacted in his life, and brought to consum-

---

[24] Rahner, *On the Theology of Death,* p. 40.

mation in his death, becomes open to the whole world and is inserted into this world as a permanent destiny of real ontological kind.[25]

To some it would appear that what is being proposed in such writing is the equivalent of equating death with the resurrection. Rahner has not escaped criticism on this point.

> ... is Rahner naively optimistic in minimizing the absurdity of death? Is not his attempt to find meaning in death totally futile or even misguided? Should he not be consistent with Heidegger's analysis of human freedom and maintain that it leads, not to fulfillment, but to nothingness?[26]
>
> Is Pannenberg right in reproaching Rahner for being too close to Bultmann in connecting Jesus' death and Resurrection?[27]

I believe that Pannenberg is indeed right not only in his criticisms of Rahner but also in his own views about the meaning of death.

> So the thesis that death brings life to its totality is to be denied. The resurrection from the dead, in which Christian hope itself rests, is more and other than only the other side of death, not only the revelation of a positive meaning for death itself; for death as such has no positive meaning. The problem becomes intelligible in the theological understanding of the death and the resurrection of Jesus Christ. According to Rahner, and also to Rudolf Bultmann, the resurrection of Jesus Christ is "the appearing of what happened in the death of Christ." For Karl Barth, also, the resurrection of Jesus was only the "revelation" of his history that was completed on the Cross. In such formulations it is no longer clear that the resurrection of Jesus is triumph over death.[28]

All Christians will indeed admit that "the problem becomes intelligible" in how one understands the death and resurrection of Jesus. Before attempting such an understanding, however, there are other things about death that must be considered.

---

[25] *Ibid.*, p. 71.

[26] Phan, *Eternity in Time*, p. 115.

[27] *Ibid.*, p. 179.

[28] Pannenberg, "Tod und Auferstehung in der Sicht christlicher Dogmatik," *Kerygma und Dogma*, 20 (1974), pp. 176-177. An English synopsis of Pannenberg's article can be found in "A Theology of Death and Resurrection," *Theology Digest*, vol. 23, no. 2 (Summer 1975), pp. 143-148.

The Theory of the Final Option

For some theologians, one aspect of the "positive" evaluation of death has been a renewed effort to defend the theory that there is in the very act of dying a moment in which the human person freely sums up a life.[29] The most extensive writing on this matter in recent times has been done by Karl Rahner,[30] although in fact the ideas put forward by him can already be substantially found in the work of Emile Mersch.[31] A particularly concise expression of their thesis runs this way.

> Death gives man the opportunity of posing his first completely personal act; death is, therefore, by reason of its very being, the moment above all others for the awakening of consciousness, for freedom, for the encounter with God, for the final decision about his eternal destiny.[32]

Alois Winklhofer, too, deals with the theme:

> The question, then, is whether we are to assume that all men are given a final moment of grace in which they look back on and judge their whole life, take stock of all their decisions and lapses in the moral and religious sphere, and so have a chance to fix their life finally, to surrender it to God, to rectify it or not in regard to him; this moment would be situated precisely at the separation of body and soul, neither before nor after. This act would occur on the threshold of the new life, and presupposes that the stepping-over it is done in full awareness, itself supernatural and an effect of grace, so that the full significance of this decisive moment is recognized.[33]

Like Mersch and Rahner, Winklhofer thinks there is such a moment in death, an instant in which we recapitulate life and freely dispose of ourselves. However, whereas Rahner claims that this theory has the authority of Aquinas behind it and can be

---

[29] Although found in others who antedate him, the modern discussion on the "final decision" is associated with the name of P. Glorieux. Cf. his article "In Hora Mortis," *Mélanges de Science Religieuse*, Lille, 1949. His position is summarized and defended by Roger Troisfontaines, *I Do Not Die*, pp. 156ff.

[30] Cf. Rahner, *On the Theology of Death* (New York: Herder and Herder, 1963); article "Death" in *Sacramentum Mundi*.

[31] Cf. Mersch, *Theology of the Mystical Body*, pp. 262-270.

[32] Boros, *The Mystery of Death*, p. ix.

[33] Winklhofer, *The Coming of His Kingdom*, p. 49.

traced back to John Damascene,[34] Winklhofer states more accurately that arguments in favor of this opinion are of "a speculative character," "not drawn from Scripture or the Fathers" and thus "not able to constitute a positive theological argument."[35] In fact the origin of the idea can probably be traced to Cardinal Cajetan, the renowned sixteenth-century disciple of Aquinas, who, commenting on the *Summa Theologica* I, q. 64, a. 2, said that there "is an immobility of both intellect and will in the soul placed outside of the state of being a wayfarer." It is then "I say that the soul is rendered obstinate through the first act that it elicits in the state of separation."[36]

The treatment by St. Thomas concerns the unwillingness of the fallen angels to change their decision against God. This fixity of will is due, says Aquinas, to the natural superiority of their intelligence and will. Their perception of good and evil is not partial and clouded as is that of humans. Thus, having acted on what was clearly perceived, their wills, unlike ours, are not fickle, fluctuating back and forth between what is really good and what is perceived as good. Cajetan applies this insight to the human race and says that such perspicacity in the intellect and determination in the will is, for humans, only finally achieved at death, when the soul, separated from the body, elicits its first act made in total clarity and self-determination.

The theory, allowing for the variations in the different authors who espouse it, has both Promethean and Platonic aspects. It is Promethean because it portrays humans as having such a power that they can freely dispose of themselves for eternity even as they are in the course of dying. It seems to posit the capability of rising above the processes that normally accompany death, whether that death be from old age, or sickness, or accident. That may be a possibility for some but, at the very least, such is not an observable phenomenon in many (most?) deaths.

---

[34] Rahner, "It seem to us—and this is an opinion which can be traced to John Damascene and which was confirmed by the authority of St. Thomas—that the finality of the personal life-decision is intrinsic to death itself, since it is a spiritual-personal act of man" (*Theology of Death*, p. 38).

[35] Winklhofer, p. 52.

[36] Cajetan, on *S. Th*, I, 64, 2, n. 18 in Leonine edition of the *Opera Omnia* of Aquinas, vol. 5 (Rome, 1889), p. 144.

More fatal for the theory, perhaps, is its fundamentally Platonic perspective on the body-soul relationship, a perspective present despite the fact that the proponents of the view, especially Rahner, frequently criticize elements of Platonic philosophy. Cajetan already revealed the Platonic underpinnings of the idea when he said that the act in question is the "first act that it [the soul] *elicits in the state of separation.*" The Platonic body/soul dichotomy is readily seen in Mersch when he writes:

> [Death] is the end of the soul's union with the body, the end of the period of formation. . . . Death, for the soul, is the passage from a formative stage to a definitive stage. The soul was made, moreover, to take its definitive form through this inner catastrophe [death].[37]

> The body has its part in the act of death, but only to be left behind, and the contribution it has to make is only that of being no longer fit for the union. Whether the body is used, whether it is unequal to psychological functions, or whether it is torn apart or crushed, matters little; or rather this matters a great deal: it will the more easily be laid aside. It is no longer required to cooperate through phantasms or feelings in the ordinary actions of the intellect or will; the series of such acts has come to an end. The body acts, not to add one more such act to the series, but to close off the series by unifying it in its definitive stage.[38]

Clearly implicit in such writing is the notion that the body is, at least to some extent, an impedance to the operation of the human soul. Indeed the soul is said to reach its "definitive form" through its separation from the body. Humans are taken to be, as Rahner's famous thesis put it, "Geist im Welt," Spirit in the world, embodied spirits, in which the body serves, at best, as "symbol" or outward manifestation of soul.

> . . . human knowledge as pre-apprehending is ordered to what is absolutely infinite, and for that reason man is spirit.[39]

> . . . man is spirit in such a way that, in order to become spirit, he enters and he has ontically always already entered into otherness, into matter, and so into the world.[40]

---

[37] Mersch, *Theology of the Mystical Body,* p. 264.
[38] *Ibid.,* p. 265.
[39] Rahner, *Spirit in the World,* p. 186.
[40] Rahner, in ch. 10 of *Hearers of the Word,* in *A Rahner Reader* (Gerald McCool, editor), p. 51.

All of these men, of course, believe in the resurrection of the body. But the importance they attach to it would almost appear to derive from a truth of Revelation grafted on, as it were, to an idealistic or Platonic conception of the soul. All in all, the theory of the final option must be judged at least improbable. As far as can be discerned, we do not die, freely disposing of ourselves, or recapitulating a life. It is part of our weakness due to sin, our fallen state, that we generally just fall or drift into death with no ability to do anything for ourselves. For most humans, at least, unconscious or semiconscious, numbed or restless with lack of comfort or with pain, beset by fear of what is ahead or regret for what is behind, death is not a summation. It is a loss, a disintegration. We are not Prometheans, but weak and devastated humans. When we die, it is the final enemy, Death, who wins the battle. A positive view of death and the death process may in effect tend to *glorify* death whereas the Christian celebration *mocks* death because Jesus conquered it.

The Second Death

St. James wrote that when an evil desire "conceives [it] brings forth sin, and when sin reaches maturity it gives birth to death" (Jas 1:15). What we know as physical death is, however, only part of the horror that the word is meant to connote for a Christian. The Book of Revelation speaks of yet another menace, the second death.

> Blessed and holy is the one who shares in the first resurrection. The second death has no power over these; they will be priests of God and of Christ, and they will reign with him for the thousand years (Rv 20:6).

> Then Death and Hades were thrown into the pool of fire. (This pool of fire is the second death) (Rv 20:14).

A Protestant scholar has written the following interesting reflections on the death endured in the lake of fire, hell.

We have presented an eschatology founded in Jesus Christ and structured by his history. In this context, hell hardly has a place. Jesus Christ is the *Savior* of the world. In him God reached his goal with the world. God's "emergency measure," perdition (Matt. 25:41), cannot be discussed *in extenso* in this context. Hell is in fact the antithesis of God's will and goal for his creation. . . .

Where should perdition be treated in more detail, since Scripture mentions this subject often? Statistically speaking, Jesus preached more frequently on hell than on heaven. It seems to me that the right place to deal with perdition is in anthropology, particularly where sin is discussed, because the human being is responsible for perdition.[41]

I think Konig is correct on several counts: Jesus did speak much of hell; it is difficult to "fit it in" with a picture of salvation and eternal life, and it probably does belong in Christian Anthropology and not in the tract on the Last Things where we usually find it. However, following the indications and terminology of the Book of Revelation, something must be said about the "second death."

As found in the New Testament, the notion of the "second death" is a development of Old Testament concepts. There the abode of the dead was *sheol*, which the Book of Job calls the "destined place of everyone alive" (Jb 30:23). The notion developed in Israel, however, that, besides sheol, there was also a place of terror and torture for evildoers—a distinct sphere of sheol. It is the Book of Daniel that seems to speak most clearly about such a domain: "Many of those who sleep in the dust of the earth shall awake; some shall live forever, others shall be an everlasting horror and disgrace" (Dn 12:2).

The idea of rising as an everlasting horror and disgrace was confirmed by the highest authority, the Lord Himself. Using various similes, Jesus spoke emphatically of the lot awaiting the wicked.

But I say to you, whoever is angry with his brother will be liable to judgment, and whoever says to his brother, "Raqa," will be answerable to the Sanhedrin, and whoever says, "You fool," will be liable to fiery Gehenna (Mt 5:22).

---

[41] Adrio Konig, *The Eclipse of Christ in Eschatology*, p. 248.

And if your right hand causes you to sin, cut it off and throw it away. It is better for you to lose one of your members than to have your whole body go into Gehenna (Mt 5:30).

And do not be afraid of those who kill the body but cannot kill the soul; rather, be afraid of the one who can destroy both soul and body in Gehenna (Mt 10:28).

And if your eye causes you to sin, tear it out and throw it away. It is better for you to enter into life with one eye than with two eyes to be thrown into fiery Gehenna (Mt 18:9).

Woe to you, scribes and Pharisees, you hypocrites. You traverse sea and land to make one convert, and when that happens you make him a child of Gehenna twice as much as yourselves (Mt 23:15).

From the netherworld, where he was in torment, he raised his eyes and saw Abraham far off and Lazarus at his side (Lk 16:23).

Do not be amazed at this, because the hour is coming in which all who are in the tombs will hear his voice and will come out, those who have done good deeds to the resurrection of life, but those who have done wicked deeds to the resurrection of condemnation (Jn 5:28-29).

"Gehenna" (cf. Is 66:24) was the "city dump" of Jerusalem where fires endlessly burned refuse. The Lord uses it as a symbol of the loss and misery of the unrepentant sinner. He associates it with weeping and gnashing of teeth and with fire. The dreadful seriousness with which Jesus spoke can be seen, especially, in Mark 3:29; 9:43-48 and Luke 13:22.

The testimonies could be multiplied many times. Paul puts it in the least metaphorical way when he speaks of being excluded from the Kingdom (1 Cor 6:10; Gal 5:19-21).

It must be admitted that it is not easy to draw up a fully coherent doctrine from the Biblical texts. The use of apocalyptic language and the fact that the texts are often hortatory or hyberbolic are indications that one must be careful in attempting to give some definitive picture of hell. However, it must be recognized that the exhortations and hyperbole have a purpose: to save the hearer from a terrible fate.

The early Fathers of the Church basically followed the New Testament teaching and terminology, although some of the popular writings, such as the *Acts of Peter*, borrowed from pagan sources. The first notable deviation in the Christian view of hell came with Origen. He was the propounder of the theory of Apocatastasis, i.e., of the universal restoration of all things. He "does not know of any eternal fire or punishment of hell. All sinners will be saved, even the demons and Satan himself will be purified by the Logos."[42] That Origen held the opinion attributed to him has been disputed,[43] but it is certain that the Christian writers close to his own time were convinced he held such an outlook.

Jerome, for a brief time, and St. Gregory of Nyssa followed Origen in the sense that they thought all men would be saved. On the other hand, Origen's contemporary, St. Cyprian of Carthage, did teach explicitly about the eternity of hell and subsequently Augustine took up the theories of Origen.

> I am aware that I now have to engage in a peaceful dispute with the merciful among us who are unwilling to believe that the punishment of Gehenna will be eternal either in the case of all those, or at least some of those, whom the completely just Judge accounts deserving of that punishment.[44]

The position of Origen or those who followed him was condemned at the Synod of Constantinople in 543, which taught:

> If anyone says or thinks that the punishment of the devils and of evil men is for a time and that there will be an end of it at some time, or that there will be a restoration [Gk. *apocatastasis*] of the devils and evil men, anathema sit (*DS* 411).

The dogmatic weight of the condemnation is not absolutely clear, although, according to the testimony of Cassiodorus,[45] it was approved by Pope Vigilius during his detention in Constantinople in the years 547-555. Augustine appears to have consid-

---

[42] J. Quasten, *Patrology*, vol. II, p. 87.
[43] Cf. Henri Crouzel, *Origen: The Life and Thought of the First Great Theologian* (New York: Harper and Row, 1989 [French, 1985]), pp. 262-265.
[44] St. Augustine, *City of God*, bk 21, ch. 17: CCSL 48, p. 783.
[45] Cassiodorus, *De institut.*: PL 70, 1111.

ered what was ultimately taught in this canon to have been, even in his time, a matter of a binding decision of the Church.[46]

The teaching on the existence of an eternal hell was later reaffirmed in the Trinitarian Creed *Quicumque.*

> At Christ's coming, all must rise in their bodies and give an account of their own deeds. Those who have done good will go to eternal life, those who have done evil to eternal fire *(DS* 76).

The *Quicumque,* the so-called Athanasian Creed, although composed by a disciple of Augustine, has long been prayed and accepted in both the East and the West as a binding expression of the Church's faith. The first credal *definition* of Faith, however, on the existence of hell and eternal damnation belongs to the *Firmiter,* the Creed of the Fourth Lateran Council in 1215.

> Christ will come at the end of the ages to judge the living and the dead and to render to each, both damned and Elect, according to their works. All of these will rise with their own bodies which they now possess in order to receive according to their works, whether good or bad. The evil will receive perpetual punishment with the devil, the good eternal glory with Christ *(DS* 801).

The teaching of the *Quicumque* and the *Firmiter* is reaffirmed in the *Benedictus Deus* of Benedict XII, January of 1336.

> Furthermore we define that, according to the general plan of God, the souls of those dying in actual mortal sin descend to hell soon after death. There they are afflicted with the pains of hell, but nonetheless on the day of judgment all will appear with their bodies before the tribunal of Christ to render an account of their own deeds so that each one may receive according to what was done in the body, whether good or evil (cf. 2 Cor 5:10) *(DS* 1002).

In our own day, the doctrines about hell and damnation have been repeated by Paul VI and the *Constitution on the Church* of Vatican Council II.

> [The Lord] ascended into heaven, whence He shall come again with glory to judge the living and the dead, each receiving according to his own merits. Those who have responded to the Love and Mercy of God will go to eternal life; those who

---

[46] St. Augustine, *City of God,* bk 21, ch. 17: CCSL 48, p. 783.

have rejected that Love and Mercy to the end will go to the fire that will have no end.[47]

Indeed since we know neither the day nor the hour it is necessary to keep vigil constantly, as the Lord warned us, so that, having completed the one course of our earthly life, we may merit to enter the marriage banquet with Him and be numbered among the blessed (cf. Mt 25:31-46) and so that we may not be commanded, like evil and lazy servants, to descend to eternal fire (cf. Mt 25:41) in the exterior darkness where there will be "weeping and the gnashing of teeth" (Mt 22:13 and 25:30). For, before we reign gloriously with Christ, all of us will stand before the "tribunal of Christ, so that each may give an account of what he has done in the body, whether good or bad" (2 Cor 5:10) and at the end of the world "those who have done good will go to the resurrection of life, those indeed who have done evil will go to the resurrection of judgment" (Jn 5:29; cf. Mt 25:46) (*Lumen Gentium*, 48).

In reference to the text from Vatican II it is to be noted that initially there was no mention of the "eternal fire." The omission was corrected at the explicit request of many bishops.[48] During the postconciliar period of theological questioning and reinterpretation, the Congregation for the Doctrine of the Faith issued, in May 1979, the *Instruction Concerning Eschatology.*

The Church, faithful to the New Testament and Tradition, believes in the happiness of the Elect who will one day be with Christ. She believes that there will be eternal punishment for the sinner who will be denied the vision of God, and that this punishment will affect the whole being of the sinner.[49]

Karl Rahner summed up the Magisterial teaching prior to Vatican II this way: "In its official teaching, the Church has defined the existence of hell and its eternity against the doctrine of the apocatastasis as put forward by Origen and other ancient writers. . . . Entry into hell takes place immediately after death. A certain distinction is made between the loss of the vision of God and the pain of sense, but apart from this there is no official declaration on the nature of the pains of hell, though the difference of punishments in hell is mentioned."[50]

---

[47] Paul VI, *Credo: AAS,* 60 (1968), p. 438.
[48] Cf. *Acta Synodalia,* vol. III, part 5, p. 59 and pp. 63-64.
[49] *AAS,* vol. 71 (1979), pp. 941-942.
[50] K. Rahner, "Hell" in *Sacramentum Mundi.*

Thus, we may say in brief that the eternal existence of hell, the "second death," is a defined dogma of Faith. Those who die in mortal sin go there, and remain there eternally.[51]

In our own day, there are some who think that, although hell in fact exists and will exist eternally for the devils consigned there, we may hope that no human being will actually be damned. This position has been defended by Hans Urs von Balthasar, among others.[52] On this question the history of Vatican Council II is able to shed some light.

We know, from the official *Relatio* of the *Acta* of Vatican II, that the text of *Lumen Gentium* #48 is not to be understood as speaking of the salvation of all humans.[53] From the same source we learn that "one bishop wanted a sentence to be included in which it would be clear that there are damned *de facto*, lest damnation remain as a mere hypothesis." The request was refused by the Theological Commission responsible for drafting the document, with the comment: "In no. 48 there are cited the words of the Gospel in which the Lord Himself speaks about the damned in a form that is grammatically future."[54] The significance of that remark is that, when she speaks of a damnation of humans, the Church speaks, as Christ Himself did, not in form of grammar that is *conditional* (i.e., speaking about something that *might*

---

[51] The denial of the "eternity" of the punishment of hell has reappeared in recent times in the form of "annihilationism," the view that those who finally reject God will be annihilated. Russell Aldwickle, who holds such a view, writes: "Gehenna is the symbol for this final separation from God. It involves suffering by that very fact of separation. However, we have contended that such suffering is not 'endless' and that God will allow to pass out of existence those who finally (that is at the End) refuse to live in His world. That if this is the case, it would constitute a defeat for God, has to be admitted. Some people would argue that such a defeat is unthinkable on Christian assumptions. This, however, can only be maintained by denying the ultimate freedom of man to repudiate his Creator, and this we have refused to do. We may permit ourselves the larger hope that no man will be finally impenitent when history comes to an end. We cannot erect this into a dogma of the necessary salvation of all men" (*Death in the Secular City*, p. 118).

[52] Cf. Urs Von Balthasar, *Dare We Hope That All Men Be Saved?* A critique of the thesis is found in J. T. O'Connor, "Von Balthasar and Salvation," *Homiletic and Pastoral Review*, vol. 89, no. 10 (July 1989), pp. 10ff.

[53] *Acta Synodalia*, vol. 3, part 8, p. 140.

[54] *Ibid.*, pp. 144-145.

happen), but in the *grammatical future* (i.e., about something that *will* happen). And it was with this understanding that the bishops of Vatican II voted upon and accepted *Lumen Gentium*. The same grammatical usage about the future of those who die in mortal sin is found in the most recent teaching of the Magisterium on this matter, viz., the *Decree on Eschatology* cited above.

It has been said that the words of Jesus [and of the Church], future as they are and not conditional, "cannot be considered as absolutely probative" since they are not intended to give us "a description of the future, a 'futurology,' but rather a knowledge of the future which is able to clarify our present."[55] It is true indeed that the future has not been *described* for us in great detail. Only enough has been revealed to stimulate our hope and desire, and to warn us that not all will share what is to be hoped for and desired. Both the indications of what is to be hoped for and the indications that not all will share those wonderful realities must be taken with equal seriousness.

An argument is sometimes made from the fact that the Church has never explicitly declared that any given individual is actually damned. This is undeniably true. Whether this fact has any bearing on the present discussion, however, is doubtful. The Church's mission is to teach the truth, preach salvation, propose models for living the Christian life well and warn against those actions and forms of living that will lead to eternal perdition. It is to be questioned whether she has been given the knowledge or power to determine and proclaim the *negative* results of any individual human life. As a community, that knowledge is reserved for the final judgment. On the other hand, although she does not mention any individual as being among the damned, she, like her Master, does not use the *conditional* but the *future indicative* mode when speaking of the outcome of human history in respect to the damnation of some.

We should recognize the beneficial aspect in having some theologians raise the question about the salvation of all humans. It forces one to pause again to ask oneself: do we really have any

---

[55] Jean-Hervé Nicolas, O.P., *Synthèse dogmatique* (Fribourg Suisse: Editions Universitaires; Paris: Beauchesne, 1986), p. 619.

nearly sufficient appreciation of how much the Lord loves us and gives of Himself for our benefit? Hell is a terrible thing, but not as terrible as the death of the God-man Who endured death to save us from hell. We never appreciate sufficiently how great God's love is. On the other hand, we must not pretend that we understand fully the nature of that love. Von Balthasar writes: "Whoever reckons with the possibility of even only *one* person's being lost besides himself is hardly able to love unreservedly."[56]

He admits that such a thesis is "practical-prescriptive and not theoretical-cognitive," but is it really true? If love is to be truly unreserved, why confine it to humans? Long ago Augustine saw the inherent difficulty in such a position and wrote:

> Now if this opinion is good and true because it is merciful, then it will be the better and the truer the more merciful it is. Then let the fountain of mercy be deepened and enlarged until it reaches as far as the damned angels. . . . Why should this fountain flow as far as the whole of human nature, and then dry up as soon as it reaches the angels?[57]

Admitting our very limited knowledge about the history of the angelic order, we know, nevertheless, that some of them rejected God in such a way as to incur eternal damnation. Von Balthasar himself admits this. Yet those spiritual beings were, like us, the work of God's creative love. Creatures of an intelligence and will greater than our own, they too were beings of beauty and, what is more, recipients of divine grace, sharers in the divine life. Nonetheless, because of their sin, their loving Creator left them to eternal damnation, *loving them still*—at least to the extent of preserving them in being. Is our love and compassion not to be extended to all those intelligent beings who inhabit this universe with us? Is our love not unreserved because we know that some of them are eternally lost to God and to us? And is it not presumptuous to imagine that we are more worthy of His compassion than they? For one who takes the existence of angels and their history seriously (as Von Balthasar does), the damnation of some of them must be a sobering reminder that the all-merciful and just God remains for us beyond our understanding.

---

[56] Von Balthasar, *op. cit.*, pp. 211f.
[57] St. Augustine, *City of God*, bk 21, ch. 17: CCSL 48, p. 783.

The Christians who think that eternal damnation is a scandal, that it contradicts the reality of an all-loving God, may appear to suffer from myopic vision. It takes a hell they have not seen to make them realize what keener observers of life and nature—including many atheists—know from their own reflections: some of life is cruel, painful, and prey to wanton, recurrent, endless violence. How can a good God permit the violence omnipresent in the animal world or the terrible suffering and misery endured by so many humans? One does not need an eternal hell to raise the question about a good and all-powerful God Who permits such things, and has permitted them since the custodians of His earth disobeyed. The answer to the question is veiled in obscurity, that of God's own being as well as the "mystery of lawlessness" spoken of by St. Paul (cf. 2 Thes 2:7). Already, however, we know in faith that God permits all such evils to draw forth greater good. The revelation of what that good is in particular cases must await the general judgment.

Augustine comments on those who admit eternal punishment for the damned, but hold out a hope that none of the human race is so damned, that all will escape.

> Moreover, the people who feel this way do not extend this opinion of theirs to the liberation or non-damnation of the devil and his angels; indeed their human mercy is concerned only with humans and they generally plead their own case . . . ; for this reason those who promise this impunity also to the prince of demons and his followers surpass such as these in preaching the mercy of God.[58]

Augustine admired the merciful intent of those who think that we may truly hope for the salvation of all human beings, but as teacher and pastor he rejected the opinion as well as its consequences. Indeed, pastorally speaking, it could prove to be, as he saw, a deceptive mercy, one that would lead to a presumption of salvation for all and end by abetting the damnation of many.

In the light of what it has been given us to know, we must suppose that (in numbers completely unknown to us) humans will be included in "the eternal fire prepared for the devil and his angels" (Mt 25:41) and that we ourselves could be among that

---

[58]*Ibid.*, 785.

number. It is such a sober awareness that the words of Jesus and the teaching of the Church would appear to inculcate, and better guides in this matter we cannot have.

It must be remembered, too, that God's revelation of the existence of hell is a salvific doctrine. It is intended to warn those who cannot be motivated by love—and such is the case, I suppose, with most of us at least some of the time. Awareness of hell's reality helps us shape decisions with an informed knowledge; it frees us from acting blindly, like actors on a stage where the plot and the possible conclusions are unknown. For all that, of course, the theme of the second death is a terrible subject and one about which more need not be said here. Let it suffice to state that death and the second death are the antithesis of all the good things God has prepared for His chosen.

Death in Christ

As the inevitable term of life in a fallen world—a world in which human death was meant to have no place—the mystery of death must be accepted. Viewed properly, from a Christian perspective, it can even, in a sense, be welcomed. Such welcoming, however, does not mean there is no pain in loss. Far from it. Undoubtedly life can be often painful and tragic, the world like an unhappy home that is filled with pain. But there is also so much of familiarity, of beauty and of joy that leaving earth itself—never mind loved ones—is a poignant thing, even leaving other emotions out of account. The moving words of an aged convert, ready to die but aware of what is relinquished, indicate some of the emotions that arise in the mind as one contemplates death.

> The hardest thing of all to explain is that death's nearness in some mysterious way makes what is being left behind—I mean our earth itself, its shapes and smells and colours and creatures, all that one has known and loved and lived with—the more entrancing; as the end of a bright June day somehow encapsulates all the beauty of the daylight hours now drawing to a close; or as the last notes of a Beethoven symphony manage to convey the splendour of the whole piece. Checking out of St. Theresa of Avila's second-class hotel, as the revolving doors take one into the street outside, one casts a backward look at the old place, overcome with affection for it, almost to the point of tears.[59]

---

[59] Malcolm Muggeridge, *Confessions of a Twentieth-Century Pilgrim*, p. 148.

Some of the same sense of affection for this earth, as well as deep appreciation for its beauty, was expressed by the saintly Pope Paul VI in his last will and testament. He wrote there how "the day is setting, and all is finishing and this stupendous, dramatic temporal and earthly scene is disappearing." That being so, the Pope felt obligated "to celebrate the gift, the good fortune, the beauty, the destiny of this very fleeting existence."[60]

The sense that existence is indeed very fleeting is what gives the tinge of melancholy to the beauties of a day or season or a period of our lives. There is the fear that what is passed is lost to us forever, the days that are no more being a death in life.

> Tears, idle tears, I know not what they mean,
> Tears from the depth of some divine despair
> Rise in the heart, and gather to the eyes,
> In looking on the happy autumn-fields,
> And thinking of the days that are no more.
>
> Fresh as the first beam glittering on a sail,
> That brings our friends up from the underworld,
> Sad as the last which reddens over one
> That sinks with all we love below the verge;
> So sad, so fresh, the days that are no more.
>
> Ah, sad and strange as in dark summer dawns
> The earliest pipe of half-awakened birds
> To dying ears, when unto dying eyes
> The casement slowly grows a glimmering square;
> So sad, so strange, the days that are no more.
>
> Dear as remembered kisses after death,
> And sweet as those by hopeless fancy feigned
> On lips that are for others; deep as love,
> Deep as first love, and wild with all regret;
> O Death in Life, the days that are no more.[61]

The words remind us—if further reminder be needed—that days are short and we are aliens here. We look "forward to the city with foundations, whose architect and maker is God" (Heb

---

[60] Paul VI, *Last Will, Origins*, vol. 8, no. 10, p. 175.
[61] Tennyson, *Tears, Idle Tears*.

11:10). This truth is well borne home to Christians by the word we use to describe the place where our life as Christians is most immediately evident, the local *parish*. The word itself comes from the Greek words *paroikia* and *paroikos* which mean a "sojourning" and "alien" and "pilgrim" (cf. Acts 7:6; 13:17; Eph 2:19; 1 Pt 1:17; 2:11). As such, the very place where the Church lives and worships is a terminal for arrivals and departures. We spend some time in a parish, a stop-over for pilgrims, like Mary and Joseph in a reluctant town. Our residence here has a note of impermanence. It has no foundation, cannot root itself in earth. For that reason, John tells us that the Word became flesh and pitched His tent among us, for the tent is a sign of impermanence. Combining somewhat the thought of St. Luke and the author of the Letter to the Hebrews, we may say that the Eternal Son was enrolled in our world (cf. Lk 2:1 where the Greek for "enroll" is the verb *apographomai*) so that we might be among the "assembly of the firstborn enrolled in heaven" (cf. Heb 12:23 where the Greek verb is the same as that in Luke). Augustine comments on this sojourn as follows:

> "One thing I have asked of the Lord, this I seek." What is this one thing? "That I may dwell in the house of the Lord, all the days of my life" (Ps 27:4). This is the one thing: for "house" is said of the place where we will always remain. In this pilgrimage "house" is spoken of, but properly speaking "tent" is what is meant; a tent is for those on pilgrimage, for those on a military campaign as it were, fighting an enemy. Therefore, when there is a tent in this life, it is manifestly because there is also an enemy. To share a tent with someone at the same time is what it means to be a comrade, and you know that this name is proper to those who are fighting side by side. Therefore, our tent is here, our home is there. But even this tent, by the abuse that comes from similarity, is sometimes called a house, and a house is sometimes in the same way called a tent. Properly speaking, however, the house is there, the tent here. . . .
>
> Thus, the psalmist says to the Lord, "I have desired this, I have asked for this, this I seek." And if we should say to him, "What will be done there; what will be your delight there; what will be the recreation *[auocamentum]* of your heart; what will be the delights that will suffice for your joys? For you will not last there unless you be happy. And that happiness, whence will it come?" Here we have different kinds of human happiness and someone is said to be miserable when what he loves is

taken away. Thus, men love different things and when someone is seen to have what he loves he is called happy. However,
he is truly happy, not if he have that which he loves but if he
loves that which should be loved. Indeed many are more miserable in having what they love than in doing without it. Loving
harmful things, they are miserable; having them they are more
miserable. . . .

And because in these earthly dwellings men are gladdened
by various delights and pleasures, and because each wishes to
live in that kind of a house where nothing will offend his soul
and there will be many things that will delight, if those things
that delight are taken away, a man wants to migrate. So, being
curious as it were, let us ask and let him [the psalmist] tell us
what we ourselves, what he, will do in that house where he
wishes, longs, desires and seeks this one thing of the Lord,
namely to dwell in it all the days of his life. "What will you do
there?" I ask you; "what is it that you desire?" Listen to what it
is. "That I may contemplate the delight of the Lord." "Behold
what I love, behold why I want to dwell in the house of the Lord
all the days of my life." He has there something great to see for
the delight of the Lord Himself is contemplated. When his night
is ended, he wants to dwell in God's light. For then, night having passed, our morning will arrive. . . .

We shall contemplate and shall enjoy great delight. Behold
I have just said this and all of you have cried out in desire for
that appearance never yet seen. Let your hearts go beyond all
customary things, let your inclination go beyond all the usual
thoughts that come from the flesh, derived from the flesh's
senses, imagining I know not what kind of phantasms. Reject
everything from your mind, deny whatever occurs to it; realize
the weakness of your heart and, because only what you are
capable of thinking of comes to your mind, say, "It is not that;
if it had been that it would not have already occurred to me."
Thus, you will desire something good. What kind of good? The
Good of all good, from which all good comes, the Good to
which nothing is added so that it might be good. A man is said
to be good, and so too a field and a good house, a good animal,
a good tree, a good body, a good soul. As often as you have said
"good" you have added something. This is the simple Good,
Good itself by which all things are good. It is this that is the delight of the Lord; it is this that we shall contemplate.

Now you see, brethren, if these good things that are called
good delight us, if goods that are not good *per se* (for everything changeable is not good *per se)* delight us, what will be the

contemplation of the unchangeable Good, the eternal Good, which always remains the same? Indeed these things that are called good would not delight us at all unless they were good, and they would not be good at all except because of Him who is simply Good. Now you know why the psalmist says, "Behold why I want to live in the house of the Lord all the days of my life."[62]

Even here in this tent, while we struggle, we are invited to remember that the good God Himself dwelt in our valley of the shadow of death, a comrade in our struggle. Then, having campaigned, He died in battle.

> The word of God was made flesh and dwelt among us. In Himself He did not possess that by which He might die for us unless He assumed mortal flesh from us. In this way the immortal was able to die, in this way He willed to give life to mortals. We would afterwards become sharers of Him Who first was made a sharer in what is ours. We did not possess of ourselves that by which we might live and He did not possess in Himself that by which He might die. Thus, by a mutual sharing He effected an exchange: ours to give Him the ability to die, His to give us the ability to live.[63]

This theme of the *divine exchange* is made much of by the Fathers. We give Him our death; He to us our life. The Second Vatican Council explicitly invites us to consider the Christological aspects of death.

> Through Christ and in Christ the enigma of sorrow and death is illuminated because apart from His Gospel this enigma overwhelms [obruit] us. Christ rose, destroying death by His death, and gave life to us so that, as sons in the Son, we cry out in the Spirit, "Abba, Father" (Gaudium et Spes, 22).

Central to the Christian understanding of death is the realization that One of the Trinity died on the Cross. The Eternal God Himself, Author of life, Life Himself died in our human flesh. As Pope John Paul II has taught:

> Let us raise our eyes first of all to Him Who is hanging on the Cross, and let us ask ourselves: Who is it that is suffering? It is the Son of God: true man, but also true God, as we know from the Creeds.

---

[62] Augustine, *Ennarr. in Ps.*, 26, Sermon 2, 7-9: CCSL 38, pp. 157-159.

[63] Augustine, "Sermon on the Passion," *Guelferbytanus 3: PLS* 2, 546.

For example, the Creed of Nicaea proclaims Him "true God from true God . . . Who for us men and for our salvation came down from Heaven, was made flesh and . . . suffered." The Council of Ephesus, on its part, declared that the "Word of God suffered in the flesh" (DS 263).

"The Word of God suffered in the flesh." It is a wonderful synthesis of the great mystery of the Incarnate Word, Jesus Christ, whose human sufferings pertain to the human nature, but must be attributed, like all His actions, to the divine Person. We have, therefore, in Christ a God who suffers!

. . . Theology has made clear that this which we cannot attribute to God as God—except in an anthropomorphic, metaphorical way whereby we speak of His suffering regrets, etc.—has been realized by God in His Son, the Word, who assumed human nature in Christ.

If Christ is God who suffers in the human nature, as a true man born of the Virgin Mary and subjected to the vicissitudes and pains and aches of every son of woman, then as the Word, a divine Person, He confers an infinite value on His suffering and death, which thus falls within the mysterious ambit of the human-divine reality, and touches, without affecting, the infinite glory and bliss of the Trinity.

Undoubtedly, God in His essence remains above the horizon of human-divine suffering: but Christ's Passion and death pervade, redeem, and ennoble all human suffering, because through the Incarnation He desired to express His solidarity with humanity, which gradually opens to communication with Him in faith and love.

. . . At Gethsemane we see how painful this obedience was to be: "Father, all things are possible to thee; remove this cup from me; yet not what I will, but what thou wilt" (Mk 14:36). In that moment Christ's agony of the soul was much more painful than that of the body (cf. St. Thomas, III, q. 46, a. 6), because of the interior conflict between the "supreme motives" of the Passion in the divine plan, and the perception which Jesus, in the refined sensitivity of His soul, has of the abominable filth of sin which seems to have been poured over Him, who had become as it were "sin" (that is, the victim of sin) as St. Paul says (cf. 2 Cor 5:21).[64]

---

[64] John Paul II, *Catechesis of Oct. 19, 1988*, translation from *L'Osservatore Romano*, English edition.

Revelation tells us that God demanded satisfaction for the sins committed by our race, and particularly for the original fall, which is the pattern of, as well as the continual, although only partial, cause for our subsequent moral failures and the personal and societal evils that flow from them. This demand for satisfaction, to have the evils committed made up or atoned for, is in itself a wonderful example of God's consideration and His condescension. It was possible for Him to have witnessed our misery, listened to our expressions of sorrow and cries for mercy (we think of David's plea in Psalm 51: "Have mercy on me, O God, in your goodness; in the greatness of your compassion wipe out my offense. Thoroughly wash me from my guilt and of my sin cleanse me") and replied with a word or gesture of pardon. In fact He did no such thing, but demanded satisfaction as the condition for forgiveness. It is a demand for justice that only at first glance hides the mercy and consideration that is its motivation. By pardoning without satisfaction, God would have left us recipients of a Divine "welfare," perpetual clients dependent on the goodwill of another. By demanding justice, satisfaction, He simultaneously ennobles us or dignifies us by establishing a situation in which, by making satisfaction, we will have *earned* His pardon and have a *right* to claim it.

This decision to ennoble us, to deal with us not as mere almoners but as possessors of rights, was not the limit of God's graciousness, however. For, in fact, the human race was not capable of making the satisfaction suited to the state of affairs produced by its sins. Since all are sinners by inheritance and by personal act, we lacked any innocent member worthy to treat with God on our behalf. Furthermore we lacked a member with the requisite dignity or status. The original fall that had affected all was an act of the preeminent members of the race, its founders and parents, Adam and Eve the first man and woman. Their disobedience was unique and universal since, through inheritance, all their descendants were left alienated from God. What progeny of theirs could act, as they had, on behalf of all? In short, God appeared to have demanded a satisfaction that we, as a race, were incapable of making. Then, having demanded the "impossible," He made it possible by becoming a human Himself. As St.

Paul wrote: "God was reconciling the world to himself in Christ" (2 Cor 5:19).

In Christ Man saves man. Two of the Prefaces of the Roman Liturgy express this truth as follows:

> We see your infinite power in your loving plan of salvation. You came to our rescue by your power as God, but You wanted us to be saved by one like us. Man refused your friendship, but man himself was to restore it through Jesus Christ our Lord.[65]

> You sent him as one like ourselves, though free from sin, so that you might see and love in us what you see and love in Christ.[66]

Truly the Incarnation is itself a redemption of the human race. By its union with the divinity in the Person of God the Son, a sinless human nature stands forth once again on our earth and within our race. In Christ a new Adam is constituted, truly human but with a personal dignity infinitely superior to that of Adam. The race is ennobled and capacitated to deal with its Creator in a way unattainable by the first Adam and his natural descendants. Moreover, in contrast with Adam and Eve, who would have been *transmitters* of grace to their descendants had they not sinned, in Christ human nature becomes not a mere transmitter but an instrumental cause of grace. In the Savior, our nature that had been sold into slavery and sin was redeemed, bought back, for God; our nature that was sick and weakened was healed and saved; our nature that was subjected to death was united to the source of life. And in that exaltation of our nature, all who share the nature were enriched. "We were by nature children of wrath. . . . But God, who is rich in mercy, because of the great love he had for us, even when we were dead in our transgressions, brought us to life with Christ" (Eph 2:3-5).

It was not God's plan to save us simply by the *presence* among us of the new Adam, a sinless Advocate worthy to deal for us before the Creator. He willed that we be saved by deeds, actions that proceeded from free human choice just as the sins, original and individual, had proceeded from freely chosen

---

[65] *The Sacramentary*, Preface III for Sundays in Ordinary Time.
[66] *Ibid.*, Preface VII for Sundays in Ordinary Time.

human deeds. This decision that we be saved by the human deeds of the God-man is, one may say, God's answer by anticipation to those who would diminish or attenuate the significance of individual actions by a false emphasis on general orientation, personal intent or "fundamental option." All Christian theology teaches this truth; it is by the deeds of the Christ, not just His presence, that we are saved. It is therefore deeds that shape and effect our relationship with God, and every deed shares in the dignity of the nature whence it flows and works either to enhance or diminish that dignity. Just as it was an act that doomed, so it is acts that saved our race.

The acts by which the Redeemer made satisfaction for the sins of His race can be seen, through the eyes of faith, to be singularly appropriate. God willed that a freely offered death of a man, along with the acts of suffering that led to that death, would be the means of our redemptive salvation. As death had been the result for us of Adam's sin, so a death, voluntarily accepted, would become the cause of sin's undoing. God willed that man, by enduring the effect of sin, should cancel out and destroy its cause. An obedient acceptance of such a death by one who was innocent would also satisfy for the act of disobedience that introduced death to our race. That such a death should be accomplished on the tree of the Cross manifests its own peculiar beauty. It evidences the harmony that exists in all God's work. He balances the tree of Eden, through which the race fell, with the tree of Calvary, through which we are saved. As Pope Urban IV wrote:

> Man fell by means of the food of the death-giving tree; man is raised up by means of the food of the life-giving tree. On the former hung the food of death, on the latter hung the nourishment that gives life. Eating of the former earned a wound, the taste of this latter restores health.[67]

The sacrifice of Christ cannot properly be portrayed as the act by which a just God, the Father, whose justice has been offended, punishes the Son in place of us. This is a type of thinking that appears to have its origins at the time of the Reformation and that finds a modern propounder in Karl Barth.

---

[67] Urban IV, *Transiturus*, Mansi, vol. 28, p. 486.

> In dying, He did not merely surrender Himself to that alienation from God which, as we learn from the Old Testament, is the climax of what man has to suffer as one whose life is over. He did this too, of course, as attested by the word on the cross: "My God, my God, why hast thou forsaken me" (Mk 15:34). It is no accident that this saying has come down to us in Aramaic and is a direct quotation of Ps 22:1. But the last "loud cry" with which Jesus died (Mk 15:37), and above all the representative character proper to this death, His vicarious bearing of the sin of all Israel and indeed the whole world, points beyond the comfortless but tolerable situation of the righteous man of the Old Testament as alienated from God in Sheol. . . . Here man— the man who is wholly and unreservedly for God—has God against him. Here God is wholly and unreservedly and in full seriousness against man. Here God metes out to man the kind of treatment he has deserved at His hand. This is how He must deal with him now in His mercy, which is "righteous" to the extent that in it He wills to establish His own right and that of man. Here He treats man as a transgressor with whom He can only deal in His wrath. Here He treats him in accordance with the enmity which man has merited from Him. . . . It is, of course, true that this man is the Son of God. In Him God Himself suffers what guilty man had to suffer by way of eternal punishment.[68]

 Even the fact that it is God Himself Who suffers in Christ does not mitigate the vengeful picture of the Father presented by this stark and fundamentally inaccurate presentation of the doctrine of satisfaction. Nor will an appeal to the cry of Jesus on the Cross, the "My God, my God, why have you abandoned me?", justify the portrayal of God the Father depicted in such a theology. As found in Matthew, the "Eli, Eli" is probably Hebrew, although the remaining words are Aramaic. In Mark the whole phrase is Aramaic. Many think that Jesus quoted the Psalm in Hebrew and that the similarity of sounds led some to think He was calling Elijah. Whatever the language, the thesis that sees in this cry a real abandonment of the Son by the Father or one that speaks about total psychological abandonment is not tenable.

The Fathers are unanimously (as far as I can determine) against any Barth-like interpretation. A few examples of Patristic interpretation may suffice.

---

[68] Barth, *Church Dogmatics*, III, 2, p. 603.

Origen sees the cry as a citation from Psalm 22 and views it as the ultimate point of the *kenosis*; the Son is robbed of the glory due Him even to the point of suffering this death, in the midst of robbers. In citing it Jesus is also showing what he has done for us. There is no notion of actual abandonment.[69]

Chrysostom sees it as citation of Psalm 22 and as Christ giving witness to the Old Testament prophecies. It is a cry in which "Christ gives honor to His Father."[70] Jerome likewise sees it as a citation of Psalm 22.[71]

Augustine views the prayer in the framework usual for his interpretation of the Psalms. The cry represents the Head praying for the members of His Body, the Church. Commenting in a similar vein on Psalm 28 (27) and its opening words "Do not be silent to me," Augustine says:

> "I have cried to You, O Lord, my God, do not be silent to me." I have cried to You, O Lord, my God, do not separate the unity of Your Word from that whereby I am man. "By no means remain silent to me; or I will be like one going down into the pit." Because the eternity of Your Word does not interrupt uniting itself to me, it happens that I am not a man like others who are born into the profound misery of this age where You, as it were, are silent, where Your Word is not known. 'Hear the voice of my cry when I pray to You, when I raise my hands to your holy temple,' namely when I am crucified for the salvation of those who, by believing, become your holy temple.[72]

Pope John Paul II has written the following on the "My God, my God, why have you forsaken me?"

> The first cry expresses the depth and intensity of Jesus' suffering, His interior participation, His spirit of oblation, and perhaps also His prophetic-messianic understanding of His drama in the terms of a Biblical psalm. . . . But on Jesus' lips the "why" addressed to God was also more effective in expressing a pained bewilderment at that suffering which had no merely human explanation, but which was a mystery of which the Father alone possessed the key. . . .

---

[69] Origen: *PG* 13, 1785-1787.
[70] Chrysostom, *Homily 88 on Matthew: PG* 58, 776.
[71] Jerome, *Commentary on Matthew: CCSL* 77, p. 274.
[72] Augustine, *Ennarr. in Ps.* 27, 2: *CCSL* 38, p. 168.

(3) In hearing Jesus crying out His "why," we learn indeed that also those who suffer can utter this same cry, but in those same dispositions of filial trust and abandonment of which Jesus is the teacher and model. In the "why" of Jesus there is no feeling of resentment leading to rebellion or desperation; there is no semblance of a reproach to the Father, but the expression of the experience of weakness, of solitude, of abandonment to Himself, made by Jesus in our place; by Him who thus becomes the first of the "smitten and afflicted," the first of the abandoned. . . .

(4) In fact, if Jesus feels abandoned by the Father, He knows however that that is not really so. He Himself said: "I and the Father are one" (Jn 10:30), and speaking of His future Passion He said: "I am not alone, for the Father is with Me" (Jn 16:32). Dominant in His mind Jesus has the clear vision of God and the certainty of His union with the Father. But in the sphere bordering on the senses, and therefore more subject to the impressions, emotions and influences of the internal and external experiences of pain, Jesus' human soul is reduced to a wasteland, and He no longer feels the "presence" of the Father, but He undergoes the tragic experience of the most complete desolation.

(5) . . . In the sphere of feelings and affection this sense of the absence and abandonment by God was the most acute pain for the soul of Jesus Who drew His strength and joy from union with the Father. This pain rendered more intense all the other sufferings. That lack of interior consolation was His greatest agony.

(6) However, Jesus knew that by this ultimate phase of His sacrifice, reaching the intimate core of His being, He completed the work of reparation which was the purpose of His sacrifice for the expiation of sins. If sin is separation from God, Jesus had to experience, in the crisis of His union with the Father, a suffering proportionate to that separation. On the other hand in quoting the beginning of Psalm 21 (22), which he perhaps continued to recite mentally during the Passion, Jesus did not forget the conclusion which becomes a hymn of liberation and an announcement of salvation granted to all by God. The experience of abandonment is therefore a passing pain which gives way to personal liberation and universal salvation.[73]

---

[73] John Paul II, "Wednesday Catechesis for Nov. 30, 1988," translation of *L'Osservatore Romano*, English edition of December 12, 1988, pp. 1 and 12.

The Pope's words capture, I think, the true meaning of the cry. "If Jesus feels abandoned by the Father, He knows however that that is not really so. He Himself said: 'I and the Father are one' (Jn 10:30)." The Lord *felt* one thing, while *knowing* another. He experienced, in the sphere of His emotions, "a suffering proportionate to that separation" from God which sin is.

The death of the Son is not an expression of God's vindictive punishment satisfying an affronted justice. It is a justice demanded for the sake of mercy, a mercy whereby God Himself will take on the consequences and punishment of our sins. The Judge undergoes the result of the crime in order to destroy it. In doing this, He gives death no value in itself. There is a text in the Old Latin translation of First Peter 3:22 that reads: "[Christ] is at the right hand of the Father, swallowing up death so that He might make us heirs of eternal life."[74] He "swallows up death" (a wonderful image), although it appeared momentarily that death had swallowed Him. Some of the paradox involved is captured by St. Ephrem of Syria (c. 305-373).

> Our Lord was trampled by death and He likewise crushed it as though it were a path. He submitted Himself to death and bore with it willingly so that He might destroy an unwilling death. For our Lord went forth carrying the Cross, that being what death willed; nevertheless He cried out from the Cross and led out the dead from the lower world although death did not will that. In the body that was His, death killed Him; using that same body as a weapon He gained victory over death. The divinity hid itself under the humanity and approached death, which killed and was killed. For death killed the natural life, and the supernatural life in turn killed it.

> Therefore, because death was not able to devour Him unless He had a body nor the underworld swallow Him up unless He had flesh, He came to the Virgin so that, taking flesh from her, He might travel to the underworld. In that assumed body He entered the underworld, broke into its treasury and laid waste its riches. . . . When death was feeding and, according to its custom, confidently approaching Him, Life, the Destroyer of death, was hidden in the mortal fruit. Thus, when death, fearing nothing, absorbed Him, it set Life free and, with Life, many others.

---

[74] The Latin text reads: *"Qui est in dextera Dei, deglutiens mortem, ut vitae aeternae nos faceret heredes."* The New Vulgate omits it since it is not in the Greek.

The wonderful Son of the carpenter raised His Cross above the underworld that swallowed up all humans and in this way the human race crossed over into the home of life. Because the human race had fallen into the underworld because of a tree it would cross into the house of life by means of a tree. . . . Glory to You Who built Your Cross as a bridge above death so that on it souls might cross from the region of death to the region of life.[75]

Ephrem's words teach what in fact is the reality. Death remains, as St. Paul teaches, "the last enemy" (1 Cor 15:26). But it has been conquered by the man Christ Jesus. "Is not Christ life? Yet Christ died. However, in the death of Christ death died because dead Life killed death, the fullness of life swallowing up death."[76] And all who belong to Christ know that they too shall mock this enemy.

Another word of Jesus from the Cross, "Father, forgive them," is as much a demand as a plea, for it comes from the man who, by personal dignity (He is the eternal Son, God Himself) and by perfect, sacrificial obedience, has the *right* to say "It is completed," satisfaction is made. "Forgive them, Father." And, in this way, God, by His mercy, has enabled the race to save itself, having become a man so that man could do so. Moreover, what Christ has achieved as man belongs to all humans for He accomplished it in our nature and as the one constituted by right as the new Adam. Yet more profoundly, He has associated us with what He accomplished by offering each of us the opportunity to be united so intimately to Him that we mystically form with Him a single person. By making us one Body with Himself through Baptism and, most especially, through the Eucharist, Christ shares Himself and all that is His by right and achievement. In Him, then, and with Him we become partakers and cooperators in the work of Redemption, even playing our part in making up what is lacking in the suffering of Christ for His Body the Church.

For this reason death, while never being a good, can be faced and even willed. The Christian knows that "if we have grown

---

[75] Ephrem of Syria, *Sermon on Our Lord*, 3-4, 9, *Liturgia Horarum*, vol. 2, for Friday of Third Week of Easter.

[76] Augustine, *In Iohannis Evangelium*, 12, 11: CCSL 36, p. 127.

into union with him through a death like his, we shall also be united with him in the resurrection" (Rom 6:5). With that knowledge, one can pray: "[I want] to know him and the power of his resurrection and the sharing of his sufferings by being conformed to his death" (Phil 3:10). The natural fear of death can no longer control the lives of the faithful. It is not that the Son of God Himself did not suffer greatly and fear death. One thinks of the Angel of the Agony. The thought is astounding that a creature should be needed to comfort the God-man. Yet such was the case. As is so often pointed out, the agony of Jesus was not like that of Socrates. The Lord gave expression to the human experience of fear. By so doing, he would ultimately conquer that fear for us.

> Now since the children share in blood and flesh, he likewise shared in them, that through death he might destroy the one who has the power of death, that is, the devil, and free those who through fear of death had been subject to slavery all their life (Heb 2:14-15).

The fear of death referred to in the text is that *servile* fear which impels us to a type of submission. Such fear gives in to death, letting it become a master whose wishes are carried out (as in the case of abortion) or a master that is run from (as in the case of euthanasia, or in those efforts to prolong life beyond its natural course as if physical life were the ultimate value). Such is the slavery caused by the fear of death. Natural fear may remain present, but the believer has overcome the fear that enslaves.

The Christian indeed is meant to live in Christ (Jn 15:4) and to die in Him. There is the understanding that one can "die in the Lord" as we read in the Book of Revelation 14:13. This death begins with Baptism (cf. Rom 6:3-11) and is constantly celebrated in the Eucharist. In this sense there is truly a "spirituality of death" for the Christian, even though death itself can be assigned no positive role. All of one's life is a dying, physically and spiritually—a severing, a breaking loose, a pulling away—and to the extent that we accept this, we participate in the Lord's own death and await a like resurrection (cf. 2 Cor 4:10ff). His death gives meaning to ours, not because the death is good but because He overcame it by His resurrection. It is often said that we die alone. This is never true for those who cling to the Firstborn from the dead. We share that event now with Him. We die in Him and He accompanies us. Thus there is hope. Our hope against death is Christ, Who holds the keys of death and the underworld. And so, in the words of a twelfth century writer, to Him we pray:

> Lest we fail with those who fail, "remain with us because evening draws on." The evening of my life is now at hand, prevailing sickness consumes my body, already fierce death threatens, fear and terror shake my soul, the terrible sentence of the judgment scares me, but You, O Lord, to Whom the Father has given all judgment, "remain with us, because evening draws on." Into Your hands I commend my spirit. Do not hand over the soul trusting in You to the powers of darkness. In You alone is our salvation; our eyes are on You lest we perish.[77]

It is with the confidence that He Who shared and overcame our death will hear us that we also pray for our dead almost joyfully:

In paradisum deducant te Angeli: in tuo adventu suscipiant te Martyres, et perducant te in civitatem sanctam Ierusalem. Chorus Angelorum te suscipiat, et cum Lazaro quondam paupere aeternam habeas requiem.	*May the angels lead you to Paradise: at your coming may the Martyrs receive you and lead you into the Holy City Jerusalem. May the choir of Angels receive you, and with the once poor Lazarus may you have eternal rest.*

---

[77] Blessed Ogerius (?): *PL* 184, 977.

III

MY FLESH WILL REST IN HOPE

DEATH is clearly a physical separation from those we love—and for many it is a spiritual separation as well. The poignancy with which we often think of those who have gone before us through death is indicated in an essay about Christmas Day by Charles Dickens.

> On this day we shut out Nothing! "Pause," says a low voice. "Nothing? Think!" "On Christmas Day, we will shut out from our fireside, Nothing." "Not the shadow of a vast City where the withered leaves are lying deep?" the voice replies. "Not the shadow that darkens the whole globe? Not the shadow of the City of the Dead?"
>
> Not even that. Of all days in the year, we will turn our faces towards that City upon Christmas Day, and from it silent hosts bring those we loved among us. City of the Dead, in the blessed name wherein we are gathered together at this time, and in the Presence that is here among us according to the promise, we will receive, and not dismiss, the people who are dear to us! . . .
>
> Lost friend, lost child, lost parent, sister, brother, husband, wife, we will not so discard you! You shall hold your cherished places in our Christmas hearts, and by our Christmas fires; and in the season of immortal hope, and on the birthday of immortal mercy, we will shut out Nothing![1]

The quotation from the *In Paradisum* at the end of the last chapter, together with this selection from Dickens, offers us the opportunity to raise the difficult questions concerned with what is called the "interim state," the condition of human beings between their bodily death and the second coming of Christ. St. Paul would appear to speak of this state in Second Corinthians 5:1-10:

> For we know that if our earthly dwelling, a tent, should be destroyed, we have a building from God, a dwelling not made with hands, eternal in heaven. For in this tent we groan, longing

---

[1] Dickens, "What Christmas Is As We Grow Older," *Christmas Stories*, pp. 23-25.

to be further clothed with our heavenly habitation if indeed, when we have taken it off, we shall not be found naked. For while we are in this tent we groan and are weighed down, because we do not wish to be unclothed but to be further clothed, so that what is mortal may be swallowed up by life. Now the one who has prepared us for this very thing is God, who has given us the Spirit as a first installment.

So we are always courageous, although we know that while we are at home in the body we are away from the Lord, for we walk by faith, not by sight. Yet we are courageous, and we would rather leave the body and go home to the Lord. Therefore, we aspire to please him, whether we are at home or away. For we must all appear before the judgment seat of Christ, so that each one may receive recompense, according to what he did in the body, whether good or evil.

It is Paul's concept of leaving the body, awaiting to be "clothed with our heavenly habitation," that has raised much discussion among Christians concerning the status of those who have departed this life. This discussion is predicated on the notion that, although the body lies buried, there is some type of continued life for those we call "dead." That there is such life is not, of course, a conviction peculiar to Christians.

Mankind never looked on death merely as the full stop at the end of the brief sentence which is life. What was the source of these intimations, these ideas, so contrary to all appearances that life furnished, to the fact presented by the whole of nature? In the beginning they derived from no revelation, whether from God or from those who had died; it was simply the self-witness of human nature, which felt itself to be other than the rest of the living world that comes and goes.[2]

The Immortality of the Soul

Plato (428-348 B.C.), through Socrates, taught the immortality of that part of our individuality which we call the soul. It was this belief that apparently enabled Socrates himself to face death with equanimity. Since Plato believed in the preexistence of souls, he judged that they were, in some sense, longing for that

---

[2] Winklhofer, *The Coming of His Kingdom*, pp. 29-30.

paradise which they had left before appearing here on earth. This idea was taken up beautifully by William Wordsworth in his *Ode: Intimations of Immortality from Recollections of Early Childhood*, which captures something of the thought not only of Plato but also of the Christian theologian Origen who adhered to Plato's idea about the preexistence of the human soul.

> Our birth is but a sleep and a forgetting:
> The Soul that rises with us, our life's Star,
> Hath had elsewhere its setting,
> And cometh from afar:
> Not in entire forgetfulness,
> And not in utter nakedness,
> But trailing clouds of glory do we come
> From God, who is our home:
> Heaven lies about us in our infancy!
> Shades of the prison-house begin to close
> Upon the growing Boy,
> But He beholds the light, and whence it flows,
> He sees it in his joy;
> The Youth, who daily farther from the east
> Must travel, still is Nature's Priest,
> And by the vision splendid
> Is on his way attended;
> At length the Man perceives it die away,
> And fade into the light of common day.
> ....
> What though the radiance which was once so bright
> Be now for ever taken from my sight,
> Though nothing can bring back the hour
> Of splendour in the grass, of glory in the flower;
> We will grieve not, rather find
> Strength in what remains behind;
> In the primal sympathy
> Which having been must ever be;
> In the soothing thoughts that spring
> Out of human suffering;
> In the faith that looks through death,
> In years that bring the philosophic mind.[3]

As heaven lies about us in infancy, so our souls that come from there are destined for that starting point. In the meantime,

---

[3] Wordsworth, "Ode: Intimations of Immortality," *William Wordsworth: The Poems*, I, pp. 525 and 528-529.

the preexistent souls are, for Plato and those who follow him more closely than Wordsworth, imprisoned in the body, and death will be a release from this prison. In his *Phaedo* Plato wrote the following about death.

> Is it anything more than the separation of the soul from the body? said Socrates. "Death is that the body separates from the soul, and remains by itself apart from the soul, and the soul, separated from the body, exists by itself apart from the body." . . .

> "And is not purification really that which has been mentioned so often in our discussion, to separate as far as possible the soul from the body, and to accustom it to collect itself together out of the body in every part, and to dwell alone by itself as far as it can, both at this present and in the future, being freed from the body as if from a prison?"

> "By all means," said he.

> "But to set it free, as we say, is the chief endeavor of those who rightly love wisdom, nay of those alone, and the very care and practice of the philosophers is nothing but the freeing and separation of soul from body, don't you think so?"

> "It appears to be so."

> "Then, as I said at first, it would be absurd for a man preparing himself in his life to be as near as possible to death, so to live, and then when death came, to object."

> "Of course."[4]

That the soul is immortal is an answer that has satisfied many in every age since Socrates spoke, for it promises the preservation of what is perceived to be the "essential self," the soul. This notion of the soul as the "real me" harmonizes well—although not by necessity—with that tendency found in those philosophies of both West and (more deeply yet) East that assign little value (and certainly no lasting value) to matter. For them, the body is ultimately disposable; only spirit counts.

Now the Church herself, while rejecting the notion of a preexistence of the soul,[5] has accepted the truth of the human

---

[4] Plato, *The Phaedo*, pp. 467-470.
[5] Provincial Council of Constantinople of 543 (*DS* 405). These canons were apparently approved by Pope Vigilius.

soul's immortality, and taught it definitively. This dogma was proclaimed in 1513 at the eighth session of the Fifth Council of the Lateran. The decree *Apostolici regiminis* reads in part:

> With the approval of this Sacred Council we condemn and reprove all those who assert that the intellective soul is mortal . . . or call this truth into doubt, since not only is the soul truly, *per se*, and essentially the form of the human body but it is also truly immortal (*DS* 1440).[6]

In our own day, the teaching of Lateran Council V has been succinctly reaffirmed by the teaching of Vatican Council II.

> Humans truly are not deceived when they recognize themselves as superior to bodily things and consider themselves not just as particles of nature or anonymous elements of the human city. Indeed, by their interiority, they surpass the universe of things. They return to this profound interiority when they turn to their heart where the God Who examines hearts awaits them, and where they themselves, under the eyes of God, discern their own fate. Therefore, recognizing in themselves a spiritual and immortal soul, they are not deceived by false illu-

---

[6] Fiorenza and Metz, writing in *Mysterium Salutis*, II, 2, say the following of the definition: "In 1513 Lateran Council V took up again the formulation of the Council of Vienne in its condemnation of the heresy of the neo-Aristotelian Pedro Pomponazzi, a follower of Averroes. According to the way of thinking of Pomponazzi, the spirit of man . . . cannot be an individual substance but rather . . . it must be universal. . . . Against this doctrine of a universal *nous* the Council underlines the unity of man. . . . In describing the individuality and the belonging of the soul to the body, the Council attributes immortality to the soul. Therefore, the intention of the words of the Council is not directed primarily to the postulating of an immortality to the soul which would separate it from the body and from history. On the contrary it tells us that the soul is immortal because, as the form of the body, it is that which essentially constitutes the individual man. As a result the Council assigns immortality to the soul because the individual man in his historical realization is immortal" (pp. 694-695). The explanation of these two theologians on this point is not accurate in light of the historical and philosophical thought of that epoch. Furthermore, it is clear from the definition itself that not only the unity of the individual is in question but also the very immortality of the soul. As the introduction in *DS* indicates correctly, Pomponazzi's book, condemned by the Council, was *Tractatus de immortalitate animae*. Of his opinion, as expressed in the book, the definition says: "According to him neither the immortality of the human soul nor its contrary can be demonstrated philosophically" (*DS* 1440). It is this that the Council is rejecting. Metz and Fiorenza were writing at a time when it was popular to see the soul/body relationship in such a way that one could not imagine the actual separation of the two. It was a position favored by Karl Rahner and passed over into his view on intermediate eschatology and the supposed immediate resurrection of the body.

sions that arise only from physical or social conditions. On the contrary, they touch the profound truth of the matter *(Gaudium et Spes,* 14).

Whether arrived at by an instinct present in nature itself, or by reason, or by a faithful acceptance of the revealing Word of God, the immortality of the soul opens up great vistas for us as we contemplate what happens at the time of death. At that moment, the horizon of the departed is both retrospective and forward looking. It is a time of discernment that is generally called the particular judgment.

The Particular Judgment

Alfred Lord Tennyson gives us a famous and beautiful description of the death of his hero-king.

> And slowly answer'd Arthur from the barge:
> "The old order changeth, yielding place to new,
> And God fulfills himself in many ways,
> Lest one good custom should corrupt the world.
> Comfort thyself; what comfort is in me?
> I have lived my life, and that which I have done
> May He within himself make pure! but thou,
> If thou shouldst never see my face again,
> Pray for my soul. More things are wrought by prayer
> Than this world dreams of. Wherefore, let thy voice
> Rise like a fountain for me night and day.
> For what are men better than sheep or goats
> That nourish a blind life within the brain,
> If, knowing God, they lift not hands of prayer
> Both for themselves and those who call them friend?
> For so the whole round earth is every way
> Bound by gold chains about the feet of God.
> But now farewell. I am going a long way
> With these thou seest—if indeed I go—
> For all my mind is clouded with a doubt—
> To the island-valley of Avilion;
> Where falls not hail, or rain, or any snow,
> Nor ever wind blows loudly; but it lies
> Deep-meadow'd, happy, fair with orchard lawns
> And bowery hollows crown'd with summer sea,
> Where I will heal me of my grievous wound."[7]

---

[7] Tennyson, "The Passing of Arthur," *Idylls of the King,* pp. 251-252.

The poet's words, indicating Arthur's request for prayer and the indication that the king's works are now hopefully to find themselves made fair in God, can remind us of a doctrine whose existence is implied by the acknowledgment that a future reward or punishment awaits the individual beyond death, namely the occurrence of the particular judgment. Although what actually occurs in the process is unknown to us, it is then that an individual life is weighed in the balance. We may consider it basically as an awareness of one's lot in the life to come. Such cognizance is something that precedes the vision of God, since not everyone will be prepared for that encounter. Indeed, the "judgment" can perhaps best be imagined as an act of insight, a sufficiently adequate realization of what awaits one. For those who die in mortal sin, estranged from God, it will be a confirmation of all the horror of death itself. For others it will be the very beginning of their victory over the death they have just experienced.

Though this name "particular judgement" more commonly brings home to us the idea of possible reprobation of individual souls, such a one-sided aspect of this act of God would leave in obscurity the most marvelous manifestation of the divine sanctity and justice. For the elect, for those who are saved, that moment which constitutes the soul in eternity is an overwhelming revelation of God's fidelity; not only does it become immensely clear to the soul that it is saved, that it is in a state of grace, that it belongs to God for ever and ever, but all the works done in the supernatural order during the mortal life are remembered by God, are brought to the knowledge of the fortunate soul, are seen in their full setting; and God rewards as only God can reward. "For I know whom I have believed and I am certain that he is able to keep that which I have committed unto him, against that day" (2 Tm 1:12). Or again: "I have fought the good fight: I have finished my course: I have kept the faith. As to the rest, there is laid up for me a crown of justice which the Lord the just judge will render to me in that day: and not only to me, but to them also that love His coming" (2 Tm 4:7-8).[8]

It is moreover at the particular judgment that we shall not only realize our fate but also fathom more profoundly the immensity of the combat in which we have been involved. It is a

---

[8] Anscar Vonier, *Death and Judgement*, pp. 65-66.

conflict that includes the angels and demons, because "our struggle is not with flesh and blood but with the principalities, with the powers, with the rulers of this present darkness, with the evil spirits in the heavens" (Eph 6:12). Pope Paul VI, in a justly famous talk, spoke powerfully of this warfare.

> Evil is not merely an absence of something but an active force, a living, spiritual being that is perverted and that perverts others. It is a terrible reality, mysterious and frightening.

> It is a departure from the picture provided by biblical and Church teaching to refuse to acknowledge the Devil's existence; to regard him as a self-sustaining principle who, unlike other creatures, does not owe his origin to God; or to explain the Devil as a pseudo-reality, a conceptual, fanciful personification of the unknown causes of our misfortunes. When the problem of evil is seen in all its complexity and in its absurdity from the point of view of our limited minds, it becomes an obsession. It poses the greatest single obstacle to our religious understanding of the universe. It is no accident that St. Augustine was bothered by this for years: "I sought the source of evil and I found no explanation" (*Confessions*, VII, 5, 7).

> Thus we can see how important an awareness of evil is if we are to have a correct Christian concept of the world, life and salvation. We see this first in the unfolding of the Gospel story at the beginning of Christ's public life. Who can forget the highly significant description of the triple temptation of Christ? Or the many episodes in the Gospel where the Devil crosses the Lord's path and figures in His teaching? And how could we forget that Christ, referring three times to the Devil as His adversary, describes him as "the prince of this world" (Jn 12:31). . . .

> Many passages in the Gospel show us that we are dealing not just with one devil, but with many (cf. Lk 11:21; Mk 5:9). But the principal one is Satan, which means the adversary, the enemy; and along with him are many others, all of them creatures of God, but fallen because they rebelled and were damned (cf. DS 800)—a whole mysterious world, convulsed by a most unfortunate drama about which we know very little.

> There are many things we do know, however, about this diabolical world, things that touch on our lives and on the whole history of mankind. The Devil is at the origin of mankind's first misfortune; he was the wily, fatal tempter involved in the first sin, the original sin. That fall of Adam gave the Devil a certain dominion over man, from which only Christ's Re-

demption can free us. It is a history that is still going on: let us recall the exorcisms at Baptism, and the frequent references in Sacred Scripture and in the liturgy to the aggressive and oppressive "power of darkness" (Lk 22:53). The Devil is the number one enemy, the preeminent tempter.

So we know that this dark, disturbing being exists and that he is still at work with his treacherous cunning; he is the hidden enemy who sows errors and misfortunes in human history. It is worth recalling the revealing Gospel parable of the good seed and the cockle, for it synthesizes and explains the lack of logic that seem to preside over our contradictory experiences: "An enemy has done this" (Mt 13:28). He is a "murderer from the beginning, . . . and the father of lies," as Christ defines him (Jn 8:44-45). He undermines man's equilibrium with his sophistry. He is the malign, clever seducer who knows how to make his way into us through the senses, the imagination and the libido, through utopian logic, or through disordered social contacts in the give and take of our activities, so that he can bring about in us deviations that are all the more harmful because they seem to conform to our physical or mental makeup, or to our profound, instinctive aspirations.

The matter of the Devil and of the influence he can exert on individuals as well as on communities, entire societies or events, is a very important chapter of Catholic doctrine which should be studied again, although it is given little attention today. . . .

This is not to say that every sin is directly due to diabolical action; but it is true that those who do not keep watch over themselves with a certain moral rigor are exposed to the influence of the "mystery of iniquity" cited by St. Paul (2 Thes 2:3ff) which raises serious questions about our salvation.[9]

We are like troops in a battle, so engrossed in our own struggle that it is easy to forget the extent of the war, the fact that others fight beside us, and that it must be won on the "grand scale." The particular judgment will immeasurably broaden our horizon. Of course, each of us individually and each skirmish is important to Him whose beneficent providence is concerned even with the fall of a sparrow to earth (cf. Mt 10:29).

---

[9] Paul VI, Wednesday Catechesis of Nov. 15, 1972, *TPS*, vol. 17, no. 4, pp. 316-318. The Wednesday Catechesis of John Paul II on August 13 and August 20, 1986, repeated all the doctrine on the devils. Cf. *Insegnamenti di Giovanni Paolo II*, vol. IX, 2, pp. 360-366 and 395-398.

When the discernment of the particular judgment is completed, the soul enters upon the first phase of its future, that form of life called, in theology, the in-between or interim state.

The Interim State

In his *Church Dogmatics*, the Protestant theologian Karl Barth, because of his notions on the body-soul relationship[10] and his views on the correlation between time and eternity,[11] envisions a situation in which there is nothing in between death and resurrection, no interim period.

> 'To fall asleep' is the characteristic New Testament term for the death which is freed from the 'second' death by the death of Jesus Christ and is therefore a wholly natural thing for the Christian. . . . The term 'fall asleep' shows that the New Testament Christians never asked independently concerning the being or state of man in death, or tried to find an answer in the postulate of an intermediate state. They simply held fast to the confession: 'I am the resurrection and the life,' and in the light of this hope they came to see in the visible process of dying the last conclusive symptom of a life surrounded by the peace of God.[12]

What Barth's final thoughts were about the relation between our individual deaths, the final coming of Christ and the resurrection of the dead is not luminously clear. However, he has been understood as saying that, in fact, because of the relation between time and eternity, we *rise at our death* in such a way that what is individual to each, namely passage from this life, is also the communal end because all arrive simultaneously in eternity. This is certainly the way Oscar Cullmann understood Barth when he wrote:

> . . . the transformation of the body does not occur immediately after each individual death. . . . This is the point where I cannot accept Karl Barth's position as a simple restatement of the original Christian view, not even his position in the *Church Dogmatics* where it is subtly shaded and comes much nearer to New Testament eschatology than in his first writings. Karl Barth

---

[10] Cf. Barth, *Church Dogmatics*, III, 2, pp. 344-346.
[11] Cf. Barth, *Church Dogmatics*, II, 1, pp. 608-640.
[12] Barth, *Church Dogmatics*, III, 2, p. 639.

considers it to be the New Testament interpretation that the transformation of the body occurs for everyone immediately after his individual death—as if the dead were no longer in time.[13]

Cullmann himself visualized an interim state that was a type of sleep. There is, according to him, a kind of survival for the just. This survival is not bodily, but spiritual, although, according to Cullmann, it is not the Greek notion of "immortality of the soul" since it is not something natural but rather caused by the Holy Spirit. What he is describing may be considered to be a type of dormition that lasts until the resurrection of all when Christ comes again. Such an outlook is not unlike that of Pope John XXII who, in sermons in 1331, gave out as his personal opinion the notion that the dead enjoy the vision of God Himself only after the Last Judgment.[14] The Pope soon retracted this opinion (cf. *DS* 990-991), but only a definition of Faith issued by his successor Benedict XII resolved the problem definitively as far as Catholic dogma is concerned.

The positions of Barth and Cullmann were not without resonance in the Catholic theological community of the twentieth century. Karl Rahner demonstrated an interesting intellectual progression in his theology concerning the "interim state," perhaps always being influenced to some extent by Barth. In early writings, Rahner defended an interpretation of Matthew 27:52 that even St. Thomas Aquinas once held (but apparently later abandoned), namely that some of those who had been dead were definitively raised at the time of the resurrection of Jesus and thus are bodily in heaven.[15] Consequently, the Assumption of Mary was not unique since there were *some* others who were bodily in heaven. Rahner wrote: "In so far as there are already

---

[13] O. Cullmann, "Immortality of the Soul or Resurrection of the Dead," *Immortality and Resurrection* (Krister Stendahl, editor), pp. 35-36.

[14] The sermons of John XXII on the matter can be found in Marc Dykmans, *Les Sermons de Jean XXII sur la vision béatifique.*

[15] On St. Thomas' opinion, see *Lectura super Evangelium S. Matthaei*, no. 2395 on Mt 27:52. "About those mentioned here it can be said that they rose not to die again because they rose to manifest the resurrection of Christ . . . they arose to enter with Christ into heaven." Thomas nowhere later repeats this opinion.

human beings (the risen Lord, our Lady and no doubt others; cf. Mt 27:52) who possess glorified bodily nature...."[16]

A somewhat fuller statement is given in volume one of his *Theological Investigations*. The footnote there sums up part of his thought at that period: "The Bull *(Munificentissimus Deus)* nowhere affirms that Mary's privilege of "anticipated" resurrection is to be understood as being unique in itself simply, as well as in its cause and title."[17]

In later works, Rahner apparently went farther, espousing a concept very like that of Karl Barth in respect to the time sequence involved when speaking of the resurrection body.

> With regard to the second Marian dogma, we could reach an easier consensus with Protestant theology. Its content does not imply that the "bodily" assumption of Mary into heaven is a privilege granted, apart from Jesus, only to her. The Church fathers, for example, felt it was obvious that the souls in limbo entered heaven with their bodies at the resurrection of Jesus. If today we use a way of thinking that differs from a platonizing interpretation of the "separation of body and soul" at the time of death and hold that everyone at death takes on his or her resurrection body already "even at that very moment" (to the extent that the use of such a temporal concept is legitimate), which view is frequently proposed even in Protestant theology, and which, with some appropriate demythologizing, can be quite legitimate, then what is stated in the dogma of Mary's assumption is not an exclusive occurrence since, as a matter of fact, it happens to all the saints. What is claimed is that what happens to Mary belongs to her in a special way because of her role in salvation-history and therefore is more readily perceived by the church's faith-consciousness than in the case of other human beings.[18]

There is no doubt that some of the Fathers, as well as St. Thomas Aquinas, thought that there were some in heaven with their bodies. Strictly speaking Rahner is also correct about the definition of the Assumption. The formula proclaiming the doc-

---

[16] Rahner, *Theological Investigations*, II, p. 215.

[17] Rahner, *Theological Investigations*, I, p. 220.

[18] Rahner, "Open Questions in Dogma," *Catholic Mind*, March 1979, vol. 77, no. 1331, p. 24. Cf. *Foundations of Christian Faith*, p. 388. The opinion is found as well in the article "The Intermediate State," *Theological Investigations*, XVII, pp. 114ff.

trine does not say that the Assumption is unique, although one may think that this was presumed. Eventually, Paul VI, perhaps to counter opinions like those of Rahner, began to teach explicitly the uniqueness of the Assumption.

> What surprises us in this mystery is its character of privilege: Mary is the only human creature, along with the Lord Jesus, her Son, who has entered paradise body and soul at the end of her earthly life (Homily for Feast of Assumption, 1975).

> Is it only the Virgin who has had this privilege of not suffering the effects of her death and of being admitted immediately, even in body, into that newness, that plenitude of life which is promised to us in the resurrection of the dead? So it is. But the resurrection of the dead, although it is not a present reality for the dead who have left time, is a reality promised to all, deferred but promised (Catechesis of May 26, 1976).

The position advocated by Rahner and by Barth concerning the time of the resurrection of the body would appear to confuse eternity with "*aevum.*" In fact, we humans never become eternal. Eternity as such and properly speaking is proper to God alone. There is and always will be some degree of measurement and thus some kind of time in the life that follows our departure from the present age. What little can be said of this form of "time" we shall discuss below.

That there is an intermediate state where only souls exist and where Mary alone is bodily resurrected with Christ is, for the Catholic, a position that must be held. The Church's teaching has indicated this in various ways and times.

It is taught in the definition of Faith mentioned earlier as being promulgated by Pope Benedict XII in 1336. The essential parts of this document, the *Benedictus Deus*, read as follows:

> By this Constitution, which is to be perpetually valid, we define what follows by our Apostolic authority. According to the common ordinance of God, the souls of all the Saints who have departed from this world before the Passion of our Lord Jesus Christ, as well as those of the holy Apostles, martyrs, confessors, virgins and of all the faithful departed who have received the holy Baptism of Christ and in whom there was nothing to be purged when they departed or in whom there will not be anything to be purged when they depart in the future, all these, we say, have been, are and will be with Christ as He is after His

Ascension in the kingdom of heaven and in the heavenly paradise, joined together with the holy Angels. If there was or will be something to be purged in them, they shall be with Christ in heaven once they have been purged after their death. Likewise, the souls of children who have been reborn by the same Baptism of Christ and the souls of children who will be baptized in the future and who depart before the use of free will are and will be with Christ in heaven. All these people soon *[mox]* after their death and after the purgation already mentioned (in the case of those who need such purgation)—even before the resumption of their bodies and the general judgment— have been, are, and will be with Christ as He is after His Ascension, in the kingdom of heaven and in the heavenly paradise, joined together with the holy Angels.

We also define that after the Passion and death of the Lord Jesus Christ those mentioned have seen and do see the divine essence with an intuitive and even face-to-face vision. No creature intervenes as an object of vision, but rather the divine essence shows itself to them immediately, in itself, clearly and openly so that, seeing this, they enjoy the divine essence itself. We define that because of such vision and joy the souls of those who have already departed are truly blessed and have life and eternal rest, as will the souls of those who have yet to depart and who will see the same divine essence and enjoy it before the general judgment. And we define that the vision of this divine essence and its enjoyment do away with the acts of faith and hope in them, inasmuch as faith and hope are proper theological virtues. We also define that, after such intuitive and face-to-face vision has or will have begun for them, the same vision and fruition has continued and will continue to exist without any interruption or end until the final judgment and after that forever.

Furthermore, we define that according to the common ordination of God the souls of those who depart in actual mortal sin soon after their death *[mox post mortem suam]* descend to hell where they suffer the pains of hell. We define that, on the day of judgment, all will appear before the tribunal of Christ with their own bodies to render an account of their deeds so that each may receive good or evil according to what has been done in the body (2 Cor 5:10) [*DS* 1000-1002].

The words "even before the resumption of their bodies and the general judgment" are clear indication that the pope was speaking of a condition wherein the soul would exist for some period of time without its body. Some would suggest that Pope

Benedict was directly defining that humans immediately enter the world to come at death, and, in the case of the Saints, see God, but that he was not directly *defining* that there is a condition or period when the human person is without his or her body. Such a distinction is possible in the sense that one can say the pope was *presuming* a disembodied soul, not *defining* it. Nonetheless, the document does presume and teach the notion of an interim state, and subsequent teaching has confirmed this. As far as the intermediate state is concerned, the Church clarified any doubt in an official declaration of 1979.

> The Church affirms the continuation and subsistence *[subsistentiam]* after death of a spiritual element endowed with consciousness and will in such a way that the "human I" itself, although lacking for a time the complement of its body, subsists *[subsistat]*. To designate this element the Church uses the word "soul" which use is received from Scripture and Tradition. Although not unaware that in the Scripture this word carries diverse meanings, nonetheless she thinks there is no valid reason why the word should be rejected. She furthermore judges it completely necessary to have a verbal instrument to sustain the faith of Christians.

> The Church excludes any ways of thinking or speaking by which her prayers, funeral rites or cult of the dead be made absurd or unable to be understood. All of these, in their substance, constitute a *"locus theologicus."*[19]

In the same document, the Church addressed the question about the uniqueness of the bodily resurrection of the Virgin Mary.

> The Church, in proposing her doctrine about the fate of humans after death, excludes any explanation that would completely eviscerate the significance of the assumption of the Virgin Mary in respect to that which belongs uniquely to her: namely that the bodily glorification of the Virgin anticipates the glorification that is destined for all the other elect.[20]

---

[19] *Letter to the Heads of the Episcopal Conferences on Certain Questions of Eschatology*, SCDF, May 17, 1979, *AAS*, 71, p. 941. Rewarding reading on the significance of this document, as well as on some of the theological positions that occasioned it, can be had by turning to Joseph Ratzinger's two appendices in *Eschatology: Death and Eternal Life*, pp. 241ff.

[20] Letter to the Heads of the Episcopal Conferences on Certain Questions of Eschatology, SCDF, May 17, 1979: *AAS*, 71, p. 941.

After those declarations a Catholic theologian has written:

> The first thing we have to infer from the Resurrection of Jesus for our own resurrection is the clear distinction between death and resurrection. Between the death and the Resurrection of Jesus lies the mysterious Holy Saturday, the deposition of Christ and the "descent into hell" of his soul. The Lord is risen *from the grave*. It is therefore irreconcilable with faith to assert that the resurrection happens *in* death. The idea that the resurrection occurs already in the moment of death contradicts the fact of Jesus' deposition and the "Resurrection on the third day."[21]

The words are strong: "it [i.e., the idea of an immediate resurrection of the body] is irreconcilable with faith," but they would seem to be accurate. A Catholic must hold and defend the existence of an intermediate state in which the soul continues to live while anticipating something more.

The Soul Without the Body

St. Thomas says of the separation of soul and body: "The soul is not the whole person, and the soul is not 'I.' The soul, departed from the body, is imperfect as long as it is without the body."[22] The statement serves to highlight the problem that Barth, Cullmann and Rahner tried to answer with their theories. How can the human soul—even granted its immortality—manage to function without the body? This is a question already raised by Augustine. "Now let anyone who can demonstrate whether the soul has some kind of a body when it departs this body; I do not think it has."[23] Although he answered that the soul did not have any kind of a body once it exited this life, Augustine also wrote:

> I do not merely opine that the soul is not corporeal; rather I openly dare to profess that I know it. Nevertheless, whoever denies that the soul has any likeness to the body or to bodily members is also able to deny that there is a soul that sees itself in dreams either walking or sitting or being carried here and there on foot and through the air and back, none of which oc-

---

[21] Christoph Schonborn, "Resurrection of the Flesh," *Communio*, vol. 17, no. 1 (Spring 1990), p. 19.

[22] Aquinas, *Lectura super Primam Epistolam ad Corinthios*, XV, lect. 2, 924, p. 411.

[23] Augustine, *De Genesi ad Litteram Libri XII*, bk, 12, 32: CSEL 28, 1, p. 426.

curs without a certain likeness of a body. Therefore, if it bears this likeness even in the underworld, a likeness which is noncorporeal but like a body, so it would seem to be that the soul, whether at rest or in suffering, is in a place not corporeal but like the corporeal.[24]

Perhaps in what he says on this point Augustine hints at an important truth and one that has frequently been evidenced in popular imagination about the disembodied soul: the soul "looks like" the body. After death the soul is not mere nebulosity; it bears a resemblance to the body whose form it is, the body that has individuated it.[25] Perhaps we may say that the departed soul is still body-related in the sense that the primary material element that has shaped and individualized the soul remains with it even as the soul is separated from the rest of the bodily material. What Winklhofer writes is in line with Augustine's conception, and would appear to be correct.

> There is always present, even in our lifetime, something that can be described as the enduring substance of the human body, as the essential element that remains, unaffected by cell-changes and the constant replacement of matter, unaltered through all the development from youth to age. Without ever being itself destroyed, it undergoes decline, old age, mutilation. It is of this that we assert that it continues in existence beyond death. . . . It becomes the 'seed' [of the resurrected body] of which St. Paul speaks.[26]

In such a conception the soul is never completely "denuded" or "dematerialized." It carries with it material aspects of its body. This element of materiality continues to relate it to the body and to individuate or distinguish the soul as "this person's soul." Thus, the soul is never "pure spirit," it is matter-oriented and, if one may put it this way, "matter-stamped" during the interim state. The persistence of this material principle also facilitates the soul's functioning in the separated state, since the human soul does not and was not intended to function naturally without the body.[27]

---

[24] *Ibid.*, bk. 12, 33: CSEL 28, 1, p. 428.

[25] That it is matter that "individuates" the soul is a characteristic principle of St. Thomas, and he indicates quite clearly that some relationship must continue to exist between the "separated" soul and its own body. Cf. *Summa contra Gentiles*, Book II, chapter 81, response to the second objection.

[26] *The Coming of His Kingdom*, pp. 224-225.

[27] Cf. Aquinas, *Summa Theol.*, I, q. 89, a. 1 c; q. 118, 3 c.

The Nature of Happiness in the "Interim State"

The "interim state" is something about which St. Augustine spoke and wrote little. That he believed in it and affirmed that, in it, the souls of the blessed enjoy God is clear.[28] But it is, says Augustine, a happiness still not complete. It is not the joy that is to come at the resurrection of the dead.

> All souls obtain, when they depart from this world, their different receptions. The good have joy; the evil, torments. But when the resurrection has taken place, both the joy of the good will be fuller and the torments of the wicked graver since they shall be tormented in the body. The holy patriarchs, prophets, apostles, martyrs, and the good faithful have been received into peace; nevertheless all of them still have to receive at the end what God has promised: for the promise also concerns the resurrection of the flesh, the destruction of death and eternal life with the angels. This all of us are to receive at the same time; for the rest, which is given immediately after death, every one, if worthy of it, receives when he dies; the patriarchs receive it first—consider from what they rest—then the prophets, more recently the apostles; still more recently the holy martyrs, and each day the worthy faithful. Some have now been in that rest for a long time, some not so long; some for a few years, and others whose time there is not recent. But when they shall wake from this sleep, they shall simultaneously receive what has been promised.[29]

> But about the holy men who are already dead it is rightly to be questioned whether they are now to be said to be in possession of [full happiness]. For they have already put off the corruptible body with which the soul is weighed down; but they themselves still await the redemption of their body. Their flesh rests in hope (Ps 15 [16]:9; cf. Acts 2:26) and does not yet shine with the incorruptibility that is to come. But this is not the place to inquire at length whether they do not have all that is needed to contemplate truth with the eyes of the heart, or as it has been said "face to face" (1 Cor 13:12).[30]

Each time he discusses the matter, the reason that Augustine assigns for the lack of perfect joy is the same. We cannot be completely happy without our bodies. The interim state is only a

---

[28] Cf. Portalie, *A Guide to the Thought of Saint Augustine*, pp. 290-295.

[29] Augustine, *In Iohannis Evangelium*, 49, 10: CCSL 36, p. 425. We have made into one the last sentence, which the Latin of the CCSL punctuates as two sentences.

[30] Augustine, *Retractationum Libri II*, I, 14, 2: CCSL 57, pp. 42-43.

"small portion of the promise."[31] "For the day of retribution is coming when, our bodies having been returned to us, the whole man will receive what he has merited."[32]

Faithful to the thought of Augustine, St. Bernard elaborated on the same doctrine.

> Unless I am mistaken, you have all noted, from what was said in the previous sermon, that there are three states of our souls: the first in this corruptible body, the second without the body, the third in the body when it has been glorified. The first state is during the struggle, the second at rest, the third in perfected happiness; the first in tabernacles, the second in the courts, the third in the house of God. "How delightful are your tabernacles, Lord of Hosts!" (cf. Ps 84:1). Much more desirable are the courts, as can be seen when the Psalm adds: "My soul longs and pines for the courts of the Lord" (cf. Ps 84:2). But, because even in the very courts there is some defect, [it is said] "Blessed entirely are those who live in Your house, O Lord" (cf. Ps 84:4). "I have rejoiced fully in what was said to me, Brothers, namely that we will go into the house of the Lord" (cf. Ps 122:1). But if you ask on what basis it is that I presume so trustingly [that we will go into the house of the Lord], it is without doubt the fact that already many of us are standing in the courts, waiting until the number of the brethren is filled up. For they will not enter into that blessed house without us nor without their bodies. . . . For it is not fitting that full happiness be given until it is given to the whole man, nor that perfection be given to an incomplete Church. Therefore, while they await the resurrection of their bodies . . . they have received the reply of God, saying, "Wait a little while until the number of your brethren is complete" (Rv 6:11).[33]

The text from the Book of Revelation cited by St. Bernard is an interesting one. It reads:

> When he broke open the seal, I saw underneath the altar the souls of those who had been slaughtered because of the witness they bore to the word of God. They cried out in a loud voice, "How long will it be, holy and true master, before you sit in judgment and avenge our blood on the inhabitants of the earth?" Each of them was given a white robe, and they were

---

[31] Augustine, *Sermon 280: On the Birthday of the Martyrs Felicity and Perpetua*, 5: *PL* 38, 1283.

[32] *Ibid.*

[33] Bernard, *Sermon Three on the Feast of All Saints*, *Opera Omnia*, vol. V, pp. 349-350.

told to be a patient a little while longer until the number was filled of their fellow servants and brothers who were going to be killed as they had been (Rv 6:9-11).

Here one is clearly dealing with the special symbolism of the Book of Revelation. The Lamb, of course, is He Who takes away the sin of the world. The seal is one of the seven on that exclusive book that only Christ can open, the book itself probably signifying the true meaning of human history as distinguished from what it appears to mean. The description of the bodies of the martyrs being "underneath the altar" is not easy to fathom. The *New International Version* of the Bible has a footnote on the text that sees the expression as a figurative way of referring to the sacrificial nature of the blood of those killed for Christ (in line with the pouring of the blood of sacrifice at the base of the altar in Exodus 29:12 and Leviticus 4:7).[34] The *New Jerusalem Bible's* note indicates that the text is speaking of the martyrs' share in Christ's sacrifice.[35] Both interpretations probably catch some of what the author was conveying by the expression. The martyrs are crying for vindication.

St. Bernard, in his sermon, notes that this cry for vindication is not, properly speaking, a cry for vengeance. It is rather a way of expressing the desire for the end to come so that the resurrection might take place.[36] This interpretation is probably not correct. Indeed, when the evil are punished, when the waters are turned to blood for them to drink, the altar (or those under the altar) cries out that such retribution is correct and true (Rv 16:7). Bernard's mitigation of the cry for vindication reflects the increasing tendency in Christianity to temper the harsh passages of the Old and New Testament that speak of the enemies of God. Such palliation is not necessary if the Biblical references be properly understood.

There is a just anger: the anger at malicious cruelty, at the persecution of the innocent, at the murder of the unborn, at those who deny the truth, at torture, racial prejudice and all social in-

---

[34] See note on the text in *The NIV Study Bible: New International Version* (Grand Rapids, Michigan: Zondervan, 1985).

[35] See note on the text in *The New Jerusalem Bible* (Garden City, New York: Doubleday and Co., 1985).

[36] Bernard, *op. cit.*, p. 350.

justice. Jesus Himself is depicted in the Gospels as exercising such anger (cf. Mk 3:5; Mt 11:20; 21:12-13; 22:7; the whole of Mt 23; etc.), and He is our model for charity. Indeed the absence of just anger is a lack of virtue. Augustine speaks of the good person's proper reaction to the evil when he comments on Psalm 30 (31):

> This man is angry at the sins of others. Who would not be angry when he sees people confessing God with their mouth and denying Him by their way of life? Who would not be angry, seeing people renouncing this age in word and not in deed? Who would not be angry seeing brother plot against brother, not keeping faith with the kiss [of peace] they imprint during the Sacraments of God? And who can enumerate all the things by which the Body of Christ is angered, that Body which lives inwardly by the Spirit of Christ and which groans as grain among chaff?. . . However, this anger must be feared lest it be such that it turn to hatred. For anger is not yet hatred. You are angry at your son, you do not hate your son; indeed you have reserved the inheritance for him who experiences your anger; and you are angry for this reason, lest he, by living badly in bad habits, lose what you have reserved for him.[37]

Anger is not hatred. Anger seeks correction of an evil, the vindication of what is good and of those who are good, a change in those who do evil. In a Christian, this must be combined with love even of one's enemy, and the realization that one's present opponent may well be one's heavenly companion as is the case with St. Stephen and St. Paul, his persecutor. There are times when a Christian who seeks redress of a wrong is doing not an evil, but a good. In that same Christian, however, there is also the sober realization that even virtuous anger, a noble zeal, can too easily go beyond bounds and flow into intemperate wrath and even hatred. In the Book of Revelation 6:9-11, it is a just anger and a noble call for vindication that the cry of the martyrs expresses. And the answer they are given is that vindication will come when the full number of those unjustly persecuted has been completed.

Such, we think, is the meaning of the symbolic passage. However, even once we have understood this symbolism, it is

---

[37] Augustine, *Ennarr. in Ps. 30*, II, s. 2, 3-4: CCSL 38, p. 204.

evident that more is being described here. There is also expressed in the text a desire for fulfillment, a longing experienced by those who have died in Christ. They are waiting for their own resurrection and the end of the Church's tribulations. Only then will the fullness of joy be theirs, a view reaffirmed by the words of Augustine and Bernard. The homily of Bernard, indeed, reminds us of the "ecclesial" nature of happiness: it is not fitting that perfection be given to an incomplete Church, he says. This is a beautiful affirmation of the communitarian nature of salvation. Even the vision of God that beatifies the souls of the just is meant to be fully appreciated within the community of all the elect.

St. Thomas Aquinas, too, could write that "the nature of the soul cannot be perfect unless it is united to the body and so the soul separated from the body is not able to attain the ultimate perfection of beatitude,"[38] and in saying this Aquinas cites not the Augustinian texts quoted above but rather the North African's remarks in the *Literal Commentary On Genesis*.[39]

Augustine's understanding of the interim state has often been modified in the theological manuals, even to the point where the resurrection of the body is described as being an "accidental" addition that offers not an "intensive" but an "extensive" growth in the happiness already possessed by the soul who already possesses the Beatific Vision.[40] Others, more correctly we think, continue to follow Augustine,[41] and the Church's prayers seem to support this view. Thus, for example, the Intercessions for Evening Prayer for Friday of the Seventh Week of Easter in the Liturgy of the Hours read: "Fill up the hope of the dead that in the coming of Christ they may acquire the resurrection."

---

[38] Aquinas, *De Potentia*, q. 5, article 10 c. Cf. *Compendium*, chapter 151.

[39] Cf. Augustine, *De Genesi ad litteram*, bk. 12, c. 35: *CSEL*, 23, 1, pp. 432-433.

[40] Cf., for example, Sagues, *Sacrae Theologiae Summa*, vol. IV, pp. 1014-1015.

[41] De Lubac, citing Bernard, writes: "Thus the saints in heaven must await together both the salvation of those still on earth and their own resurrection. These views link up with those of St. Bernard, who, as we have seen, connects together the two conditions of perfect happiness: the resurrection of the body and the completion of the number of the elect" *(Catholicism: Christ and the Common Destiny of Man*, p. 130). Pozo, *Teología del Más Allá*, p. 78, also favors this view.

If then we can presume the accuracy of the Augustinian position, we can say that, even in the interim state, there is room and even a certain necessity for *some version of the virtue of hope,* in the sense of the expectation experienced by the blessed as they await the resurrection of their bodies and the completed growth of the Church.[42] When the *Benedictus Deus* taught that hope did not exist in the souls in heaven, it meant hope for salvation, not that hope which longs for the resurrection of the flesh and the filling up of the company of the Elect. While charity always remains, we may also say that an aspect of the virtue of hope does not disappear immediately upon death. In the interim state, the souls who see God find it possible to ask the Eternal Watchman, " 'Watchman, how much longer the night? Watchman, how much longer the night?' The Watchman replies, 'Morning has come, and again night. If you will ask, ask; come back again' " (Is 21:12).

The Future of Time

When thinking about the Saints waiting for the resurrection, one is easily led to reflect on the nature of time in the afterlife. Will there be time, and, if so, what kind of time? We ask this because it is common for people to speak of the life to come as *"eternal* life." Even our Lord and the Liturgy of the Church use this expression. Properly speaking, however, "eternity is the very measure appropriate to the duration of the divine life."[43] Or, as Augustine put it, "true eternity is where there is nothing of time."[44] When one combines this truth, therefore, with the normal way of speaking about the "eternal life" of the blessed, one can easily be enticed to conclude that the passage through death is an entrance into the very eternity of God Himself. In such a view, because of their share in God's life, the blessed will be swept up out of time. Traces of this opinion are recognizable in what we have already seen of Karl Rahner's views on the interim

---

[42] De Lubac, following the Augustinian view, speaks of a type of hope in Christ Himself in *Catholicism: Christ and the Common Destiny of Man,* pp. 131-133.

[43] Kenneth L. Schmitz, "Traces of Eternity," *Communio,* vol. XV, no. 3, p. 303.

[44] Augustine, *In Iohannis Evangelium,* 23, 9: CCSL 36, p. 239.

state. Prescinding from such theories, the question of time in the life to come, of course, long predates the present century.

St. Thomas had already considered the question of time in relation to the life to come, and he came to the conclusion that the saints, in some way, participate in eternity itself.

> ... it is apparent that the created intellect becomes a partaker of eternal life through the [beatific] vision. For, eternity differs from time in the fact that time has its being in a certain succession while the being of eternity is a simultaneity of everything *[totum simul]*. As we have shown there is no succession in the beatific vision. Rather everything that is seen through it is seen simultaneously, in one look. Therefore this vision is made perfect by a certain participation in eternity.[45]

Scheeben is a faithful disciple of Thomas when he develops the idea at greater length:

> The natural life of the created spirit, though imperishable, is subject to the flight of time. It cannot unfold all its power in a single act, but must advance by a continuous succession of distinct acts. But the life which the spirit lives in God resembles the divine life; everything concerning this life is centered in God and around God; all that the spirit knows and loves, it knows and loves in God and through God. In its natural life, while gravitating toward God in various ways, the spirit incessantly rotates around God, so to speak, like a planet around the sun. But in its supernatural life it comes to rest, with unalterable peace, in God Himself, embracing in a single act of knowledge and love of God all the stages of development that in natural life are dispersed over a lengthy and diversified course. The spirit that lives in God and with God rises superior to the laws of the earthly flight of time (*tempus* in the narrower sense), and also is above the flight of time that measures the duration of the spiritual creature (*aevum*), and shares in the prerogative of changeless repose which is unattainable by the natural creature and is proper to God alone. Since the life of the glorified spirit is wholly divine and flows from God in whom it has its source, it is eternal in the manner of God's life, and so its eternity is at once the consequence and a distinctive mark of its divine charater. To emphasize the perfection of this life, and its relation to the life of the divinity, the Son of God could well content Himself with designating it as eternal life.[46]

---

[45] Aquinas, *Summa Contra Gentiles*, III, q. 61.
[46] Scheeben, *Mysteries*, p. 664.

Francis Sylvester of Ferrara, one of the classic commentators on Aquinas, saw the difficulties in a position that purported to have humans enter into eternity, and he attempted to answer them, striving to put to rest the objections Duns Scotus had placed against Thomas' position.[47] The specifics of such arguments are not essential to us here. It may be sufficient to note that, whatever may be said of Aquinas' position vis-à-vis a participation in God's eternity, it is also true that the Common Doctor of the Church envisioned some movement in the life to come. This would, in turn, imply the ability to measure such motion and thus some kind of time. Perhaps it is for this reason that he qualified his remarks about the participation in eternity with the word "certain." The Saints will enjoy, he says, a certain participation in God's eternity.

For all the truth contained in the insight that the Saints, who share God's life, also share in some way His eternity, it still must be maintained, as Thomas himself did, that there is some form of duration, and therefore time, in the life that lies before us. Admittedly it will be time that is not measured by the standards we normally use now. However, "if life is meaningful now because our time is filled with the activity of God, there seems to be no reason why a temporal process after death should not acquire a similar or greater meaningfulness because the same God is active in it."[48]

Although the notion of temporal relativity as we view it post-Einstein was unknown, the Medievals recognized a certain relativity in the measurement of duration and had an appreciation for a "time" different from what we are aware of here on earth. They spoke readily of three "types" of "time": eternity, time as we experience it here on earth, and what they called the "aevum." Of this last Aquinas writes as follows:

> Time has a before and after; the "aevum" does not have in itself a before and after, but these can be joined to it; eternity does not have a before and after nor is it compatible with them.

---

[47] See the commentary of Ferrara on q. 61 on pp. 169-171 of the Leonine edition.
[48] Russell Aldwinckle in his *Death in the Secular City*, p. 160. Aldwinckle is one of the few modern theologians to deal at any length with the question of time in the life to come in a good and reflective discussion on pp. 150-165.

[As an example of "*aevum*" we have the Angels.] It is clear that Angels have unchangeable existence together with the ability to change in respect to choice, which is something pertaining to their nature; they also have the ability to change their understanding, their affections and their place according to their own manner.[49]

The Angels already enjoy the Beatific Vision. Yet this fact does not do away with a measurement of duration for them, the *aevum*. Indeed as Aquinas notes, their understanding, affection and places can change. Thus, despite his remarks about the participation of the Elect in the eternity of God there was, for St. Thomas, no intrinsic opposition between duration and a beatific participation in God's life. This lack of opposition would be confirmed for Thomas by the fact that even during His time as wayfarer Jesus possessed the Beatific Vision, yet operated in earthly time. There are other truths that also militate against a view that would hold for the cessation of all time. Chief among them is the concern of the Saints for us and their present prayers for us, as well as their own longing for the resurrection. Since these things are so, it would probably be better to cease speaking in a way that suggests the cessation of all time for those who behold God face to face.

The idea that in the life to come we enter a kind of eternity or total timelessness should likely be considered a vestigial and dispensable aspect of Greek philosophy. It develops from the notion that perfect happiness is achieved in repose and in a type of communion with God that is best described as ecstasy. It is true, of course, that some of the great mystics and spiritual writers of the Church speak of their experiences in prayer by using such terms. Such expressions, therefore, are hallowed by usage in the Church. Nonetheless, it must be remembered that these writers are attempting to describe an experience that happens in this life. Such periods in prayer last briefly and occur to them in a body whose senses still partake of the form of this passing world. As a result, these intense episodes of prayer cannot be considered normative for the knowledge of God that will be had in the life to come. What the mystics are describing is not the future, but the present, and the present of a transient, ineffable experi-

---

[49] Aquinas, *Summa Theol.*, I, q. 10, a. 5 c.

ence in which an unadapted body and soul are brought to still point by the overwhelming presence of the God Who draws near. Such blessed moments cannot be employed to make direct comparisons with the experiences of the Saints who will have been especially graced to enjoy perpetually the vision of God.

Let us return to something of which our age, since Einstein, is particularly aware, namely the relativity involved in the way we measure. How we gauge time on earth is not the method one would use in a galaxy other than our own, nor in the universe at large were we able now to do such a thing from a vantage different from our present one. Indeed, even within our solar system, time is not the same for all.[50] As *perceived* duration a minute or an hour can vary considerably.

> Time is a queer thing and memory a queerer; the tricks that time plays with memory and memory with time are queerest of all. From maturity one looks back at the succession of years, counts them and makes them many, yet cannot feel *length* in the number, however large. In a stream that turns a mill wheel there is a lot of water; the millpond is quiet, its surface dark and shadowed, and there does not seem to be much water in it. Time in the sum is nothing. And yet, a year to a child is an eternity, and in the memory that phase of one's being—a certain mental landscape—will seem to have endured without beginning and without end. The part of the mind that preserves dates and events may remonstrate, "It could have been like that for only a little while"; but true memory does not count nor add; it holds fast to things that were and they are outside of time.[51]

In the life to come the perception of time will be like that possessed by children. It will not be calculated so much by movement external to the Saints as it will be measured by their treasured memory of events, meetings, conversations, and by the succession of new events, meetings and conversations. They will no longer be slaves to years, months, days, hours and minutes. Punctuality will have no place. Like children they will be free from the burdens of time, while enjoying its benefits. Indeed, it will only be then that those who will possess endless life shall

---

[50] A fascinating book by Anthony F. Aveni (*Empires of Time: Calendars, Clocks, and Cultures,* Basic Books, 1990) teaches us that even on earth there have been and are various (and some exotic) ways of measuring duration.
[51] Helen Santmyer, *Ohio Town* (New York: Berkeley Books, 1985), p. 278.

fully realize what it means to have a share in "the fullness of time" (Gal 4:4).

In a real way the future of time is already present to those who share in the flesh of the risen Lord in the Eucharist. Under the veil made by appearances of bread and wine, the Lord Who Himself already lives in the age to come is present to us. Indeed the appearances are less substantial than gauze separating us from the world ahead. As He draws us to Himself we are gradually being attracted to the age ahead. In truth, the Eucharist is the past, present and future of time. The One Who is the Eucharist comes to us as Victim marked with the past wounds that heal our universe; He is present to us here and now; He pulls us gently into the future that He already possesses and that will be ours.

Redeeming the Time

Flannery O'Connor gives us an idea of the reversal that will take place with the change and discernment that take place in dying and judgment. She does this in a short story wherein she describes one of the self-righteous good. The character, Mrs. Turpin, is a hard-working, neat, overbearing Christian who disdains "niggers and white-trash" as unindustrious, disorderly and uncouth. By God's grace, she is the recipient of a shock of grace that leads to a vision that lets her see others from the Lord's viewpoint.

> There was only a purple streak in the sky, cutting through a field of crimson and leading, like an extension of the highway, into the descending dust.... A visionary light settled in her eyes. She saw the streak as a vast swinging bridge extending upward from the earth through a field of living fire. Upon it a vast horde of souls were rumbling toward heaven. There were whole companies of white-trash, clean for the first time in their lives, and bands of black niggers in white robes, and battalions of freaks and lunatics shouting and clapping and leaping like frogs. And bringing up the end of the procession was a tribe of people whom she recognized at once as those who, like herself and Claud, had always had a little of everything and the God-given wit to use it right. She leaned forward to observe them closer. They were marching behind the others with great dignity, accountable as they had always been for good order and

common sense and respectable behavior. They alone were on key. Yet she could see by their shocked and altered faces that even their virtues were being burned away.[52]

"Even their virtues were being burned away." It is surely sobering to realize that much that we consider virtue in ourselves is in fact custom or social convention, or good manners. We will die with these "virtues" only to experience the need to become truly good. This exigency is met by the reality the Church calls Purgatory.

The scriptural evidence for the existence of a state of purification is meager. Traditionally the text most appealed to is the one found in the Second Book of Maccabees.

> Next day they came to find Judas (since the necessity was by now urgent) to have the bodies of the fallen taken up and laid to rest among their relatives in their ancestral tombs. But when they found on each of the dead men, under their tunics, objects dedicated to the idols of Jamnia, which the Law prohibits to Jews, it became clear to everyone that this was why these men had lost their lives. . . . The valiant Judas . . . took a collection amounting to nearly two thousand drachmas, and sent it to Jerusalem to have a sacrifice for sin offered, an action altogether fine and noble, prompted by his belief in the resurrection. For had he not expected the fallen to rise again, it would have been superfluous and foolish to pray for the dead, whereas if he had in view the splendid recompense reserved for those who make a pious end, the thought was holy and devout. Hence, he had this expiatory sacrifice offered for the dead, so that they might be released from their sin (2 Mc 12:39-45; *NJB*).

What is considered to be of central importance in the above passage is the notion that expiatory sacrifices would have value for those already dead, for those indeed who had died in sin. If such men were damned because of their sin, sacrifice would be fruitless; if they were already pardoned and with God, such sacrifice would be unneeded. Judas, therefore, was convinced that, after death, there is a condition or state in which some can yet be aided on their way to God. His conviction the Church has made her own.

---

[52] Flannery O'Connor, "Revelation," *The Complete Stories*, p. 508.

There is also a New Testament text that is frequently appealed to as giving evidence of the doctrine of Purgatory.

> If anyone builds on this foundation [Christ] with gold, silver, precious stones, wood, hay, or straw, the work of each will come to light, for the Day will disclose it. It will be revealed with fire, and the fire itself will test the quality of each one's work. If the work stands that someone built upon the foundation, that person will receive a wage. But if someone's work is burned up, that one will suffer loss; the person will be saved, but only as through fire (1 Cor 3:12-15).

St. Augustine gave this an interpretation that saw in it a reference to purification after death, a cleansing that involved a suffering more arduous than any normally undergone in this life.

> "O Lord, do not rebuke me in Your anger." May I not be among those to whom it will be said, "Enter the eternal fire that has been prepared for the devil and his angels." "And do not correct me in Your wrath." Rather, may You cleanse me in this life and make me such that I have no need of the cleansing fire such as exists for those who will be saved, but in such a way as if "by fire." Why is this said except for the fact that they built here on foundations of wood, hay and straw? If they had built on gold, silver and precious stones they would be secure from either fire; not only from the eternal fire that forever torments the evil, but also from that fire which cleanses those who are saved through fire. For it is said, "He will be saved, but as if through fire." Because it says, "he will be saved," this fire is disdained [by some]. Clearly, although saved by fire, nevertheless this fire will be more serious than anything a person is able to suffer in this life. . . . The evils that are here are much easier [to endure]; nevertheless see how people will do whatever you order them to do so as not to suffer such evils. How much more should they do what God commands so they won't suffer graver things?[53]

Despite the interpretation of Augustine and other theologians, whether this text really refers to what we call Purgatory is difficult to decide. Paul is speaking metaphorically, and it is not evident that the purging of which he is speaking occurs in a period after the Day of discernment. The exact meaning of the text may be left an open question. It is sufficient to note that some of the Fathers found in it a witness to something that the

---

[53] Augustine, *Ennarr. in Ps. 37*, 4: CCSL 38, p. 384.

Church, in her understanding of Revelation, has perceived to be true, namely that some of the dead are in a condition that can be helped by prayers.

There are some indirect references to a purification after death in Christian writers of the third and fourth century. A text of Tertullian, for example, written around 210, seems to speak of a retribution after death, in the underworld, which however is not eternal punishment.

> To sum up: when we understand the prison that the Gospel talks about (cf. Mt 5:25-26) as being the underworld and the "last penny" as being the slight fault being cleansed there in the wait for the resurrection, [then] no one will doubt that the soul makes recompense in the underworld, the fullness of resurrection being saved for the sake of the body also.[54]

In addition to his commentary on First Corinthians, chapter 3, seen above, Augustine speaks of the purification of souls after death in his *City of God*.

> Some suffer temporary punishments only in this life, others after death, still others both now and after death, although they do so before that severe and final judgment. Moreover not all who sustain temporary punishments after death will come to the eternal punishments that will follow that judgment. For some, whatever is not remitted in this life will be remitted in the future age, that is, they will not suffer eternal punishment in the future age.[55]

> [If a child who is not yet capable of obeying the Commandments] and has received the Sacraments of the Mediator dies in these years of youth, . . . not only is it not destined for eternal punishment, but it is not even afflicted by any purgatorial torments after death.[56]

It is from this last citation, with its mention of "purgatorial torments,"[57] that we ultimately derive the word "Purgatory." It describes the state of purification after death, a condition in which the dead can be succored by the prayers of those still living on earth. In fact it is the Christian practice of prayer for the

---

[54] Tertullian, *De Anima*, LVIII, 8: *CCSL* 2, p. 869.

[55] Augustine, *City of God*, bk. 21, ch. 13: *CCSL* 48, pp. 779-780.

[56] *Ibid.*, p. 782.

[57] In *Enchiridion*, XVIII (69), he refers to these torments as *ignem purgatorium*, purgatorial fire *(CCSL* 46, p. 87).

departed that is itself the chief evidence for the faith of the Church in a Purgatory. Already around 213, Tertullian mentions expiatory prayers for the dead, references that express the conviction that the dead could be helped by such prayers.[58] The Jerusalem Catechesis (late fourth century or early fifth century) contains the same notion when the catechist (probably St. Cyril) tells his hearers:

> Then we make remembrance of those who have fallen asleep, and so first of all of the patriarchs, the prophets, the Apostles and the martyrs. . . . Then we pray for all the holy Fathers and bishops who have fallen asleep and for all those in general among us who have fallen asleep. We do this trusting that it will be of great benefit to the souls for whom our prayer is offered while the holy and awesome sacrifice is present.[59]

The doctrine has long been denied by some. In the Middle Ages, the Albigensians disowned it. At the time of the Reformation, Luther, who at first accepted it but said it could not be found in the Scriptures, had repudiated the teaching by 1530. Most traditional Lutherans follow him, and his denial is consistent with what was, at least in common estimation, Luther's ideas on justification. Man in himself, Luther thought, is a sinner and thus cannot be purified as such. Covered over with the merits of Christ alone, the deceased either enter heaven immediately or are eternally damned.

For many Protestants there is what might be called a practical ambiguity in their belief. Although the Protestant communities deny the existence of any purification after death, very many individual Protestants continue the early Christian practice of offering prayers for their departed loved ones.

After the break between East and West there arose in the thirteenth century a dispute about Purgatory with the separated Eastern Churches. Some Eastern bishops and theologians thought that the doctrine about purgatorial fire smacked of

---

[58] Cf. Tertullian, *De Corona*, III, 3: *CCSL* 2, p. 1043: "We make offerings for the dead on the annual observance of their death"; *De Monogamia*, 10, 4: *CCSL*, 2, p. 1243.

[59] *Mystagogic Catechesis*, V, 10, *Sources Chrétiennes*, vol. 126, p. 158. A like reference is found in Theodore of Mopsuestia, *Homily XV*, 43, *Studi e Testi*, vol. 144-145 (Rome: Polyglot Press), pp. 527-529.

Origenism, a "universalism" by which all would be saved and no human actually damned. By the time of the Council of Florence in 1439, their objections centered on two chief points: Purgatory as a place and the idea of fire. No mention of either was made by that Council in its decree on Purgatory (cf. *DS* 1304-1306) where it essentially repeated a doctrine already taught in the *Benedictus Deus* of 1336.

Following in all its essentials the decree of Florence, the Council of Trent in 1547 and 1563 solemnly taught the existence of a purgatorial state (cf. *DS* 1580 and 1820). The dogma of these Councils has been succinctly reaffirmed by the Second Vatican Council.

> Therefore, until the Lord comes in His majesty and all His Angels with Him (cf. Mt 25:31), and until death has been destroyed and all things have been subjected to Him (cf. 1 Cor 15:26-27), some of His disciples are on earthly pilgrimage; others, having finished this life, are being purified, while others indeed are glorified, clearly looking upon the one and triune God as He is. All of us, however, in different degrees and modes communicate in the same love of God and neighbor and sing the same hymn of glory to our God. For all who belong to Christ and have His Spirit coalesce into one Church and adhere to each other in Him (cf. Eph 4:16). Therefore the union of the wayfarers with those who have fallen asleep in the peace of Christ is by no means interrupted but rather, according to the perennial faith of the Church, is strengthened by the sharing of spiritual goods *(Lumen Gentium, 49).*

> This Sacred Synod receives with great devotion this venerable faith of our elders concerning the living fellowship with those who are in heavenly glory or who are still being purified after death, and proposes again the decrees of the Councils of Nicaea II, Florence and Trent *(Lumen Gentium, 51).*

Pope Paul VI reiterated the same faith in his Creed in 1968.

> We believe that the souls of all those who have died in the grace of Christ—both of those who still must be purified by the fire of Purgatory and of those who are taken into Paradise by Jesus as soon as separated from their bodies, as was the Good Thief—constitute the People of God after death.[60]

---

[60] *AAS,* 60 (1968), p. 444.

The Congregation for the Doctrine of the Faith likewise repeated the essence of this teaching in its declaration of 1979.

> The Church, adhering faithfully to the New Testament and tradition, believes in the happiness of the just who will someday be with Christ. She likewise believes that eternal punishment is prepared for sinners who will be deprived of the vision of God and that this punishment will have a repercussion on the whole being *[esse]* of the sinner. As far as concerns the Elect, she believes also that there is possible, previous to the vision of God, a purification that nonetheless is totally different from the punishment of the damned.[61]

In the renowned series of conferences that he gave as a retreat to Pope Paul VI, Karol Wojtyla spoke with insight on the mystery of the purification that occurs after a person's departure from this present world.

> The law of purification and the reality of purgatory certainly have a profound objective meaning from which their subjective meaning stems. Both arise out of the need for man to be spiritually prepared for union with the living God in charity. In one sense, this union expresses the degree of purity attainable by the created human spirit. Here, obviously, we are presupposing a whole order of grace, because union with the living God far exceeds the dimensions and the entitlement by right of any created being. God himself wills this union. It is he who leads man towards it in Christ and in the Holy Spirit, so it is he who determines the degree of perfection required for this union. Therefore the mystery of purgatory is explained not only by the order of justice but also—and perhaps primarily—by the order of charity and union with God.[62]

In speaking of the "order of charity," the pope is making a crucial point. The pains of purification are caused by love, the burning desire to change oneself to be suitable for Love. In such pains, those who suffer are not alone. It is part of Catholic Faith, professed again in the texts of the Second Vatican Council seen above, that those who have left this life and are still in the process of purification are linked both to the Saints in heaven and to us in this life by those unimaginably intimate bonds that bind together all who live in Christ. From early times those here have

---

[61] *Letter to the Heads of the Episcopal Conferences on Certain Questions of Eschatology*, SCDF, May 17, 1979: *AAS*, 71, pp. 941-942.
[62] Karol Wojtyla, *Sign of Contradiction*, p. 170.

prayed for the departed. Although denied by St. Thomas, it is also the common belief of the faithful that those being purified pray efficaciously for us.[63] Death cannot separate us from Christ or from those who are His members, nor can it prevent the mutual assistance that member renders member. Love is stronger than death.

In his letters to the Colossians and Ephesians, St. Paul has an injunction that is capable of various interpretations. He speaks of "buying back the time" or "redeeming the time" or, in a looser translation, "making good use of the time" (cf. Col 4:5; Eph 5:16—NAB: "making the most of the opportunity"). When we think of how often we lament time wasted, time in which we could have done so much more for others, it is a consolation to know that, in some way, we can perhaps "buy it back," redeem what we wasted. This, too, is an aspect of Purgatory. It is an opportunity to recoup unappreciated and squandered opportunities. Through it the Lord of all ages redeems time itself.

The Final Battle and the Coming of the Lord

In Catholic thought Purgatory has always been viewed as a period of waiting, the expectation of souls preparing to partake in the glory reserved for them. As we have already indicated, however, there is an *Advent* aspect to the whole of the interim state. The teaching of the *Benedictus Deus* in 1336,[64] although it was surely necessary, has had at times unintended consequences. While defending the existence of the interim state and the fact that the souls of the just enjoy the vision of God and are happy, and that the virtues of faith and hope, in the sense explained above, do not exist for those who share that vision, it has often caused theology to treat the life to come as though it were simply the equivalent of the interim state, to which the resurrected body has been "tacked on." As is so often true of this life, what is ephemeral is given undue importance. The sense of incompleteness, as well as the *transitory* nature of the in-between period, is frequently lost sight of.

---

[63] On St. Thomas' position, cf. *Summa Theol.*, IIa, IIae, q. 83, a. 11, ad 3.
[64] Cf. pp. 111-112 for the text.

The Church's official teaching does not make the same mistake. If one reads the documents of Vatican II, especially *Lumen Gentium* and *Gaudium et Spes*, one can see that the emphasis is placed where it should be, namely on the definitive state that will come at the return of Jesus. For all the immense happiness enjoyed by those souls now in heaven, there is nonetheless present in them, more intensely than among us Christians still here, a longing for the end, a desire to see God's plans for His creation reach their goal. The duty of those still here is to recognize and foster that desire. On the other hand, it is true to say that, at times, a strong awareness of the final state makes itself felt in our present history, but not infrequently such periods have given rise to various aberrant conjectures as to how and when the Lord shall achieve His purposes. A recurrent example of such mistakes is the opinion known as chiliasm or millenarianism (from the Greek and Latin words for one thousand).

The villainous monk in Browning's *Soliloquy in a Spanish Cloister*, plotting the overthrow of his hated Brother Lawrence, thinks of using a difficult text in Scripture to doom his enemy.

> *There's a great text in Galatians,*
> *Once you trip on it, entails*
> *Twenty-nine distinct damnations,*
> *One sure, if another fails.*[65]

It is not only Galatians, of course, that offers stumbling blocks for even those adept at interpreting Scripture. There are still passages, with all the real or imagined advances of modern exegesis, whose meaning is cloaked. One such is found in chapter twenty of the Book of Revelation.

> Then I saw an angel come down from heaven, holding in his hand the key to the abyss and a heavy chain. He seized the dragon, the ancient serpent, which is the Devil or Satan, and tied it up for a thousand years and threw it into the abyss, which he locked over it and sealed, so that it could no longer lead the nations astray until the thousand years are completed. After this, it is to be released for a short time.

---

[65] Robert Browning, "Soliloquy in a Spanish Cloister," *Robert Browning: The Poems*, Volume One, edited by John Pettigrew and Thomas Collins (New York: Penguin Books, 1981), p. 358.

Then I saw thrones; those who sat on them were entrusted with judgment. I also saw the souls of those who had been beheaded for their witness to Jesus and for the word of God, and who had not worshiped the beast or its image nor had accepted its mark on their foreheads or hands. They came to life and they reigned with Christ for a thousand years. The rest of the dead did not come to life until the thousand years were over. This is the first resurrection. Blessed and holy is the one who shares in the first resurrection. The second death has no power over these; they will be priests of God and of Christ, and they will reign with him for the thousand years.

When the thousand years are completed, Satan will be released from his prison. He will go out to deceive the nations at the four corners of the earth, Gog and Magog, to gather them for battle; their number is like the sand of the sea. They invaded the breadth of the earth and surrounded the camp of the holy ones and the beloved city. But fire came down from heaven and consumed them. The Devil who had led them astray was thrown into the pool of fire and sulfur, where the beast and the false prophet were. There they will be tormented day and night forever and ever.

Next I saw a large white throne and the one who was sitting on it. The earth and the sky fled from his presence and there was no place for them. I saw the dead, the great and the lowly, standing before the throne, and scrolls were opened. Then another scroll was opened, the book of life. The dead were judged according to their deeds, by what was written in the scrolls. The sea gave up its dead; then Death and Hades gave up their dead. All the dead were judged according to their deeds. Then Death and Hades were thrown into the pool of fire. (This pool of fire is the second death.) Anyone whose name was not found written in the book of life was thrown into the pool of fire (Rv 20:1-15).

This difficult text has given rise to various interpretations. Among the more significant was that of Joachim of Fiore in the twelfth century whose exegesis of the Book took it to be speaking of a thousand-year period during which the Holy Spirit would guide the Saints in ruling the earth. Joachim even set a date for the beginning of this period. Later, in the early 1500's during the time of the Reformation in Germany, Thomas Münzer preached the coming of a millennial kingdom, and the resultant fanaticism flamed the violence of the Peasants' Revolt. Closer to our own time, William Miller (1782-1849), the founder of the

"Millerites," also understood the text to be speaking of a thousand-year kingdom and preached that the appearance of this kingdom was proximate. Its failure to appear did not discourage the followers of Miller. His disciples, now known as the Seventh-Day Adventists, have carried on his convictions about the millennial kingdom.[66]

Even in the Early Church the text was a source of difficulty and contention. The Church historian Eusebius (c. 325) tells us that Bishop Papias of Hierapolis was a believer in the millennial reign of Christ on the earth.[67] St. Justin Martyr held similar views, as did St. Irenaeus. The exegesis given by Irenaeus is typical.

> It is necessary to say that the just, when the world is recreated after they have been resurrected at the appearance of Christ, will receive the inheritance that God promised to the fathers, and will reign in it; only after that will the judgment of all take place. For it is just that they should receive the reward of their sufferings in the very creation in which they labored or in which they suffered; that they should return to life in the creation in which they were slain because of their love for God; and that they should reign in the creation in which they endured servitude.[68]

What the great Saint of Lyons is saying is that, before the final return of Christ and the Last Judgment, there will be a period during which the Saints will reign in triumph with their Lord here on the earth.

The North African theologians, Origen and Augustine, disagreed with the millennial interpretation of the text in the Book of Revelation. Augustine's exegesis of Revelation 20:1-15 is classic and sets the pattern for all later interpretation by orthodox theologians and for the decisions of the Church's Magisterium.

---

[66] For a modern exegesis of the Book of Revelation in a millenarianist sense, cf. Vernard Eller, *The Most Revealing Book of the Bible* (Grand Rapids, Michigan: William Eerdmans Pub. Co., 1974), esp. pp. 184-190.

[67] Eusebius, *Ecclesiastical History*, III, 39, 11-13.

[68] Irenaeus, *Adversus Haereses*, V, 32: *Sources Chrétiennes*, 153, pp. 397-399. Irenaeus continues his interpretation, along the same line, in chapter 33 of Book V of the *Adversus Haereses*.

Those who because of the words in this book think that the first resurrection will be corporeal have been especially moved, among other things, by the number of one thousand years, as if it should happen that there be a sabbath of such an amount of time for the Saints, a holy vacation, that is. . . . This opinion would be tolerable in a way if it were believed that some spiritual delights would be present for the Saints in that sabbath because of the presence of the Lord. Even we were once of this opinion. But, since they say that those who rise then will have a vacation of immoderate carnal meals in which there will be so much food and drink that not only do they not maintain any moderation but even exceed the measure of credulity itself, in no way can these things be believed except by those who are carnal. Those who are spiritual call those who believe such things *chiliasts,* using a Greek word; translating it word for word, we can call them Millenarians. It would take too long to refute them on every point; rather we now ought to show how this Scripture should be understood. . . .

As far as I can see, the thousand years can be understood in two ways: either that this event takes place in the final thousand years, that is, in the sixth millennium of years, as if in the sixth day, whose final periods are now flying past, to be followed by a sabbath that has no evening, namely the rest of the Saints that has no end . . . ; or else [the author] uses a thousand years to stand for all the years of this age so that by a perfect number the very fullness of time might be signified. . . . It is thus that we understand the psalm when it says, "He has been mindful of the word of His covenant forever, the word He gave unto a thousand generations," by which is meant "unto all generations."[69]

In the interim, while the devil is bound for a thousand years, the Saints also reign with Christ for a thousand years—that is, already in this time of His first coming. . . . [When Revelation 20:4 speaks of those "who reign with Christ for a thousand years," it speaks] of the souls of the martyrs who have not yet had their bodies restored to them. For the souls of those who die first are not separated from the Church, which even now is the Kingdom of Christ. . . . Only the souls of the martyrs are mentioned because they, in a special way, reign in death. But from the part we are to understand as well all the other dead belonging to the Church, which is the Kingdom of Christ.[70]

---

[69] Augustine, *City of God,* bk. 20, ch. 7: *CCSL* 48, pp. 709-710. His earlier view can be seen in *Sermon 259: PL* 38, 1197.

[70] Augustine, *City of God,* bk. 20, ch. 9, *op. cit.,* pp. 717-718.

It is interesting to note that Augustine admits he once held a view that was a form of millenarianism without the grosser ideas that came to be associated with it. Perhaps for that reason, he is quite lenient in this criticism of the type of millenarianism held by Irenaeus and some of the other Fathers. What he repudiates strongly are forms of the doctrine that envision a period of carnal delights for the chosen before the final coming of Christ. Nonetheless, while speaking leniently of what might be called moderate millennial views, he ultimately destroys the basis of the doctrine by presenting an interpretation of the Book of Revelation that favors the symbolic understanding of the passage. And this is what the Church recognized as being her own understanding. Everyone is left free to read the symbolism of the chapter in various ways (Augustine himself gives two possibilities), but the notion of a literal reign of one thousand years here on earth before the Lord's coming is rejected.

Forms of millenarianism are still found among various religious groups. In addition to the Adventists already mentioned, the Jehovah's Witnesses and the Mormons advocate forms of this doctrine.[71] Within the Church herself, there was need to repeat in 1944 the warning that even modified forms of millennial doctrine cannot be safely taught as aspects of the Catholic Faith (cf. *DS* 3839).

The section on the one thousand years in the Book of Revelation is intended, at the least, to keep alive hope in the victory of Christ and those who belong to Him. That hope will never die completely. Indeed it is true that, looking for that victory, "all creation waits in expectation" (cf. Rom 8:19). Without doubt there have been and are many who have given up all hope that

---

[71] John Paul II has had to warn Catholics of the dangers to true Faith presented by the sects, some of which employ the attractive appeal of millennial doctrine. "The sects and the new religious movements today place before the Church a noteworthy pastoral challenge both because of the spiritual and social malaise into which their roots reach and because of the religious elements which they use as instruments. These elements, taken out of their context in Catholic doctrine and tradition, are often employed for purposes far removed from their original scope. The widespread millenarianism, for example, evokes the themes of Christian eschatology and the problems related to human destiny . . ." ("Message for World Migration Day—July 25, 1990," *L'Osservatore Romano*, English edition, August 6, 1990, p. 1).

human history as we know it has any purpose. It is not "going anywhere," they claim, "it just happens." History, for them, has become like a play whose author fails to show when called for. As Shakespeare wrote:

> All the world's a stage,
> And all the men and women merely players;
> They have their exits and their entrances,
> And one man in his time plays many parts—
> Last scene of all,
> That ends this strange eventful history,
> Is second childishness, and mere oblivion,
> Sans teeth, sans eyes, sans taste, sans everything.
>
> (As You Like It, Act II, scene 7)

Hilaire Belloc, completing the thought in his own sonnet, wrote:

> We drink behind the scenes and pass a jest
> On all our folly; then, before we go
> Loud cries for "Author" . . . but he doesn't come.[72]

In fact, of course, the Author will come. And the Biblical descriptions of the period that will precede His coming indicate that insistent cries for "Author" will arise from the lips of His persecuted faithful. It will be a time when even the faith of the just will be so sorely tried that they will be tempted to despair of His coming. So great will be the test that He Himself wondered aloud whether there would be any faith left when He came (cf. Lk 18:8). Jesus also says of that period, "Because of the increase of evildoing, the love of many will grow cold" (Mt 24:12). It is to be deduced, therefore, that the period immediately preceding His appearance will be an epoch in which faith and charity will be severely challenged. The Bible likewise depicts the end times, with the ambivalent and traditionally symbolic signs that will presage them, as a period of persecution for the followers of Christ. Whether that persecution will be physical oppression or the more subtle and insidious tyranny exercised by the enticements of Babylon the Great[73] is not clear. And it is quite useless to speculate on the specifics of the time and nature of the trials.

---

[72] Hilaire Belloc, "Sonnet XXIX," *Sonnet and Verse* (London: Sheed and Ward, 1944), p. 31.

[73] See below under Chapter VI: "The City of Compact Unity," pp. 247ff.

What is very clear, however, is that there will finally be one last great assault of the Devil and all that is allied with him against Christ and His Church. The forces of death, the Antichrist, the Beast, Babylon the Great, and Gog and Magog (cf. 1 Jn 2:18; 2:18-22; 2 Thes 2; Rv 20:8) will rise against the Author of Life, attempting as it were to kill Him again, at least in His members. The assurance that faith gives comforts us with the awareness that those who persevere will share the triumph of the Lord as He snatches victory from death once more. Then will come the final harvest.

> Then I looked and there was a white cloud, and sitting on the cloud one who looked like a son of man, with a gold crown on his head and a sharp sickle in his hand. Another angel came out of the temple, crying out in a loud voice to the one sitting on the cloud, "Use your sickle and reap the harvest, for the time to reap has come, because the earth's harvest is fully ripe." So the one who was sitting on the cloud swung his sickle over the earth, and the earth was harvested.
>
> Then another angel came out of the temple in heaven who also had a sharp sickle. Then another angel came from the altar, who was in charge of the fire, and cried out in a loud voice to the one who had the sharp sickle, "Use your sharp sickle and cut the clusters from the earth's vines, for its grapes are ripe." So the angel swung his sickle over the earth and cut the earth's vintage. He threw it into the great wine press of God's fury. The wine press was trodden outside the city and blood poured out of the wine press to the height of a horse's bridle for two hundred miles (Rv 14:14-20).

The scene, of course, is symbolic. However, the role of the Angels is significant. Jesus Himself said that the Angels would have a special function at the end, at the harvest. It will be their duty to segregate the evil from the good (cf. Mt 24:31ff). Now that image, too, is probably symbolic, but it does intend to tell us that the various orders of creation, the visible and invisible, will have their part to play in the final act, and that the Angels will serve Christ in the terrible times that we generally refer to as the "end of the world."

At the appearance or "Parousia" of the Son of Man at this last harvest, there will be, as the Book of Revelation assures us, a final battle, Armageddon (cf. Rv 16:16). It is then that the present epoch of human history will come to its term. One of the most powerful descriptions of that "end"—still used by the Church in her Divine Office for the last week of the Liturgical Year—is the famous *Dies Irae*. (Stanzas 1-4, 8, 10-11 of the twenty-one-stanza work are given below.)

Dies irae, dies illa
solvet saeclum in favilla
teste David cum Sibylla.

Quantus tremor est futurus
quando iudex est venturus
cuncta stricte discussurus!

Tuba mirum spargens sonum
per sepulcra regionum,
coget omnes ante thronum.

Mors stupebit et natura,
cum resurget creatura
iudicanti responsura.

Quid sum miser tunc dicturus,
quem patronum rogaturus,
cum vix iustus sit securus?

Recordare, Iesu pie,
quod sum causa tuae viae,
ne me perdas illa die.

Quaerens me sedisti lassus,
redemisti crucem passus;
tantus labor non sit cassus.

The day of wrath, that day,
will reduce this age to ash
as David and the Sibyl attest.

What trembling there will be
when the judge shall come
to examine all things closely.

The trumpet, sounding mightily
through the tombs of the world,
gathers all before the Throne.

Death and nature will marvel
when creation rises
to respond to judgment.

What, in misery, shall I say;
what patron shall I invoke
when barely the just will stand secure?

Remember, kindly Jesus,
that I am the cause of Your life's work.
Let me not perish on that day.

Looking for me You sat and rested, weary;
suffering the Cross You redeemed me.
Let not such effort be in vain.

The poetry of the *Dies Irae*, especially the penultimate verse quoted, reminds us that the finale is, in a special sense, the "day of the Lord." This "day" is an important theme in both the Old and the New Testaments and is marked by contrasting characteristics. At times, it is portrayed as a day of terror and judgment, aspects well captured by the words and music of the *Dies Irae*.

Howl, for the day of the Lord is near; as destruction from the Almighty it comes (Is 13:6).

Lo, the day of the Lord comes, cruel, with wrath and burning anger; to lay waste the land and destroy the sinners within it! (Is 13:9).

> The Lord raises his voice at the head of his army; for immense indeed is his camp, yes, mighty, and it does his bidding. For great is the day of the Lord, and exceedingly terrible; who can bear it? (Jl 2:11).

> Woe to those who yearn for the day of the Lord! What will this day of the Lord mean for you? Darkness and not light! (Am 5:18).

Jesus Himself indicates that, for some, the day will indeed be one of judgment, more terrible than the destruction of entire cities.

> I tell you, it will be more tolerable for Sodom on that day than for that town (Lk 10:12).

And the Second Letter of Peter tells us that not only humans, but all creation, the very elements of the universe, will face the awesome judgment of that day, destined for their own purification by fire.

> [You are] waiting for and hastening the coming of the day of the Lord, because of which the heavens will be dissolved in flames and the elements melted by fire (2 Pt 3:12).

Paul, who refers to that time not just as the "day of the Lord," but the "day of the Lord Jesus," or quite simply "the day" (cf., for example, 1 Cor 5:5; 2 Cor 1:14, Phil 1:6; 1 Thes 5:2; etc.), recalls the other facet of the Old Testament theme. He indicates that, for those who have loved God, it will be a day of vindication and reward.

> From now on the crown of righteousness awaits me, which the Lord, the just judge, will award to me on that day, and not only to me, but to all who have longed for his appearance (2 Tm 4:8).

The day, then, will be one of judgment, but not necessarily a judgment to condemnation. For some, those who have appealed from their heart to Him Who wearily sat by a well in Samaria seeking sinners, it will be the judgment of acquittal and vindication.

Apparently, when the day occurs, there will be those who have not previously departed this life. It is of these that some Christians are speaking when they talk of the "rapture," basing themselves on Paul's words in First Thessalonians 4:17 ("Then we who are alive, who are left, will be caught up together with them [the dead] . . ."). Even for those thus caught up or "rapt"—if Paul literally means that some will live through the end times—the day of the Lord Jesus will see the determination of their ultimate fate, a discernment equivalent to the particular judgment undergone by all who died before the Lord's return. For those who will have lived through the final period there shall, of course, be no Purgatory. The anguish endured through the final temptations and trials, as well as the cosmic events that herald the end, will have produced in the faithful whatever purification was yet to be achieved. For those who died in mortal sin and already tasted the wormwood of eternal bitterness, as well as for those who will persevere through the last times in grave sin, the second death will then become definitive. All the rest of humanity shall enter the Kingdom prepared for them from all eternity.

The Final Judgment, rendered by Him Who will come to judge the living and the dead, will be, above all, the fully transparent revelation of God's love, mercy and justice as they have existed—often unrecognized—in human history. At that point, the meaning of human history itself—with everything in it that has appeared to be inexplicable or inconsistent with the existence of a loving and all-powerful God—will become clear. Then will God's ways with man be vindicated in the sense that all will recognize His wisdom.

There is a thought-provoking comparison to be made between two Biblical accounts of the reign of King Abijah of Judah. Of him and his work, the First Book of Kings says:

> He imitated all the sins his father had committed before him, and his heart was not entirely with the Lord, his God, like the heart of his grandfather David (1 Kgs 15:3).

The Second Book of Chronicles, on the other hand, makes no such blanket judgment, and includes a speech made by the King that defends Judah's worship of the Lord God (cf. 2 Chr 13:4-12). In short, Second Chronicles displays the King in a rather favorable light. Looking at the two accounts it would be facile to dismiss the differences as just another example of what some suppose to be the contradictions among the Scriptural books. However, it is to be remembered that the author of Second Chronicles knew the First Book of Kings and frequently in-

dicates that he expected his readers to be familiar with the previous account. The distinctive emphasis therefore is intended.
Furthermore, it is inspired by God, Who perhaps is using Abijah
to teach us how impossible it is to assess adequately any person's
life and place in history. The lives of individuals and indeed all of
history are filled with ambiguity and with enigmatic motives that
defy easy categorizing. Our tendency to pass a judgment and
then close ourselves to further examination is a sinful failure to
remember this.

Another example of the same thing can be derived from the
Twelve. How often negative sentence is passed on them for their
blindness and weak faith during the ministry of Jesus. Indeed, He
Himself rebukes them for such failures. On the other hand, on the
very night of His betrayal, during which they will abandon Him,
He gives Himself to them in the Eucharist, praising them as having
been the ones who stood by Him in His trials (cf. Lk 22:28). Being
God, Jesus can reconcile such apparently disparate judgments. He
knows that they and we are not all of one piece. We differ among
ourselves and are individually complex. It is for that very reason
that no absolute judgment is to be passed before the day, for only
the Lord, just judge that He is, can bring to light all that is required
to put individuals and human history in proper perspective.

How the Last Judgment can take place in a way that all
those who have ever lived will simultaneously experience it has
always been difficult to imagine. Perhaps it will not be the
gathering of all in one place but rather the presence of all the
saved in God that will locate the judgment scene. In Him, too,
through the knowledge that comes to all through the Beatific Vision, the judgment will be made plain. For the damned, such
awareness will not be necessary. They will not care. Cognizant
of the consequences of their past choices they shall continue to
choose their own way—but of that terrible mystery we have committed ourselves to say no more.

The last battle, the final harvest, the appearance of Christ
and the judgment are often referred to as the end of the world
and of human history. They are—as we shall see—no such thing,
but rather the inauguration of an uninterrupted life in which the
good are everlastingly free of all danger of unhappiness.

The Role of the Saints in the Judgment

During His ministry, Jesus had said to His disciples, "You who have followed me . . . will yourselves sit on twelve thrones, judging the twelve tribes of Israel" (Mt 19:28). This was repeated by His followers. Paul wrote: "Do you not know that the holy ones will judge the world?" (1 Cor 6:2; cf. 1 Thes 3:13 and Rom 12:13). Exercising such a role will be the culmination of the share already held by the faithful who participate in Christ's triple office of priest, prophet and king, described this way by Pope John Paul II:

> They exercise their kingship as Christians, above all, in the spiritual combat in which they seek to overcome in themselves the kingdom of sin (cf. Rom 6:12), and then to make a gift of themselves so as to serve, in justice and in charity, Jesus who is Himself present in all His brothers and sisters, above all in the very least (cf. Mt 25:40).
>
> But in particular, the lay faithful are called to restore to creation all its original value. In ordering creation to the authentic well-being of humanity in an activity governed by the life of grace, the lay faithful share in the exercise of the power with which the risen Christ draws all things to Himself and subjects them along with Himself to the Father, so that God might be everything to everyone (cf. 1 Cor 15:28: Jn 12:32).[74]

It is by what they do through prayer, example and labor that Christians help "restore to creation all its original value." That restoration will be achieved, as the Pope citing St. Paul indicates, when Christ restores the Kingdom to His Father at the end. Then, by their own presence at the Judgment, Christians will themselves bear witness to how this restoration has been achieved. They will make manifest what has been achieved in their lives through God's grace. In fact, their very lives and works will be the "open scroll" with its seals broken (cf. Rv 5) in which is contained the explanation of history's true meaning. Then too all will see how the activities of each prepared the world to come, a theme to which we shall return below.

There is another aspect of the "day of the Lord" that has been revealed to us through the Books of the Bible. Speaking of

---

[74] John Paul II, *Christifideles Laici: The Vocation and Mission of the Lay Faithful in the Church and the World*, 14, TPS, vol. 34, no. 2 (1989), p. 113.

that day, Isaiah indicates that the traditional enemies of God's People will also come at last to see the truth and share in the blessings showered on the chosen people.

> The Lord shall make himself known to Egypt, and the Egyptians shall know the Lord in that day; they shall offer sacrifices and oblations, and fulfill the vows they make to the Lord.... On that day there shall be a highway from Egypt to Assyria: the Assyrians shall enter Egypt, and the Egyptians enter Assyria, and Egypt shall serve Assyria. On that day Israel shall be a third party with Egypt and Assyria, a blessing in the midst of the land (Is 19:21-24).

The Church of the living God, the new Israel, has never forgotten this truth. She knows that salvation is offered to all, including those outside the bond of unity and truth with which she has been blessed. There exist, in a number known to God alone, those who, responding to His grace to act in conformity with an upright conscience, can find eternal life on the day of Christ Jesus Who died "to gather into one the dispersed children of God" (Jn 11:52; cf. *Lumen Gentium,* 16). For such people, the day will be one of great recognition as they acknowledge Jesus of Nazareth, the Incarnate God, and His Church, the sacrament of His salvation for all peoples.

The Resurrection of the Flesh

We know, through faith, that, when Jesus returns, it is not merely spirit that is destined to survive. Everything of beauty and joy that belongs to Nature, and especially the marvel of our own human bodies, is ordained, having passed through fire, to share in the wonders of those times. Through Isaiah, God promised Israel:

> But your dead shall live, their corpses shall rise; awake and sing, you who lie in the dust. For your dew is a dew of light, and the land of shades gives birth (Is 26:19).

This is the pledge of Him Who had just said through the same prophet, "[God] will destroy death forever" (Is 25:8).

Both these citations came from what is often called the "Apocalypse of Isaiah." Because of the hope expressed therein for the conquest of death, there are those who think that the prophecies are not from the eighth-century prophet Isaiah, but from someone in the sixth or fifth centuries writing in the Isaian tradition. The reason some date the sections so late after the time of Isaiah himself is that they are of the opinion that the notion of a life after death was not revealed to Israel until during or after the captivity in Babylon (c. 597-530). In fact, it is more probable that the ideas about an everlasting life arose in Israel much earlier than is often thought, but the question of dating is of no direct concern here. What is important is that gradually Israel's trust in the living God came to be such that He was seen as giving a life that survived the death He had never intended for us. Texts like the ones above began to crystallize such a trust; others, like that in Ezekiel 37:1-16, developed an imagery that portrayed a bodily resurrection. Through Ezekiel the faithful are told by the Lord God, "Then you shall know that I am the Lord, when I open your graves and have you rise from them, O my people!" (Ez 37:11).[75] By the time of the writing of the Book of the prophet Daniel (the date of the Book is disputed; many would place it in the second century before Christ), this conviction was for many Israelites a deeply rooted truth.

> Many of those who sleep in the dust of the earth shall awake; some shall live forever, others shall be an everlasting horror and disgrace (Dn 12:2).

Despite the prophetic indications, in the times of the New Testament not all the Jews had come to accept the notion of a life after death. Jesus had to teach the Sadducees that God is indeed a God of the living (cf. Mt 22:23ff). Then, in the events of the First Easter, God did open a tomb, and from it One came forth Who holds the power to renew the bodies of His brothers and sisters, conforming them to His own glorious body. He rose incorrupt; He would give incorruptibility to His own.

St. Luke tells us that a key element of the earliest preaching of both Peter and Paul was the use of Psalm 16 as a prophecy of

---

[75] For the full text of the passage in Ezekiel, cf. below under Chapter VII: "To Gaze on the Beauty of the Lord," p. 316.

the Messiah's Resurrection. Verses nine through eleven of that psalm read:

> Therefore has my heart been glad,
> indeed my heart has rejoiced;
> even my flesh will rest in hope.
> For You will not abandon my life to the underworld
> nor let Your Holy One see corruption.
> You will make known to me the ways of life,
> the fullness of joy before Your face,
> delights at Your right hand forever *(New Vulgate)*.

Peter (Acts 2:22-32) and Paul (Acts 12:32ff), attributing the psalm to David's authorship, point to the fact that the prayer of hope was not fulfilled for David himself. His body is still buried. The flesh of the lion of Judah, the root of David, however, was not abandoned to the underworld nor did it see corruption. Raised, it now beholds the face of the Father and delights at His right hand forever. And what is true of Jesus the Lord will be true of all those who belong to Him. Not only are their souls saved: their flesh rests in hope. During the whole of the interim period the flesh of the just rests in hope. For they await the day when the resurrection of the Head will be shared by the members. Paul takes this great truth and develops it at length in the most extensive passage on the resurrection in the New Testament.

> But if Christ is preached as raised from the dead, how can some among you say there is no resurrection of the dead? If there is no resurrection of the dead, then neither has Christ been raised. And if Christ has not been raised, then empty [too] is our preaching; empty, too, your faith . . . , and if Christ has not been raised, your faith is vain; you are still in your sins. Then those who have fallen asleep in Christ have perished. If for this life only we have hoped in Christ, we are the most pitiable people of all.
>
> But now Christ has been raised from the dead, the firstfruits of those who have fallen asleep. For since death came through a human being, the resurrection of the dead came also through a human being. For just as in Adam all die, so too in Christ shall all be brought to life, but each one in proper order: Christ the firstfruits; then, at his coming, those who belong to Christ. . . .
>
> But someone may say, "How are the dead raised? With what kind of body will they come back?"

You fool! What you sow is not brought to life unless it dies. And what you sow is not the body that is to be but a bare kernel of wheat, perhaps, or of some other kind; but God gives it a body as he chooses, and to each of the seeds its own body.

Not all flesh is the same, but there is one kind for human beings, another kind of flesh for animals, another kind of flesh for birds, and another for fish. There are both heavenly bodies and earthly bodies, but the brightness of the heavenly is one kind and that of the earthly another. The brightness of the sun is one kind, the brightness of the moon another, and the brightness of the stars another. For star differs from star in brightness.

So also is the resurrection of the dead. It is sown corruptible; it is raised incorruptible. It is sown dishonorable; it is raised glorious. It is sown weak; it is raised powerful. It is sown a natural body; it is raised a spiritual body. If there is a natural body, there is also a spiritual one.

So, too, it is written, "The first man, Adam, became a living being," the last Adam a life-giving spirit. But the spiritual was not first; rather the natural and then the spiritual. The first man was from the earth, earthly; the second man, from heaven. As was the earthly one, so also are the earthly, and as is the heavenly one, so also are the heavenly. Just as we have borne the image of the earthly one, we shall also bear the image of the heavenly one.

This I declare, brothers: flesh and blood cannot inherit the kingdom of God, nor does corruption inherit incorruption. Behold, I tell you a mystery. We shall not all fall asleep, but we will all be changed, in an instant, in the blink of an eye, at the last trumpet. For the trumpet will sound, the dead will be raised incorruptible, and we shall be changed. For that which is corruptible must clothe itself with incorruptibility, and that which is mortal must clothe itself with immortality. And when this which is corruptible clothes itself with incorruptibility and this which is mortal clothes itself with immortality, then the word that is written shall come about:

"Death is swallowed up in victory.
Where, O death, is your victory?
Where, O death, is your sting?"

The sting of death is sin, and the power of sin is the law. But thanks be to God who gives us the victory through our Lord Jesus Christ (1 Cor 15:12-57).

With this presentation of Christian doctrine, Paul establishes a pattern that will be adhered to by the Fathers of the Church. The Apostle of the Gentiles uses natural analogies (the seed and growth, the varieties of bodies) as well as revealed truths, the analogy of Faith, to buttress his presentation of the resurrection. Nonetheless, his attempt at clarity has left many puzzled. The words of verse fifty, which state that "flesh and blood cannot inherit the kingdom of God," have, because of their starkness (like those of Jesus in John 6:63), often been used by theologians and exegetes to attenuate the *physical* or *material* nature of the resurrected body. Such is not the intention of St. Paul. What he means when he speaks of "flesh and blood" can be better understood by comparing the text in First Corinthians with the way he uses the same terminology in chapter eight of his Letter to the Romans. There he writes:

> Those who are in the flesh cannot please God. But you are not in the flesh; on the contrary, you are in the spirit, if only the Spirit of God dwells in you (Rom 8:8-9).

In this text in Romans, Paul is speaking to Christians who are still in this world, men and women who have material bodies of flesh and blood. Nonetheless, he reminds them that, while those who are "in the flesh" are not able to please God, they by contrast can please Him because they are "not in the flesh" if they possess the Spirit. It is clear that flesh is not opposed to material bodiliness, but refers rather to <u>a way of life.</u> So, too, in the famous text from his First Letter to Corinth. "Flesh and blood cannot inherit the kingdom of God" is referring not to material bodiliness but to a merely natural way of life and of living. That "flesh and blood" which are "in the spirit," on the other hand, are inheritors of the Kingdom.

Augustine correctly exegetes the meaning of First Corinthians 15 when he writes:

> Therefore God will bestow a wonderful facility, a wonderful lightness. Not without cause are those bodies called spiritual. They are not called spiritual because they will be spirits and not bodies. The bodies we now have are called "souled" bodies and yet they are not souls but bodies. As they are now said to be "souled" and yet are not souls, so they will then be called spiritual but not be spirits, because they will be bodies. Why,

therefore, dearly beloved, is it called a spiritual body except for the fact that it will serve at the spirit's pleasure? Nothing of yourself will contradict yourself, nothing in you will rebel against you.[76]

In his *Retractions* he corrects the impression that one could possibly gain from his *Book on Faith and the Creed (De Fide et Symbolo Liber Unus)* where he stated that "our bodily members and the substance of flesh" would not exist once "the earthly body we now have had been changed into a heavenly body." Our resurrection, he says in the *Retractions*, will make our bodies like that of the resurrected Jesus Who could eat and be touched.

> Thus it is clear that the Apostle [in 1 Cor 15:50] is not denying that the substance of flesh will be in the Kingdom of God; it is rather that either he calls "flesh and blood" those who live according to the flesh or he speaks of the very corruption of the flesh, which then indeed will not exist.[77]

For Paul and those who follow him the resurrection of Jesus is both the cause and the pattern of all life from the dead. It is both an assertion and a prayer.

> If we have grown into union with him through a death like his, we shall also be united with him in the resurrection (Rom 6:5).

> [I want] to know [Christ] and the power of his resurrection and the sharing of his sufferings by being conformed to his death, if somehow I may attain the resurrection from the dead (Phil 3:10-11).

The Church Fathers on the Resurrection

The North African Doctor was not, of course, the only or first of the Church Fathers to understand that St. Paul's preaching of the mystery of the resurrection of the dead was intended to convey the resurrection of a material body. As one may well imagine, the theme of resurrection is found very frequently in the writings of the Fathers of the Church. We present a few excerpts here as representative selections, and texts that highlight especially the dignity of matter, the human flesh.

In one of the earliest extant, non-Biblical Christian documents, St. Clement of Rome, writing to the Corinthians between

---

[76] Augustine, *Sermon 242 a (147)*, 11: PL 38, 1142.
[77] Augustine, *Retractationes*, bk. 1, ch. 16: CCSL 57, p. 53.

69 and 96 A.D., referred to the resurrection and used the legend (although he apparently thought it was real) of the phoenix to illustrate the doctrine.

> Beloved, let us consider how the Master continually points out to us the future resurrection, the firstfruits of which He made the Lord Jesus Christ by raising Him from the dead. Let us see, beloved, the resurrection that happens regularly. Day and night manifest the resurrection; night sleeps, the day rises; the day departs, the night comes on. [He then uses the example of the sown seed that brings forth fruit.]
>
> Let us see the glorious sign that happens in Eastern lands, that is, in the lands around Arabia. For there is a bird that is named phoenix. This, being the only begotten, lives for five hundred years. When it comes to die, it makes a nest for itself out of frankincense and myrrh and other spices, into which it goes. When its time is fulfilled, it dies. A kind of worm is born from its rotten flesh that, feeding on the fluid of the dead animal, grows wings. After it has grown strong, it takes the nest that contains the bones of its progenitor and carries them from Arabia to Egypt and a city called Heliopolis.[78]

Clement begins where all consideration of the future resurrection must begin: with the resurrection of Jesus. It is to be noted, too, that Clement speaks of the resurrection of the *flesh*, not simply the resurrection of the dead. He uses the Greek word *sarx*, thus making the materiality of the future resurrection quite explicit. In doing this Clement is following the Greek of the New Testament and the Greek citations of Psalm 16 as used in the texts of Acts given above. This usage will be followed by the Creeds of the Western Church. By the fourth century, the Roman Baptismal Creed (basically the Apostles' Creed as we know it) and its variants as used at Milan by Ambrose and in North Africa by Augustine confess faith in the "resurrection of the flesh" or "of the body." The Creed of Nicaea, on the other hand, speaks simply of the resurrection of the dead. They are all teaching the same truth, but the Western texts, like Clement, have the advantage of highlighting the perdurance of flesh itself in the risen body.

Clement continues his reflection on this doctrinal truth by employing natural analogy to make an apologetic for the resurrection. He takes the daily events of the rising and setting of the

---

[78] Clement of Rome, *Letter to Corinth*, 24-25: Funk, I, p. 132.

sun and the growth of seed as illustrative of the resurrection. His use of the phoenix as a comparison to aid acceptance of the resurrection begins beautifully. He deliberately heightens the similarities between the marvelous bird and Christ. The phoenix is described as "only begotten." Clement's Greek for this is *monogenes*, the word St. John uses to describe the Son in John 1:14, 18. Clement then recalls the gifts of the Magi, frankincense and myrrh, and the anointing of the Lord with spices for his burial (cf. Mt 2:11; Jn 19:39-40). Subsequently, however, adhering to his version of the legend of the phoenix, he describes the rebirth/resurrection of the bird in terms that are not well calculated to parallel the resurrection of the Lord. Nonetheless, his point is made, and the legend itself was picked up and used frequently, especially by Tertullian, Eusebius and the poet Lactantius.

There developed around the name of Clement of Rome a whole body of Christian literature. Among it was an early Christian sermon, long entitled the Second Letter of Clement. Written sometime around 150 A.D., it defends the resurrection of the body and does so by listing all the other blessings that the Lord has showered on the flesh. It is in and through the flesh that we "recovered sight" (i.e., were baptized); it is in the flesh that Christ came to save us; it is the flesh that the Spirit will vivify for the resurrection.

> And let none of you say that this flesh will not be judged nor rise. Know this: in what were you saved, in what did you recover your sight? Was it not in this flesh? Thus it is necessary that we guard the flesh as the temple of God. For, as you were first called in the flesh, so shall you come forth in the flesh. If the Lord Christ Who saved us, although formerly He was spirit, was made flesh and so called us while in the flesh, so also shall we receive our reward in this flesh.[79]

> The flesh is able to receive so great and incorruptible a life when the Holy Spirit is joined to it. . . .[80]

That the present blessings bestowed by God on the flesh are an indication of what He will yet do for the flesh is a form of theologizing that will reach a new high-point in St. Irenaeus, the great Bishop of Lyons. In his treatment, Irenaeus uses both natural analogy and the analogy of Faith to present the doctrine of

---

[79] *Homily of the Second Century (II Clement)*, 9: *Funk*, I, p. 194.
[80] *Ibid.*, 14: *Funk*, I, p. 202.

the resurrection of the flesh. He returns to the familiar theme of the seed and vegetative growth but employs most fruitfully revealed mysteries to cast light on our resurrection. Writing around 190 A.D., Irenaeus reminds the faithful that God became flesh and that He gives us this very Flesh as our Food. If our bodies are so dignified in eating, will not that Food nourish these bodies not merely for temporal existence but for eternal life as well? Indeed it will, says Irenaeus.

> Vain in every respect are they who reject the entire dispensation of God, and deny the salvation of the flesh, and spurn its regeneration, saying that it is not capable of incorruption. But if this flesh is not saved, then neither did the Lord redeem us by His Blood, nor is the cup of the Eucharist the communion of His Blood, nor the bread that we break the communion of His Body. For blood can only come from veins and flesh and whatever else makes this human substance. Having truly become this human substance, the Word of God redeemed us by His own Blood, as His Apostle says: "In Him we have redemption through His blood, the remission of sins" (Col 1:14). And because we are His members and are nourished by means of the creation—a creation that He Himself offers to us making the sun to rise and letting it rain as He wills—He has declared that the cup that is taken from creation is His own Blood, from which He makes our blood increase, and He has decreed that the bread, taken from creation, is His own Body, by means of Which our bodies grow.
>
> 3. When, therefore, the cup that has been mixed and the bread that has been made receive the word of God and become the Eucharist and the Body of Christ, from which the substance of our flesh is increased and supported, how can they affirm that the flesh is incapable of receiving the gift of God that is life eternal, which flesh is nourished from the Body and Blood of the Lord, and is a member of Him? . . . And just as the vine planted in the ground fructifies in its season, and as a grain of wheat falling into the earth and decomposing rises with manifold increase by the Spirit of God Who contains all things and then, through the wisdom of God, serves for the use of men, and having received the word of God becomes the Eucharist, which is the Body and Blood of Christ; so also our bodies, having been nourished by this Eucharist and then placed in the earth and suffering decomposition there, shall rise at their time, the Word of God granting them resurrection unto the glory of God the Father. . . . [81]

---

[81] *Adversus Haereses*, V, 2, 2-3. The critical text of the Latin and the surviving Greek fragments is to be found in *Irénée de Lyon, Contre les Hérésies, Livre V*, volume 153 of *Sources Chrétiennes*, pp. 28-32.

The main themes that appear in previous writers occur again in Tertullian, the first great Christian writer in the Latin language. Tertullian faced a virulent form of Gnosticism that denied any value to material reality and, consequently, to the flesh. For Christians influenced by such notions, only spirit counted. The soul was all-important. Vigorously Tertullian combated such attractive but aberrant "spirituality." The worth of the flesh, he reminds us, is plainly seen in the care taken by the Creator in forming it, and, even more, in the fact that He made the flesh His own. It is that flesh of His and ours which will know the resurrection.

> A great thing was being done when God constructed humans from matter. It was honored as often as it experienced the hand of God, when He touched it, when He pulled at it, when He formed and shaped it. Reflect on God, totally occupied and given over to it, with His hand, His senses, His work, His counsel and wisdom, His providence, and especially His affection that guided its features. For, whatever was expressed in clay, it was Christ, the future man, that was thought of, for He, the Word made flesh, was then clay and earth.[82]

The Patristic evidence could be multiplied at length, and there would be much value in doing so. However, let a final word, which captures the spirit of the Fathers, be said by one who was a recognized expert in the field.

> The dust around us will one day become animate. We may ourselves be dead long before, and not see it. We ourselves may elsewhere be buried, and, should it be our exceeding blessedness to rise to life eternal, we may rise in other places, far in the east or west. But, as God's word is sure, what is sown is raised; the earth to earth, ashes to ashes, dust to dust, shall become glory to glory, and life to the living God, and a true incorruptible image of the spirit made perfect. Here the saints sleep, here they shall rise. A great sight will a Christian country then be, if earth remains what it is; when holy places pour out the worshippers who have for generations kept vigil therein, waiting through the long night for the bright coming of Christ![83]

---

[82] Tertullian, *De Resurrectione Mortuorum*, VI, 2-4: CCSL 2, p. 928.

[83] John Henry Newman, "The Resurrection of the Body," in *Parochial and Plain Sermons* (San Francisco: Ignatius Press, 1987), p. 176.

The testimonies are all a wonderful hymn of praise to the One Who died and conquered death and Who has promised to share that conquest with His own. "Once I was dead, but now I am alive forever and ever. I hold the keys to death and the netherworld" (Rv 1:18). The keys of the Kingdom of heaven He gave to Peter. He retains for Himself the keys of Death and of the netherworld, keys to get out, not to enter. And hence He shall bring our bodies.

"You are God's field," says Paul in First Corinthians 3:9. It might better be translated, "You are God's planting." In a special sense this is true of those of us who have already fallen asleep in Christ. They are planted in the earth, God's planting. And He Who stood by a tomb and was thought to be a Gardener is tilling until that planting flower. And what He will reap for the just is not simply a spiritual harvest, but their very bodies. In this way, just as the old creation began in a garden, and the new creation began by a garden tomb, the eighth day will be a garden. It is at that garden which we must now look since it will be the homeland for those whose flesh rests in hope.

IV

THE NEW GENESIS

SPEAKING of Abraham, Sarah and the patriarchs, the author of the Letter to the Hebrews observes:

> They . . . acknowledged themselves to be strangers and aliens on earth, for those who speak thus show that they are seeking a homeland. . . . They desire a better homeland, a heavenly one (Heb 11:13-16).

The faithful of the Old Testament beheld with obscured vision the country that awaited them, and so God, in guiding them, strove to keep alive their hope for that better homeland. To encourage the Israelites during their captivity in an alien land, He said through Isaiah: "Your eyes will see a king in his splendor, they will look upon a vast land" (Is 33:17). The prophet was referring to the return from the exile in Babylon, a going home that would let the people worship the Lord in a restored temple in their beloved country. For Christians, that land and the temple wherein the Lord dwelt among the Jews so that His beauty could be contemplated (cf. Ps 27:4) foreshadow (cf. 1 Cor 10:6) the homeland where those who have imitated the meekness of Christ shall inherit the whole earth (cf. Mt 11:29 and 5:5).

The Lord Almighty is the creator of all things visible and invisible, Who made them to exist and have life. "For God did not make Death, he takes no pleasure in destroying the living. To exist—for this he created all things" (Wis 1:13-14; *NJB*). This giving of being, the New Testament writers tell us, was done in and through Christ, "through whom all things were made" (cf. Jn 1:3; 1 Cor 8:6; Col 1:16; Heb 1:2).

The Book of Revelation appropriately thanks the Lord for the creation: "Worthy are you, Lord our God, to receive glory and honor and power, for you created all things; because of your will they came to be and were created" (Rv 4:11). So marvelous is what He has brought to existence that, in a singularly profound sentence, Alan of Lille (died around 1202) has nature say,

157

"I am the vicar of God the Creator."[1] The vicar of God! In fact so prodigious in power, so enchanting in beauty is this vicar that she can be—and not infrequently has been—mistaken for the Regent Himself. She disclaims such honor.

> Lest because of the prerogatives of my power it seem that I arrogantly derogate from God, I confess myself to be the humble disciple of the supreme Teacher. For, when I work, I am not able to follow expressly in the footsteps of God the Worker; rather like one in admiration, from afar I watch Him working. His working is simple, mine multiplex; His sufficient, mine lacking; His work marvelous, mine mutable. He is unborn, I born; He creating, I what is created; He the maker of my work, I the work of the Maker. He works from nothing, I a beggar work from something. He works in His own name, I work in His name.[2]

The disclaimer is true, but God has indeed made nature wonderful and awesome, a participant with Him in His prerogatives. Moreover, He loves her, taking a complacency in His creation, comparable to the delight He takes in the new Adam, His Son through Whom that very creation exists (cf. Mt 3:17; 17:5). Some part of our own duty in life is to share God's delight in nature, to enjoy a complacency in it, to let it fascinate us. Such a duty is also a gift. For without the gift we are often not able to see nature so as to appreciate her and thank her Author for the fruit of His hands.

> The charity of God is poured out in our hearts through the Holy Spirit Who has been given to us and through Whom we see that whatever is, in any way, is good.[3]

> We see these things and each of them is good, and all of them together very good.[4]

> Your works praise You so that we may love You, and we love You so that Your works may praise You.[5]

> We see all these things and they are very good because You see them in us, You Who have given us Your Spirit so that we might see them and love You in them.[6]

---

[1] Alan of Lille, *Liber de Planctu Naturae: PL* 210, 442: "*Dei Auctoris vicaria.*"
[2] *Ibid.*, 445.
[3] Augustine, *Confessions*, bk. 13, ch. 31: CCSL 27, pp. 269-270.
[4] *Ibid.*, ch. 32, p. 270.
[5] *Ibid.*, ch. 33, p. 270.
[6] *Ibid.*, ch, 34, p. 272.

"So that we might see them and love You in them!" Supreme Teacher that He is, God instructs us through creation, which is in itself a kind of revelation. The question put by an anonymous skeptic,

> *Why does the sun, when 'bout to set*
> *Emit a scarlet flame,*
> *Which makes a marquee of the sky—*
> *Like Broadway, but I see no name?*

received its answer already from St. Paul. It is blindness caused by sin that produces our failure to recognize the Creator in and through His creation.

> Ever since the creation of the world, [God's] invisible attributes of eternal power and divinity have been able to be understood and perceived in what he has made. As a result, they have no excuse (Rom 1:20).

The thought expressed here by Paul has been made the object of a definition of Faith by Christ's Church. The First Vatican Council taught that, by the light of natural reason, we humans are able to arrive at the knowledge of the existence of a good Creator (cf. *DS* 3004: "God, the origin and end of all things, can be known with certainty by the natural light of human reason from the things that He created"). However, although the powers of reason in and of themselves are sufficient, our nature has been harmed. For this "nature wounded in its natural powers and subject to the dominion of death,"[7] *revelation is morally necessary in order to know these truths.* This necessity for the aid of revealed truth was affirmed by Pope Pius XII in the encyclical *Humani Generis* of August 12, 1950 *(DS* 3876). His thought there basically follows St. Thomas Aquinas in his articles in the *Summa Theologica* and the *Summa Contra Gentiles.*[8]

For the eye with light, however, nature magnifies her Lord. Dante was aware of this and, reflecting on the garden of Paradise, reminds us how what God has created can serve to turn our thoughts and love to Him.

---

[7] Paul VI, *Creed: AAS*, 60, p. 440.
[8] Cf. Aquinas, *Summa Theol.*, I, a. q. 1; *Contra Gentiles*, I,

Le fronde onde s'infronda tutto l'orto
de l'ortolano etterno, am' io cotanto
quanto da lui a lor di bene e porto.

The leaves by which the whole garden
of the Eternal Gardener is enflowered I love to the extent
that they bear the good received
from Him (Paradiso, canto 26, 64-66).

The gift is needed to take all this in, because sin has ruined our relation with nature, and distorts both nature's own beauty and the Beauty to which nature can guide us. In some cases, there are those who never really see the earth, although they trick themselves to the extent of thinking or pretending to see it.

An infant who has just learned to hold his head up has a frank and forthright way of gazing about him in bewilderment. He hasn't the faintest clue where he is, and he aims to learn. In a couple of years, what he will have learned instead is how to fake it: he'll have the cocksure air of a squatter who has come to feel he owns the place. Some unwonted, taught pride diverts us from our original intent, which is to explore the neighborhood, view the landscape, to discover at least *where* it is that we have been so startlingly set down, if we can't learn why.[9]

Nature's inability to be seen for what it really is and what it can teach is not totally due to our lack of perception. There is now in nature herself a certain opaque element that partially hides what she was fashioned to reveal. For nature too has been touched by sin. As C.S. Lewis wrote:

There are elements of evil in [nature]. To explain that would carry us far back: I should have to speak of Powers and Principalities and all that would seem to a modern reader most mythological. . . . It is enough to say here that Nature, like us but in her different way, is much alienated from her Creator, though in her, as in us, gleams of the old beauty remain.[10]

The notion expressed by Lewis runs through the prophets of Israel. They tell us that punishment for the sins of our race is shared by the whole creation (cf. Gn 3:17-18; Jer 4:23-28; 9:9;

---

[9] Annie Dillard, *Pilgrim at Tinker Creek*, pp. 11-12.
[10] C.S. Lewis, "On Living in an Atomic Age," *Present Concerns*, p. 79.

12:4; 14:2-6; Hg 1:6-11; 2:16-17, and many more).[11] Especially clear expressions of their thought are the following:

> Hear the word of the Lord, O people of Israel, for the Lord has a grievance against the inhabitants of the land: There is no fidelity, no mercy, no knowledge of God in the land. False swearing, lying, murder, stealing and adultery! in their lawlessness, bloodshed follows bloodshed. Therefore the land mourns, and everything that dwells in it languishes: the beasts of the field, the birds of the air, and even the fish of the sea perish (Hos 4:1-3).

> The earth is utterly laid waste, utterly stripped, for the Lord has decreed this thing. The earth mourns and fades, the world languishes and fades; both heaven and earth languish. The earth is polluted because of its inhabitants, who have transgressed laws, violated statutes, broken the ancient covenant. Therefore a curse devours the earth, and its inhabitants pay for their guilt; therefore they who dwell on earth turn pale, and few men are left. The wine mourns, the vine languishes, all the merry-hearted groan. . . . Thus it is within the land and among the peoples, as with an olive tree after it is beaten, as with a gleaning when the vintage is done. . . . "The earth will burst asunder, the earth will be shaken apart, the earth will be convulsed. The earth will reel like a drunkard, and it will sway like a hut; its rebellion will weigh it down, until it falls, never to rise again." On that day the Lord will punish the host of the heavens in the heavens, and the kings of the earth on the earth. They will be gathered together like prisoners into a pit; they will be shut up in a dungeon, and after many days they will be punished. Then the moon will blush and the sun grow pale, for the Lord of hosts will reign on Mount Zion and in Jerusalem, glorious in the sight of his elders (Is 24:3-23).

What beautifully poetic, yet sad language. Because of the sins of humanity, "the land mourns," "the beasts of the field . . . and even the fish of the sea perish," "the wine mourns, the vine languishes," the earth herself reels "like a drunkard." The Second Vatican Council, Biblically rooted, makes the essence of this teaching its own when it proclaims that the original Fall has disturbed the relationship between our race and all created things—everything suffers for our transgression:

---

[11] Cf. Gustave Martelet, *Libre Réponse à un scandale. La faute originelle, la souffrance et la mort* (Paris: Editions du Cerf, 1986). Martelet, it would appear, denies the share that creation experiences in the Fall. Cf. Jean-Hervé Nicolas, O.P., "Le Péché Originel et le Problème du Mal," *Revue Thomiste*, vol. 89, no. 2, pp. 289-308.

> Although created in justice by God, humans, at the instigation of the Evil One, abused their freedom from the beginning of history, raising themselves against God and desiring to attain their own end apart from God. . . . Frequently refusing to recognize God as its beginning, humanity has also disrupted its proper relation to its last end, as well as the whole relationship to self, to other humans and to all created things (*Gaudium et Spes*, 13).

Citing the first of the above texts from Scripture and summarizing the teaching of Scripture and the Church in Council, Pope John Paul II has written:

> When man turns his back on the Creator's plan, he provokes a disorder which has inevitable repercussions on the rest of the created order. If man is not at peace with God, then earth itself cannot be at peace: "Therefore the land mourns and all who dwell in it languish, and also the beasts of the field and the birds of the air and even the fish of the sea are taken away" (Hos 4:3).[12]

Redemption of the Universe: the New Earth

When God, after the Fall, first chose a people as His own, the promise of the land—a land flowing with milk and honey—was always set before their eyes as the great blessing that would be their inheritance. For their sins the original generation was not allowed to take possession of that land. Even the most meek of men, Moses, because of his lack of trust, was not permitted to reach the promise. From Mt. Nebo he was given from afar the vision of the inheritance. So, too, with us. We see from afar the land promised us. What is amazing is this: it is not a different land. *It is the land we already know and love,* although we know it now only as twisted and misshaped in its own degree and manner by our sins.

Despite our sins, we have been bought back, our inheritance restored by Christ, and the land has been redeemed with and for us. Speaking about the glorification of Christ's flesh at His resurrection, Augustine said: "What was owed to earth was paid off as soon as the Lord was glorified after the war with death had been waged."[13] This "what was owed to earth" means for Augustine that earth, dust, which had given flesh to the Eternal Word,

---

[12] John Paul II, *Message for World Day of Peace, 1990, TPS*, vol. 35, no. 3, p. 201.
[13] Augustine, *Ennarr. in Ps. 23, 7: CCSL* 38, p. 136.

deserved to be glorified. And so it was. Now, together with us, creation itself awaits a better future, a future that will not only restore what belonged to it at the beginning but also renew it in a superior degree. As God promised through Isaiah:

> Yes, in joy you shall depart, in peace you shall be brought back; mountain and hills shall break out in song before you, and all the trees of the countryside shall clap their hands. In place of the thornbush, the cypress shall grow, instead of nettles, the myrtle. This shall be to the Lord's renown, an everlasting imperishable sign (Is 55:12-13).

The resonance of nature with the work of redemption and salvation, an idea found throughout the Scriptures, is inculcated by St. Paul who tells us that this harmony among the elements of the creation will be *everlasting* because even non-intelligent being awaits its own share in what God has planned for humanity.

> Creation awaits with eager expectation the revelation of the children of God; for creation was made subject to futility, not of its own accord but because of the one who subjected it, in hope that creation itself would be set free from slavery to corruption and share in the glorious freedom of the children of God (Rom 8:19-21; cf. Is 11:6; Jl 4:18).

On this passage Aquinas writes:

> The word "creation" in this passage can be understood of sensible creation itself, namely the elements of this world. This type of creation can be said to "expect" something in a double sense. ... In the first sense, God imprints a certain natural aspect of creation that inclines it to some natural purpose, as when a tree "expects" the bearing of fruit. ... In the second sense, sensible creation is ordained by God to some end that surpasses its natural form. For as the human body will be endowed with a certain form of supernatual glory, so the whole of sensible creation, in that glory of the sons of God, will attain a certain newness of glory, as the Book of Revelation tells us when it says, "I saw a new heaven and a new earth."[14]

St. Thomas' exegesis here was better than that of Peter Lombard (and many others before and since) who maintained that the word "creation" in the Pauline text referred to humans only.[15]

---

[14] Aquinas, *Super Epistolam ad Romanos Lectura*, ch. 8, lec. IV, no. 660.
[15] Peter Lombard, *In Ep. ad Romanos: PL* 191, 1445. The same Lombard at the end of his *De Sent. IV*, dist. XLII, says nothing about the new heaven and new earth, simply treating of man's resurrection *(PL* 192, 1112).

Modern exegesis has, in the main, confirmed Aquinas' view of the meaning of Romans.[16]

Pertinent to the concept of nature's resonance to the mystery of salvation is an obscure text in the Book of Revelation:

> But the earth helped the woman and opened its mouth and swallowed the flood that the dragon spewed out of its mouth (Rv 12:16).

Here the earth is seen as helping the woman against the Devil. The land expresses in its own way a revolt against him who became by robbery, not by right, the "ruler of this world" (Jn 12:31), who, having been hurled to earth, led the whole world astray (Rv 12:9). For in sad fact, the earth has been made subject not only to futility, meaningless existence, but to the Devil. Its help to the woman is protest, as well as a manifestation of its expectation for a future when it will share the freedom of its inhabitants.

By God's mercy, this expectation of the creation is not going to be frustrated. Throughout the Bible God has promised that there is indeed a future for the creation itself.

> Lo, I am about to create new heavens and a new earth; the things of the past shall not be remembered or come to mind. Instead, there shall always be rejoicing and happiness in what I create. . . . No longer shall the sound of weeping be heard there (Is 65:17-19).

> Then I saw a new heaven and a new earth. The former heaven and the former earth had passed away, and the sea was no more. . . . He will wipe away every tear from their eyes, and there shall be no more death or mourning, wailing or pain, for the old order has passed away (Rv 21:1, 4).

We must intepret the texts as meaning not literally a *new* but rather a transformed earth. There will be no new creation out of nothing, but rather one from preexisting material. Like humans,

---

[16] Cf. S. Lyonnet, "La rédemption de l'univers," *Lumière et Vie,* vol. 9, no. 48 (1960), pp. 43-62. Lyonnet praises St. Thomas' treatment of the issue in the *Contra Gentiles.* Pope John Paul II has agreed. In his message for the World Day of Peace, 1990, the pope writes: "All of creation became subject to futility, waiting in a mysterious way to be set free and to obtain a glorious liberty, together with all the children of God" *(Origins,* vol. 19, no. 28, p. 465).

the non-intelligent creation will go through its own death throes, so vividly described by St. Peter.

> But the day of the Lord will come like a thief, and then the heavens will pass away with a mighty roar and the elements will be dissolved by fire, and the earth and everything done on it will be found out. . . . Because of [that day] the heavens will be dissolved in flames and the elements melted by fire. But according to his promise we await new heavens and a new earth in which righteousness dwells (2 Pt 3:10-13).

The future life of the just will be enjoyed in a transformed earth. Humans are called to live their future

> *Not in Utopia—subterranean fields,—*
> *Or some secreted island, Heaven knows where!*
> *But in the very world, which is the world*
> *Of all of us,—the place where, in the end,*
> *We find our happiness, or not at all![17]*

It will indeed be on this earth that we will find our happiness or not at all. That happiness will not come *from* the earth, at least not primarily, but it will be on the earth. Peter says that all this will happen "according to [God's] promise." It was a promise made to the disinherited, those from whom the earth had been taken. "Blessed are the meek, for they will inherit the land" (Mt 5:3). The land will be restored to them, wrested from the Devil and from those few rich who have presently and always arrogated so much of it to themselves.

References to the theme of a transformation of the material universe are present, but mostly undeveloped, in the Apostolic Fathers. Angelo O'Hagan is, I believe, correct in his conclusion, which states:

> . . . belief in material re-creation of the world was widespread during the sub-apostolic age. In the dogmatic sense, it could be said to be "present" in the Church during that era. However, the rarity of explicit reference to this belief, together with the certain presence of strong and growing Greek-Hellenistic notions unfavorable to earthly renewal, forces us to regard the concept as of secondary significance to the age of the Apostolic Fathers, as something already showing signs of being neglected.[18]

---

[17] Wordsworth, *The Prelude*, books X-XI, lines 724-729 (140-144).
[18] Angelo O'Hagan, *Material Re-Creation in the Apostolic Fathers*, p. 141.

St. Irenaeus, however, had beautiful passages, one of which we have already seen, but that is worth repeating.

> It is necessary to say that the just, when the world is recreated after they have been resurrected at the appearance of Christ, will receive the inheritance that God promised to the fathers, and will reign in it; only after that will the judgment of all take place. For it is just that they should receive the reward of their sufferings in the very creation in which they labored or in which they suffered; that they should return to life in the creation in which they were slain because of their love for God; and that they should reign in the creation in which they endured servitude.[19]

The quotation, as we saw, is tinged with the millenarianism espoused by Irenaeus. Perhaps it was this millennial viewpoint that first induced a cautious approach to any theological treatment of the new creation. This, in conjunction with those factors that stressed a Hellenistic preference for immortality and "spirituality," caused the idea of a material re-creation to be less and less prominent a part in the theology of the life to come. After the twelfth century, the classical treatises on the future life normally made little reference to the renovation of the universe.[20] The Second Vatican Council, however, has recognized as part of God's Revelation this expectation of a new creation.

> ✳ The Church, to which we are all called in Christ Jesus and in which we acquire holiness through the grace of God, will only be perfected in the glory of heaven when the time for the restitution of all things arrives (cf. Acts 3:21) and when, together with the human race, the whole world, which is intimately joined with humanity and through it approaches its own goal, will be perfectly restored in Christ (cf. Eph 1:10; Col 1:20; 2 Pt 3:10-13). . . .

> ✳ Already the end of the ages has come upon us (cf. 1 Cor 10:11) and the renovation of the world has been irrevocably determined and even anticipated in this age in some real way. . . . The Church herself . . . dwells among creatures that groan and labor even now and expect the revelation of the sons of God (cf. Rom 8:19-22) *(Lumen Gentium,* 48).

---

[19] Irenaeus, *Adversus Haereses,* V, 32, *Sources Chrétiennes,* 153, pp. 397-399.
[20] In our century, a theologian of the stature of Fr. R. Garrigou-Lagrange, for example, in his *Life Everlasting,* has but one reference to the "beauties of the renovated world" with a footnote reference to Isaiah 65:17 and Revelation 21:1, and this occurs in his chapter entitled "Accidental Beatitude" (p. 255).

We do not know the time when earth and humanity will be completed, nor do we know the manner by which the universe will be transformed. Indeed the figure of this world, deformed by sin (cf. 1 Cor 7:31), passes away but we are taught that God is preparing a new dwelling place and a new earth in which justice dwells (cf. 2 Cor 5:2 and 2 Pt 3:13), and whose happiness fulfills and surpasses every desire for peace that arises in human hearts (cf. 1 Cor 2:9 and Rv 21:4-5). At that time, when death has been destroyed, those who are sons of God in Christ will be raised, and that which was sown in weakness and corruption will put on incorruption (cf. 1 Cor 15:42 and 53). While charity and the works of charity remain (cf. 1 Cor 13:8), all that creation, which God created for the sake of humanity, will be freed from its servitude to vanity (cf. Rom 8:19-21) *(Gaudium et Spes*, 39).

The teaching of the Council is reflected at the end of the Fourth Eucharistic Prayer as the Church prays: "Merciful Father, grant to us, Your children, that we may attain our heavenly inheritance, with the Blessed Virgin Mary, Mother of God, with Your Apostles and Saints in Your kingdom where, with all creation that has been freed from the corruption of sin and death, we may praise You" *(ubi cum universa creatura a corruptione peccati et mortis liberata)*. In this sense what Pope John Paul II has written can be understood in its deepest meaning:

> Bread and wine, water and oil, and also incense, ashes, fire and flowers, and indeed almost all elements of creation have their place in the liturgy as gifts to the Creator and as a contribution to the dignity and beauty of the celebration.[21]

The material elements used at Mass are offered to God as, in a sense, the firstfruits of the material creation that will itself, having been offered, be transformed when Christ comes. That final transformation both is anticipated at Mass in the offering and finds its cause in the Eucharistic Christ Who changes some of what is offered, the bread and wine, into Himself. As we have already seen, the Conciliar teaching is not something new in Catholic theology. Although the theme was never a major one, the doctrine of Vatican II had been foreshadowed by some Christian theologians, going back to Irenaeus. Even those later theolo-

---

[21] John Paul II, *Apostolic Letter on 25th Anniversary of the Liturgy Constitution, Origins*, vol. 19, no. 2 (May 25, 1989), p. 21.

gians who were most grounded in the Patristic tradition kept this view alive. Matthias Scheeben, for example, wrote:

> Not only the human body, but the whole of material nature, is moving toward a state of glorification, in which it is to realize its final purpose and attain its eternal repose.
>
> We have to view this transformation according to the analogy of the glorification of the human body, with which it is closely connected. For as the body is the domicile of the soul, material nature is the domicile of the whole man. The human body is derived from material nature and does not abandon its organic connection with matter even when united to the spirit. By a natural conformity, therefore, the glorification of the human body must be communicated to the nature which encompasses it and is bound up with it, so that this nature may become a worthy dwelling place for glorified man, and in its totality have a share in the glory shed over man, its highest pinnacle.
>
> If the glorification of material nature in general must be represented after the analogy of the glorification of the human body, it is manifestly an absolutely supernatural mystery. For this transfiguration will result in a glory that infinitely surpasses all the powers and exigencies of nature, and hence can be neither known nor conceived by the natural intellect. . . .
>
> Pursuing the analogy of the transfiguration of the human body, we must stop at saying that it consists, on the one hand, of a suppression and repression of materiality, particularly of the corruptibility, inconstancy, and perishableness resulting therefrom, and on the other hand, of a communication of supernatural beauty and energy.[22]

And Walter Kasper writes:

> On the contrary, the wonderful orders in the world are in their own way the reflection of the wonder of being in general. For God's action is indeed always new but also always faithful. God's faithfulness does not only concern the history of salvation, but also the steadfast existence of the orders of nature (Gen. 9:8-17), which again and again demand amazement from the observer and praise of the Creator from the pious. Both aspects, historical contingency and enduring orders, were connected with one another in late Old Testament and early Jewish apocalyptic. The Apocalypse includes nature and its orders in God's historical salvific action. Thus, according to Paul, all cre-

---

[22] M. Scheeben, *The Mysteries of Christianity*, pp. 682-683.

ation waits in longing and in birth pains for the coming of the kingdom of the freedom of the children of God (Rom. 8:19-22). In this historical dynamic ordering of nature to salvation history and to its perfection in Jesus Christ, one can recognize an indication that the Bible thinks of being as time and thus comes very close to our present understanding of reality or is at least open to it.[23]

Scheeben's sentence "For this transfiguration will result in a glory that infinitely surpasses all the powers and exigencies of nature, and hence can be neither known nor conceived by the natural intellect" is, of course, an exaggeration. The transformed universe cannot really *infinitely* surpass present realities. The remark must be understood as poetic hyperbole that stresses the marvelous nature of the perfected state of the universe. In fact, the transformation of the universe will give us a recast, not a totally different material reality.

Given the Patristic teaching and that of the Second Vatican Council, the coming existence of a new earth and new heaven is, for the Catholic, an element of one's faith. On this point, all the major theologians of the Church have agreed. But the questions must then be asked: What about the specific aspects of this transformed universe? What will the new earth be like? On these questions there is and has been much difference of opinion.

Although there are great limits to what we can say with certainty, it is natural and beneficial to ruminate with Augustine: "While the Truth which You are was present, we were wondering what the future, eternal life of the Saints would be like."[24]

"We were wondering." This should always be part of our attitude to what God has made known. And a docile wondering about the life before us and about the shape of the material universe to come is a powerful stimulant to hope. Therefore, with Augustine and following him, we will attempt to consider the question: What will that land be like?

We must realize that non-Christians also have reflected on this question. Determined to accept the truth wherever God has

---

[23] W. Kasper, "The Logos Character of Reality," *Communio*, vol. XV, no. 3 (Fall 1988), p. 282.

[24] Augustine, *Confessions*, bk. 9, ch. 10: *CCSL* 27, p. 147.

permitted it be found, let us look first to see how one of the most famous of the pagans envisioned the life to come. Virgil described Elysium this way:

His demum exactis, perfecto munere divae
devenere locos laetos, et amoena virecta
fortunatorum nemorum sedisque beatas.
Largior hic campos aether et lumine vestit
purpureo, solemque suum, sua sidera norunt....
... passimque soluti
per campum pascuntur equi: quae gratia currum
armorumque fuit vivis, quae cura nitentis
pascere equos, eadem sequitur tellure repostos.
Conspicit ecce alios dextra laevaque per herbam
viscentis, laetumque choro paeana canentis
inter odoratum lauri nemus, unde superne
plurimus Eriadani per silvam volvitur amnis.

With these things done and their duty to the goddess finished, they came to happy places, pleasant green places in the fortunate forests, the home of the blessed. Here the fields are clothed with abundant air and bright-colored light since the place knows its own sun and stars.... Everywhere horses were grazing loose upon the plain; for the pleasure in chariots and weapons and their care in grazing brilliant horses follows them when they have rested from earth. And behold he [Aeneas] sees other souls to his right and left picnicking upon the grass and singing happy hymns in chorus, a sweet-scented forest of laurel, from which the mighty River Po winds, through the woodland, to the world above. (Aeneid, VI, 640-659)

Elysium, in short, was seen as a place of fragrant forests, verdant pastures, springs and rivers, as well as abounding in animal life. It was a realm where our pleasant occupations here on earth would continue. This fair picture failed to influence St. Thomas Aquinas in any way. His writing on the transformed universe reveals that there were limitations to his usually robust defense of matter. Although he established a general principle that stated: ". . . [in the life to come] the entire bodily creation will be appropriately changed to be in harmony with the state of those who will then exist"[25] and cited the Book of Wisdom ("God created all things that they might exist") as scriptural witness for the principle, he nonetheless taught that not all of creation as we

---

[25] Aquinas, *Contra Gentiles*, IV, ch. 97.

know it will be restored. Only the "elements" of the material universe will find a place in the new Genesis. By these elements he meant fire, air, water and earth. All else will fail to be reborn after the death of the universe. "Animals, plants, and the mixed bodies, which are entirely corruptible in whole and in part, will not remain at all in that state of incorruption."[26] He calls upon First Corinthians 7:31 ("The world in its present form is passing away") as evidence for this view.

> The material universe cannot remain in existence without its essential parts. But the essential parts of the universe are the heavenly bodies and the elements, for the entire world machine is made up of them. Other bodies do not, apparently, pertain to the integrity of the material universe, but contribute rather to its adornment and beauty. They befit its changeable state in the sense that, with a heavenly body acting as efficient cause, and with the elements as material causes, animals and plants and minerals are brought into being. But in the state of final consummation another kind of adornment will be given to the elements, in keeping with their condition of incorruption. In that state, accordingly, there will remain men, elements, and heavenly bodies, but not animals or plants or minerals.[27]

In essence his teaching had not changed from the time he wrote his commentary on the *Sentences* of Lombard. His treatment on that occasion is found verbatim in the Supplement to the *Summa Theologica*, q. 91, a. 5. There he wrote:

> Since the renovation of the world will come about for the sake of humans it is necessary that it be conformed to their renovation. They, however, are renewed from a state of corruption to a state of incorruption and perpetual rest *(perpetuae quietis)*. Thus the world will be renewed in such a way that, all corruption being done away with, it will remain in perpetual rest. Therefore only those things that have an ordination to incorruption can be part of that renovation. Such things are the heavenly bodies, the elements and human beings. The heavenly bodies are, by their nature, incorruptible in whole and in part. The elements are corruptible in part, but incorruptible taken as a whole. . . . Animals and plants and minerals and all mixed bodies are corruptible in whole and in part in respect to both their matter and their form. As such they do not in any way have an ordination to incorruption, and so shall not remain in the renovation.

---

[26] *Ibid.*
[27] Aquinas, *Compendium*, ch. 170: Vollert translation.

Faced with the objection that animals and plants serve as adornments for the elements and should remain, St. Thomas answered that plants and animals belong to the perfection of the elements in the present age, not in the future. Furthermore, the movements of the heavenly bodies will cease in the re-creation. It is this movement that causes the generation of the plants and animals, and, when it ceases, so will their natural appetite for existence (ad 3). In short, St. Thomas imagines a bald universe, a universe without the adornment of grass, trees, fields, or animals. All in all, it is, I think, not a pleasant description of the future work of the great Artist.

It seems likely that this view which would deny the presence of vegetative and animal life in the new earth arose in part as a result of certain appendages to the rich philosophy inherited from the Greeks. For all its great value, part of Greece's aesthetic and metaphysical thought viewed change as a lack of perfection. Change was described as being either the acquiring of a perfection not yet possessed or the loss of a perfection already possessed. Thus motion was an imperfect state. An additional factor was the Aristotelian notion, shared by Thomas, that the heavenly bodies were, of themselves, incorruptible, and immobile. Given these presuppositions, motion was viewed as less than ideal, and the Biblical and Patristic notion of "heavenly rest" came to be interpreted as *immobility*, an unchanging complacency in a perfection fully attained. In such a perspective, in the renovation of the last times, all the heavenly bodies would be fixed in place, all their motion ceasing. As a consequence any change of seasons on earth would be ended, as would all growth. Faithfully following Aquinas, and adding no new arguments, Suarez (1548-1617) would write of the heavenly bodies: "They will cease to be moved and become perpetually quiescent because there will have ceased every necessity for their movement, namely their service to man. . . ."[28]

Both Suarez and St. Thomas thought that this conclusion followed logically from their interpretation of Romans 8:20 ("For creation was made subject to futility . . ."). Their understanding

---

[28] Suarez, *Commentarii et Disputationes in IIIam Partem D. Thomae*, q. 59, a. 6, disp. 57, sec. 2 in *Opera Omnia*, vol. 19, ed. Carolo Berton (Paris: Vives, 1877).

of the word "futility" saw it as meaning "change."[29] So, having been made subject to change because of sin, creation must be free of change in the life to come. Duns Scotus (c. 1266-1308) agreed with these conclusions, although he wisely maintained that the various theological and philosophical positions that defended them were not conclusive.[30]

This view of an immobile future universe carried over into the understanding of how the Saints participated in the Beatific Vision. That Vision was perceived as a type of ecstasy in which everything the Blessed were to know was known instantaneously, without any variation in degree or aspect. To this opinion we shall return later. Owing to St. Thomas' influence, this view about the non-existence of animal and vegetative life in the world to come became practically universal in Catholic theology for a long time. Only in our own century has it begun to be questioned, and then only when consideration is given to the matter at all, and that is infrequently.

St. Thomas failed to correct Aristotle in this area—something he did frequently in other areas—because there was no overwhelming tradition or Biblical evidence to the contrary. Nevertheless, previous to Aquinas the opinions concerning the renovation of the vegetative and animal life were not so negative, granted that the matter was rarely treated specifically.

Early in Christian literature, in the marvelous third-century account of the *Martyrdom of Perpetua and Felicity*, one finds a description of heaven that portrays it as "a vast space, a garden of pleasure, having trees of roses, as well as every other kind of flowers, the height of the trees being like that of a cypress."[31] There was a pleasant nourishing smell everywhere and in its midst a city of light.[32]

St. Jerome, in his exegesis of Isaiah 65:17ff, understood the new heavens and new earth as a change of the old heaven and

---

[29] Cf. St. Thomas, *In Romanos*, 8, lec. 4, *op. cit.*, no. 668, p. 121. Suarez, *Commentarii et Disp. etc.*, q. 59, a. 6, disp. 58, sec. 3, *op. cit.*, p. 1117.
[30] Duns Scotus, *In Lib. IV Sententiarum*, dist. 48, q. 2, *Opera Omnia*, vol. 20 (Paris: Vives 1894), pp. 523-542.
[31] *Martyrdom of Perpetua and Felicity: PL* 3, 44.
[32] *Ibid.*, 45-46.

earth for the better, not a total annihilation of the same,[33] and he cites Romans 8:19 as evidence from Sacred Scripture for this interpretation.[34] While in this he can be said to support a view of the continuance of animal and vegetable life, there is a marked tendency in his exegesis to allegorize the texts, referring what is said about the material conditions of the new heaven and new earth to the heavenly Jerusalem or to the Church and the spiritual delights found therein.[35] In this use of allegory, he set a pattern followed by later theologians, including St. Thomas, who annihilated all but the "elements." Jerome's contemporaries, Chrysostom and Augustine, were more positive.

Commenting on Romans 8:21, Chrysostom writes:

> What is this creation [that shall be delivered]? Not only you, but also that which is inferior to you. That which does not share with you reason or sense perception will share with you the good things [to come]. . . . It will no longer be corruptible, but will follow after the beauty of your body. As you were rendered corruptible, it too was made corruptible. Thus when you are made incorruptible, it too will follow.[36]

Augustine was still more optimistic. He wrote of a new heaven and a new earth that *would exist for the sake of beauty,* a loveliness that would delight the mind and lead the Saints to praise the Source of all delights. It would be a universe where rest did not equal a cessation of motion, but where motion itself would be an aspect of beauty.

> . . . together with all the great and wonderful things that will be seen there, our rational minds will be inflamed, by the delight of a beauty conformed to reason, to praise the great Artisan. What the movement of such bodies will be there I do not dare to delineate, nor am I able to think of; nevertheless both movement and stasis, just like the appearance of everything, will be beautiful there where everything which is not beautiful will not exist.[37]

---

[33] Jerome, *Commentariorum in Esaiam Libri XVIII*, XVIII, 17-18: CCSL 73a, pp. 759-760.

[34] *Ibid.*, IX, 26: CCSL 73, pp. 395-396.

[35] *Ibid.*, IV, 6-9: CCSL 73, pp. 150-152; XVIII, 20-25: CCSL 73a, pp. 762-769.

[36] Chrysostom, *In Epist. ad Romanos*, XIV: PG 60, 530.

[37] Augustine, *City of God*, bk. 22, ch. 30: CSEL 40, 2, p. 665.

For a while subsequent theologians, without many specifics, followed the positive Augustinian tradition. Primasius of Hadrumentum (sixth-century bishop of what is now Sousse in Tunisia) thought that the universe would be cleansed by fire and that heaven and earth would be changed for the better, in conformity with the incorruption and immortality of the bodies of the Saints.[38] This same position was taken by Julian of Toledo in the seventh century in a work that is almost unique since it deals ex professo with the afterlife, the *Prognostikon Futuri Saeculi*. It is essentially a compendium of Augustine's thought on the subject. Speaking of the new earth, Julian writes: ". . . the world, having been renewed for the better, will be suitably accommodated to humans who will also have reen renewed for the better in the flesh."[39]

Rabanas Maurus (c. 780-856) viewed what was to come as a new paradise, a garden of delights. "Paradise, i.e., the garden of delights, mystically signifies either the present Church or the land of the living where those who have merited it by correct faith and good works will live forever."[40]

Arnold of Bonneval (died c. 1156) has left us an idealized description of the paradise of Eden that must rank among the most beautiful in medieval literature. It was a place of intimacy with God; of trees and flowers that delighted man's sense of touch and smell; where nothing would harm and all would enchant; and where work would be effortless creativity.[41] In all this, of course, Arnold saw a type of spiritual realities: the paradise of the soul in grace and the paradise of the world to come. What the new earth will be filled with, he explicitly says, revelation has not told us.[42] Yet, as one reads his description of the earthly Eden, one cannot but sense that he intended to whet the appetite for what lies ahead, not to make it dwell sadly on what was lost. He even seems to imply that the first Genesis will happen again, given back to us in a perfected condition, for he completes his treatment by saying:

---

[38] Primasius of Hadrumentum, *Commentarius in Apocalypsin: CCSL*, 92, pp. 284-285.

[39] Julian of Toledo, *Prognostikon*, bk. II, ch. 46: *PL* 96, 518,

[40] *De Universo Libri*, bk. 12, ch. 2: *PL* 111, 334.

[41] Arnold, *De Operibus Sex Dierum: PL* 189, 1535-1538.

[42] *Ibid.*, 1531-1532.

> Adam is led out of the place of delight in order to do pen-
> ance. . . . Nevertheless he is placed before paradise in order to
> make satisfaction so that, seeing frequently whence he de-
> parted and thinking upon what was and what would have
> been, . . . he might experience . . . what great good there is in
> subjection and obedience through which even he who had
> fallen and been repelled might not despair of a future of return
> and restitution.[43]

Other medieval theologians stressed the aspect of pleasure
that would be found in the life to come, a pleasure arising in
some part from the restored universe. A sermon, whose author is
unknown although it was once attributed to Peter Damian (1007-
1072) and is from the same period, reads:

> The heavenly paradise [will be] a blessed and glorious region,
> full of pleasure *(voluptatis)* and of the glory of pleasantness
> and joy, grace and kindness. There is rest from labor, pleasure
> arising from what is new *(iucunditas de novitate)*, and eternal
> security. There is the City of the Great King.[44]

Rupert of Deutz (c. 1080-1129) is even more descriptive in
his portrayal. We will do what is good, he writes, simply for the
sake of pleasure.

> In heaven, made happy by an eternal resurrection, our soul
> alone will feed on the happy vision of the Divinity; our body,
> however, if it wishes, will eat from every beautiful and pleasant
> tree, not out of any necessity, but simply for the sake of the
> great and ineffable pleasure *(magna et ineffabili voluptate)*.[45]

And Rupert sets it as a principle that the Paradise to come
was the pattern for the earthly Eden: "It should be known that
this earthly paradise was made according to the pattern of the
heavenly Paradise."[46]

These writers are using a "spiritual" sense in their exegesis
of the Book of Genesis, and one can say that, in doing so, they
are only doing what the Book of Revelation itself does when it
depicts the life to come in terms of Old Testament imagery. We

---

[43] *Ibid.,* 1568-1569.

[44] Peter Damian, Sermon 59: *PL* 144, 838. On the unauthentic nature of the sermon (59) of Peter Damian, cf. Jn. Lucchesi (editor), *CCCM* 57, p. VIII.

[45] Rupert of Deutz, *De Sancta Trinitate et Operibus Eius,* bk. II, 26: *CCCM* 21,
p. 214. Cf. Rv 2:8.

[46] Rupert of Deutz, *op. cit.,* 27, p. 215.

must not think that the mystical sense excludes the real sense; rather it enhances it. In reality, what Rupert and the others do is not without great insight. As has frequently been observed, "protology," our understanding of the beginning of everything, is eschatology, our thought about the end. The end is included in some way in the beginning, and the beginning is understood more clearly retrospectively. Newman writes in this regard: ". . . there are traces of paradise still left among us, yet, it is evident, Scripture says little of them in comparison of its accounts of human misery."[47] There is present in us a certain longing for what has been lost, even though we may not recognize it as something that was possessed. A modern author in a beautifully composed meditation on the first three chapters of Genesis writes along the same lines when he speaks of Adam, after the Fall, thinking back on Eden.

> He saw in imagination the garden again as he remembered it— as he would always remember it: the brown slope . . . jewelled with the dew upon it, and the morning sun over the forest; the riverfalls and the hanging willows, the grassglades and hairferns and the purple fruit clusters; the saplings and cedars and the little leaves that stood against the sun: the bird that stood on his hand and the bush-tail leaping, and every creature. . . .

> And of all the scenes of the garden remembered, only one remained to trouble him, there by the river; which had stood at the gate of his mind from the day of his disobedience, and would remain with him all the days of his life, and with his seed forever: . . . the man and the woman walking hand in hand, naked and unashamed: Adam and Ishah as they had been, and might have been always, and were no more.[48]

One can say that a universe restored without its accompanying adornment would be a creation very different from the one made by God, and from the world in which He Himself, having become man, lived. As imagined by St. Thomas and many after him, it would be almost a dreary creation, with a type of desolation portrayed in the Bible as a chastisement by God for unfaithfulness: "I will make the land a waste, because they have broken

---

faith, says the Lord God" (Ez 15:8). It is difficult to think that what God considers a curse for the world in its present state is to become a permanent condition in the revitalized and transformed universe He has promised. The cosmos is to be one brought to perfection, even in its natural beauties. We can make our own the remark that "we may suppose that all life on earth, in whatever form, will be involved in the renewal of the human race, and so belong to the new earth."[49] This was the view of the greatest of the Church's theologians who, lover of beauty that he was, surveyed the charms of the earth and then anticipated how those same delights would enchant us in a perfected state.

> What discourse can define the beauty and usefulness of the creatures that the Divine generosity has given to humans to gaze upon and to use even while we have been cast into and condemned to our present labors and miseries? Think of the multiform and various beauty found in the heavens and on land and in the sea; the great quantity and marvelous variety of light itself as found in the sun and moon and stars; the darkness of forests; the colors and the scents of flowers; the multitude of singing and colored birds; the multiform variety of so many and such great animals, among whom we admire those least in size (since we are stupefied more by the works of ants and bees than by the immense bodies of whales); the great spectacle of the very sea when it dresses itself, as it were, with clothes of diverse colors, sometimes green in its many forms, sometimes purple, sometimes blue. Indeed, what a delight it is to watch the sea even when it is stirred up, a pleasure that becomes greater because it gently strokes the watcher without tossing him about and crushing him as it does the sailor. And what shall we say of the abundance of food found everywhere to ward off hunger; or of the diversity of flavors to ward off disgust, flavors spread abroad by the riches of nature instead of by the skill and work of cooks? Think of what aids there are in so many things for the preservation and recuperation of health! Reflect on the pleasant change that comes from the alternation of day and night, the gentle tempering of the winds . . . ! And all these wonderful things are solace for us while we are miserable and condemned, not the rewards of the blessed. What therefore shall those rewards be like, if these are so many, so wonderful and so great?[50]

---

[49] Winklhofer, *The Coming of His Kingdom,* p. 248.
[50] Augustine, *City of God,* bk. 22, ch. 24: CSEL 40, 2, pp. 648-649.

As we read that Augustinian hymn of praise to the beauties of the world, one can only think of how fully he would agree with the poetry of another great admirer of the Artisan's masterpieces in nature.

> *. . . here I stand, not only with the sense*
> *Of present pleasure, but with pleasing thoughts*
> *That in this moment there is life and food*
> *For future years. And so I dare to hope,*
> *Though changed, no doubt, from what I was when first*
> *I came among these hills; when like a roe*
> *I bounded o'er the mountains, by the sides*
> *Of the deep rivers, and the lonely streams,*
> *Wherever nature led: more like a man*
> *Flying from something that he dreads than one*
> *Who sought the thing he loved. For nature then*
> *(The coarser pleasures of my boyish days,*
> *And their glad animal movements all gone by)*
> *To me was all in all.—I cannot paint*
> *What then I was. The sounding cataract*
> *Haunted me like a passion: the tall rock,*
> *The mountain, and the deep and gloomy wood,*
> *Their colours and their forms, were then to me*
> *An appetite; a feeling and a love,*
> *That had no need of a remoter charm,*
> *By thought supplied, nor any interest*
> *Unborrowed from the eye.—That time is past,*
> *And all its aching joys are now no more,*
> *And all its dizzy raptures. Not for this*
> *Faint I, nor mourn nor murmur; other gifts*
> *Have followed; for such loss, I would believe,*
> *Abundant recompense. For I have learned*
> *To look on nature, not as in the hour*
> *Of thoughtless youth; but hearing oftentimes*
> *The still, sad music of humanity,*
> *Nor harsh, nor grating, though of ample power*
> *To chasten and subdue. And I have felt*
> *A presence that disturbs me with the joy*
> *Of elevated thoughts; a sense sublime*
> *Of something far more deeply interfused,*
> *Whose dwelling is the light of setting suns,*
> *And the round ocean and the living air,*
> *And the blue sky, and in the mind of man:*
> *A motion and a spirit, that impels*
> *All thinking things, all objects of all thought,*
> *And rolls through all things. Therefore am I still*

A lover of the meadows and the woods,
And mountains; and of all that we behold
From this green earth; of all the mighty world
Of eye, and ear—both what they half create,
And what perceive; well pleased to recognise
In nature and the language of the sense
The anchor of my purest thoughts, the nurse,
The guide, the guardian of my heart, and soul
Of all my moral being.[51]

The beauty—both awesome and terrible—so appreciated by Augustine and Wordsworth, comes alive verbally in our day in such deservedly honored works as Annie Dillard's *Pilgrim at Tinker Creek*. For many, unfortunately, both the outer mystery and the inner depth of meaning are lost. For those who are sympathetic to her lessons, however, nature can still grant an almost intuitive and even therapeutic wisdom that suggests her Creator. Such is one of the advantages of growing up in a rural environment. In her book that so poetically evokes this type of nurturing, Helen Santmyer delineates the opportunities presented to those raised in such surroundings.

At first hand they know the local earth and all that thereon lives and grows. Wandering free as the wind, left to their own devices, they are neither led nor hindered by the consciousness of being overseen. . . . Before they read poetry they have found the stuff of which it is made, and they come to its pages at last with a fine sense of recognition—recognition of those truths that are based on evidence long and familiarly known. They accept the poet's testimony as to an "always": always the firmament of stars by night, the arched bow of the sky by day, and the line of a hill against it, trees and growing fields, wild flowers, streams and the cattle that go down to them to drink, lambs and colts and the birds that fly: these in the verses of the Psalmist, in Theocritus and Horace, in Milton and Wordsworth, are the same as in the days and nights, so many centuries later, when they first saw and noted them. They accept also therefore

---

[51] William Wordsworth, *Lines Composed a Few Miles above Tintern Abbey*, *William Wordsworth: The Poems*, I, p. 360.

such philosophies—such conceptions of God and man—as are based by the poets on this immutability.[52]

In just such an environment was Jesus of Nazareth reared. He drew from rural life many of the images He used to communicate His teaching. For, who better than the creator of nature would realize that in nature itself "our elementary feelings co-exist in a state of greater simplicity, and, consequently, may be more accurately contemplated, and more forcibly communicated"?

> Why are you anxious about clothes? Learn from the way the wild flowers grow. They do not work or spin.... If God so clothes the grass of the field, which grows today and is thrown into the oven tomorrow, will he not much more provide for you, O you of little faith? (Mt 6:18-30).

> He proposed another parable to them. "The kingdom of heaven may be likened to a man who sowed good seed in his field" (Mt 13:24).

> Learn a lesson from the fig tree (Mt 13:28).

> A sower went out to sow his seed. And as he sowed, some seed fell on the path, and birds came and ate it up (Mt 13:3).

> Foxes have dens and birds of the sky have their nests, but the Son of Man has nowhere to rest his head (Mt 8:20).

> In the evening you say, "Tomorrow will be fair, for the sky is red"; and, in the morning, "Today will be stormy, for the sky is red and threatening." You know how to judge the appearance of the sky, but you cannot judge the signs of the times (Mt 16:2-3).

---

[52] Helen Hooven Santmyer, *Ohio Town* (New York: Berkeley Books, 1985), pp. 307-308. Her thoughts in this passage are very similar to those suggested by Wordsworth in his justly famous "Prelude to Lyrical Ballads": "Low and rustic life was generally chosen, because in that condition, the essential passions of the heart find a better soil in which they can attain their maturity, are less under restraint, and speak a plainer and more emphatic language; because in that condition of life our elementary feelings co-exist in a state of greater simplicity, and, consequently, may be more accurately contemplated, and more forcibly communicated; because the manners of rural life germinate from those elementary feelings; and, from the necessary character of rural occupations, are more easily comprehended; and are more durable; and lastly, because in that condition the passions of men are incorporated with the beautiful and permanent forms of nature" *(Poems,* vol. I, pp. 869-870).

Jesus drew from that same pastoral and village life many other examples that He used to great effect (cf. Mt 13:33; 11:16; Lk 15:8-9; 2:8). The human eye of the Creator readily observed the charm and mystery of nature and used it to guide us to the Father. This is the nature—in all its seasonal and climatic variations—that He Himself, to Whom all power is given, will restore when He comes again.

The Greater and Lesser Lights

Of the heavenly bodies, Holy Scripture tells us that the Father of lights (cf. Jas 1:17) exhibits them to be seen: "he leads out their army and numbers them, calling them all by name" (Is 40:26). Indeed, before Him, "the morning stars sang in chorus" (Jb 38:7). In turn, the loveliness of those bodies has often been sung.

> I kiss my hand
> To the stars, lovely-asunder
> Starlight, wafting him out of it; and
> Glow, glory in thunder;
> Kiss my hand to the dappled-with damson west;
> Since, tho' he is under the world's splendour and wonder,
> His mystery must be intressed, stressed;
> For I greet him the days I meet him, and bless when I understand.[53]

The Book of Revelation would seem to indicate that, in the life to come, there will exist no sun or moon, and that the night, the moon's time to appear, will likewise disappear (cf. Rv 21:23; 22:5). Similar indication is found in the Lord's own prophecy about the final tribulations when He teaches that "the sun will be darkened, and the moon will not give its light" (Mt 24:29). Commenting on this latter passage, St. Thomas wrote:

> At the coming of Christ [the sun and moon] will not be changed according to their substance, but by comparison because so great will be the brightness of Christ and of the Saints that the

---

[53] G.M. Hopkins, "The Wreck of the Deutschland," in *A Hopkins Reader*, edited with an introduction by John Pick, Image Books (Garden City, NY: Doubleday, 1966), p. 36.

brightness of the sun and moon will not appear. . . . But after
the day of judgment the brightness of the sun and moon will be
increased, thus fulfilling what is said in Isaiah 30:26: "The
moon will shine like the sun, and the sun will be seven times
brighter. . . ."[54]

Thus, in respect to the heavenly bodies Thomas reconciles
apparently contradictory passages, properly understanding the
symbolic aspect present in the prophecies. By so doing, and in
line with Tradition and other passages in Scripture, he defends
the transformation of the heavenly bodies in the re-creation of
the universe. It must be added, however, that the continued existence of the galactic bodies, as well as our own sun and moon,
will include—unlike what Thomas and others thought—their
natural motion. This being so, it is natural to expect a change of
seasons. Furthermore, the motion and the concomitant processes
it causes will have a duration, thus giving the Elect, if they
wanted it, another way to mark time. As indicated, however,
such measuring of time will have no importance in the life to
come. Measurement of duration then will only exist to serve Augustine's law: it will be present to the extent that it adds to the
beauty of the life to come, or permits that beauty to manifest itself in various phases.

And what loveliness there will be. And how much of it! The
present gives us some indication. Who can look at the pictures
sent back by Voyager I and II without some astonishment? Only
now are they racing out of our solar system into deep space with
its galaxies beyond counting. Already a contemplation of the
universe gives us some idea of its immensity. And our current
view is telescopic—not even "bird's-eye." The cosmos is in fact so
vast that it is either a provocation to doubt or an invitation to reflect on the wildness of God's "imagination," or look for reasons
in His prodigality. Why so much? Why so much that appears useless? Why such differences in type and kind? It is as if He were
an impressionistic Artist who stood back from the canvas and
threw onto it all his pigments in their every hue, and then everything else as well. Vast, unnecessarily vast so it would seem, yet
science begins to detect more fully the intricate bonds that link it
all together and make it a pattern. It was perhaps planned as a

---

[54] Aquinas, *In Matt. Lectura*, ch. 23, lec. III, no. 1958.

playground, a resort, a museum of art and science, and more; all at the same time: to be enjoyed more in the future than it can be even now.

On the Earth's Embellishment

There is a book of passionate poetry in the Bible wherein the lovers use the flowered and verdant adornments of the earth to describe as well as to entice each other. Tradition, both Jewish and Christian, has most often understood this Spouse and His Bride to be the Lord Almighty Himself and His people, the community He has created and redeemed. She says to Him and of Him, and of herself:

> My lover is for me a cluster of henna from the vineyards of En-gedi (Song 1:14).

> As an apple tree among the trees of the woods, so is my lover among men (Song 2:3).

> His eyes are like doves beside running waters, his teeth would seem bathed in milk, and are set like jewels. His cheeks are like beds of spice with ripening aromatic herbs. His lips are red blossoms; they drip choice myrrh (Song 5:12-13).

> Arise, north wind! Come, south wind! blow upon my garden that its perfumes may spread abroad. Let my lover come to his garden and eat its choice fruits (Song 4:16).

Of her, the Bride, it is said,

> Who is this that comes forth like the dawn, as beautiful as the moon, as resplendent as the sun, as awe-inspiring as bannered troops? (Song 6:10).

And He, Who made all the analogies possible by creating the beauty of this earth, says of her:

> Ah, you are beautiful, my beloved, ah, you are beautiful! Your eyes are doves behind your veil. Your hair is like a flock of goats streaming down the mountains of Gilead (Song 4:1).

> How beautiful is your love, my sister, my bride, how much more delightful is your love than wine, and the fragrance of your ointments than all spices! Your lips drip honey, my bride, sweetmeats and milk are under your tongue; and the fragrance of your garments is the fragrance of Lebanon. You are an enclosed garden, my sister, my bride, an enclosed garden, a fountain sealed (Song 4:10-12).

You are a garden fountain, a well of water flowing fresh from Lebanon (Song 4:15).

The life to come will bring consummation to this love and in that fulfillment all the same imagery of love will be available, serving both as a memory of the courtship here and now and as an enduring source from which the imagination may draw comparisons to express love for the one who infinitely outshines Solomon. As St. Bernard, describing the joys of heaven, said, all earth's beauties will be present so that "seeing Him in all creatures" He may be praised.[55] In hope we anticipate such possibilities when we use Nature to praise Him now.

I see His Blood upon the rose
And in the stars the glory of His eyes.
His Body gleams amid eternal snows,
His tears fall from the skies.

I see His face in every flower;
The thunder and the singing of the birds
Are but His voice—and carven by His power
Rocks are His written words.

All pathways by His feet are worn,
His strong Heart stirs the ever-beating sea.
His crown of thorns is twined with every thorn,
His cross is every tree.[56]

C.S. Lewis in that wonderful book, *The Great Divorce*, describes his traveler's first impressions of heaven as the "level, grassy country through which there ran a wide river."

The light and coolness that drenched me were like those of a summer morning. . . . I had the sense of being in a larger space, perhaps even a larger *sort* of space, than I had ever known before: as if the sky were further off and the extent of the green plain wider than they could be on this little ball of earth. . . . It was the light, the grass, the trees that were different; made of some different substance, so much solider than things in our country that men were ghosts by comparison.[57]

---

[55] St. Bernard, *"In Festivitate Omnium Sanctorum; Sermo 4,"* Opera Omnia, vol. V, p. 357.
[56] Joseph Mary Plunkett in Kilmer's *Anthology of Catholic Poets*, p. 171.
[57] C.S. Lewis, *The Great Divorce*, pp. 27-28.

It is a universe both more vast and more solid. Apart from the notion that what is there will be "made of some different substance," all the "fantasy" of Lewis' description may be presumed to be an insightful but insufficient foretaste of the reality. The spaciousness of this world of ours in its transformed state will be necessary since all humans who have been saved from the beginning of time will inhabit it. What is more, these people shall inhabit it without crowding, without that kind of population density that leaves trees, grass, shrubbery and animals confined to parks and zoos. The restored universe will be more "solid" simply because it is more real. It will be like the difference between a painting by Monet seen from a distance and that same painting viewed "close up." Only a close inspection reveals the solidity of the brush strokes, the texture and quantity of the paint. It is all much more substantial than the impression it gives. And so with the earth, but from the opposite perspective. Now everything here appears solid, while what is to come is but vague impression. Then, however, there will be nothing ethereal about it, nor any danger of any of its reality and beauty passing away like a mist. Lewis' description of the plain, grass and trees owes something perhaps to Virgil, but we are not to discount them for that reason. Revelation takes the truths perceived by the pagans and purifies them, not disowns them.

The Good Things of the Lord

The Creator of all things promised Israel, His chosen, the blessings of nature: verdant pastures, rich fields and peaceful valleys, a land destined to flow with milk and honey, wine and oil. And, when they came into what had been promised, "they found abundant and good pastures, and the land was spacious, quiet, and peaceful" (1 Chr 4:40). The land itself and the good things it produced became a sign of blessing.

> He will love and bless and multiply you; he will bless the fruit of your womb and the produce of your soil, your grain and wine and oil, the issue of your herds and the young of your flocks, in the land which he swore to your fathers he would give you (Dt 7:13).

They became, as well, an object of prayer:

> May there be an abundance of grain upon the earth; on the tops
> of the mountains the crops shall rustle like Lebanon; the city
> dwellers shall flourish like the verdure of the fields (Ps 72:16; cf.
> Zec 10:1).

The longed-for good pasture eventually took on a symbolic
aspect: it was where the great Shepherd fed His own, the sheep
of His flock (cf. Ps 95:7; 79:13; 74:1). In fact God Himself was
seen as the pasture in Whom His people grazed.

> Whoever came upon them devoured them, and their enemies
> said, "We incur no guilt, because they sinned against the Lord
> [their true pasture],[58] the hope of their fathers" (Jer 50:7).

The wandering away of His people from their "true pasture"
brought loss of field, plain and their produce. Often enough such
misfortune is described as being a punishment for the sins of mankind (cf. Jer 12:4; 48:8 and 33; 50:45). Their restoration, on the other
hand, was a sign of renewed favor, the portent of better times.

> I will lead them out from among the peoples and gather them
> from the foreign lands; I will bring them back to their own
> country and pasture them upon the mountains of Israel, in the
> land's ravines and all its inhabited places. In good pastures will
> I pasture them, and on the mountain heights of Israel shall be
> their grazing ground. There they shall lie down on good graz-
> ing ground, and in rich pastures shall they be pastured on the
> mountains of Israel (Ez 34:13-14; cf. Is 49:9; Jer 23:3).

When He assumed our human nature, God reaffirmed the
promise made through Ezekiel, promising that there was yet a
more verdant pasture for His own. "I am the gate. Whoever enters through me will be saved, and will come in and go out and
find pasture" (Jn 10:9). Even before the Incarnation the perspective of nature's restoration had been enlarged and taken on
idealized aspects.

> On that day, the mountains shall drip new wine, and the hills
> shall flow with milk; and the channels of Judah shall flow with
> water: a fountain shall issue from the house of the Lord, to
> water the Valley of Shittim (Jl 3:18).

---

[58] The NAB text does not have the words in brackets. However, they are found
in the NIV version and the *New Revised Standard Version* (which has "the true
pasture"); "true pasture" is also the reading of John Bright in his Anchor Bible
translation and commentary, *Jeremiah* (Garden City, NY: Doubleday and Co.,
1965), p. 340.

> I will open up rivers on the bare heights, and fountains in the broad valleys; I will turn the desert into a marshland, and the dry ground into springs of water. I will plant in the desert the cedar, acacia, myrtle, and olive; I will set in the wasteland the cypress, together with the plane tree and the pine (Is 41:18-19).

Although such idealization may have been merely imagery for the human authors of the Scriptures, it was nonetheless a symbol of the new creation and contained the notion that what the Lord had made would not only endure but be perfected: ". . . the new heavens and the new earth which I will make shall endure before me, says the Lord" (Is 66:22). In that context even Israel's prayers for the benefits of the land took on a fuller meaning, one directed toward a future not yet realized. It was only then that the Creator-Shepherd would indeed make His flock "repose" in "verdant pastures," leading them "beside restful waters" (Ps 23:2). And those pastures will be forested, the still waters bounded by trees.

Sacra Dionaeae matri divisque ferebam
auspicibus coeptorum operum, superoque nitentem
caelicolum regi mactabam in litore taurum.
Forte fuit juxta tumulus, quo cornea summo
virgulta et densis hastilibus horrida myrtus.
Accessi, viridemque ab humo convellere silvam
conatus, ramis tegerem ut frondentibus aras,
horrendum et dictu video mirabile monstrum;
nam, quae prima solo ruptis radicibus arbos
vellitur, huic atro liquuntur sanguine guttae
et terram tabo maculant. Mihi frigidus horror
membra quatit, gelidusque coit formidine sanguis.

I was offering sacrifices to Venus and the gods
for their auspices on the work undertaken
and I was slaughtering on the shore a bull to the supreme king of the heavenly beings.
As it happened there was a mound nearby on the very top of which
stood a thicket of dogwood and a glistening myrtle tree thick with leaves.
When I approached, attempting to pluck the green growth from the ground so that I could cover the altar with flowery branches.
I saw a marvelous thing, but horrible to speak of;
for from the first tree which is plucked by its roots from the ground
there flow drops of dark blood which stain the earth. I was cold with horror,
my limbs shook, and my blood congealed with dread.

(Aeneid, III, 19-30)

Not only does the wondrous tree bleed; it speaks, as Aeneas describes for us how one of his own countrymen, Polydorous, murdered by the King of Thrace, lies buried at the roots of the myrtle. Dante later imitated his Mantuan guide and has one of the trees in Hell speak to him as he unwittingly plucks it.[59] Like Virgil before him and others since, he saw the "human-like" aspects of a tree. It is the poetic recognition that, for many humans, there is some special attraction to the beauty of trees, as well as to their role in our life and history. That insight is not lacking in the Bible as well. As healthy voyeurs, watching the more captivating among them dress and undress in Spring and Fall, we can forget that there is Another Who watches. The role that God assigns to trees in sacred history is worthy of reflection, and is indicative of the honored place they will hold in the new earth. As we have seen already, it is not complete error that led the Magdalene to perceive the God-man on the day of His resurrection as a gardener (cf. Jn 20:15). Already in the opening chapters of the Book of Genesis we see the Divine Horticulturalist at work. "Out of the ground the Lord God made various trees grow that were delightful to look at and good for food" (Gn 2:9). "God looked at everything he had made, and he found it very good" (Gn 1:31). Indeed what Ecclesiastes said of himself can be applied with greater propriety to the Lord God: "I made gardens and parks, and set out in them fruit trees of all sorts. And I constructed for myself reservoirs to water a flourishing woodland" (Eccl 2:5-6).

And what God rooted He took care to protect, even from the destruction wrought against trees by the noblest of His creatures, man. He laid the injunction on warring humanity: "When you are at war with a city and have to lay siege to it for a long time before you capture it, you shall not destroy its trees by putting an ax to them. You may eat their fruit, but you must not cut down the trees. After all, are the trees of the field men, that they should be included in your siege?" (Dt 20:19).[60] Such a blessing of God are trees that their useless destruction is portrayed over and over again as a deprivation for humanity, even as a special sign

[59] Cf. Dante, *Hell,* canto XIII, lines 31-33, 43-50.
[60] *The New Oxford Annotated Bible* comments appropriately on this passage: "This stipulation limits wanton destruction of natural resources which, unlike the city and its booty, are gifts from the Lord" (p. 241).

of God's chastisement. As punishment for Egypt "he struck down their vines and their fig trees and shattered the trees throughout their borders" (Ps 105:33). So, too, for Assyria:

> The Light of Israel will become a fire, Israel's Holy One a flame, that burns and consumes his briers and his thorns in a single day. His spendid forests and orchards will be consumed, soul and body; and the remnant of the trees in his forest will be so few . . . that any boy can record them (Is 10:17-19).

The Book of Revelation, depicting the final rebellion of our world against God's, warns of the horror of a de-forested earth.

> Do not damage the land or the sea or the trees until we put the seal on the foreheads of the servants of our God (Rv 7:3).

> When the first [angel] blew his trumpet, there came hail and fire mixed with blood, which was hurled down to the earth. A third of the land was burned up, along with a third of the trees and all green grass (Rv 8:7).

If their destruction is a sign of chastisement, so too is their very existence and nature figurative. Trees are a symbol of the person who is justified and holy. "I will pour out my Spirit upon your offspring, and my blessing upon your descendants. They shall spring up amid the verdure like poplars beside the flowing waters" (Is 44:3-4). To such an extent are the just comparable to trees that the first psalm, as prologue for the entire Psalter—which itself, according to St. Athanasius, is "like a paradise that contains in it the fruits of all the other Books [of the Bible]"[61]—can proclaim of the just man that "He is like a tree planted near running water, that yields its fruit in due season, and whose leaves never fade" (Ps 1:3). The Incarnate Word uses a similar comparison (cf. Mt 7:15-20).

It is not only of good human beings that the tree is a symbol. The Song of Songs—at least in its traditional reading as being the love song of God and Israel—depicts the Bride as saying to her Lord: "As an apple tree among the trees of the woods, so is my lover among men. I delight to rest in his shadow, and his fruit is sweet to my mouth" (Song 2:3). Nor is the Bride's comparison completely fanciful because the Lord God had compared Himself to a tree, saying, "I am like a verdant cypress tree—because of

---

[61] Athanasius, *Epistola ad Marcellum*, 2: PG 27, 12.

me you bear fruit!" (Hos 14:9).[62] To show His predilection for trees, the Spouse of Israel often—and ultimately fully—reveals Himself in association with them. He walks among them in the cool of the day (cf. Gn 3:8); He appears to Abraham by the trees of Mamre (cf. Gn 18:1); He lets us watch Him in anguish in a garden of olive trees (cf. Lk 22:39-44); He draws all to Himself, being lifted up on a tree, for, as Peter preached, we "put him to death by hanging him on a tree" (Acts 10:39).

Of this greatest of trees Pope Urban IV wrote:

> Man fell by means of the food of the death-giving tree; man is raised up by means of the food of the life-giving tree. On the former hung the food of death, on the latter the nourishment of life. Eating of the former earned a wound; the taste of this latter restored health. Eating wounded us and eating healed us.[63]

It is this same tree that Venantius Fortunatus, the great sixth-century poet, so extolled in his *Vexilla Regis* and *Pange Lingua Gloriosi*. The latter hymn follows:

Arbor decora et fulgida,	*O Tree, beautiful and glorious,*
Ornata Regis purpura,	*adorned with the purple of the King,*
Electa digno stipite	*chosen in your worthy trunk*
Tam sancta membra tangere.	*to touch such holy Members.*
Beata, cuius brachiis	*O blessed Tree, on whose boughs*
Pretium pependit saeculi,	*hung the world's Price,*
Statera facta est corporis,	*that was made the balance for His Body*
Praedam tulitque tartari.	*and bore away the loot of hell.*
Crux fidelis, inter omnes	*O faithful Cross,*
Arbor una nobilis:	*one noble tree among them all;*
Silva talem nulla profert	*no forest offers such as you*
Fronde, flore, germine:	*in leaf or flower or fruit:*
Dulce lignum, dulce clavum,	*sweet the wood, sweet the nails,*
Dulce pondus sustinet.	*sweet the Weight it bears.*
Sola digna tu fuisti	*Only you were worthy*
Ferre mundi pretium;	*to bear the Ransom of the world*
Atque portum praeparare	*and be an ark to offer harbor*
Arca mundo naufrago,	*to a shipwrecked world.*
Quam sacer cruor perunxit,	*The sacred blood, poured from*
Fusus Agni corpore.	*the body of the Lamb, washed you.*

---

[62] The full significance of the image of God as tree can be seen by comparing God's application of the image to Himself with Ezekiel 31:3-7.

[63] Urban IV, *Transiturus, Mansi*, vol. 28, p. 487.

Genesis 2:9 tells us that in the middle of the garden were "the tree of life . . . and the tree of the knowledge of good and bad." Those trees of Eden were but a sign of the Tree to come. It is the tree of Calvary that becomes indeed the Tree of Life, as well as the Tree of knowledge. For it is from the wood of the Cross that definitive life comes to mankind. It is by contemplation of the tree of Golgotha that we understand the true nature of good and evil. This sign of the tree will not be absent even at the end of history's current phase.

"And then the sign of the Son of Man will appear in heaven" (Mt 24:30). Explaining this text, St. Thomas Aquinas, like others, writes:

> The sign of the Son is the sign of the victory of Christ because when the whole world is renewed it will be a sign that He obtained victory over all through His passion. Or it can be taken to mean the sign of the Cross in order to show that all this glory comes about through His passion.[64]

The trees of heaven, that is to say the trees of the new earth, will be for the Saints a perpetual reminder of that Cross. Meanwhile the trees, like all creation that groans, await their future. When that future appears, "then shall all the trees of the forest exult before the Lord, for he comes: he comes to rule the earth" (1 Chr 16:33; cf. Ps 96:12; Is 44:23). Indeed, "mountains and hills shall break out in song before you, and all the trees of the countryside shall clap their hands" (Is 55:12). At that time, says the Seer of the Book of Revelation, what Ezekiel foretold will be fulfilled:

> Then the angel showed me the river of life-giving water, sparkling like crystal, flowing from the throne of God and of the Lamb down the middle of its street. On either side of the river grew the tree of life that produces fruit twelve times a year, once each month; the leaves of the trees serve as medicine for the nations. Nothing accursed will be found there anymore. The throne of God and of the Lamb will be in it, and his servants will worship him. They will look upon his face, and his name will be on their foreheads (Rv 22:1-4; cf. Ez 47:7-12).

---

[64] Aquinas, *Super Evangelium S. Matthaei Lectura*, XXIV, lec. III, no. 1961. Peter Lombard held that it was the Cross (*De Sent.*, IV: *PL* 192, 1112). It is common today to interpret the sign as being simply the Lord Himself. Cf. John Meier, *Matthew*, p. 287.

"To the victor I will give the right to eat from the tree of life that is in the garden of God" (Rv 2:7), says the Lord. On the other hand, from anyone who does not heed the Gospel "God will take away his share in the tree of life" (Rv 22:19).

The story of trees—the use God had made of them and the future He promises them—are indication enough that the Creator does not look on all His creatures indifferently. As is true with His treatment of humankind, the Almighty has a love of predilection for particular non-human vegetative and animal life. Nor is it trees alone that He loves particularly. It is clear from His activity, for example, that He loves the yield of the grape.

As fruit of the earth and the work of human hands comes "wine to gladden our hearts" (Ps 104:15), for which God is to be blessed. So great a cause of delight is it that only God's love can be said to fill the heart with "more joy than they have when grain and wine abound" (Ps 4:7). Indeed only the love of husband and wife and of Israel for her Lord is superior by comparison. "Let him kiss me with kisses of his mouth! More delightful is your love than wine!" (Song 1:2).

It is the part of the wise man to recognize the enchantment of wine since Wisdom itself prepares this drink for him. "She has dressed her meat, mixed her wine. . . . To him who lacks understanding [she says], Come eat of my food, and drink of the wine I have mixed!" (Prv 9:2-5). In fact, the Eternal Wisdom promises free drink to the parched: "All you who are thirsty, come to the water! You who have no money, come, receive grain and eat; come, without paying and without cost, drink wine and milk!" (Is 55:1). And what He promises to give freely, He will also provide in abundance. The mountains will drip with it and it will flow from all the hills: "Yes, days are coming, says the Lord, when the plowman shall overtake the reaper, and the vintager, him who sows the seed; the juice of grapes shall drip down the mountains, and all the hills shall run with it" (Am 9:13). And wine, free and abundant, is what He provided at Cana in Galilee when His mother called His attention to the need for more (Jn 2:1-10).

In no greater way can the divine Vintner's love for the fruit of the grape be seen than by what He does with it and for it at His Supper of the New Covenant. There He assimilates the wine to

Himself and makes it His own Blood so as to intoxicate us, render us heady, on His love. At that same meal He promises to drink with us again, new wine in the eternal Kingdom: "I tell you, from now on I shall not drink this fruit of the vine until the day when I drink it with you new in the kingdom of my Father" (Mt 26:29). With these words He reaffirms the pledge found in Isaiah: "On this mountain the Lord of hosts will provide for all peoples a feast of rich food and choice wines, juicy, rich food and pure, choice wines (Is 25:6).

Ecology

An appreciation for what the good things of the earth *are and will be* should be a constitutive element of mankind's own moral dimension, as well as being the true reason for a Christian ecological sense. In this regard Pope John Paul II has written:

> Nor can the moral character of development exclude respect *for the beings which constitute* the natural world, which the ancient Greeks—alluding precisely to the order which distinguishes it—called the "cosmos." Such realities also demand respect. . . .

> One cannot use with impunity the different categories of beings, whether living or inanimate—animals, plants, the natural elements—simply as one wishes, according to one's own economic needs. On the contrary, one must take into account *the nature of each being* and of its *mutual connection* in an ordered system, which is precisely the "cosmos."[65]

> When the ecological crisis is set within the broader context of the search for peace within society, we can understand better the importance of giving attention to what the earth and its atmosphere are telling us: namely, that there is an order in the universe which must be respected, that the human person, endowed with the capability of choosing freely, has a grave responsibility to preserve this order for the well-being of future generations. I wish to repeat that the ecological crisis is a moral issue.[66]

---

[65] John Paul II, *Sollicitudo Rei Socialis*, no. 34 (Boston: St. Paul Editions, 1988), pp. 61-62.

[66] John Paul II, *Message for World Day of Peace 1990*, TPS, vol. 35, no. 3, p. 206. Cf. *Christifideles Laici*, 43, TPS, vol. 34, no. 2, p. 146.

As the pope indicates, it is not only vegetative life that is to be respected because of its part in the ordered beauty that is the cosmos. Along with the transformation of vegetative life in the new earth, we may also anticipate the preservation of animal life. Stratford Caldecott writes:

> In material nature we must include the animal kingdom: heaven does not post a sign saying "No Pets Allowed."
>
> The fundamental lesson of these texts is a profound one. A Resurrection Body must bring with it a Resurrection Earth. Its appearance remains beyond our capacity to imagine, but we know that the whole of nature, the entire cosmos, has been redeemed, and not a blade of grass will be lost "when the perishable puts on the imperishable" (1 Cor 15:54). This must surely change our behavior, especially when we reflect that, in Jesus Christ, the Resurection has already taken place.[67]

The prophet Isaiah foretold a transformed animal life for the kingdom of peace he envisioned.

> The fox and the lamb shall graze alike, and the lion shall eat hay like the ox, but the serpent's food shall be dust. None shall hurt or destroy on all my holy mountain, says the Lord (Is 65:25).

Now the Seer's words are symbolic, of course. Nonetheless, there is no solid reason for excluding animal life from the restoration of the universe. And this is true for two reasons: their own intrinsic value as part of the varied beauty of the cosmos, and as reminders of their symbolic role in our own salvation.

Is the lamb to be denied a place in the renewed universe called into being by the power of Christ's sacrifice, for which the lamb was the preeminent symbol (cf. Ex 29:41; Lv 4:32; Is 53:7; Mk 14:12; Jn 1:29; 19:14, 36; Rv 5:6)?

And what of the eagle? In the life to come the sight of the eagle will remind the Saints of how God identified Himself with its majesty and beauty in flight, how He carried His people on eagle's wings (cf. Ex 19:4; Dt 32:11), and how, as the great Eagle, He led to safety the Mother of the Messiah and the Messianic people (cf. Rv 12:14). The eagle's presence then will be a re-

---

[67] Stratford Caldecott, "Cosmology, eschatology, ecology: Some reflections on *Sollicitudo Rei Socialis,*" *Communio,* vol. XV, No. 3 (Fall 1988), p. 312.

minder, as well, of how many times in the trials of this life, when the struggle seemed too arduous and failure certain, the Eagle's brood was consoled and given courage by the words He inspired.

> He gives strength to the fainting; for the weak he makes vigor abound. Though young men faint and grow weary, and youths stagger and fall, they that hope in the Lord will renew their strength, they will soar as with eagles' wings; they will run and not grow weary, walk and not grow faint (Is 40:29-31).

God tells us indeed that our "youth [will be] renewed like the eagle's" (Ps 103:5), which means, of course, that He will give those who live in Him a share in His own youthfulness. The Saints, seeing the eagles of the life to come, will remember how, when He came among us, He wished to spread His own wings (cf. Mt 23:37) to protect His brood, and how He invited those who were faint, saying, "Come to me, all you who labor and are burdened, and I will give you rest" (Mt 11:28). The presence of the eagle will also remind the Blessed of the paradox involved in His use of such imagery for Himself. The eagle was an animal that had been declared "unclean" and "detestable" (cf. Lv 11:13). Nevertheless He deigned to employ it as a fit image for Himself, anticipating in this way His humility and His ultimate revelation about the nature of clean and unclean that He would make to Simon Peter (Acts 10:9-15).

Nor will the presence of the animals fail to recall to us how God chooses the lowly and outcast of the earth. Think of the poor donkey, a byword for stupidity and stubbornness. To be buried like a donkey was, for Jeremiah, a sign of ultimate disgrace (Jer 22:19). Yet it was through this beast that the Lord of all instructed an errant prophet in an unforgettable story (cf. Nm 22:21ff and 2 Pt 2:16). And it was this poor creature that He associated with the triumph of One Who was to come from the family of Judah:

> The scepter shall never depart from Judah, or the mace from between his legs, *until he comes to whom it belongs,* and he receives the people's homage. He tethers his donkey to the vine, his purebred ass to the choicest stem. In wine he washes his garments, his robe in the blood of grapes (Is 49:10-11, with alternative NAB text given in italics).

Rejoice heartily, O daughter Zion, shout for joy, O daughter Jerusalem! See, your king shall come to you; a just savior is he, meek, and riding on an ass, on a colt, the foal of an ass (Zec 9:9; cf. Mt 21:1-9).

When they drew near to Jerusalem, to Bethpage and Bethany at the Mount of Olives, he sent two of his disciples and said to them, "Go into the village opposite you, and immediately on entering it, you will find a colt tethered on which no one has ever sat. Untie it and bring it here." So they brought the colt to Jesus and put their cloaks over it. And he sat on it. Many people spread their cloaks on the road, and others spread leafy branches that they had cut from the fields. Those preceding him as well as those following kept crying out: "Hosanna! Blessed is he who comes in the name of the Lord!" (Mk 11:1-10).

Chesterton placed himself in the mind of that poor colt, representative of all his type. He portrays it as recognizing the fact that, in a sense, it is an aberration, good for little more than to be pulled, kicked and beaten into service. The animal exults, nonetheless, in a day of imagined glory—glory that it thinks was its own—and, in a sense, was.

> Fools! For I also had my hour;
>   One far fierce hour and sweet:
> There was a shout about my ears,
>   And palms before my feet.[68]

When we think of the animals in the life to come, we should cast a realistic view on aspects of their existence in the present eon. Tennyson's poem *In Memoriam*, which we quoted earlier, observes that nature only appears to be "careful of the type" and "careless of the single life." In fact she says, "I care for nothing, all shall go." Certainly this seems the case of so much of animal life. Not only do individual creatures die, entire types and species that once made this earth their habitat have disappeared completely. Like toys enjoyed for a time and discarded, it seems as if the Lord grows bored with some, leaving their relics to fill our museums or vie for some vicarious existence in human memory or textbook. Will these bones live? The Lord alone knows, and we would be foolish to predict a survival of every type in the life

---

[68] G.K. Chesterton, *Stories, Essays, and Poems*, Everyman's Library (New York: E.P. Dutton and Co. Inc., 1957), p. 283.

to come. On the other hand, humanity has lived a shorter time here than did some of the species that are now "extinct" to all except to Him Who is the God of the living, and Who gives life, and Who loves what He creates even though He permits suffering and death and loss to memory. In short, we cannot know, but we can have a justified hope that "the river of life-giving water, sparkling like crystal, flowing from the throne of God and of the Lamb" (Rv 22:1), will refresh even the lowly animals. For all who praise Him then, the canticle of the Three Young Men will have its full meaning:

> Bless the Lord, all you works of the Lord,
>   praise and exalt him above all forever.
> Angels of the Lord, bless the Lord, . . .
> You heavens, bless the Lord, . . .
> All you waters above the heavens, bless the Lord, . . .
> Sun and moon, bless the Lord; . . .
> Stars of heaven, bless the Lord; . . .
> Every shower and dew, bless the Lord; . . .
> Lightnings and clouds, bless the Lord; . . .
> Let the earth bless the Lord,
>   praise and exalt him above all forever.
> Mountains and hills, bless the Lord; . . .
> Everything growing from the earth, bless the Lord; . . .
> You springs, bless the Lord; . . .
> Seas and rivers, bless the Lord; . . .
> All you birds of the air, bless the Lord; . . .
> All you beasts, wild and tame, bless the Lord (Dn 3:57-81).

Addressing His Apostles about what was to happen, the Lord spoke of His own final coming as the herald of a "new birth," a new genesis (in Greek *palingenesia*: Mt 19:28; cf. Ti 3:5). And indeed that is what the heavens and new earth will be: a new Genesis, an Eden whose beauties cannot be destroyed again. This new Paradise will be the material setting for the life that God has promised. For all the Elect the words of the Psalm will be fulfilled: "Pleasant places were measured out for me; fair to me indeed is my inheritance" (Ps 16:6). Purified and transformed, none of the universe's beauty will be lost to the Blessed: the smell of a field after a Spring shower, the sense of abandon and joy when walking in a gentle rain, the scent of nature in its flowers and woodlands, the idle pleasure and lack of anxiety that comes of sitting beside a gently flowing brook or under a tree, the majesty of mountains, the wonder of the sun rising and declining, the kaleidoscope of colors in Autumn, the intricacies of snow when the individual patterns of each flake can be discerned. In truth, when thinking of the good things God has prepared for those who love Him, one must follow Augustine's advice to "take away corruption and add what you want."[69] In that land of the incorrupt, everything will exist to enthrall those who, free of the concerns that now often keep one from experiencing or enjoying nature's loveliness, can abandon themselves to delight and praise.

There will also be, of course, that immense part of reality to be enjoyed which we cannot imagine: the spiritual aspect of the universal creation, the realm of the angels, and all the wonders and beauty contained therein, such as can hardly be less than we experience in the material creation. Although it is surely not an adequate image, we can conceptualize it in terms of light. We humans are capable of seeing only a very small part of the light that comes from the rays of the sun. The spectrum of light is so broad that what we see is like the limited vision of a four-year-old looking through a chink in a fence at a construction site two blocks wide. And there are aspects of light, such as the infrared, that we cannot see at all. Some of earth's other living creatures, without our intelligence, see a far wider range on the spectrum than we do. So with the invisible part of the universe. A vast spectrum of light and color and beauty already exists—and what more we cannot even guess—waiting to be enjoyed. Like the land, so the invisible universe will be at rest, to be enjoyed, and to serve as a means by which and in which to praise the King.

Honorius of Autun (c. 1090-1159), in his catechism on the Christian faith, has left us the following description of the life to come, which says succinctly and beautifully what we have said poorly and at length:

> The sun will shine seven times brighter than it now shines. The moon and the stars will be clothed with unspeakable splendor. Water, which merited to touch the body of Christ and washed

---

[69] Augustine, *Sermon 242 (147)*, 4: PL 38, 1140.

the Saints in Baptism, will surpass all the beauty of crystal. The earth, which cherished the body of Christ in its womb, will in its entirety be like Paradise. And, because this earth was watered with the blood of the Saints, it will be perpetually decorated with sweet-smelling flowers, with unfading lilies, roses and violets. This change will be wrought by the hand of the Most High, because the earth, which was cursed and given over to thorns, will then be blessed forever by the Lord, and labor and sorrow will exist no more.[70]

[70] Honorius of Autun, *Elucidarium*, bk. III, 15: *PL* 172, 1168.

V

THE SAINTS WHO ARE IN THE LAND

THE old creation was completed on the sixth day as the Lord God breathed spirit into the dust of the earth. Before Adam and Eve, God had brought forth the land and waters and their adornment. The New Creation occurs in a reverse process. The new Adam and the new Eve appear first, not last. Then a new day is inaugurated, which would ultimately be lethal to the unvarying cycle of seven. The proverbial wisdom that there is nothing new under the sun is proved false as the sun of Easter morning dawns upon something truly new: immortal life out of death, and the birth of the eighth day, the New Creation's first and everlasting day.

It is to the new pair, Christ and His Mother, and to this day, Easter, that we must always look if we wish to discern what spirit and matter will become in the new Genesis. However, Christ and Mary are more than just exemplars for the life to come. As Firstborn of the dead, to Whom all things have been made subject, Christ Himself brings the New Creation into existence. Mary, His Mother and unique associate, becomes the Woman, Mother of all who will live in the universe remade by her Son. All those who dwell in the land of the living will be His members and her children, who, still struggling in the valley of death, are consoled by the assurance that "those who sow in tears will reap with cries of joy" (Ps 126:5).

Having considered the restored universe, we can now ask what those who will dwell in the courts of the Lord forever will be like. What will be the condition and abilities of the "saints who are in the land" (Ps 16:3; *New Vulgate*)? What is it that the Blessed will reap for themselves with songs of joy? And what will they do in the Paradise God has prepared for them?

Augustine's Principle of Beauty

About the Elect and their status, present and future, our knowledge is limited. Of necessity much of what follows will be speculation, but it will be rooted in what Revelation tells us, especially in what we can learn from the resurrected condition of the Lord and His Mother, and in what great Christian Saints and theologians have concluded. We shall see that what can be said will speak in a special way in *praise of the body*, for as Augustine wrote:

> Porphyry, a bitter enemy of the Christian faith . . . said and wrote, "Every body is to be fled." He said "every" as if each body were the miserable prison of the soul. But, with God as teacher, our faith praises the body. . . .[1]

It is a wonderful truth and one sadly often overlooked: our Catholic faith *praises* the body. And the man whose words have now reminded us of this great truth is the very one so often inaccurately criticized for Manichaean and "anti-body" tendencies. A far better appraisal of Augustine has been given in our own time by an eminent scholar. Peter Brown, drawing a necessary distinction between Augustine and earlier writers, especially Jerome, Ambrose, and Chrysostom, declares that, in respect to the body, Augustine is much more positive than they. "The fatal flaw of concupiscence would not have seemed so tragic to Augustine, if he had not become ever more deeply convinced that human beings had been created to embrace the material world. The body was a problem to him precisely because it was to be loved and cherished."[2]

In dealing with what he thought worthy of being "loved and cherished," Augustine applies his own use of the *via pulchritudinis*, the principle of beauty, to the human body resurrected.

> If there is no perceivable member of the body (and no one doubts this) that is merely accommodated to some task without also being beautiful, there are nevertheless some members whose purpose is only beauty and not usefulness. Thus, I think it can be easily understood that in the creating of the body *dignity was more important than necessity*. Indeed necessity and the time for usefulness is going to pass away and then we shall enjoy only the beauty of each other without any lust. . . .[3]

---

[1] Augustine, *Sermon 242*, 7: *PL* 38, 1137.

[2] Peter Brown, *The Body and Society*, p. 425. The entire section of pp. 387-427 is most valuable reading.

[3] Augustine, *City of God*, bk. 22, ch. 24: *CSEL* 40, 2, p. 647. One can see how very different are the views of Augustine and those of Origen as described by Crouzel. Cf. above, p. 29.

There could hardly be a clearer enunciation of the claims of beauty over utility. We can readily notice how Augustine differs from those Christian theologians who, in considering the life to come, tend to decide what will perdure only by the principle of necessity. For the Bishop of Hippo, on the contrary, what is to be preserved is what was created beautiful and not simply useful. When it comes to questions of the next life, the determining principle is not the answer to the question, "What *purpose* will this or that serve?" but rather the answer to the question, "How much of the beauty that He originally created does God intend to preserve forever?" For the Doctor of Grace, the fact that there will be a renewed universe signified that Beauty Himself will bring all other created splendor to perfection, especially that of the human body.

> I do not think anything that naturally belongs to the body will perish. That which was born deformed (and this happens only for the sake of showing that the present condition of mortals is a penalty) will be restored in such a way that the deformity will perish while the integrity of the substance will be preserved. For if a human artist is able to reshape a statue that, for some reason, he made deformed, and render it beautiful in such a way that nothing of the substance but only the deformity perishes . . . what must we think of the Artist Who is almighty? Will not He, therefore, be able to remove and destroy any deformities of the human body—not only the usual ones but also the rare and horrible ones that are congruent with our miserable life here but are abhorrent to that future happiness of the Saints?[4]

Nature of the Risen Body

According to Augustine, the identical body that has died is destined for resurrected life. Even the matter in the risen body is the same as that which formerly was its own. In the *Enchiridion*—which, like the final sections of his *City of God*, was one of his mature works, being written around 421—the Bishop of Hippo Regius spoke of the material identity between the present and the risen body.

---

[4] Augustine, *City of God*, bk. 22, ch. 19: *CSEL* 40, 2, pp. 629-630.

> For God the earthly material from which mortal flesh is created does nor perish; ... in a moment of time it returns to the human soul that first animated it in order that the person might be, grow, and live.[5]

> God, the marvelous and ineffable builder, will, with marvelous and ineffable swiftness, restore everything from which our flesh was constituted. For its reintegration it will not matter at all whether what was hair returns as hair, or what were nails as nails, or whether any of these things that perished be now changed into flesh or other parts of the body since the providence of the Builder will see to it that there will be nothing unbecoming.[6]

The second paragraph of the quotation intends to address some of the difficulties caused by efforts to imagine how the restoration of the body takes place. In many cases, the body will have disintegrated, its elements having been absorbed by the earth from which it came or even having been taken up, in some form, into another body. The imagination is useless in trying to picture how everyone will receive his or her own matter. And Augustine is too smart and too faithful to get bogged down in specifics about such things. The Almighty, Who made everything from nothing, will be able to achieve the restoration by His ineffable power. What is more, that Power will achieve His purposes in a suitable manner.

Not infrequently the following type of objection is raised against the numerical identity of the human body: The matter of the body is changing constantly. Obviously it cannot all be restored. Therefore at what stage will it be when resurrected? The purpose of such questions, often enough, is to make the doctrine of a material resurrection look ridiculous. Augustine, not as aware as subsequent ages were of the constant changes in the body, had already anticipated the proper answer: Leave this to the power of God. Aquinas, more cognizant of the material changes regularly undergone by the body, explained the truth this way.

---

[5] Augustine, *Enchiridion*, XXIII, 88: CCSL 46, pp. 96-97.
[6] *Ibid.*, 89: CCSL 46, p. 97.

> That which does not hinder numerical unity in humans while
> they live will clearly not hinder numerical unity for those resur-
> rected. . . . As far as its matter is concerned, the parts [of the
> body] come and go: this however does not hinder a person from
> being one in number from the beginning of life to its end. . . .
> Humans are not, therefore, numerically different according to
> their different ages, even though not everything that is mate-
> rially in a person at one age is also there at another. Thus it is
> not required that whatever was materially present during the
> whole space of a person's life be materially present so that he
> or she be numerically one at the resurrection. . . . And again, if
> something is lacking it can be supplied by the power of God.[7]

If one studies carefully the compacted reasoning of St.
Thomas in question eighty-one of the *Contra Gentiles*, it is evident that, for the great Doctor, a person is made numerically one
and individual by the original union of spirit and matter. This
unity and individuality is never later able to be lost: the soul remains the form of this individual body and remains itself individualized by the matter whose form it is. In some way the indi-
vidualizing function of matter endures even through death because of the relation or exigency that the soul has for its own
matter. We have already seen how Augustine explains this: after
death, some matter in an attenuated condition continues to exist
with the immortal soul. This opinion we accept and it is, in essentials, not far from the thought of Aquinas.

In any case, what is crucial for both Doctors of the Church is
the fact that God Who created each of us as an individual will restore us as the identical persons, body and soul, we now are. This
teaching is in fact the faith of the Church, defined in the Creed of
Lateran IV in 1215.

> Christ will come at the end of the ages to judge the living and
> the dead and to render to each, both damned and Elect, accord-
> ing to their works. All of these will rise with their own bodies
> that they now possess in order to receive according to their
> works, whether good or bad (DS 801).

The doctrine about the numerical unity of the risen body is
set in its proper perspective, I think, by a remark made by Fr.
Vonier. "Resurrection from the dead is the act of God by which

---

[7] Aquinas, *Summa Contra Gentiles*, Lib. IV, cap. 81, *Opera Omnia*, XV, p. 254.

He gives back ... the whole realm of sense activity, which had ceased to be."[8]

It is this *restoration of the senses* that Augustine attempted so strenuously to defend. It is true that a fair amount of his thinking on the conditions and activities of the resurrected flesh finds parallels in the Fathers who wrote before him or during his own lifetime and was continued in subsequent theologians. For, on essentials, all are in the great stream of Catholic Tradition. Nevertheless, on matters where the Church has passed no definitive decision, there are often significant differences between his thought and that of others. We shall attempt to show where he differs from others and try to illustrate, as well, how later generations agreed with, modified, or rejected his views.

The principle of beauty, linked with God's resolution to perfect what He created, states that there will be no defect at all in the bodies: "... what is not fitting will not exist."[9]

> The flesh rises incorruptible; the flesh rises without defect, without deformity, without mortality, without being burdened or weighed down.[10]

God's intention to preserve and make flawless what He originally created may be better appreciated by reflecting on the miracle of the virginal birth (as distinguished from the virginal conception) of Christ, which is often considered a difficult doctrine to accept. The continued physical integrity of a woman who has become a mother seems to serve no purpose. For some it is even thought to be incompatible with true motherhood. As a result, there is a temptation to give this doctrine a purely symbolic or "spiritual" interpretation. The fact, however, that Pius XII, in his Bull *Munificentissimus Deus,* which defined the doctrine of the physical assumption of Mary to the next life, associated the virginal birth with her assumption, may give an insight into one of the significant aspects of the doctrine. Citing St. John of Damascus, Pius XII wrote:

---

[8] Anscar Vonier, *The Life of the World To Come,* p. 150.
[9] Augustine, *City of God,* bk. 22, ch. 30: CSEL 40, 2, p. 665.
[10] Augustine, *Sermon 240, 3: PL* 38, 1131-1132.

St. John Damascene, who among others is an outstanding herald of this truth [the Assumption] that has been handed down, compares the bodily Assumption of the dear Mother of God with other gifts and privileges, and says with fervent eloquence: "It was necessary that she who preserved her virginity intact in giving birth should preserve her body without corruption even after death."[11]

What is implied here is once again the principle of beauty, the *via pulchritudinis*. True beauty is found in a harmony and integrity of various parts of the entirety. Having created Mary in a particular way, the almighty Artist preserved her—not only spiritually by an immaculate conception but also physically by a virginal birth and bodily assumption—so that her privileges, in spirit and body, might teach us that He plans an unbroken creation. She is that part of the first creation which is preserved from the universal fall into brokenness. As the new Eve come perfect from the hands of the Creator, she is kept physically integral so that, at her Assumption, she might be the best of the old creation raised to its everlasting condition. In this way the Mother of God becomes a pledge for the fallen earth, promising that it and not something completely new will have an unblemished future. Mary is therefore, both for us who share her nature and for the lower ranks of the material order as well, boast and hope.

The Virgin

Mother, whose virgin bosom was uncrost
With the least shade of thought to sin alied;
Woman! above all women glorified,
Our tainted nature's solitary boast
Purer than foam on central ocean tost;
Brighter than eastern skies at daybreak strewn
With fancied roses, than the unblemished moon
Before her wane begins on heaven's blue coast;
Thy Image falls to earth. Yet some, I ween,
Not unforgiven the suppliant knee might bend,
As to a visible Power, in which did blend

---

[11] Pius XII, *Munificentissimus Deus: AAS*, 42 (1950), p. 761.

All that was mixed and reconciled in Thee
Of mother's love with maiden purity,
Of high with low, celestial with terrene![12]

The physical integrity anticipated in Mary will be shared by all the Elect. Nothing will be left shattered. Writing of his friendly adversary, George Bernard Shaw, with whose thinking he often profoundly disagreed, G.K. Chesterton observed, "Bernard Shaw is like the Venus of Milo; all that there is of him is perfect."[13] Such a remark will never be able to be made about the resurrected. In them there will not just be a beauty of individual parts, but the perfection of the totality of the human person, arms and all. Furthermore, it has to be noted that, when we speak of perfection in this regard, we are not intending to indicate that all those who enter the joys of the life to come will be remade according to some ideal image, a kind of Hollywood type of beauty with its vapid sameness. Far from it. Each will be very different.

> It is not to be feared by either fat people or thin people that they will then be such as they would not have chosen to be now were they able. For all beauty of the body is a harmony of parts united with a certain pleasantness of color. When there is no harmony of parts something offends either because it is distorted or because it is too much or too little. Therefore the kind of deformity that causes a lack of harmony in the parts will not exist when whatever is less than fitting will be supplied as the Creator knows how, and what is more than fitting is taken away even while the integrity of the matter is preserved.[14]

In an age where a "trim" body is almost a cult object and where great amounts of social pressure and propaganda are exerted on those who are heavy, the humane realism of those words should be a consolation. The quotation reminds us as well that notions of beauty are often imposed on us by others and that for the Saints part of the form of this world that will pass away is the false desire to be what they were not intended to be.

---

[12] Wordsworth, in *Ecclesiastical Sonnets*, Part II, no. XXV, *William Wordsworth: The Poems*, II, p. 474. The increasing awareness of Mary in Wordsworth's life can be seen by comparing bk. 2, lines 60-64 of *The Prelude* in its 1805 and 1850 editions.

[13] From Chesterton's book on Bernard Shaw, quoted in Maisie Ward's *Gilbert Keith Chesterton* (London: Penguin Books, 1958), p. 164.

[14] Augustine, *City of God*, bk. 22, ch. 19: CSEL 40, 2, p. 630. He discusses the same question more tentatively in *Enchiridion*, XXIII: CCSL 46, p. 97.

Weight watching, an almost obsessive and even "religious" devotion to exercise, the anxiety to appear "fit," steroids, cosmetic surgery and the like will have no part in the life to come, except as objects of amusement to memory.

While considering the form of the body in the life to come, Augustine is led to a reflection on women. He lived in an age that still suffered from the Greek notion that male beauty is the model of perfection. It was also an age whose philosophies at times depicted the female as a defective male. Moreover, for some of the Fathers of the age, sexuality was viewed as totally functional. As a consequence, they apparently thought that bodies would rise sexless.[15] Augustine's convictions were quite different.

> Defects will be taken away from those bodies, nature will be preserved. Moreover, the female sex is not a defect, but natural. . . . Therefore the female as well as the male is a creature of God; inasmuch as she comes from the man, unity is commended; inasmuch as she comes from the man in that way [i.e., from his side] Christ and the Church were prefigured.[16]

Not only is the female body not a defect; it is a part of the natural order willed by God. It is, furthermore, part of a complex sign that indicates deeper realities: the unity in companionship of man and woman, and the unity in flesh of Christ and the faithful. As natural and as symbolic, both sexes will remain in the life to come. "He who established both sexes will restore both."[17] Augustine is quite explicit: the life to come is not androgenous. His opinion on this matter is consistent with his general views on women. A noted Augustinian scholar has done a study on these views, and a portion of his conclusions are worth citing since, in this area (as in so many others), Augustine is frequently misunderstood and quoted out of context.

> Some of the positive elements of his thought are taken over from his predecessors; others are corrections of the opinions of his predecessors. [Augustine's] idea of the moral superiority of women is borrowed from the best of Christian tradition. In the

---

[15] Winklhofer, *The Coming of the Kingdom*, cites St. Basil and Gregory Nazianzen (p. 227). Crouzel says that such a doctrine can readily be drawn from Origen's principles (*Origen*, pp. 252-253).

[16] Augustine, *City of God*, bk. 22, ch. 17: CSEL 40, 2, pp. 625-626.

[17] *Ibid.*, p. 626.

question of woman as the image of God, he corrects the opinion of several theologians who wrote before him. . . . The same must be said regarding the presence of the female body and sex in the resurrected state of the human being. This had been denied by influential authors before him. . . . Augustine's own and most important contribution to a change within the relationship between husband and wife is, according to me, his emphasis on love in married life, and even more his interpretation of the conjugal relationship as friendship. In the Christian tradition before him this was seldom or never done.[18]

Augustine, so positively influenced by women in his own life, especially by his mother and by the mother of his son, neither demeaned them nor idealized them beyond the lot of fallen humanity. He was capable of realistic appraisal, even while never losing sight of the beauty. Undoubtedly his groundbreaking reflections on the Mother of the Lord and on the Church as Christ's Bride owe something to his appreciation of the dignity of womankind. In that he was not far from the balance between realism and idealization that Wordsworth attempted to capture when writing of his own wife.

> She was a Phantom of delight
> When first she gleamed upon my sight;
> A lovely Apparition, sent
> To be a moment's ornament;
> Her eyes as stars of Twilight fair;
> Like Twilight's, too, her dusky hair;
> But all things else about her drawn
> From May-time and the cheerful Dawn;
> A dancing Shape, an Image gay,
> To haunt, to startle, and way-lay.
>
> I saw her upon nearer view,
> A Spirit, yet a Woman too!
> Her household motions light and free,
> And steps of virgin-liberty;
> A countenance in which did meet
> Sweet records, promises as sweet;
> A Creature not too bright or good
> For human nature's daily food;
> For transient sorrows, simple wiles,
> Praise, blame, love, kisses, tears, and smiles.

---

[18] T.J. van Bavel, "Augustine's View on Women," *Augustiniana* (Annus 39 [1989] Fasc. 1-2), p. 53.

And now I see with eye serene
The very pulse of the machine;
A Being breathing thoughtful breath,
A Traveller between life and death;
The reason firm, the temperate will,
Endurance, foresight, strength, and skill;
A perfect Woman, nobly planned,
To warn, to comfort, and command;
And yet a Spirit still, and bright
With something of angelic light.[19]

Both male and female then shall continue to exist as such in the life to come. This is so because the Creator originally planned the race this way, because of the dignity of each individual who has always existed as one or the other sex, because of the beauty manifest in such a plan and because of what is symbolized by such diversity of sexes. This established, one can then ask further questions about the resurrected body.

In respect to age, Augustine thought that "the bodies of the dead will rise neither less than nor beyond the form of youth, but rather in the age and vigor that we know Christ to have reached here."[20]

This is an opinion that would be later followed by many, including St. Thomas Aquinas, who estimated that the risen would all be youthful, although not all of the same numerical age.[21] Augustine, however, was not fully satisfied with such a view, even though he expressed it himself. In another writing, he seems to admit the possibility that the resurrected will be reestablished at the fullness of age that they were destined to reach, without however the miseries that might have accompanied that age on earth.[22] He was willing to admit even other opinions, among them the possibility that each shall rise with a body that possesses the age it had achieved before dying to the present life.

There would be no difficulty if the form of the body were young or old since there will remain in the life to come no weakness

---

[19] Wordsworth, *She Was a Phantom*, in *The Poems*, vol. I, p. 603.

[20] Augustine, *City of God*, bk. 22, ch. 15: CSEL 40, 2, p. 623.

[21] Aquinas, *Summa Theologica, Supplementum*, q. 81, a. 1 c, and a. 2, ad 1.

[22] Augustine, *Sermon 242 a (147)*, 3: PL 38, 1140.

of body or mind. Therefore, even if someone contends that each one will rise in that form of body in which he or she died, he is not to be argued with in any laborious discussion.[23]

This last opinion is attractive. In the Middle Ages, Honorius of Autun accepted it and gave reasons that make it at least plausible.

It is credible that in the future life it will be more pleasant to behold different ages and different sizes of both men and women, just as here it is more pleasant to hear different sounds on musical instruments or the lyre. Therefore it is more to be believed that all will rise and appear in the age and size that they had when they migrated from here.[24]

There is a congruity about this opinion—and opinion is all that one can claim for it—that recommends it. The human person develops in such a way that age and experience generally go together. This is not always to our benefit, of course. It is true that "there is no fool like an old fool," nor none so evil as those who have grown old in their sins. The remarks of the young Daniel to the evil old men are true.

How you have grown evil with age! Now have your past sins come to term: passing unjust sentences, condemning the innocent, and freeing the guilty. . . . Offspring of Canaan, not of Judah, . . . beauty has seduced you, lust has subverted your conscience (Dn 13:52-57).

On the other hand, age can be a gift, the heritage of youth.

Therefore I summon age
To grant youth's heritage,
Life's struggle having so far reached its term;
Thence shall I pass, approved
A man, for aye removed
From the developed brute; a god through in the germ.
Youth ended, I shall try
My gain or loss thereby;
Leave the fire ashes, what survives is gold:
And I shall weigh the same
Give life its praise or blame;
Young, all lay in dispute; I shall know, being old.

---

[23] Augustine, *City of God*, bk. 22, ch. 16: *CSEL* 40, 2, p. 624.
[24] Honorius, *Elucidarium: PL* 172, 1169.

So, take and use Thy work:
Amend what flaws may lurk,
What stain o'the stuff, what warpings past the aim!
My times be in Thy hand!
Perfect the cup as planned!
Let age approve of youth, and death complete the same!
                                    (Browning, *Rabbi Ben Ezra*)

Age, of course, faces its own battles for the reconciliation of conflicts within us.

As we look towards the autumn shores,
the struggle in us runs along
the same divide
which every man carries in him,
when his body is the past of his own future—
every man
if he cannot link his future
with his body.[25]

For many, however, especially those who, through faith, can link their future with their body (the pope's phrase is a beautiful one: the body is the past of one's own future), the passage of years and the gaining of experiences are an enrichment, a process often enough mirrored in the physical appearances, the manners, and mannerisms of the elderly. They become in their bearing the distillation of the goodness they have achieved, purified by the sufferings they have endured, refined to a richness of character missing earlier in their lives. In age they are like a flower in full bloom. And all these qualities can be reflected in the body, as is so often recognized. All this should not be lost. Let disappear—as they will—weakness, infirmity, the stiffness of old age, the tendency to be intractable in outlook, and the like, but let the flower itself be preserved as it has come to full life here. But, one may ask, what about those aspects of youth that age itself cannot replace, and the joys associated with that period that cannot be compensated for by age?

O pleasant exercise of hope and joy!
For great were the auxiliars which then stood
Upon our side, we who were strong in love!
Bliss was it in that dawn to be alive
But to be young was very Heaven![26]

---

[25] Karol Wojtyla, *Collected Poems*, pp. 149-150.
[26] Wordsworth, *The Prelude*, books X-XI, lines 690-694 (105-109).

Those experiences will not be lost in the life to come. If the bodies of the Elect do indeed then reflect the maturity of their earthly history, itself purified and perfected, they shall also reflect the life of the soul whose "youth has been renewed by the Lord" (cf. Opening Prayer for Third Sunday of Easter).[27]

As far as the stature of the risen is concerned:

> They will receive the stature that either they had in youth, even if they died old, or that they would have had, if they died early.[28]

These questions about age and size helped Augustine reflect on the condition of those who had died as little children or as infants in the womb.

> Therefore, what are we to say about infants except that they will not rise in that smallness of body in which they died, but rather that what would have come to them slowly in time they will receive by a marvelous and quick work of God.[29]

This will happen, he says, because the potentiality for such growth is already present in the body even from the moment of conception.

> All have this measure of perfection since they are conceived and born with it; but they have it in potency (ratione) not in size (non mole).[30]

Augustine is applying here his renowned theory of the *rationes seminales*. These "rationes" are, as St. Thomas explained them, "the active and passive powers that God has given to creatures, through whose instrumentality natural effects come into existence."[31] What Augustine has divined by his philosophical theory is something we now know to be true in the case of the child even in the womb. Present from the beginning is the genetic makeup that will determine so many factors of an individual's life, among them basic size.

---

[27] Cf. below under Chapter VII: "To Gaze on the Beauty of the Lord," pp. 281ff.

[28] Augustine, *City of God*, bk. 22, ch. 15: *CSEL* 40, 2, p. 623.

[29] *Ibid.*, ch. 13: *CSEL* 40, 2, p. 622.

[30] *Ibid.* Augustine's use of the word *ratione* here serves to recall his theory of the *rationes seminales* by which he explained the evolutive coming to be of aspects of the creation that did not manifest themselves all at once. There were present in creation elemental potencies that would develop in time.

[31] Aquinas, *De Veritate*, q. 5, a. 9, 8.

More is able to be said about those separated "untimely" from this life than simple reference to their age and size in the life to come. The fact that infants and young people die reminds us of the truth that there are relationships that are never capable of developing in this life. Early death of child or parent, total geographical or emotional separation even while living, misunderstandings, hatred and the like are among the many causes of aborted relationships. The future life will see that many of these will not only come to their full term but also be perfected along with all other relationships. One can think of parents meeting children whom they had never known here but for more than a few weeks, months or years. Children will meet parents who died before they were born or before they were old enough to know them well. It is not only in age and size that the resurrected will reach their due term but also in all that should have been theirs here but was left incomplete.

Sex, age, size and shape are components of the body as we know it. They are part of the present, fallen creation, and, as such, remnants of a loveliness that lacks its original luster. They will survive and be perfected in the life to come, enriched with the gift of immortality and impassibility.

It is a certain teaching of Christianity that, once resurrected, the living will never again die. The fruit of the tree of life will be forever theirs, and be incapable of being lost. St. Thomas, consistently carrying out his own philosophical and theological insights, saw that immortality should belong to the body. Since, he said, the soul is naturally immortal, and since humans are only full persons when both their "component parts" are present, it was fitting that, even at the beginning, God should have intended immortality for the body that, considered simply in itself as matter, is mortal. Due to sin, that promised immortality was lost. The resurrection restores by perfecting what had been originally promised.

We have shown already that human souls are immortal. Separated from their bodies, therefore, they remain in existence when the body dies. Moreover, it is also clear from what was said above that the soul is naturally united to the body: it is by its very essence the form of the body. Thus, it is contrary to the nature of the soul to be without a body. And nothing that is contrary to nature can exist perpetually. Therefore, the soul will not forever be without a body. Since the soul is perpetual, it is necessary that it be joined again to a body, which is what the resurrection does. Thus, the immortality of the soul seems to demand the future resurrection of bodies.[32]

The astonishing gift of immortality will be accompanied by an inability to suffer sickness or pain or any form of mental or bodily infirmity. As the Word of God assures us:

He will wipe every tear from their eyes, and there shall be no more death or mourning, wailing or pain, for the old order has passed away (Rv 21:4).

Death and suffering are part of this "old order" in which we live. Immortality and impassibility will be their death in the world to come. These, however, will not be the only qualities that will complete the bodies of the Blessed. The flesh of those who live forever will be endowed with a special type of clarity or glory. The Book of Wisdom, speaking of the immortality of the just, says:

In the time of their visitation they shall shine, and shall dart about as sparks through stubble; they shall judge nations and rule over peoples, and the Lord shall be their King forever (Wis 3:7-8).

Jesus Himself repeats this idea when, explaining the parable of the weeds, He concludes: "Then the righteous will shine like the sun in the kingdom of their Father" (Mt 13:43). He did not confine this promise to words. He confirmed it by giving His disciples an indication of their own future when He was transfigured before their eyes on the holy mountain. The Church's prayer in the Liturgy for the Feast of the Transfiguration indicates the prognostic aspects of that mystery and prays for their achievement: "O God, Who by the testimony of the fathers strengthen the mysteries of the Faith in the glorious Transfiguration of Your Only-Begotten, and marvelously prefigure the perfect adoption of Your children, grant to us Your servants that, listening to the voice of that same beloved Son, we may merit to become His coheirs."

The quality of being filled with and reflective of light comes from the soul's goodness exhibiting itself in a physical way

---

[32] Aquinas, *Summa Contra Gentiles*, bk. IV, q. 79, *Opera Omnia*, vol. XV, pp. 248-249.

through the resurrected body.[33] It is in fact an intensification of something we experience at times in this world, that luminous quality possessed by some good people (one thinks of a Mother Teresa of Calcutta or a Pope Paul VI). Because of it, even a face that lacks the normal harmony that denotes beauty can become wonderfully attractive. It is like the glow of life in the face of a pregnant mother. This transparency of life and goodness all the resurrected will enjoy as their own. Such clarity or lightsomeness as it flows from the soul to and through the body reminds us that it is the whole person of which we are speaking, not just the body.

The luminosity evident in the Saints will not, however, be simply a revealing of their own perfected goodness. It will be as well a reflection of the glory they will behold. For it is the sight of God that will cause them to "shine like the sun in the kingdom of their Father" (Mt 13:43). This is a truth first recognized in the case of the great Lawgiver of the Old Covenant. Having asked to see the glory of the Lord God of Israel, Moses was rewarded. "But," God said to him, "my face you cannot see, for no man sees me and still lives. . . . You may see my back; but my face is not to be seen" (Ex 33:19-23). Subsequently, "when Aaron . . . and the other Israelites saw Moses, [they] noticed how radiant the skin of his face had become. . . . When [Moses] finished speaking with them, he put a veil over his face. Whenever Moses entered the presence of the Lord to converse with him, he removed the veil until he came out again. On coming out, he would tell the Israelites all that had been commanded. Then the Israelites would see that the skin of Moses' face was radiant; so he would again put the veil over his face until he went to converse with the Lord" (Ex 34:30-35). For the Elect who will see not God obliquely but face to face there will be no need for the veil. It will be a brilliance shared by them all in varying degrees and for all to see. It will be furthermore the total unveiling of a glory that is theirs even now, although only partially. Paul strove to remind the faithful of this truth.

> We [are] not like Moses, who put a veil over his face so that the Israelites could not look intently at the cessation of what was fading. . . . All of us, gazing with unveiled face on the glory of

---

[33] Aquinas, *Summa Theol.*, *Suppl.*, q. 85, a. 1 c.

the Lord, are being transformed into the same image from glory to glory.... For God who said, "Let light shine out of darkness," has shone in our hearts to bring to light the knowledge of the glory of God on the face of Jesus Christ (2 Cor 3:13, 18; 4:6).

The radiance of the Saints, then, is the final consummation of the glory that is already theirs, that majesty of God which shines on the face of Christ and that constantly, however imperfectly, radiates in the members of His Body, the Church.

The Knowledge of the Saints

Giving us his views on the end of universal evolution—above all of human evolution—Teilhard wrote:

> Because it contains and engenders consciousness, space-time is necessarily of *a convergent nature*. Accordingly its enormous layers, followed in the right direction, must somewhere ahead become involuted to a point which we might call *Omega*, which fuses and consumes them integrally in itself.[34]

Teilhard, despite the fact that this "noogenesis" appeared to call for the absorption and disappearance of individual consciousness, insisted that the end of the universe would not be monadic or pantheistic because *"union differentiates."*[35]

> The conclusion is inevitable that the concentration of a conscious universe would be unthinkable if it did to reassemble in itself *all consciousness* as well as all *the conscious*; each particular consciousness remaining conscious of itself at the end of the operation, and even (this must absolutely be understood) each particular consciousness becoming still more itself and thus more clearly distinct from others the closer it gets to them in Omega.[36]

The learned anthropologist, inaccurate as his views sometimes were, does not miss the mark here. What he wrote is especially important because sometimes descriptions of the life to come—as well as of states or experiences of prayer—can easily give the impression that when God is truly all in all, He will totally absorb His creatures. Such is in no way a Christian under-

---

[34] Teilhard de Chardin, *The Phenomenon of Man*, p. 259.
[35] *Ibid.*, p. 262.
[36] *Ibid.*, p. 261.

standing of the life to come. In knowing God, the Elect will continue, as individual persons, to know themselves, and others, and
indeed all creation.

The radiance of the Saints is what comes to them because of
the knowledge of God's glory shining in the face of Christ. This
knowledge of God's glory will in turn illumine fully the minds of
the Elect. The mental capacities of the Saints will be—like everything else about their personalities—greatly enhanced. In this
life, our intellects are weakened and even darkened owing to
original sin and our own personal sins. As Augustine said rather
matter-of-factly, "The mind, after sin, has been made more feeble
(imbecillior)."[37] In his footsteps, Aquinas wrote:

> The race in common suffers diverse punishments, both bodily
> and spiritual. Among the bodily, the most potent is death to
> which all the others are ordered. . . . Among the spiritual the
> most potent is the weakness of reason, because of which it hap-
> pens that the human race comes to truth with difficulty and eas-
> ily falls into error.[38]

Having hid itself from the Light of truth that is God, the human mind dwells in great obscurity. As previously noted, even
some of those things that we can and should know by natural reason—especially those that pertain to God, His existence and His
eternal law—remain ungrasped, so that, as the Church teaches, we
have a need for God to intervene as Teacher in such matters.[39]

Apart from its proclivity to fall easily into error and with
equal ease to be led to that misapprehension of the good which
leads to sin, the thoughtful are aware of the lassitude of their intellects, and of the labor it takes to learn, to retain what is
learned and to use well what has been retained. Some of the
time, the very effort at intellection is such a task that we simply
let the mind "drift." It goes its way, undisciplined, floating with
the imagination, too lazy even to integrate the information
passed on through the senses. Indeed we not infrequently leave
the mind "disengaged," as it were, living for the most part from
sense knowledge, instinct, and emotions. So obvious is all this

[37] Augustine, *De Musica Libri Sex*, ch. V: *PL* 32, 1170.
[38] Aquinas, *Summa Contra Gentiles*, bk, IV, ch. 52, *Opera Omnia*, XV, p. 163.
[39] Cf. Pius XII, *Humani Generis: AAS*, 42 (1950), pp. 561-562.

that one should not need the light of revelation to know the infirmity of the human intellect. Long ago the pagan Plato recognized it. In Book VII of his *Republic*, he narrates for us Socrates' famous story of the cave. Those in its darkness are an example of the necessary struggle to acquire the philosophic mind. Such intellectual disorder and the struggle needed to improve the mind will not be the fate of the Saints. In the life to come the intellect will operate with accuracy, aided by an acuity that comes from God Himself. Then in all truth will it be able to be said, "In your light we see light" (Ps 36:10). Reason will be immune to distraction, incapable of error, unimpeded by bodily fatigue.

How often the Bible refers to our mind's need for help and light. We are a people walking in darkness and only the Lord God is the light that can illumine that obscurity. His Revelation is our aid, for "the command of the Lord is clear, enlightening the eye" (Ps 19:8). The believer can pray in truth: "Your word is a lamp for my feet, a light for my path" (Ps 119:105). The old law, however, was not bright enough to enlighten the obscurity effectively. It had the great advantage of making us aware of the darkness, but more was needed. The word that was a light to our feet and was, as John tells us, "the light of the human race" (Jn 1:4) needed to come into the darkness that could neither understand nor overcome it (cf. Jn 1:5). He came and promised: "Whoever follows me will not walk in darkness, but will have the light of life" (Jn 8:12). He later makes the promise an invitation to those still blind, "Buy [from me] ointment to smear on your eyes so that you may see" (Rv 3:18). Now the ointment that makes everything visible is Christ Himself. That is why it is said: "Awake, O sleeper, and arise from the dead, and Christ will give you light" (Eph 5:14).

> The Lord illumines the blind. Therefore, brethren, let us be illumined, having the ointment of faith. He mixed His saliva with earth and anointed the one who was born blind. We are born blind from Adam and we need Him to enlighten us.

> We shall enjoy the truth when we shall see face to face because that is what is promised us. For who would dare to hope for what God had not deigned either to promise or to give?

We shall see face to face. As the Apostle says, "Now we know in part, now we know obscurely through a mirror: then we shall know face to face" (1 Cor 13:12). And the Apostle John in his epistle writes: "Beloved, now we are children of God, and what we will be has not yet appeared. We know that, when He appears, we will be like Him because we shall see Him as He is" (1 Jn 3:2). This is the great promise.[40]

It is a traditional view that when the great promise has been fulfilled then all the knowledge to be possessed by the Saints will come to them immediately. Since they know at that point as they are known, they will, as it were, apprehend or know everything at once in the Beatific Vision. Such was St. Thomas' opinion.

. . . the created intellect, seeing the divine substance, knows, in the very substance of God, all the kinds of reality; . . . it is necessary that the intellect that sees the divine substance contemplate all things not in succession but simultaneously. Therefore, those things that are seen through the vision of the divine substance, by which we are happy, are all seen in their actuality. Therefore, one is not seen first, another later. All the things that the intellect sees in the divine substance, it sees simultaneously. That is why Augustine says, "Then our thoughts will not be changeable, moving from some things to others and returning to them: rather we shall see all our knowledge in one simultaneous vision."[41]

It must be admitted that Thomas quotes his own favorite theologian loosely in this citation, working perhaps from a defective manuscript. In fact, Augustine envisioned the possibility of what St. Thomas taught; he did not however affirm it. What Augustine actually wrote was: "Perhaps our thoughts will not be changeable, moving from some things to others and returning to them; rather we shall see all our knowledge in one simultaneous vision. Still, when even this shall happen—if indeed it shall happen. . . . "[42]

---

[40] Augustine, *In Iohannis Evangelium Tractatus*, 34, 8-9: CCSL 36, pp. 315-316.

[41] Aquinas, *Summa Contra Gentiles*, III, q. 60.

[42] Augustine, *De Trinitate*, XV, 16: CCSL 50a, p. 501. Augustine's Latin reads: "*Fortassis etiam non erunt volubiles nostrae cogitationes, ab aliis in alia euntes atque redeuntes, sed omnem scientiam nostram uno simul conspectu videbimus. Tamen cum et hoc fuerit, si et hoc fuerit. . . .*" Aquinas quotes him as reading: "*Non erunt tunc volubiles nostrae cogitationes, ab aliis in alia euntes et redeuntes: sed omnem scientiam nostram uno simul conspectu videbimus*" (Leonine edition, p. 167). The omission of the "*fortassis*" and the "*si et hoc fuerit*" gives a different cast to Augustine's thought.

St. Augustine's "perhaps" and "if indeed it shall happen" are omitted in Thomas' quotation of the text. And they make a difference. Now St. Thomas' own judgment in this matter is consistent with his general explication of the Beatific Vision, which for him is a type of ecstasy in which we know all things immediately and perfectly.[43] It must be noted, though, that Thomas does not appear to be fully consistent with himself. We say this because he saw that the Angels, who possess the Beatific Vision, are still able to teach one another. Indeed, he even speaks of a certain ability to learn in heaven when he treats of the knowledge already possessed by the Angels.

> It must be said that both the higher and the lower ranks of Angels immediately see the essence of God and in this respect one does not teach the other. . . . But the reasons of the divine works that are known in God as their cause are all known by God in Himself because He comprehends Himself; in respect to others who see God, it can be said that the more perfectly one sees Him the more one will know of His reasons. Therefore, a higher Angel knows in God more things about the reasons in His divine works than a lower Angel and informs the other about them.

> One Angel does not illumine another by handing over to it the light of nature or of grace or of glory, but rather by strengthening its natural light and showing it the truth about those things that pertain to the states of nature, grace and glory.[44]

The implication of Thomas' teaching is significant. The vision of God face to face fully beatifies each and all who share it, and, since it is immediate, no creature can augment that direct vision for another. However, there are different capacities in each

---

[43] This view is held also by many in our day. Typical is Candido Pozo. "We conceive of the [beatific] vision as an ecstasy in God. There is in it a certain participation in the immobility of God that is not the quietude of death but the plenitude of life: thus there is in the Blessed a certain participation in the eternity of God" (*La Teología del Más Allá*, p. 170). He appears not fully content with such a position, however, for he adds: "Because participation is not equality, the situation of the Blessed does not lose all temporal relation. . . . We are not dealing—one cannot—with a notion of time univocal with our own, but we also cannot suppress all notion of temporality for this would be equivalent to confusing eternity with the 'aevum' (the only participation in eternity of which the creature is capable)" (*ibid.*). Scheeben, too, held a similar view. Cf. *The Mysteries of Christianity*, p. 664, and above, in Chapter IV: "The New Genesis," p. 168.

[44] Aquinas, *Summa Theol.*, I, 106, 2, ad 1. Cf. I, Iiae, 5, 6, ad 3.

creature and thus, although each sees the same reality, some will see more in that reality than others. It is like two people looking at a work of Monet, both fully seeing and enjoying the painting. One, however, will discern aspects not directly grasped by another and will be able to guide the other to a fuller appreciation. Something similar, we may surmise, will be true of the knowledge of the Saints who possess the Beatific Vision. The wonders of the New Creation—to say nothing of the immensity of the Godhead—will always afford an opportunity for one to point out to another a new aspect or insight. And those who are closer to God, whose perfection in charity was greater here and will be in the life to come, will be the better teachers. The best of them, therefore, will be the Seat of Wisdom herself.

When Augustine was thinking about the knowledge of the Angels, he made a distinction that subsequently became famous in theology, namely the contrast between "morning" and "evening" knowledge.

> There is such a great difference between knowledge of any thing in the Word of God and knowledge of the thing in its own nature that the former is rightly considered as belonging to day, the latter to evening. For, in comparison with that light which is seen in the Word of God, all knowledge by which we know any creature in itself cannot without reason be called night. . . .
>
> Thus, the holy Angels, with whom we shall be equals after the resurrection, if until the end we hold fast to the Way—that Way which Christ has become for us—always see the face of God and enjoy the Word that is His Only Son and the Father's equal . . . ; without doubt they know every creature, among which they themselves were made at the beginning, first of all in the Word Himself in Whom exist all the eternal causes [rationes] of all the things that are made in time. . . . There [i.e., in the Word] their knowledge is like the day . . . ; here, however, it is like the evening.[45]

It is imagery, of course. The Angels, like the Blessed in heaven, in knowing the Word know, in Him, all other things since He is the pattern and cause of all things. This knowledge

---

[45] Augustine, *De Genesi ad Litteram Libri 12*, bk. IV, ch. 23 and 24: *CSEL* 28, 1, pp. 122-124. Aquinas picks up this imagery and uses it, for example, in his commentary on the Epistle to the Romans. Cf. *Super Epistolas S. Pauli Lectura, Ad Romanos*, XIII, lect. 3, no. 1066.

which is theirs, in Him, is possessed with the clarity of day, the brightness and freshness of morning. However, they also know things in themselves. This latter knowledge is less brilliant and clear than the same knowledge that they have of the same thing in the Word, and thus Augustine calls it "evening" knowledge. There is, writes Augustine, a vast difference between the two forms of knowing.

> The knowledge possessed by the creature, considered in itself, is, if I may put it this way, more lacking in color than when something is known in the Wisdom of God as in the Art by which it was created. Therefore, it can more fittingly be described as evening. . . . This evening, however, becomes morning when this knowledge is used to praise and love the Creator.[46]

St. Thomas commented on these passages of Augustine when he wrote his own treatment on Angels in the *Summa*. And it is interesting and important to note that Aquinas maintained that the same person/Angel could possess both types of knowledge and that the morning knowledge did not make the evening knowledge superfluous. He comments:

> When what is perfect comes, that which is imperfect is done away with if the imperfect is opposed to the perfect. In this way, faith, which concerns those things that are not seen, is done away with when vision comes. However, the imperfection of "evening" knowledge is not opposed to the perfection of "morning" knowledge. The fact that something is known in itself is not opposed to the fact that it be known in its cause. Again, that which is known by two means—one of which is perfect, the other imperfect—has nothing contradictory about it. We are able to hold the same conclusion because of demonstrative evidence and because we have reasoned to it.[47]

In this comment we have yet another indication that the Saints, in possessing the Vision of God, will nonetheless possess other forms of knowing as well. If these considerations are correct, there can be some growth in knowledge even when one possesses the sight of God face to face. It might be worth remembering, as well, that Thomas' views on the Beatific Vision at one time led him to assert that there was no experimental knowledge

---

[46] Augustine, *City of God*, bk. 11, ch. 7: CCSL 48, p. 327.

[47] Aquinas, *Summa Theol.*, I, q. 58, a. 7, ad 3.

in Christ Who, on earth, possessed that vision. The possession of the vision would have seemed to obviate the need for acquired knowledge. Upon reflection, Thomas admitted in the *Summa* that he had changed his mind on this.[48] Might he have changed his mind on the nature of the knowledge in the Saints if he had ever completed the sections on the life to come in the *Summa*? There is for now no way of knowing, but one may follow him to the extent of recognizing for the Elect what he admitted for the Angels: the vision of God does not exclude all further learning and insight.

The knowledge of the Blessed will, of course, be the special wisdom that belongs to those who appreciate the foolishness of God's ways and, above all, the foolishness of the Cross. In other words, when speaking of the knowledge possessed by those in the age to come, it is good to remember that there will be in it a certain inversion of values. Jesus Himself assured us that true wisdom is hidden from "the wise and the learned," and revealed to "the childlike" (Mt 11:25). Commenting on this Paul wrote:

> Where is the wise one? Where is the scribe? Where is the debater of this age? Has not God made the wisdom of the world foolish? . . . We proclaim Christ crucified. . . . For the foolishness of God is wiser than human wisdom (1 Cor 1:20-25).

Indeed, it must be said that what we now often consider wisdom and knowledge will have totally disappeared in the future. The Lord has a very strong statement about the value we place on some things: "What is of human esteem is an abomination before God" (Lk 16:15). The word in the Greek of this text is the same word He uses when He speaks of the "desolating abomination" (Mt 24:15), indicating that often the value we place on things is the equivalent of idolatry. In what is ahead, many present values will be turned upside down and reality will be seen as it is in fact, which is to say that it will be seen as God sees it and not as we, in the blindness we often take for light, imagine it to be. It is then that the Saints will fully "have the mind of Christ" (1 Cor 2:16).

The knowledge of the Blessed—and the happiness that flows from it—will not be something totally new or unprepared for. By

---

[48] On Thomas' admission of his change, cf. *Summa Theol.*, III, q. 9, a. 4 c.

His gifts of grace God already gives Himself to the faithful in such a way that He is to be known and delighted in. The knowledge and enjoyment of the Saints will be the flowering of what is possible here through grace, charity and what we call the intellective gifts of the Holy Spirit, wisdom, knowledge and understanding. These gifts accommodate our minds to God in such a way that a certain experience of Him is possible already in this life. It is an experience that develops from faith and must always be grounded in faith but that is able at times to do what Augustine describes as "touching" Eternal Wisdom.[49] Experiential knowledge like this, always obscure now, will only come to perfection when what Jesus prayed for is realized: "That they [may] know you, the only true God, and the one whom you sent" (Jn 17:3).

Memory

Along with fuller knowledge and a progressive deepening of insight, the Blessed will have flawless memories. Memory was a theme particularly dear to Augustine, and he treats of it extensively in Book Ten of the *Confessions*. For most of us—except when it functions poorly or is lost—it is a power generally taken for granted. It is, nonetheless, a "vast cloister" (ch. 8), and an "immense and immeasurable sanctuary" (ch. 8), in which we store all that comes to us or that we ourselves fashion. As a consequence it can also be for us a dark well of much shame and sorrow. It can, on the other hand, be a treasure-trove, the font of so much joy recalled and relived. Like all the faculties of the resurrected Saints, memory too will be purified, sharpened and freed from the whims of selectiveness and forgetfulness. In the life to come, the Blessed will remember people, places, occasions and things of the present life. All these will be recollected then in a way that makes their true significance transparent through the application of a perfected reason. With memory thus shot through with deeper understanding, the Saints will relive the past. And that, in itself, will become a source of joy, a poetry all its own. As Wordsworth wrote:

---

[49] Cf. below in Chapter VI: "The City of Compact Unity," p. 270.

Poetry is the spontaneous overflow of powerful feelings: it takes its origin from emotion recollected in tranquillity: the emotion is contemplated till by a species of reaction the tranquillity gradually disappears, and an emotion, kindred to that which was before the subject of contemplation, is gradually produced, and does itself actually exist in the mind. In this mood successful composition generally begins, and in a mood similar to this it is carried on; but the emotion, of whatever kind and in whatever degree, from various causes is qualified by various pleasures, so that in describing any passions whatsoever, which are voluntarily described, the mind will upon the whole be in a state of enjoyment.[50]

What he is describing would, of course, be impossible without the employment of memory. It is memory that first stores an event, along with the emotion that accompanies it. It is memory that is later capable of calling up for us that same "emotion recollected in tranquillity." Analogously, this will be a function of our memories in the world to come. Even what was pain here or in itself shameful will be then numbered among the remembered joys, for to those who love God all things work for good, even repented sins. In truth, for those who are saved, *everything* that is now painful to remember will then be seen in such a light that Virgil's intimation will be realized: *"Forsan et haec olin meminisse iuvabit."*[51] With a memory and imagination cleansed by their new condition, those in heaven even now recall their own lives here on earth, the persons and events that were important to them and the help they received from others (even during their period of purgation). It is these memories that in part nourish their concern for us. Likewise it is such recollections that aid them in longing for the total renewal of everyone and everything that they loved and enjoyed here.

Memory of this kind will be operative in the land of the living. Then, as they contemplate the natural beauties of the restored earth, the Saints who live that life will each be able to say, "I have owed to them . . . feelings of unremembered pleasure."[52]

---

[50] William Wordsworth, "Preface to Lyrical Ballads" in *The Poems*, vol. I, pp. 886-887.

[51] *Aeneid*, I, line 203: "Perhaps some day it will be a joy to remember even these things."

[52] William Wordsworth, *Lines Composed a Few Miles above Tintern Abbey, The Poems*, I, p. 358.

As we are all aware some joys, even moments of happiness with those we love, are indeed unremembered until summoned to mind by some association with nature. That will be true in the life to come. In remembering, the Blessed shall find additional grounds for delight and thus for praise of Him Who is the One Who causes all things worth treasuring and pondering in the heart (cf. Lk 2:19, 51).

The Glorious Freedom of the Children of God

In the eighth chapter of his Letter to the Romans, St. Paul speaks of the "glorious freedom of the children of God" (Rom 8:21). This freedom will be one of the greatest gifts of those who are among the Elect. It will be a liberation that gives them something far more unfettering than mere freedom of choice. It will be an emancipation that will unchain the will and the passions, leaving them to indulge themselves without restraint in all that will be truly delightful.

> There will exist in that City free choice . . . , freed from every evil and filled with all good, enjoying without end the delight of eternal joys.

> And it should not be thought that because sin will not be able to delight them they do not have free choice. Indeed choice will be more free when it has been freed from delight in sinning in order to delight unfailingly in not sinning. For the first freedom of choice that was given to humans when they were created in justice was an ability not to sin, although they were also able to sin. The last freedom of choice, by which they will not be able to sin, will be more powerful, a gift of God, not a possibility of nature itself. It is one thing to be God, another to participate in God. By His nature, God is not able to sin; one who participates in God receives from Him the gift of not being able to sin. . . . But because this nature sinned when it was able to sin, it is freed by a greater gift whereby it is led to that freedom in which it is not capable of sinning. Just as the first immortality, which Adam lost by sinning, was an ability not to die, so the last immortality will be an inability to die. It cannot be denied, can it, that God Himself has free choice, although He cannot sin?[53]

---

[53] Augustine, *City of God*, bk. 22, ch. 30: CSEL 40, 2, pp. 666-667.

Notice how Augustine distinguishes free choice from freedom itself. In doing this he follows the Lord Who assured us that it is only the truth, namely Himself, that makes us free (cf. Jn 8:31-32), not the illusory freedom that comes from choosing what is evil and thus against our own best interests.

Freedom in the land of the living will be also a sign that the effects of Original Sin and concupiscence and all personal sin will have been overcome. We only imperfectly understand the effects of sin in us. We are distorted personalities, bent in our will, our emotions, our passions, our knowing, our judgments. So weakened are we that we have only the minimum amount of insight into what we ourselves might be when freed from the murkier depths of our personalities. On this matter Chesterton wrote perceptively:

> ... very few people in this world would care to listen to the real defence of their own characters. The real defence, the defence which belongs to the Day of Judgment, would make such damaging admissions, would clear away so many artificial virtues, would tell such tragedies of weakness and failure, that a man would sooner be misunderstood and censured by the world than exposed to that awful and merciless eulogy. One of the most practically difficult matters which arises from the code of manners and the conventions of life, is that we cannot properly justify a human being, because that justification would involve the admission of things which may not conventionally be admitted. ... Thus the decencies of civilization do not merely make it impossible to revile a man, they make it impossible to praise him.[54]

To be properly defended we would have to permit the confession of things that convention forbids. It is such "unmentionables," says Chesterton, that would actually place us in a different light. What cannot be mentioned are the miseries and evils we are pulled to or have to struggle against, the unpleasant and even demonic hidden aspects of our disordered personalities. It is only in recognizing them, in admitting what we would be like without what Christ's grace achieves even in our reluctant wills, that a real defense can be made for what we are. In the life to come, once the judgment has done just what Chesterton claims

---

[54] G.K. Chesterton, *Robert Browning* (New York: The Macmillan Co., 1916), pp. 188-189.

needs to be done, the personalities of those saved will have been purified like gold in a furnace. Emotions will be perfectly integrated and as a result much more spontaneous because they will not need the constraints now applied to defend goodness against attack; judgments will be clear and unprejudiced, inhibitions and fears and phobias gone; the tendency to disorder in all the appetites abolished. It is presently quite impossible to imagine what sexual love is like without lust (that is with no self-seeking in it), what temperance is when it is truly, as Augustine surprisingly described it, "love giving itself integrally to that which is loved."[55] But that is what love and temperance—and all the emotions and virtues—will be in the future.

In the homeland there will be qualities that here on earth we considered admirable or noteworthy or important or, in some cases, even essential that will be totally absent from the personalities of the Saints: sagacity, cunning (the wisdom that goes with being as "wise as serpents"), skill in negotiations and making compromises, business acumen, deftness in persuasion and salesmanship and preaching, the ability to turn a witty phrase at the expense of others. Such characteristics and others like them are attributes often admired here. However, when they are not actually the result of sin, original and personal, they are means of "making do" or "getting by" or "passing the time" in a fallen world. They all, in their own ways, either are used to advance us at the expense of others or are the virtues necessary for dealing with the conflicts that arise from competition of one kind or another as it exists in this life.[56] All such traits of the present life will disappear, there being no need for them, and since nothing in them can add to the beauty or harmony of the life ahead.

Who will the Elect be and what will they be like? We may answer in general by saying that they will be those who are or will have become practitioners of the Beatitudes of the Lamb and received the promises attached to those Beatitudes.

---

[55] Augustine, *De Moribus Ecclesiae Catholicae*, ch. XV: *PL* 32, 1322.

[56] Cardinal Newman has this insight on the "virtues" that will not exist in the coming life in his sermon "The State of Innocence," *Parochial and Plain Sermons*, pp. 1021ff. It is a fine insight, although one would want to qualify much that appears in the sermon.

> Blessed are the poor in spirit,
>> for theirs is the kingdom of heaven.
> Blessed are they who mourn,
>> for they will be comforted.
> Blessed are the meek,
>> for they will inherit the land.
> Blessed are they who hunger and thirst for righteousness,
>> for they will be satisfied.
> Blessed are the merciful,
>> for they will be shown mercy.
> Blessed are the clean of heart,
>> for they will see God.
> Blessed are the peacemakers,
>> for they will be called children of God.
> Blessed are they who are persecuted for the sake of righteous-
> ness,
>> for theirs is the kingdom of heaven.

> Blessed are you when they insult you and persecute you and utter every kind of evil against you falsely because of me. Rejoice and be glad, for your reward will be great in heaven. Thus they persecuted the prophets who were before you (Mt 5:3-12).

When they are come upon for the first time or rediscovered with a fresh vision, one realizes that these "blessings" are certainly an oddity. They are an illustration of something we saw earlier when considering the knowledge of the Saints. In the outlook of Jesus—and therefore of those who follow Him and to the extent they follow Him—the world is seen upside down as it were. Nothing is the way one would "naturally" look at it. The contrast with our ordinary ideas of what makes for happiness is increased when we add to the Beatitudes spoken by the Lord on the mountain those He revealed to John.

> Blessed is the one who reads aloud and blessed are those who listen to this prophetic message and heed what is written in it, for the appointed time is near (Rv 1:3).

> I heard a voice from heaven say, "Write this: Blessed are the dead who die in the Lord from now on." "Yes," said the Spirit, "let them find rest from their labors, for their works accompany them" (Rv 14:13).

> "Behold, I am coming like a thief." Blessed is the one who watches and keeps his clothes ready, so that he may not go naked and people see him exposed (Rv 16:15).

> Then the angel said to me, "Write this: Blessed are those who have been called to the wedding feast of the Lamb." And he said to me, "These words are true; they come from God" (Rv 19:9).

> Blessed and holy is the one who shares in the first resurrection. The second death has no power over these; they will be priests of God and of Christ, and they will reign with him for the thousand years (Rv 20:6).

> Blessed is the one who keeps the prophetic message of this book (Rv 22:7).

> Blessed are they who wash their robes so as to have the right to the tree of life and enter the city through its gates (Rv 22:14).

The various Beatitudes can help us make an "indentikit" of the Elect, a kind of profile of what they will be like. Of course, many of the virtues practiced by those blessed by Jesus will no longer be necessary when the vicissitudes of the present age have passed. A longing for justice, concern for the poor and oppressed, peace-making and other such qualities are values that will all have taken their leave along with the world that made them necessary. In such cases the blessings will remain, the virtues that merited them will have lost their purpose. Nonetheless, in the Saints there will be recognizable the virtues that distinguished them in a particular way during this life. They will then—even as now—be definable in "groups." There will exist the virgins, the confessors, the great doctors, the holy men and women who were repentant sinners. The general types, however, will exist to highlight what is individual. Each man and woman will be an irreplaceable and unique image of the Word, more different from each other in possessing the fullness of holiness than they were in this life.

Nor will they be "pale-faced" creatures, meek, gentle, loving and the like in the sense that a secularized but formerly Christian world counterfeits these virtues and misuses the words that identify them. For, in the land of life, although everything that smacks of selfishness, pride and a lack of love will have been purged from the personality, every other facet of an individual's uniqueness will stand out as more richly individual. Aquinas' equanimity will be greater, not less; More's wit sharper, not blunter; Philip Neri's laughter unalloyed by penance; Teresa's determination unaffected by hesitation; the physical attractiveness of an

Agnes heightened, and so forth. In seeing the Lord the Saints will come to a full understanding of themselves and simultaneously take on all His characteristics that, as individuals, they were meant to reflect. As the Second Vatican Council teaches:

> In reality only in the mystery of the Incarnate Word is the mystery of humans truly clarified. For Adam, the first man, was a figure of the future man, namely of Christ the Lord. Christ, the last Adam, in the very revelation of the mystery of the Father and His love, fully manifests humanity to itself and opens up its highest vocation (*Lumen Gentium*, 22).

In knowing the risen Christ, humanity will be recognized in its perfection even as each person's share in that humanity is brought to its own particular fulfillment by being conformed to Him. That conformity will be according to the unique pattern for each person, a pattern that always existed in the Eternal Word. For those who were chosen in Him before the creation of the world to be adopted as sons through Jesus Christ have been predestined according to the plan of Him Who works out everything in conformity with the purpose of His will (cf. Eph 1:4-11).

The total integration of the personalities of the resurrected will be manifested in the body. Not only will there be the glory of the gift of clarity, there will exist as well what is known as the quality of subtlety. St. Thomas describes this as "the dominion of the glorified soul over the body, by reason of which the glorious body is said to be spiritual, completely subject as it were to the spirit."[57] It is a quality evident in the accounts of the appearances of the Risen Jesus. He had the power to let Himself be recognized or not, and to appear to His disciples even through closed doors. His material body showed itself malleable in ways our bodies presently do not seem to be. As Aquinas indicates at length, this subtlety does not mean that the body becomes "spiritual" or "ghostly." It will still occupy its own place, be able to be seen and touched when it wills and exhibit all the other qualities of its materiality, but do so in such a way that the harmony of body and soul, the integrity of the whole person, is evident. Thomas speaks of this quality of subtlety as an exercise of total dominion by the soul over the body. This, of course, is a kind of theological

---

[57] Aquinas, *Supplementum*, q. 83, a.1.

shorthand in which he is using the common body/soul language. Employing the same terminology, St. Paul describes the present situation.

> When I want to do right, evil is at hand. For I take delight in the law of God, in my inner self, but I see in my members another principle at war with the law of my mind, taking me captive to the law of sin that dwells in my members. Miserable one that I am! (Rom 7:21-24).

If not correctly understood, it can appear that the body is the negative element that pulls against the soul. This is an over-simplification of what is intended by both Paul and St. Thomas. Body/flesh and soul/spirit are in a sense "code" words that describe tendencies that affect both body and soul. The body can be "spiritual"; the soul can be "carnal" or "fleshy" or "live according to the desires of the body." Already in his day Augustine warned against understanding the "shorthand" or code language in a simplistic way. Writing on the gift of continence, he said:

> Without doubt those who wish to define continence as restraining only the lusts of the body make too narrow a demarcation; they do better who do not add "of the body" but rather say that the control of lust or cupidity in a general sense belongs to the virtue of continence. This cupidity is found as a vice not only of the body but of the soul as well. If cupidity of the body exists in fornications and revelings, are enmities, contentions, jealousies . . . not exercised in the movements and disturbances of the soul?[58]

Seen in this its proper light, the gift of subtlety is not some form of Platonic domination of the noble soul over the sinful body. Rather, it actually means that the Saints as persons will not be impeded in their self-expression and activity as we some-times are here by the infirmities of this life. These infirmities are present in the soul and its powers as well as in the body and its powers. Thus, it might be better to define the gift of subtlety as the power that overcomes everything in the human person that "pulls against" the better self.

At times of anxiety or stress, or when one is trying to con-front various emotional or psychological problems, we com-monly say we are trying to "get it all together." The phrase is not

---

[58] Augustine, *De Continentia,* 13, 28: CSEL 41, p. 178. Dates as varied as 395 and 412 are given for this work.

an inappropriate one. Sin and the consequences of original sin in us are disorders that work toward a type of disintegration in the personality; virtue tends to integration and unity. Thus, in the life to come, which will be a life of total virtue, the Saints will have attained an integration and unity in personality that, except in the cases of Christ and His Mother, is never fully realized in this life by anyone.

Closely aligned with the gift of subtlety will be that other aptitude which is spoken of as agility, the ability to move from place to place at will. It is an idea that flows from the facility that the Risen Christ possessed of making Himself present apparently out of nowhere. This gift should be easier for us to assent to than it may have been formerly. We now know so much more of the properties of matter than did the ancients who had to accept ideas such as that of bodily agility on a faith greatly lacking in natural analogies. Modern science, however, already hints at the possibility of a matter/energy type of conversion that would theoretically enable the body to operate in marvelous ways. In this area even science fiction only approximates what theology has long posited for the body when it speaks of the gift of agility.

The full harmony of soul and body, evidenced in these gifts, indicates that the very beauty of the body will be enhanced. Furthermore, this enrichment, we are told, will be of different degrees in the Saints. Such a "gradation" in glory among the Elect should not surprise. Even the traditional way of speaking about the soul's "dominion" over the body can help us understand why the Saints will have different degrees of glory. The history of the growth of their personalities will have been one of differentiated development. They will have been created with varied potential to begin with and will have had that potential fulfilled by God's grace working through charity. Others will have developed their potential to a greater or lesser degree, depending on their correspondence with grace. Such personality development, totally dependent on the love possessed and exercised by each one now, will find its reflection in the glory of the risen body. The differences in degree, however, will actually enrich all.

> Who is capable of thinking of, much less speaking of, the degrees of rewards, honors and glory given for merit? That such will exist is not to be doubted. That blessed City will see in itself this great

good, namely that no inferior will envy any superior just as now the other Angels do not envy the Archangels. No one will want what has not been received; each will be bound by the closest bond of harmony with whoever has received, just as in the body the finger does not want to be the eye since the intimate linkage of the flesh contains both members. And so it will be that someone who has a gift less than someone else will also receive as a gift the fact that no more than what one has will be desired.[59]

The Activities of the Saints

It will be the Lord's Day, the eternal eighth day, that is sanctified by the resurrection of Christ that prefigures the eternal rest not only of the spirit but also of the body. There we shall be at leisure and we shall see, we shall see and we shall love, we shall love and we shall praise. That is what the end that has no end will be. For what other end is there for us than to reach the Kingdom that has no end?[60]

Rest is the word we perhaps most often employ when speaking of the life ahead. "Grant them eternal rest," we pray for the departed. Or we speak of them as "having gone to their rest,"[61] and of resting in peace. Providentially, rest is characteristic of the life to come, and, like so much of that life, it finds its beginnings here. In fact an injunction to rest was given to our race at its beginnings. Having Himself rested on the seventh day, God imposed on His chosen ones for their own good the sabbath command.

For six days work may be done; but the seventh day is the sabbath rest, a day for sacred assembly, on which you shall do no work. The sabbath shall belong to the Lord wherever you dwell (Lv 23:3).

He extended this command to include the year-long rests of the seventh and jubilee years.

But during the seventh year the land shall have a complete rest, a sabbath for the Lord, when you neither sow your field nor prune your vineyard (Lv 25:4).

We say that He gave these commands "for their own good." One would think that humanity, by necessity or common sense,

---

[59] Augustine, *City of God*, bk. 22, ch. 30: *CSEL* 40, 2, p. 666.

[60] *Ibid.*, p. 670.

[61] Eucharistic Prayer II, *The Sacramentary*, (New York: Catholic Book Publishing Co., 1985), p. 551.

would have known enough to rest from labor even without a command to do so from the Lord. And certainly there was a time and there are yet cultures where a command appears superfluous. For some, however, where capitalism is the only truly successful economic system and where production, consumption, increased earnings, profits and improving one's standard of living have become, if not the only purpose, then at least the only way of life, the injunction to rest is more indispensable than ever. In many of the societies of the "first world," the "workaholic" is recognized as a neurotic, driven person. On the other hand the type is often secretly admired, and, even when not admired, emulated. Paradoxically, people enter therapy to learn how to relax, and the therapy itself becomes another form of "doing something." A frenetic, productive society has emerged and appears now to have at least the potential to become global.

In such an ambient all the perennial anxieties remain, and new ones appear. They are often fled by means of liquor, drugs and illicit sex in ever more exotic and unnatural forms; by travel where much is seen and little appreciated, or during which one is so busy taking photographs that the interior delight in what is seen is lost. "Where is the Life we have lost in living?/ Where is the wisdom we have lost in knowledge?"[62] The restlessness built into our nature seems to augment itself constantly. To counteract such ills was surely part of God's intention in commanding us to rest. But there was yet a deeper purpose. We must, as Paul VI said, "pause to enjoy God,"[63] for our restlessness finds no ultimate relief and our activity no ultimate purpose except in Him.

In blessing the tribes of Israel, Moses prayed for Benjamin:

> Benjamin is the beloved of the Lord, who shelters him all the day, while he abides [rests] securely at his breast (Dt 33:12).

At the foretaste of the heavenly supper, John the Evangelist, heeding the invitation ("Come to me, all you who labor and are burdened, and I will give you rest"—Mt 11:28-29), entered uniquely into that promise made to Benjamin, and so will all who come to realize that God alone is our rest.

---

[62] T.S. Eliot, *Choruses from the Rock*, in *The Wasteland and Other Poems*, Harvest Books (New York: Harcourt Brace Jovanovich, 1962), p. 81.

[63] Paul VI, *The Priest* (Baltimore: Helicon Press, 1965), p. 138.

> My soul rests in God alone, from whom comes my salvation (Ps 62:2).

> You who dwell in the shelter of the Most High . . . abide [rest] in the shadow of the Almighty (Ps 91:1).

It is rest the Lord promises those who mourn and weep in this valley of tears, who even in the midst of a fascinating world find life burdensome at times, or who have struggled to no apparent purpose, or who have never been allowed to participate in the good things of this world. All such as these are invited to that repose spoken of by the author of the Letter to the Hebrews.

> Therefore, let us be on our guard while the promise of entering into his rest remains, that none of you seem to have failed. . . . For we who believed enter into that rest, just as he has said: "As I swore in my wrath, 'They shall not enter into that rest,' " and yet his works were accomplished at the foundation of the world. . . . Therefore, since it remains that some will enter into it, and those who formerly received the good news did not enter because of disobedience, he once more set a day, "today," when long afterwards he spoke through David, as already quoted: "Oh, that today you would hear his voice: 'Harden not your hearts.' ". . . Therefore, a sabbath rest still remains for the people of God. And whoever enters into God's rest, rests from his own works as God did from his (Heb 4:1-10).

It is this same cessation of toil that was promised to the visionary of the Book of Revelation:

> I heard a voice from heaven say, "Write this: Blessed are the dead who die in the Lord from now on." "Yes," said the Spirit, "let them find rest from their labors, for their works accompany them" (Rv 14:13).

In that rest not only will our agitated lives and our burdensome labor end, but also the sensation we so often have of being fidgety and what we call "ill at ease." For some people these are conditions they live with almost all the time, sometimes termed an inability "to unwind." Such conditions of inquietude are states that impel many to narcotic efforts dangerous to themselves and others. All this too will disappear in the rest that will be the unchanging prerogative of those who inhabit the land of the living.

The great Sabbath rest will also have as its purpose that which is part of its rationale here, the praise of God.

Work Without Labor

Rest, with the prayer and contemplation that accompany it, may seem to exhaust the future possibilities. Indeed St. Thomas could write: ". . . it can be seen that all the occupations of the active life cease [in the life to come]. . . . Only the occupation of the contemplative life will remain for the resurrected."[64]

We must disagree with this. The great rest and perfect contemplation do not necessitate inactivity. As Vonier wrote:

> Far from us all such interpretations of the rest of our departed fellow-Christians, which savor more of narcotics than of faith in eternal life; which come from weariness of thought rather than from a desire to see good days. Eternal rest is the unchanging contemplation of the beauties of God, not somnolency of the spirit. It is the joy of work, the exhilaration of eternal freshness of mind; it is work without fatigue, because it is the creature's best portion busy with the most perfect object; it is the fixity of the created mind on the uncreated Truth.[65]

Pope John Paul II has written, when reflecting on the Incarnate Word Who, at Joseph's side, learned the skills of a workman: "Work has been taken up in the mystery of the Incarnation, and *has also been redeemed in a special way*."[66] Thus work is part of the redeemed order and shall always be part of it, but only *as fully redeemed*. The Saints shall work and shall enjoy it, finding in it the outlet for their heightened creativity, as well as a means by which they may glorify the Creator Who "is at work until now" (Jn 5:17).

The fact that the Saints will work can be discerned partially in a truth that is a matter of faith. We know through Revelation that the departed even in the interim state are concerned for us and aid us. It is the mystery that we call the Communion of Saints. They work for us.

Cyprian of Carthage wrote long ago that those in heaven are "still solicitous for our salvation."[67] This notion finds its way into

---

[64] Aquinas, *Summa Contra Gentiles*, bk, IV, ch. 83, *Opera Omnia*, XV, p. 265.

[65] Anscar Vonier, *The Life of the World To Come*, pp. 110-111.

[66] John Paul II, *Guardian of the Redeemer, TPS*, vol. 35, no. 1 (1960), p. 16.

[67] Cyprian, *De Mortalitate*, no. 26: CCSL 3A, pp. 31-32. The full text of Cyprian is found below in Chapter VI: "The City of Compact Unity," p. 264.

the Votive Mass for All Saints in the *Roman Missal* where the Church prays in the Prayer Over the Gifts "that we may be aware that those who we believe are already secure in their own immortality are solicitous about our salvation." Likewise Paul VI, quoting *Lumen Gentium,* number 49, confesses in his creed that the Saints "intercede for us and greatly help our weakness by their fraternal solicitude."

 Thus, even now, as they await the resurrection of their bodies and the restoration of the universe, the dead are active, especially in manifesting their concern for us. This solicitude on their part is a truth that even some pagans recognized.

> The notion that the dead are not affected at all by the fortunes of their descendants or any of those whom they love seems unduly heartless and contrary to accepted beliefs. . . . It appears that the dead are affected to some extent by the good fortunes of those whom they love, and similarly by their misfortunes; but that the effects are not of such a kind or so great as to make the happy unhappy, or to produce any other such result.[68]

A reference to the same idea, i.e., the care of the dead for us, is found, from a Christian perspective, in Ruricius, Bishop of Limoges, who died about 499. Writing to console the parents of a young girl who has died, he says:

> Therefore, leaving aside something of present realities, let us think on future things so that those whom the present makes weak the future may strengthen. . . . For us Christ is our hope and our portion, our hope here in the land of the dying, our portion in the region of the living. For us this death is not the death of our natures but merely the end of this present life, because we believe that she has been renewed unto better things. . . .
>
> So, let a ready faith wipe away your tears because we believe that our dear ones have not lost life but changed it. We discern that they have left this age that is filled with struggles and have hastened to a region of beatitude; they have gone forth from a laborious pilgrimage and arrived at the homeland (*patriam*) of peace. Believe me, my dear brethren, she is already sure of her peace and solicitous for our salvation. . . . There we will all be able to rejoice together in joys that are not false but true, not temporal but eternal.[69]

---

[68] Aristotle, *Ethics*, bk. I, section XI, translated by J.A.K. Thomson; revised by Hugh Tredennick (New York: Penguin Books, 1986), p. 85.

[69] Ruricius, *Epistolae*, libri II, Epis. IV: *PL* 58, 84-85.

The words of Ruricius are almost identical with those of Cyprian: "solicitous for our salvation." St. Bernard, too, speaking of the face-to-face vision of God, said that the Saints would be "absorbed but not forgetful of the cry of the poor."[70] St. Thomas More, in his *Utopia*, expresses a similar notion, locating it within a society that is not Christian.

> But when a person dies in a cheerful and optimistic mood, nobody mourns for him. They sing for joy at his funeral, and lovingly commend his soul to God. Finally, more in a spirit of reverence than of grief, they cremate the body, and mark the spot by a column engraved with an epitaph. Then they go home and discuss the dead man's character and career, and there's nothing in his life that they dwell on with such pleasure as the happy state of mind in which he left it. This method of recalling his good qualities is thought the best way of encouraging similar virtues in the living, and also of pleasing the dead—for the subject of these discussions is believed to be present at them, though invisible to human eyes. After all, perfect happiness implies complete freedom of movement, and no one with any feeling would stop wanting to see his friends when he dies, if they'd been really fond of one another while he was alive. On the contrary, the Utopians assume that a good man's capacity for affection, like every other good thing about him, is increased rather than diminished by death. So they believe that the dead mix freely with the living, and observe everything they say and do. In fact they regard them almost as guardian angels, and this gives them greater confidence in tackling all their problems. Also, the sense of their ancestors' presence discourages any bad behavior in private.[71]

This concern of the departed for the well-being of those temporarily left behind is a matter of faith for a Catholic, part of the mystery of the union in charity and good works that exists in the Communion of Saints. Summarizing earlier teaching, the Second Vatican Council taught:

> Moreover it is not only for the sake of their example that we cultivate the memory of those in heaven, but even more so that the union in the Spirit of the whole Church might be strengthened by the exercise of fraternal charity (cf. Eph 4:1-6). Just as Christian communion among those who are on the way leads us more closely to Christ, so our fellowship with the Saints joins us to Christ from Whom, as font and head, every grace

---

[70] St. Bernard, "Sermon on the Feast of St. Victor," *Opera Omnia*, vol. VI, p. 35.
[71] Thomas More, *Utopia*, Book Two, Penguin Classics edition, trans. by Paul Turner, 1970, p. 121.

and the very life of the People of God flow. Therefore it is extremely fitting that we love these friends and coheirs of Jesus Christ, who are also our brethren and benefactors, that we give God due thanks for them and that "we suppliantly invoke them and flee to their prayers, influence and help in obtaining benefits from God through His Son Jesus Christ our Lord Who is our only Redeemer and Savior."[72] Every genuine testimony of love shown by us to those in heaven tends toward and, by its very nature, terminates in Christ Who is the "crown of all the Saints"[73] and, through Him, terminates in God Who is wonderful in His Saints and is magnified in them *(Lumen Gentium,* 50).

We invoke them, seeking their assistance and influence. That they are capable of and do give such help indicates an activity on their part, even while perfect contemplation is theirs. Such solicitude, here and now, for those on earth cannot leave those in heaven unaffected. St. Thomas at one time in his career held that the Angels and Saints can merit a certain increase in their own happiness during the interim state, and do so by leading others to salvation.

Some say that before the day of judgment the blessed are able to merit and the damned are able to demerit. But this cannot be in respect to the one's essential reward or the other's principal punishment because in relation to these things each has already arrived at his or her goal. Nevertheless, it can happen in respect to a person's accidental reward or secondary punishment. These are able to be increased up to the day of judgment. This is especially so in respect to the demons and the good Angels. The task of the good Angels is to lead others to salvation and through achieving this task the joy of the good Angels grows. The role of the demons is that of leading some to damnation and, in achieving this, their own punishment is increased.[74]

Later in life he appears to have modified his view, denying any increase in merit or demerit on the part of those, including

---

[72] This quotation within the text is taken from the Council of Trent, *DS* 1821.

[73] This quotation within the text is taken from the Invitatory for the feast of All Saints in the *Roman Breviary* (pre-Vatican II edition). It is also an invocation of the Litany of the Saints.

[74] Thomas Aquinas, *Summa Theol.,* Supplementum, q. 98, a. 6 c.

the Angels, who partake of "face-to-face" life with God.[75] Such a change—although it still allowed for an "accidental" growth in happiness for the Angels and Saints—would seem to be consistent with his views on time, knowledge, activity and the like among the Blessed. As we have seen, he tended to imagine the perfected state of the universe and mankind as a type of relative immobility. We think this way of looking at the matter is to be rejected, choosing with Augustine and others to foresee a universe that preserves its own natural motions, forms of life, and a humanity that, while enjoying the Vision of God, is enhanced in its intellectual and creative processes, not frozen into a type of ecstatic trance (although such a pejorative description would hardly do justice to Aquinas' view of the Beatific Vision).

What Thomas said in his earlier text quoted above we think to be both true and defensible. In the interim state the good can and do increase their own happiness as they see their activity on our behalf bear fruit. This growth in happiness—accidental as one would have to call it in scholastic terms—is real, nonetheless, and fully consonant with the Patristic evidence and the Church's prayers, which describe the Blessed as solicitous for our welfare.

The activity of the Elect in respect to their brothers and sisters still on pilgrimage will not be needed when the pilgrimage is over for everyone. Then there will other forms of activity.

> Nothing prevents our visualizing the mighty host of the elect human race as developing untold powers of activity with a freedom of will and resourcefulness of genius unknown to the sons of Adam while they dwell on this planet; their liberty—shall we say their initiative—will be heightened to an unknown power; and may we not think of them as doing things truly worthy of a race of giants for the glory of God and His Christ?[76]

As Arnold of Bonneval wrote, speaking of the earthly paradise:

---

[75] Aquinas, *Summa Theol.*, II, IIae, q. 13, a. 4, ad 2. "Merit and demerit belong to the state of pilgrimage. Thus the good deeds of those on the way are meritorious, evil deeds lacking in merit. In the Blessed, however, good deeds are not meritorious, but belong rather to the reward of their happiness. And likewise evil deeds among the damned are not lacking in merit but belong to the punishment of damnation." On the Angels, cf. *Summa Theol.*, I, q. 62, a. 9, ad 3.

[76] Anscar Vonier, *The Life of the World To Come*, p. 128.

The rational intellect would have, in the Creator, if it had not fallen, a fullness of truth and peace, and the vision of that one goodness would fill his whole mind.... Nothing there was sad, nothing corruptible.... There was a certain ecstasy—which however did not enervate or call man away from his proper duties but which sharpened and cleansed his mind for every work and study. Humans would work, not building something new with laborious effort but illuminating or shading something with delightful cultivation.... Without tedium, without bother would man the cultivator be able to work diligently....[77]

The God Who fashioned us with incredible talents of body and mind, Who indeed made us co-creators, will not suddenly cancel all the creativity with which He has endowed the human race. All traditional theology held that Christ enjoyed the Beatific Vision even while sojourning with us on earth, doing the work of the Father. And Jesus Himself told us that even now the Angels work while enjoying the Beatific Vision (cf. Mt 18:10), thus indicating that the Vision is not such as to immobilize humans in all but their intellective faculties. Creative work is fully consonant with the vision of God.

Creative activity will not, of course, fill all the time of the life to come. The Saints will travel! "For we should believe that we will have such bodies that we will be in any place where and when we want."[78] This ability will be greatly enhanced by the gift of agility, about which Aquinas says: "Just as by the gift of subtlety the body is completely subject to the soul ... so by the gift of agility it is subject to the soul as its mover so that it is prompt and suited to obey the spirit in all the movements and actions of the soul."[79] Even now, as the Doctor of Charity noted, "our soul is not moved by our feet but by our affections."[80] St. Thomas, who, in the case of the planets and stars, considered movement to be some form of imperfection or, at least, not necessary, did grant that the resurrected will move about. Such motion, he says, will not be instantaneous movement, but rather a form of swift, unimpeded and laborless motion. And what would be the need for instantaneous movement? There will be no rush, no sched-

---

[77] Arnold, De operibus, op. cit., 1535-1536.
[78] Augustine, Sermon 242 a (147), 5: PL 38, 1140.
[79] Aquinas, Supplementum, q. 84, a. 1.
[80] Augustine, In Iohannis Evangelium Tractatus, 48, 3: CCSL 36, p. 413.

ules to meet, no fear that anything will be missed by a tardy arrival. Travel in the life to come will serve the purposes of praise,
beauty and pleasure. St. Thomas gives us a partial reason for
such travel when he writes that this will take place so that "their
vision might be refreshed by the beauty of creatures in their diversity since in those creatures the wisdom of God will shine
forth in an eminent way."[81]

By "creatures," Thomas clearly means here Angels, other
humans or the planets and stars, since he has denied that plant
and animal creation will continue to exist. His reason, however,
is a good one. The living will move about in order to see God's
beauty and wisdom reflected in the diversity of His creatures.
Granted a greater diversity of creatures than St. Thomas envisioned, so much the greater variety of beauty. The whole universe will exist for the Saints to travel in, and to enjoy to their
hearts' content. Humans will not be alone, of course, in that universe. There will surely be the company of the blessed Angels,
and, perhaps, of other intelligent beings. Teilhard could write
with more assurance than is currently warranted:

> [Formerly] it was possible to amuse oneself with the still purely
> arbitrary idea of the plurality of inhabited worlds.
>
> The position is now completely and permanently reversed.
> There has been such a simultaneous advance in our physical
> and biological knowledge that what was pure imagination . . .
> is seen by us in the twentieth century to be *by a long way the
> most probable* alternative. . . .
>
> At an average of (at least) one human race per galaxy, that
> makes a total of millions of human races dotted all over the
> heavens.[82]

Of course, what he means to speak of is other "intelligent
races," not "human" since the human race is only our own.
Whether he ultimately proves to be correct is not our direct concern here—not even to raise the matter as an interesting speculative possibility. It is inserted simply to indicate that the Elect will
dwell in a universe so vast that it offers possibilities for travel,
cultivation and enjoyment not yet even considered or imagined.

---

[81] Aquinas. *Supplementum*, q. 84, a. 2.
[82] Teilhard, "A Sequel to the Problem of Human Origins," *Christianity and
Evolution*, pp. 231-232.

The new heaven and new earth will thus be a delight for the senses, the imagination, the memory and the intellect.

> O what pleasure sight will have! The Saints will discern the King of glory in His beauty; they will behold all the Angels and Saints, the glory of God, the glory of the Angels, the patriarchs, the prophets, the apostles, the martyrs, the confessors, the virgins. . . . They will look into their eyes, and see their faces . . . and discern their very thoughts. They will contemplate all the things that exist in the new heaven and new earth.[83]

---

[83] Honorius of Autun, *Elucidarium*, bk. III: *PL* 172, 1172.

VI

THE CITY OF COMPACT UNITY

T HE life ahead is often evoked in Sacred Scripture by the image of the New Jerusalem, the heavenly city. It is not a vision likely to appeal to all, since, for many of us, cities are not attractive places. Not infrequently, we associate them with decay, drugs, violence, disconnected and anonymous living, noise and other maladies. In truth, cities are all too often a "large-as-life" portrait of human sin and misery at their most manifest. On the other hand, there are people who find it difficult to imagine life outside of the city. For them the metropolis is synonymous with a fullness or abundance in human living.

Jerusalem and Babylon

Augustine saw the possibilities in such disparate conceptions, and his use of the contrast to describe history as the growth of two cities, the city of God and the "earthly" city, is justly famous.

> Two cities, one of the unjust, the other of the Saints, go their way from the beginning of the human race to the end of this age; they are mixed bodily but separated in will, and are to be separated even bodily on the day of judgment. For all who love pride and temporal domination, together with the empty figure and pomp of arrogance . . . and seek their own glory by the subjection of others, all these are bound together in one society. . . . And all humans and all spirits who humbly seek the glory of God and not their own, and who follow God devoutly, likewise belong to one society.[1]

> Two loves create the two cities: love of self to the contempt of God creates the earthly city; love of God to the contempt of self the heavenly city. The earthly city glories in itself, the heavenly in the Lord. The earthly seeks its glory from men; God gives to the heavenly the test of a good conscience as its greatest glory.[2]

> As Jerusalem signifies the city and society of the Saints, so Babylon signifies the city and society of the unjust.[3]

---

[1] Augustine, *On Catechizing the Uneducated (De Catechizandis Rudibus)*, XVIIII, 31: CCSL 46, p. 156.

[2] Augustine, *City of God*, bk. 14, ch. 28: CCSL 48, p. 451.

[3] Augustine, *On Catechizing the Uneducated*, XXI, 37: CCSL 46, p. 161.

It is clear that the two cities are prototypical. They are both real and symbolic. Indeed they have a symbolic value because of their reality. As Augustine recognized, his teaching on the two cities is anticipated in the Bible and especially in the Book of Revelation. There an earthly city serves in reality and in symbol as the epitome of all that is evil in human society. It is the terrible and alluring Babylon the Great, enemy and captor of Israel, as well as present and future predator that stalks God's New People. She is, however, an enemy whose fate is sealed, destined for devastation.

> After this I saw another angel coming down from heaven, having great authority, and the earth became illumined by his splendor. He cried out in a mighty voice: "Fallen, fallen is Babylon the great. She has become a haunt for demons. She is a cage for every unclean spirit, a cage for every unclean bird, a cage for every unclean and disgusting beast. For all the nations have drunk the wine of her licentious passion. The kings of the earth had intercourse with her, and the merchants of the earth grew rich from her drive for luxury."

> Then I heard another voice from heaven say: "Depart from her, my people, so as not to take part in her sins and receive a share in her plagues, for her sins are piled up to the sky, and God remembers her crimes. Pay her back as she has paid others. Pay her back double for her deeds. Into her cup pour double what she poured. To the measure of her boasting and wantonness repay her in torment and grief. . . ."

> The kings of the earth who had intercourse with her in their wantonness will weep and mourn over her when they see the smoke of her pyre. They will keep their distance for fear of the torment inflicted on her, and they will say: "Alas, alas, great city, Babylon, mighty city. In one hour your judgment has come." The merchants of the earth will weep and mourn for her, because there will be no more markets for their cargo: their cargo of gold, silver, precious stones, and pearls; fine linen, purple silk, and scarlet cloth; fragrant wood of every kind, all articles of ivory and all articles of the most expensive wood, bronze, iron, and marble; cinnamon, spice, incense, myrrh, and frankincense; wine, olive oil, fine flour, and wheat; cattle and sheep, horses and chariots, and slaves, that is, human beings. "The fruit you craved has left you. All your luxury and splendor are gone, never again will one find them."

> The merchants who deal in these goods, who grew rich from her, will keep their distance for fear of the torment inflicted

on her. Weeping and mourning, they cry out: "Alas, alas, great city, wearing fine linen, purple and scarlet, adorned in gold, precious stones, and pearls. In one hour this great wealth has been ruined."

Every captain of a ship, every traveler at sea, sailors, and seafaring merchants stood at a distance and cried out when they saw the smoke of the pyre, "What city could compare with the great city?" They threw dust on their heads and cried out, weeping and mourning: "Alas, alas, great city, in which all who had ships at sea grew rich from her wealth. In one hour she has been ruined. Rejoice over her, heaven, you holy ones, apostles, and prophets. For God has judged your case against her" (Rv 18:1-20).

The characteristics of the earthly city, Babylon, are worth noting. She is the center of commerce and trade, to whom has been given the power of the Devil for the final struggle against God's people. She will be most lamented by the earth's businessmen who "grew rich from her drive for luxury." Her children are greed, consumerism, economic and social injustice and all the immorality that accompanies an overly rich and selfish society. Rightly do the just say of her: "Fair Babylon, you destroyer, happy those who pay you back the evil you have done us! Happy those who seize your children and smash them against a rock" (Ps 137:8-9).

Every actual earthly city shares something of Babylon, and to that extent should be an object for distaste and even loathing. Once that is recognized and said, however, one must right the balance, as it were, by recalling the sage observation of Sherlock Holmes to Watson when the latter waxed eloquent on the beauties and serenity of a scenic countryside. "It is my belief, Watson, founded upon my experience, that the lowest and vilest alleys in London do not present a more dreadful record of sin than does the smiling and beautiful countryside."[4] Holmes' assertion has been expertly confirmed by Jane Marple who observes, "There is a great deal of wickedness in village life";[5] indeed "human nature is much the same everywhere, and, of

---

[4] Arthur Conan Doyle, "The Adventure of the Copper Beeches" in *The Complete Sherlock Holmes* (Garden City, NY: Doubleday and Co., Inc., 1988), p. 323.

[5] Agatha Christie, "The Bloodstained Pavement," in *Miss Marple: The Complete Short Stories* (New York: Berkeley Books, 1986), p. 57.

course, one has opportunities of observing it at closer quarters in a village."[6] One need not visit the city to see evil. The placid loveliness of St. Mary Mead is in reality a microcosm of the emotions and passions operative in all human communities.

In their comments, the two eminent detectives display a fine theological sense. Watson, entranced with the apparent, exhibits the unreflective mind. And at times we are not unlike the good doctor. There is a tendency to confuse what is beautiful and "nice" with what is "good." We observe a person of prepossessing features, well groomed, well dressed, attentive to art and literature, marked by unostentatious sophistication, courteous in speech and action. How readily we mistake these endowments for moral virtue, and how far from reality such a judgment may be and often is! One need only think of those mannered gentlemen, devotees of Mozart and Beethoven and the best in graphic arts, who ordered and even participated in the extermination of millions of people in Nazi concentration camps; or of the well-spoken and refined doctors, some of them patrons of culture, most of them rich, who murder unborn babies every day. "Dignity, and even holiness too, sometimes, are more questions of coat and waistcoat than some people imagine."[7] We are so easily deceived by appearances, ever needful of God's reminders that "man sees the face, but God sees the heart" and that if we speak with the tongues of men and Angels or even give our bodies to be burned but do not have charity, it profits nothing (cf. 1 Cor 13:1-4).

So it is with the apparent contrast between the city and rural life. Correctly perceived, both sites are marked by the ambivalence introduced into human affairs by Original Sin. What is present everywhere is only more obvious in cities because of the greater number of humans living in close proximity. Cities are often vice undisguised, while the rural landscape conceals the same iniquity under a God-made cloak of beauty. Earthly cities and rural landscapes are both marked by the ambivalence of a fallen world. They both have their share in Babylon, but they also partake of something of the heavenly city.

---

[6] Agatha Christie, "The Thumbmark of St. Peter," in *Miss Marple: The Complete Short Stories, op. cit.,* p. 72.

[7] Charles Dickens, *Oliver Twist,* ch. 37, p. 322.

As Augustine so clearly saw, the two cities are at times indistinguishable. Jerusalem is a good example. The earthly Jerusalem, as the Bible portrays her, was, in Augustine's words, a *"corpus mixtum,"* what we would call "a mixed bag." She is, apparently simultaneously, the holy city, the city of sin; city of beauty, city of desolation; city in which God is enthroned, city in which God has been killed (cf. Rv 11:8). She is Ariel (cf. Is 29:1-2), and Zion, but also Sodom and Egypt (cf. Rv 11:8); a city praised and condemned by the prophets; a city lauded in song and psalm, but also the theme of lamentation, the most poignant of which was composed by her Builder Himself Who cried over her, "Jerusalem, Jerusalem, you who kill the prophets and stone those sent to you, how many times I yearned to gather your children together as a hen gathers her brood under her wings, but you were unwilling! Behold, your house will be abandoned" (Lk 13:34-35).

Because she partook of Babylon, Jerusalem was chastised. However, in the midst of the tribulations that she suffered for her own sins, she was never completely abandoned by her Lord. Instead she was promised a better future "once the Lord has rebuilt Zion and appeared in glory" (Ps 102:17). And when He fulfilled that promise, those who had been exiled from her during her ruin would rejoice.

> Those whom the Lord has ransomed will return and enter Zion singing, crowned with everlasting joy; they will meet with joy and gladness, sorrow and mourning will flee (Is 51:11).

In that day, Jerusalem would become a "city of . . . festivals" (Is 33:20). Indeed, in the promised days of glory, the city would not be exclusively urban for it would be "in a place of rivers and wide streams" (Is 33:21). To her would come her king, "a just savior" (Zec 9:9). But this opportunity, too, we know she missed because she did not recognize the time of her inspection by that very King (cf. Lk 19:44).

Because of the geographical situation of the earthly city, one always approached her on the ascent. Whether one went to her from North or South, one always *went up* to Jerusalem: "that is where the tribes go up, the tribes of the Lord" (Ps 122:4 NIV). Therefore one prayed "Rise up, let us go [up] to Zion" (Jer 31:6); "let us climb the mount of the Lord" (Mi 4:2; cf. Is 2:3, etc.). She

was a city "on high," and so, since she she missed the time of her
visitation, it was easy enough for the disciples of Jesus to view
her as being indeed "on high." They transposed the good qualities of the earthly Zion and the promises made to her to the
heavenly city, heiress to the promises made to the earthly abode
of the Lord God. There would be a *new* Jerusalem. The creation
of God and not man, she would come from His hands intact,
beautiful and richly endowed.

> I also saw the holy city, a new Jerusalem, coming down out of
> heaven from God, prepared as a bride adorned for her husband
> (Rv 21:2).

> I heard a loud voice from the throne saying, "Behold, God's
> dwelling is with the human race. He will dwell with them and
> they will be his people and God himself will always be with
> them as their God. . . ." The one who sat on the throne said, "Be-
> hold, I make all things new." Then he said, "Write these words
> down, for they are trustworthy and true" (Rv 21:3-5).

In a certain sense, she is not completely "from above." She
exists already, this city, not completed it is true, but living here
and now, as Augustine saw, "mixed in body" with Babylon. As
such she strives to win the earth from Babylon so that it can be
saved. For Babylon is an image of what is evil in our earthly existence; it is not earthly existence itself. There are features of the
earthly city that will in fact form part of the heavenly realm. In
that sense, while the natural creation in its restoration will mirror the marvels of the Creator, the existence of the heavenly City
will always indicate that the Architect of the new Jerusalem
willed to share His creative powers with humankind. The
heavenly City—although it comes from God—will also be partly
our work, as we shall see below.

Following Augustine, the Second Vatican Council in its *Constitution on the Church in the Modern World* could say:

> Proceeding from the love of the eternal Father, founded in time
> by Christ the Redeemer, made one in the Holy Spirit, the
> Church has a saving and eschatological purpose that can only
> be fully achieved in the future age. However, she is now present
> on earth, made up of men and women, members of the earthly
> city. . . .

> The Council encourages Christians, citizens of two cities, that they strive to fulfill their earthly duties faithfully and to do so led by the spirit of the Gospel *(Gaudium et Spes,* 40 and 43).

The various communities of the earth must become ever less Babylon, ever more Jerusalem. However, until the end of this age, everything on earth is marked by elements of both Jerusalem and Babylon. Even the Jerusalem that is above is not yet fully part of the restored material creation but exists seminally in those who are already her citizens. As Isaiah says, those who live there will be called "holy" (Is 4:3). She will not come fully into existence until the "earthly city," the city of those estranged from God, is destroyed. For the time will come when the great King will have this city "burned" (Mt 22:7) and raise from it, like a phoenix, the new city that both comes down from heaven and ascends from earth. Being built already from her members who are "living stones" (cf. 1 Pt 2:5), this new city is still the object of pilgrimage. To her continue to go up the tribes of the Lord.

> No, you have approached Mount Zion and the city of the living God, the heavenly Jerusalem, and countless angels in festal gathering, and the assembly of the firstborn enrolled in heaven, and God the judge of all, and the spirits of the just made perfect, and Jesus, the mediator of a new covenant, and the sprinkled blood that speaks more eloquently than that of Abel (Heb 12:22-24).

The citizens of that City will have the physical and spiritual qualities we have already considered, and which were summarized by Honorius of Autun this way:

> They will have seven special glories of the body, and seven of the soul. In the body: beauty, swiftness, strength, freedom, delight *(voluptas),* health, immortality; in the soul, wisdom, friendship, harmony, power, honor, security, joy.[8]

The Church as the New Jerusalem

Any metropolis at its best symbolizes and helps effect the coming together of people that we call community or society, the Latin *societas.* It is, at least ideally, constituted by a variety of people who differ in nationality, race and language, and who live

---

[8] Honorius, *Elucidarium,* bk. II, ch. 17: *PL* 172, 1169.

communally and civilly, mutually enriching one another. And so it will be in the heavenly city, the City of God, the new and eternal Jerusalem. It will be, as the psalm says, a city of compact unity (cf. Ps 122:3) whose citizens are polyform.

> After this I had a vision of a great multitude, which no one could count, from every nation, race, people, and tongue. They stood before the throne and before the Lamb (Rv 7:9).

This Jerusalem will witness the end of all individualism, and the perpetual establishment of the great Catholic principle of community. By nature and by the creative purpose of God our race is social, created to live in community. And this aspect of our being is as true of the supernatural order as it is of the natural.

> It pleased God to sanctify and save men not individually, cut off from any mutual connection, but to constitute them in a people who would acknowledge Him in truth and serve Him in holiness *(Lumen Gentium, 9; cf. Gaudium et Spes, 32).*

The heavenly Jerusalem will be the Catholic Church brought to fulfillment in her catholicity and unity. As Vatican II says:

> When Christ shall appear and the glorious resurrection of the dead take place, the brightness of God will illuminate the heavenly City and its light will be the Lamb. Then the whole Church of the Saints, in the greatest happiness of charity, will adore God and "the Lamb Who was killed" (Rv 5:12), proclaiming with one voice: "To the One Who sits on the throne, and to the Lamb, blessing and honor and glory and power forever and ever" *(Lumen Gentium, 51).*

The glory of the Church then will be the end of a long and wondrous history, a record partially but beautifully outlined by a non-Catholic.

> There is not, and there never was on this earth, a work of human policy so well deserving of examination as the Roman Catholic Church. The history of that Church joins together the two great ages of human civilization. No other institution is left standing which carries the mind back to the times when the smoke of sacrifice rose from the Pantheon, and when camelopards and tigers abounded in the Flavian amphitheatre.
>
> The royal houses of Europe are as of yesterday, when compared with the line of the Supreme Pontiffs. That line we

trace back in an unbroken series, from the pope who crowned Napoleon in the nineteenth century to the pope who crowned Pepin in the eighth; and far beyond the time of Pepin the august dynasty extends, till it is lost in the twilight of fable. The republic of Venice came next in antiquity. But the republic of Venice is gone, and the papacy remains. The papacy remains, not in decay, not a mere antique, but full of life and youthful vigor.

The Catholic Church is still sending forth to the farthest ends of the world missionaries as zealous as those who landed in Kent with Augustine, and still confronting hostile kings with the same spirit with which she confronted Attila. The number of her children is greater than in any former age. Her acquisitions in the New World have more than compensated for what she has lost in the Old. Her spiritual ascendancy extends over the vast countries which lie between the plains of the Missouri and Cape Horn, countries which, a century hence, may not improbably contain a population as large as that which now inhabits Europe.

Nor do we see any sign which indicates that the term of her long dominion is approaching. She saw the commencement of all the governments and of all the ecclesiastical establishments that now exist in the world; and we feel no assurance that she is not destined to see the end of them all. She was great and respected before the Saxon had set foot in Britain, before the Frank had passed the Rhine, when Grecian eloquence still flourished in Antioch, when idols were still worshipped in the temple of Mecca. And she may still exist in undiminished vigour when some traveller from New Zealand shall, in the midst of a vast solitude, take his stand on a broken arch of London Bridge to sketch the ruins of St. Paul's.[9]

As we watch in our own day the Church arising in parts of the world where she had been mercilessly persecuted—even as Christian culture dies in many of the lands it created—one is tempted to add to Macaulay's chronicle. Honesty, however, reminds us that there is a dark side to the picture painted by Macaulay. Since the earthly members of the Church are citizens of two cities, Babylon has often left its mark on them, thus marring her beauty and obscuring the historical record for those who study it. Reality, moreover, tells us that the triumph is not won. The victory, although certain, is not yet. As we have already seen, the last battle is yet to come.

---

[9] Thomas Lord Babington Macaulay, "Essay on Von Ranke's History of the Popes," *Works of Macaulay*, vol. 6, pp. 454-455.

The Church and Israel

The Church is and will be, as Paul VI reminded us in his Creed, "the heiress of the divine promises, and the daughter of Abraham according to the Spirit, through that Israel, whose sacred Books she lovingly guards and whose patriarchs and prophets she piously venerates."[10] That first People, the vine unto whom we have been grafted, will travel with the Church until the end, fulfilling not the role she should have had but a function significant for the world's salvation nonetheless.

> Israel plays a dual part with regard to the history of the world and the salvation of the world. In what *directly* concerns this salvation, Israel has given the Saviour to the world—and is itself, through time, a living and indestructible depository of the promise of God.
>
> In what *indirectly* concerns this salvation of the world, Israel is obedient to a vocation which I think above all deserves emphasis, and which supplies a key for many enigmas. Whereas the Church is assigned the task of the supernatural and supratemporal saving of the world, to Israel is assigned, in the order of temporal history and its own finalities, the work of the *earthly leavening* of the world. Israel is here—Israel which is not of the world—at the deepest core of the world, to irritate it, to exasperate it, to *move* it. Like some foreign substance, like a living yeast mixed into the main body, it gives the world no quiet, it prevents the world from sleeping, it teaches the world to be dissatisfied and restless so long as it has not God, it stimulates the movement of history. . . .
>
> "The history of the Jews," said Leon Bloy, "dams the history of the human race as a dike dams a river, in order to raise its level."[11]

Abraham's offspring according to the flesh has experienced "a hardening . . . in part, until the full number of the Gentiles comes in" (Rom 11:25). When that happens, as Paul said in prophecy, all Israel will itself enter into what is its own by right. Indeed their coming in will be the very sign of "life from the dead" (cf. Rom 11:15), and thus, in the Church to come, Israel and

---

[10] Paul VI, *Creed: AAS*, 60 (1968), p. 440.
[11] Jacques Maritain, "The Mystery of Israel," *The Social and Political Philosophy of Jacques Maritain: Selected Readings,* Joseph Evans and Leo Ward, (Notre Dame, Ind.: University of Notre Dame Press, 1955), pp. 205 and 210.

the Gentiles will be one, the barrier having been fully broken down through the blood of Jesus the Messiah (cf. Eph 2:13-18).

Already the final state of the Church, the New Jerusalem, as exemplified in the perfection of the Beatitudes, is anticipated in the Jewish Virgin Mother of the Messiah, and in her alone, because of her bodily resurrection in the mystery of the Assumption.

> In this interim, the Mother of Jesus, just as she, already glorified in body and soul in heaven, is the image and beginning of the Church, which is to be perfected in the age to come, so she shines forth here on earth as the sign of certain hope and solace for the pilgrim People of God until the Day of the Lord arrives *(Lumen Gentium, 68).*

This city of the Elect will be the city of peace, Salem, unlike the city of this world where each of us can say:

> I see violence and strife in the city making rounds on its walls day and night. Within are mischief and evil; treachery is there as well; oppression and fraud never leave its streets (Ps 55:11-12).

What truth there is in Clement of Rome's remark, "Jealousy and contention have overturned great cities."[12] There will be no fear of such things in the heavenly city, that Jerusalem which is from above. It will be a society without institutional corruption of any kind, because it will be a community of perfected persons. Nothing will be tainted, and the harmony within each will extend to and be reflected in the entire body, when every wall of separation will have been definitively destroyed.

The Future of Our Works

As one thinks of the heavenly Jerusalem it is natural to wonder what the present city contributes to the one that is to come. What will happen to all the great achievements of our race in this present eon? Are they all to perish? Will nothing but the "moral" value of humanity's creativity perdure?

---

[12] Clement of Rome, *Ad Cor.,* VI, 4: Funk, I, p. 108.

Thou also, man! hast wrought,
For commerce of thy nature with herself,
Things that aspire to unconquerable life;
And yet we feel—we cannot choose but feel—
That they must perish. Tremblings of the heart
It gives, to think that our immortal being
No more shall need such garments; and yet man,
As long as he shall be the child of earth,
Might almost 'weep to have' what he may lose,
Nor be himself extinguished, but survive,
Abject, depressed, forlorn, disconsolate.
....

The consecrated works of Bard and Sage,
Where would they be? Oh! why hath not the Mind
Some element to stamp her image on
In nature somewhat nearer to her own?
Why, gifted with such powers to send abroad
Her spirit, must it lodge in shrines so frail?[13]

Humanity need not succumb to sorrow before such an imagined loss. What is best in the earthly city, we must presume to have its part in the city to come. The new Jerusalem will be a crystal palace showcase to display human creativity; it will be the reserve of culture and art. Although that City will come down from heaven and be God's work, humankind will have contributed to it. For not only shall men and women work creatively in it, but some of what they have created here will be preserved for the everlasting society. In a poem which, in Chesterton's words, was written "to describe the most perfect soul of music,"[14] Robert Browning vigorously affirmed the survival of our works.

Therefore to whom turn I but to thee, the ineffable Name?
Builder and maker, thou, of houses not made with hands!
What, have fear of change from thee who art ever the same?
Doubt that thy power can fill the heart that thy power expands?
There shall never be one lost good! What was, shall live as before;
The evil is null, is naught, is silence implying sound;
What was good shall be good, with, for evil, so much good more;
On the earth the broken arcs; in the Heaven a perfect round.

---

[13] Wordsworth, *The Prelude*, bk. V, lines 18-48.
[14] G.K. Chesterton, *Robert Browning* (New York: The Macmillan Co., 1916), p. 23.

All we have willed or hoped or dreamed of good shall exist;
Not its semblance, but itself; no beauty, nor good, nor power
Whose voice has gone forth, but each survives for the melodist
When eternity affirms the conception of an hour.[15]

Eternity shall affirm the conception of an hour. It is a sagacious way to anticipate the answer given by Him to Whom we pray to establish and prosper the works of our hands (cf. Ps 90:17). There is nothing of worth that shall not endure, that shall not rise into the new heavens and new earth. Much the same affirmation was made by Teilhard when he wrote:

> It is certainly a very great thing to be able to think that, if we love God, something of our inner activity, of our *operatio*, will never be lost. But will not the work itself of our minds, of our hearts, and of our hands—that is to say, our achievements, what we bring into being, our *opus*—will not this, too, in some sense be 'eternalised' and saved.
>
> Indeed, Lord, it will be—by virtue of a claim which you yourself have implanted at the very centre of my will! I desire and need that it should be. . . .
>
> Show all your faithful, Lord, in what a full and true sense 'their work follows them' into your kingdom—*opera sequuntur illos.*[16]

The words of the French theologian Rondet echo the same sentiments.

> What would the risen Gutenberg be with a body which is identical with his earthly body of flesh, but without any relation to the discovery for which he is famous? What would a Christian painter be without his work, a musician without his symphonies, a poet without his poems? And is nothing to remain of the tremendous efforts of modern industry, of engineers and workmen? Do we have to continue to say with medieval theology: '*solvet saeculum in favilla*'?[17]

The Second Vatican Council, responding to the various efforts to find some lasting value in human works, touches on this mystery in its constitution *Gaudium et Spes*:

---

[15] Robert Browning, "Abt Vogler," in *the Poems*, vol. I, edited by John Pettigrew; supplemented by Thomas Collins (New York: Penguin Books, 1981), p. 780.

[16] Teilhard de Chardin, *The Divine Milieu*, pp. 55-56.

[17] Rondet, *La théologie du travail*, quoted by Auer in Vorgrimler, vol. V, p. 197.

Although earthly progress must be sedulously distinguished from the growth of Christ's Kingdom, neverthelss, inasmuch as it is able to contribute to a more human society, such progress is of very great importance to the Kingdom of God.

The goods of human dignity, fraternal union, and liberty, that is all these goods of nature and the fruits of human industry, after we have produced them on earth in the Spirit of the Lord and according to His command, we will find again later on, but cleansed from all stain and illumined and transfigured when Christ gives back to His Father the eternal and universal Kingdom, a "Kingdom of truth and life, a Kingdom of holiness and grace, a Kingdom of justice, love and peace." Already the Kingdom is present in mystery on earth; it will be completed when the Lord comes *(Gaudium et Spes, 39)*.

One theologian notes that the "in mystery" of the last sentence of the quotation refers to the Lord's sacrifice.[18] This observation is probably correct because the preceding paragraph of *Gaudium et Spes* refers to the matter that is transformed in the celebration of the Eucharist.

The Lord has left to His own the pledge of this hope and viaticum for the journey in that Sacrament of faith in which the elements of nature, formed by men, are changed into the glorious Body and Blood, a table of fraternal communion and a foretaste of the heavenly banquet *(Gaudium et Spes, 38)*.

The idea that what happens to the bread and wine used in the celebration of Mass is like what will happen to all that we have to offer to God finds some echo in the thought of Pope John Paul II. He comments on *Gaudium et Spes*, 39, in his *Sollicitudo Rei Socialis,* saying:

However imperfect and temporary are all the things that can and ought to be done through the combined efforts of everyone and through divine grace, at a given moment of history, in order to make people's lives "more human," nothing will be *lost or will have been in vain.*[19]

To the extent that we look forward to the City to come, to that same degree do we realize how Babylon holds us captive. We weep by the streams of Babylon (cf. Ps 137), while we long for the gently flowing waters of Siloam (cf. Is 8:6, called

---

[18] Alfons Auer in Vorgrimler, vol. V, p. 198.
[19] John Paul II, *Sollicitudo Rei Socialis,* no. 48 (Boston: St. Paul Editions, 1988), p. 92.

"Shiloah" there). In such exile, and even while longing, the great consolation must be that, of our works done in and for the new Jerusalem, "nothing will be lost or will have been in vain."

The Society of Friends

For St. Augustine, the earthly city has its origin in friendship. Indeed, he saw friendship as the foundation stone of society. Marriage arose from friendship and the family was a society of friends.

> Two things are needed in this world: health and a friend. . . . God made us that we might exist and live: this is health; but, lest we exist alone, friendship was required. Therefore friendship begins from one's wife and children and extends itself to others.[20]

> A person opens his eyes to his parents, and life takes its start from their friendship.[21]

He repeats such thoughts in the very first words of his great treatment on marriage, the *De bono coniugali:*

> Because each person is a part of the human race and human nature indeed is social and has as a great and natural good the power for friendship, God willed to create all humans from one man, but also willed that they should be held together by the bond of relationship. Therefore the first natural bond of human society is that of man and wife.[22]

Thus, the Doctor of Charity is teaching that marriage is the first natural society and is a society of friends. As he noted, this primal society of friends extends itself to others, and he has left us a memorable description of some of the happiness that comes from such companionship.

> There were a wide range of things that captivated the soul in friendships: conversing and laughing together, mutually complying with one another in goodwill, reading the same books and discussing them pleasantly, wasting time together or spending it seriously, disagreeing at times without rancor as one disagrees with oneself, solidifying the very many agree-

---

[20] Augustine, Sermon Denis XVI, "On the Feast of the Scillium Martyrs," *Miscellanea Agostiniana,* I, p. 75.
[21] Augustine, *Sermon 9,* 7: CCSL 41, p. 121.
[22] Augustine, *De bono coniugali: CSEL* 41, p. 187.

ments by that very rare disagreement, mutually teaching and learning from each other, bothered by a desire for absent friends and welcoming their return with joy. By these things and by signs of this type that are like kindling wood, souls are forged together and made one out of many, for such things proceed—whether spoken or through a look or a thousand other pleasant gestures—from hearts that love and are loved in return.[23]

Augustine may be said to have summed up his thoughts on friendship when he wrote: "In all human existence there is nothing for the person who has no friend."[24] And, indicating that such friendship must be rooted in honesty, he says, "No one is able to be truly a person's friend unless he is first a lover of the truth. . . ."[25] In all this he reflects what the Lord God Himself has revealed.

A faithful friend is a sturdy shelter; he who finds one finds a treasure. A faithful friend is beyond price, no sum can balance his worth. A faithful friend is a life-saving remedy, such as he who fears God finds; for he who fears God behaves accordingly, and his friend will be like himself (Sir 6:14-17).

Augustine, of course, was not the first great thinker to reflect on the meaning and nature of friendship. Aristotle has a developed treatment of the theme in book eight of *The Nicomachean Ethics*.[26] Subsequently, the Roman philosopher and politician, Cicero, dealt with it in his *De Amicitia*. There Laelius gives as a definition: "Friendship is nothing other than harmony in respect to all human and divine matters united with benevolence and charity."[27] He expands on this when he goes on to say that friendship should be "a community of will in all things and all plans."[28] In praise of friendship, Laelius says he doubts anything greater has been given to mankind by the gods, except wisdom, and continues with the following observations.

---

[23] Augustine, *Confessions*, bk. 4 ch. 8: CCSL 27, p. 47.

[24] Augustine, *Letter 130*, 4 (To Proba): CSEL 44, p. 44.

[25] Augustine, *Letter 155*, 1: CSEL 44, p. 431.

[26] A good translation of Aristotle's work can be found in the Penguin edition, *Aristotle: Ethics*, Thomson and Tredennick (translators), London, 1976.

[27] *De Amicitia*, VI, I, 21: *Est autem amicitia nihil aliud nisi omnium divinarum humanarumque rerum cum benevolentia et caritate consensio.*

[28] Cicero, *De Amicitia*, XVII, 61.

What more pleasant than to have someone with whom you dare to speak as you would with yourself?[29] Whoever looks upon a true friend looks upon a certain likeness of the self.[30] One would seem to take the sun from the world who would take friendship from life, since we have received from the gods nothing more pleasant than friendship.[31]

Following his usual guides, Augustine and Aristotle, St. Thomas Aquinas often wrote on friendship. He did a full commentary on Aristotle's treatment of it and skillfully used the theme in his own treatments of the Eucharist and charity in the *Summa*.

Not all love has the definition of friendship, but only that love which is accompanied by benevolence, i.e., when we love someone so that we wish him good. . . . But even more than benevolence is required for friendship. There is required a certain mutual love because a friend is friend to a friend. Such mutual benevolence is founded on some kind of communication.[32]

Since true friendship is founded on the virtues, whatever is contrary to virtue in a friend is an impediment to friendship, and whatever is virtuous is evocative of friendship.[33]

Five things are proper to friendship: Each friend wishes a friend to be and to live; wishes good things for the friend; does good to the friend; lives with that friend in delight *(delectabiliter)*; agrees, delighting and sorrowing over the same things.[34]

Honorius of Autun, speaking of the fact that friendship will last in the life to come, compares the friendships that will exist there to the friendship of Scipio and Laelius.[35] In this way, he invites us to reflect upon the friendships of that great city, for the love of friendship will be one of the greatest delights of the New Jerusalem. It is there that "no one will make an enemy and no

---

[29] *Ibid.*, VI, 15: *Quid dulcius quam habere quicum omnia audeas sic loqui ut tecum?*

[30] *Ibid.*, VII, 8: *Verum enim amicum qui intuetur, tamquam exemplar aliquod intuetur sui.*

[31] *Ibid.*, XIII, 47: *Solem enim e mundo tollere videntur qui amicitiam e vita tollunt, qua nihil a deis immortalibus melius habemus nihil iucundius.*

[32] Aquinas, *Summa Theol.*, IIa, IIae, q. 23, a. 1 c.

[33] *Ibid.*, q. 106, 1, ad 3.

[34] *Ibid.*, q. 25, 7, c

[35] Honorius, *Elucidarium: PL* 172, 1170.

one will lose a friend."[36] Already the Fathers of the Church realized this truth, and saw it as an additional reason to long for that homeland.

> We must consider, beloved brethren, and reflect again and again on the fact that we have renounced the world and that we dwell here for the duration as guests and pilgrims. Let us embrace the day that assigns each of us his dwelling and that, having rescued us from here and released us from the snares of the world, restores us to paradise and the kingdom. What person, having been in a foreign country, would not hasten to return to his native land? Who, when hurrying to sail to his loved ones, would not hope more eagerly for a favorable wind so that he might more quickly embrace his dear ones?
>
> We consider Paradise to be our country; we have already begun to have the patriarchs as our parents; why do we not hasten and run to see our country, so that we can greet our parents? There a great number of our loved ones await us; a thronging and plentiful crowd of parents, brothers and children desires us, already secure in their inability to be harmed yet still solicitous for our salvation. What a great joy it is both for them and for us together to come into their sight and embrace! What pleasure there in the heavenly kingdom without the fear of dying, and what a great and perpetual happiness with an eternity for living!
>
> There are the glorious choir of apostles, there the throng of exulting prophets, there the innumerable group of martyrs, crowned because of the victory of their struggle and passion; there the triumphant virgins who have subdued the concupiscence of the flesh and body by the strength of their continence; there the merciful are rewarded who have done works of justice by giving food and alms to the poor, who, observing the precepts of the Lord, have transferred their earthly patrimony to the heavenly treasures.
>
> Let us hurry to them, beloved brethren, with eager longing, and let us pray that we may quickly be with them and that we may come speedily to Christ. May God see this as our thought. May Christ the Lord, Who will give more ample rewards of His glory to those whose longings for Him have been greater, look upon this resolution of our mind and faith.[37]

---

[36] Augustine, *Sermon 256*, 3: PL 38, 1193.
[37] Cyprian of Carthage, *De Mortalitate*, no. 26: CCSL 3A, pp. 31-32.

Cyprian is encouraging the faithful to look forward to the resumption of perfected friendships in the life to come. In this life, unfortunately, we know that friendships are not without their difficulties. The obstacles to concordant human relationships are many indeed. Augustine, himself aware of this, said:

> There is a dire necessity in the human race: to be unaware of what is in another's heart, and so frequently we think badly of a faithful friend, and frequently we think well of an unfaithful friend. O harsh necessity! . . . What can you do so that today you can see into the heart of your brother? There is nothing you can do.[38]

Shakespeare wrote one of his great plays, *Othello,* on the ideas captured in those words of Augustine. He sets before us Iago, friend to no one but himself; friend self-made according to the mold of him who kissed his Friend to death after Satan had entered in; false friend to Othello whom he served for gain:

> *Were I the Moor, I should not be Iago.*
> *In following him, I follow but myself.*
> *Heaven is my judge, not I for love and duty,*
> *But seeming so, for my peculiar end;*
> *For when my outward action doth demonstrate*
> *The native act and figure of my heart*
> *In complement extern, 'tis not long after*
> *But I will wear my heart upon my sleeve*
> *For daws to peck at, I am not what I am.*
>
> (*Othello,* Act I, scene 1.)

False friend to Cassio, whose goodness rankled him, and to Roderigo whom he uses as a dupe to kill Cassio.

> Now, whether he kill Cassio
> Or Cassio him, or each do kill the other,
> Every way makes my gain. Live Roderigo,
> He calls me to a restitution large
> Of gold and jewels that I bobbed from him
> As gifts to Desdemona.
> It must not be. If Cassio do remain,
> He hath a daily beauty in his life
> That makes me ugly.
>
> (Act V, scene 1.)

---

[38] Augustine, Second Commentary on Ps. 30 [*Ennarr. in Psalmos,* Ennarr. II in Ps. 30, 13]: CCSL 38, p. 200.

It is partly a fear of such false friendships that often impedes the very beginnings of fellowship in this life. What will the other be like? Can he or she be trusted? We are all too acquainted with the fact that even some "friends" who have nothing of the full evil of Iago in them cannot always be relied upon. The experience described by Hugo is all too common.

> Some people are malicious from the mere necessity of talking. Their conversation, chatter in the drawing room, gossip in the antechamber, is like those fireplaces that rapidly burn up wood; they need a great deal of fuel; the fuel is their neighbor.[39]

As Hugo intimates, there are not too many things more detrimental to human relations than the evils done by speech. A loose tongue, with its off-handed backbiting, its delight in rumor and idle gossip, is a threat to harmony, and is powerfully portrayed as a monster by Virgil.

Extemplo Libyae magnas it Fama per urbis,
Fama, malum qua non aliud velocius ullum.
Mobilitate viget virisque adquirit eundo;
parva metu primo, mox sese attollit in auras,
ingrediturque solo, et caput inter nubila condit,
....
—pedibus celerem et pernicibus alis,
monstrum horrendum, ingens, cui, quot sunt corpore plumae,
tot vigiles oculi subter (mirabile dictu),
tot linguae, totidem ora sonant, tot subrigit auris.
....
tam ficti pravique tenax quam nuntia veri.
Haec tum multiplici populos sermone replebat
gaudens, et pariter facta atque infacta canebat.

At once Gossip travels through the great cities of Libya,
Gossip, than which no other evil is swifter.
It thrives on movement and gathers strength as it goes;
small at first through fear, soon it moves into the open,
it treads the earth and places its head among the clouds.
....
—swift of foot and agile of wing,
a monster to be feared, and powerful, the feathers of whose body
are as numerous as the vigilant eyes beneath (a marvel to speak of),
with as many tongues, as many mouths, as many attentive ears.
....
as tenacious a messenger of lies and perversity as of truth.
It fills the peoples with multifold talk
and, rejoicing, sings equally of what is fact and fiction.
(Virgil, Aeneid, bk. IV, lines 173ff)

---

[39] Victor Hugo, *Les Miserables*, Fantine, bk. V, "The Descent," VIII, p. 178.

Like Virgil, most of us are aware of how such gossip, once started, cannot be stilled; it thrives on movement. Even knowledge that it is false does not check it. "What does the world, told truth, but lie the more?"[40] St. James was moved to give stern warning about the evils that flow from the tongue (cf. Jas 3:1-12), and notes that "if anyone does not fall short in speech, he is a perfect man, able to bridle his whole body also" (3:2). And such shall the Saints be, with mouths that speak out of the abundance of hearts filled with charity, and that, thereby, build up rather than tear down the tranquility of the new Jerusalem.

In addition to the sins of the tongue, what harms our peace here, and always threatens friendships, are our congenital insecurities. Will others like us? Can we trust our hearts, our thoughts, our secrets to them. We realize how suspicion and misunderstanding destroy relationships, and so even with our closest friends there is often a reticence, a holding-back, an inability to communicate or express all that we think or feel or are. No such limitations to friendship will exist in heaven. There,

> You will all know everyone. Those who are there will not be known because you will see their faces; in the life to come there will exist mutual recognition because of greater awareness. . . . When they are filled with God, they will see in a divine way. There will not exist anything that offends nor anything that hides knowledge.[41]

When he says that there will be nothing that hides knowledge, Augustine is addressing a common difficulty. People do not always reveal what they truly think or feel. There can be "hidden agendas" in relationships, and the recognition that such can happen readily fosters doubt. The future, he says, will preserve the Saints from such things. Each will be to the other an "open book" in the life to come. There will be nothing to hide where mutual love and perfect happiness will be shared by all. On the contrary, the next life will be all the good things we experience in friendship brought to completion. In that land will be reunion with those known and loved here (including reunions with those we never knew in the flesh but who became our

---

[40] R. Browning, "The Pope," *The Ring and the Book*, line 672.
[41] Augustine, *Sermon 243, 6: PL* 38, 1146.

friends in the Communion of Saints); there will be as well friendships newly formed with all the saved.

> Trusting on a most sure promise we hope that we in this life—from which we will migrate and from which we have not lost, but merely sent ahead, those of our own who have migrated before us—will arrive at that life where they will be to us more dear since they will be better known and more lovable since there will be no fear of separation.[42]

The just will recognize their own and delight in seeing them again. Already St. Ignatius of Antioch referred to this truth when he wrote to Polycarp: ". . . I am full of thanksgiving to God that I was worthy to see your holy face, which I hope to enjoy forever in God."[43]

In this community of friendship, the civilization of love spoken of by Paul VI, people shall learn from one another, as we have already indicated when treating of the question of knowledge in the future life.

The Order of Charity

In thinking of friendship, it may be important to note that in the life to come everyone will be loved by each, but not in the same way or to the same degree. Christian charity is frequently depicted as an undifferentiated love, wherein we feel or will the same for everyone. This in fact is not the case. There is an order of charity, according to which we must love some more than others. What is more, this order will continue to exist in heaven. St. Thomas teaches this explicitly.

> Even according to the order of affection we should love one more than another. The reason for this is that, since the principle of love is God and the one loving, it is necessary that, according to their greater nearness to one or the other of these two, the greater is the affection of love.[44] Thus it is not necessary to love all equally.[45] In the homeland the order of love will be determined by a person's closeness to God. Thus the better will be loved more by us. Nevertheless it happens that in the

---

[42] Augustine, *Letter 92, To the Lady Italica,* 1: CSEL 34, 2, p. 437.
[43] Ignatius of Antioch, *Ad Polycarpum,* I, 1: Funk, I, p. 288.
[44] Aquinas, *Summa Theol.,* IIa, IIae, 26, 6 c.
[45] *Ibid.,* ad 1.

homeland people will love those united to them for many reasons, for the motives of virtuous love will not cease to exist in the souls of the blessed. Nevertheless to all these reasons the reason for love that is derived from nearness to God will be incomparably preferred.[46]

Those closest to God will be most loved, but there will exist as well special ties that will exist as "motives of virtuous love" uniting the Saints in particular ways. Writing further on the order of charity, Thomas says that "the affection of charity that comes from grace is no less ordered than natural appetite that is an inclination of nature since both inclinations proceed from divine wisdom."[47] This is an important statement for it shows the congruence between the natural and the supernatural, and it bears on all that we have been considering. Nature carries within itself the stamp of divine wisdom and mirrors grace and the supernatural. So much more will nature do this in the life to come. Life here is prologue; it has a sequel, and that sequel will build on what exists and is developed now. For that reason, although loves will be purged of all selfishness and every evil aspect of exclusivity, husbands and wives who are among the Elect will love each other in a way not shared with others. So too will those who are friends here love one another distinctly there. We see this truth reflected now in a simple but significant sentence in the Roman Canon of the Mass. Having remembered in the first place the "Blessed Virgin Mary, Mother of Our Lord and God, Jesus Christ," we remember next "Joseph, her Spouse." We remember not him who *was* her spouse, but who even yet and forever *is* her spouse.

Among those who will be loved for their closeness to the Lord will be those poor whose willing endurance and sufferings promoted the salvation of others more abundantly blessed now with the good things of this world. Often neglected or even scorned in the present, such people will be recognized and thanked in the future for the great good they have done for others. Speaking of their role there in relation to us, St. John Chrysostom said that "they are the ones who build our heavenly homes."[48]

---

[46] *Ibid.,* 13 c.
[47] *Ibid.,* 6 c.
[48] Chrysostom, *In Epist. ad Hebraeos,* Homily 32: *PG* 63, 223.

Conversation

We have already said something about time and travel in the life to come. Some of that travel will be for no more profound but also for no more pleasant reason than for the sake of visiting others, and spending time with them. Hoping for our own share in the life to come, we can anticipate with delight the conversations to be enjoyed in the life ahead with those we have loved here and others we will learn to love there. Thinking of what such pleasurable discourse has meant to us, we recall the record our guide has left us of one of the more memorable conversations in human history.

> The day—known to You, unknown to us—on which she was to depart from this life was close, and it happened (brought about, I believe, by Your hidden ways) that she and I were standing alone, leaning on a certain window that looked out on the garden that was within the house where we stayed. This was at Ostia on the Tiber where, removed from the crowds after the labors of a long journey, we were resting ourselves before sailing. In this way we were speaking alone most pleasantly, forgetting what lay behind us and intent on what lay ahead. Between ourselves and in the presence of the Truth, which You are, we were asking what the future and eternal life of the Saints might be like, that life which neither eye has seen nor ear has heard nor has it entered into the heart of man. Nevertheless, we opened the mouth of our hearts, longing for the heavenly waters of Your fountain, the fountain of life that is with You, so that, sprinkled by it, we might in some manner and according to our powers of comprehension think about so great a reality.
>
> And when our talk was led to the conclusion that the delight of our bodily senses—whatever that delight might be, viewed in whatever corporeal light You wish—was not comparable to the pleasure of that life and did not even seem worthy of mention, we raised ourselves up with a more ardent effort, and traveled little by little beyond all bodily things and even heaven itself from which the sun, moon and stars shine on the earth. And still we climbed interiorly, thinking of, speaking about and wondering at Your works. We came to our own souls and transcended them so that we might touch the region of unfailing fullness where You feed Israel forever on the food of truth. There life is the Wisdom through which all these things come to exist, the things that are and were and will be, although this Wisdom itself does not come to be but is now as it was and always will

be. Rather, better to say that "was" and "will be" are not in that Wisdom, but only the present since that Wisdom is eternal; for to have been and to be are not eternal. And while we spoke and longed for that Wisdom, we touched it momentarily, in the beat of a heart. We sighed, and left the first fruits of the spirit bound there, and came back to the sound of our own mouth where a word begins and has an end. For what is like Your Word, O Lord, which remains in itself without aging and renewing all things?[49]

I would more prefer to have overheard that conversation than all the dialogues of Socrates. It has so much of what occurs on those occasions in which we are, in Wordsworth's words, "surprised by joy." Two persons who love one another, complementary in spirit, capable of enjoying the beauties of creation, more blessed yet in being able to see beyond creation to its Creator, and, most wonderful of all, sharing God—if only momentarily—together. Such levels of dialogue as that given Augustine and Monica are beyond us, but most of us are capable of recalling periods of communication with those we love that stand out and rise above what ordinarily passes for conversation. In the best of such discourse we find joy, a sense of solidarity, food for the imagination and mind and (it is to be hoped) God. Especially blessed are those conversations that not only are held in Him but aver to Him directly. This, of course, will always be the case in the life to come since then the immediate vision of God will be enjoyed by all of the Elect at all times. In each converse He will be the Presence that facilitates the discourse and causes its joys, even while He is being delighted in for Himself.

What will one talk about there? Surely the Saints will reminisce, making use of the heightened power of memory and the better perception of the events of this life. They will speak of the beauties of the restored nature and of their current activity and creative efforts in that restored world. They will speak of God, always present to each and all "face to face" but capable of being shared in different perspectives with different people and at different times. And all such conversations will take place, as St. Thomas wrote in one of his own more exuberant moods, *delectabiliter,* in delight.

---

[49] Augustine, *Confessions*, bk. 9, ch. 10: CCSL 27, pp. 147-148.

The Angels and the Saints

Those saved will enjoy the company of the Angels with whom they have prayed so often here on earth. Finally they will be truly recognized as having been companions in prayer. The Blessed will acknowledge their Guardian Angels who have enlightened, watched over and guided them home. And, if there should be in the life to come other creatures, non-human but material and intelligent like ourselves, it will be no great surprise to many of the Blessed. They have always anticipated such a possibility in their acceptance of the reality of the angelic spirits. Indeed the Angels help us understand that the wonders of matter and even the Incarnation itself do not encompass all the possible expressions of God's grandeur. As *expressed* His beauty is imitable without limit.

In raising the question about other beings, we may as well ask ourselves about the variety of creatures that we already know as existing, some of them—to our way of looking at things—far from beautiful. Why, for instance, the existence of cockroaches? Will they and all the other creatures that we individually and perhaps collectively find ugly exist in the new creation? We have already noted the great number of species that have become extinct in the course of the history of our own planet. Others face the same fate. Will they all be restored—at least as a species—for the life to come? If not, are there others that God will let disappear forever? To such questions we have no answers.

Perhaps some of the creatures for which we can see no need or that we find repulsive would never have existed if our race had not fallen. If so, then one may surmise that the Fall, with its consequent blinding of the human intellect and perception, rendered us incapable of seeing and appreciating things for what they are. We know this from experience. Some people never detect the nuances in anything; things must be large or flashy to be appreciated. One tree is like another, one flower like every flower, one body like any other: all to be enjoyed, if they are truly enjoyed, without any appreciation of the finer variations in each. And, to an extent, we all share in such lack of perception. It is perhaps because of this very obtuseness, our slowness to appreciate the degrees of beauty in being, that God created the enormous constrasts in the universe: so that what is deemed ugly would help to highlight the beautiful.

In the life to come such vast contrasts of type will not be needed. The slightest difference will be greatly magnified; nothing will be missed and every aspect even of what was familiar will take on new contours of meaning and beauty. Blade of grass will clearly differ from blade of grass. So it is already with the Angels; each is a separate species, says Aquinas. This is so, not because they are different things, but because what we discern simply as "Angel" is so rich in variety from its companions that we can only describe it by calling it a different species. That too will be the experience of those who see and know them. They, like all the invisible creation, will offer as much variety as the material order offers now and will offer more abundantly then. And the Saints will be like the Angels, the most minute differences in each personality being regarded and relished in a way we repeatedly fail to do now because of our opaque or narcissistic vision.

The Mother of All the Living

In the company of the Angels and together with all who may share the life to come, the citizens of the New Jerusalem will share life with her who "on an earth covered over with the dirt of sin opened out as the most beautiful flower that has ever blossomed in the garden of mankind."[50] They will take a special pride and delight in Mary who—with but the exception of her Son— surpasses all the beauties and wonders of creation, even while adding a unique luster to everything else. The words of St. Anselm of Canterbury's *Prayer to Our Lady* speak of this loveliness and surpass even the words put by Dante on St. Bernard's lips in the *Paradise.*

> O Begetter of the Life of my soul, the one who nourished the Restorer of my flesh, the one who gave milk to the Savior of my whole being, what shall I say of you? My tongue is deficient because the mind is insufficient. . . . What shall I worthily say to

---

[50] Pope Paul VI, "Sermon '*E motivo*' of Sept. 8, 1964," *New Horizons for the Women Religious* (Boston: St. Paul Editions), p. 6.

the Mother of my Creator and Savior, through whose holiness my sins are purged, through whose integrity incorruptibility is given to me, through whose virginity my soul is loved by its Lord and espoused by its God? What, I ask, shall I say to the Mother of my God and Lord, through whose fecundity I am a ransomed captive, through whose birth-giving I am freed from eternal death, and through whose Offspring I, lost, am found and led back from the exile of misery to my homeland of happiness? . . . O Lady, portal of life and gate of salvation, way of reconciliation and doorway of restoration, I beg you through your saving fecundity to see that pardon for my sins and the grace of living well be granted to me, and that this your servant may be protected to the end in your custody. . . .

Heaven and the stars, earth and waters, day and night and whatever is subject to the power or use of the human race congratulate themselves that through you, my Lady, they have been raised up in a certain way to their lost beauty and been given a certain new and ineffable grace. For all things, as it were, were dead; having lost their native dignity to please God and their ability to sing His praises, for which purposes they had been made, they were clothed over with oppression and discolored by being used by those who serve idols, for which purposes they were not made. Restored, as it were, they truly rejoice; for now they are ruled by those who confess God and His dominion and they are made beautiful in being used. They rejoice as it were with a new and inestimable grace since they experience God Himself, the Creator Himself, not only ruling over them invisibly but even behold Him visibly among themselves and using them for sanctification. And all these good things have come to the world through the blessed fruit of the blessed womb of blessed Mary. . . .

O Woman marvelously singular and singularly marvelous, through whom the elements are renewed, the lower regions are repaired, the demons are trampled, humankind is saved and the Angels are reintegrated! . . . O blessed and more than blessed Virgin, through whose blessing every nature is blessed, not only created nature by the Creator, but the Creator by created nature as well! . . . O Woman, beautiful to look at, lovely to contemplate, delectable to love! . . .

Nothing is equal to Mary, nothing, God excepted, is greater than Mary. . . . All nature is created by God, and God is born of Mary. God created all things, and Mary gave birth to God. The God Who made all things is Himself made from Mary and in this way He remakes all that He had made. He Who was able to make everything from nothing did not wish to remake what had been ruined unless He first be made the Son of Mary. Thus, God is the Father of things created, Mary the Mother of things re-created. God is the Father of the construction of all things, Mary the Mother of the reconstruction of all things. God begot Him through Whom all things were made, and Mary bore Him through Whom all things are saved. God begot Him without Whom there is nothing at all, and Mary bore Him without Whom there is nothing at all that is good. Oh, truly "the Lord is with you" to whom the Lord granted that all nature should be as much in debt as to Himself. . . .

The Mother of God is our Mother. The Mother of Him in Whom Alone we hope and Whom Alone we fear is our Mother. The Mother of Him Who Alone saves . . . is our Mother. . . . O Mary, how much we owe you! Lady and Mother, through whom we have a Brother such as Him, what thanks or praise can we give you?[51]

Since the days long ago when St. Justin (c. 150) and St. Irenaeus (c. 190) recognized her as the New Eve, the Church has ever more fully come to realize that the new creation, with its new earth and new heaven, is to be peopled by those who are children of the Mother of all the living (cf. Gn 3:20). Like the first Eve and the sleeping Adam, Mary is born from the side of the new Adam. It is the sleep of Jesus on the Cross, the redemptive death of the Messiah, that preserved His Mother by anticipation from all stain of sin, original and personal. That sleep of the Lord was immediately preceded by His giving over of the Spirit Whose activity, with Mary's cooperation, makes the renewed race and prepares the new Eden.

The Church too is born from the side of the sleeping Christ. Like Mary, the Church is mother, although Mary is so in a more eminent way for the Church herself learns motherhood from Mary, and indeed only cooperates with Mary in giving birth to the members of Christ. As Vatican Council II teaches, "Mary is Mother to us in the order of grace" *(Lumen Gentium,* 61).

Furthermore this maternity of Mary in the economy of grace lasts uninterruptedly from the consent that she faithfully offered at the Annunciation and sustained without hesitation beneath the Cross until the perpetual consummation of all the Elect. Assumed into heaven, she does not lay aside this salvific

---

[51] Anselm, *Oratio VII: Ad sanctam Mariam pro impetrando eius et Christi amore, Opera Omnia,* vol. 3, pp. 19-24.

office, but by her multifold intercession continues to obtain for us the gifts of eternal salvation. With her motherly love she takes care of the brothers and sisters of Christ who are still on pilgrimage in the midst of dangers and sorrows *(Lumen Gentium,* 62).

When the Council says that Mary's maternal function lasts "until the perpetual consummation of all the Elect," the *until* must be understood in the same sense that Matthew used when he wrote that Joseph "had no relations with [his wife] until she bore a son" (Mt 1:25). As is clear from a consideration of Greek as well as English usage, the word "until" does not necessarily mean that there is a change once the "until" arrives. When we say that so-and-so was faithful to her husband until the day she died, we do not mean that she began to be unfaithful to him after she died. What the Council is teaching is that Mary's maternal role will always continue, but that it is especially important now while some of her children are still on pilgrimage.

One can rightly distinguish two aspects to Mary's motherhood, an active and passive one. Until the consummation of all the Elect, her role continues to be one of active maternity, by which we mean that she is *still giving birth.* By her necessary cooperation with the Holy Spirit she brings to birth not only Christ the head of the Body but all the members of the Body as well. This parturition will not end until this age has wholly passed over into the everlasting Kingdom. As intercessor and Mediatrix of grace, the Mother of the Church is the channel for the life of charity in those who belong to her Son. When the Body has come to full stature, then Mary's active motherhood will stop; she will however continue to be the Mother who has given life and nurtured and guided all those who conquer the dragon, her enemy. Then she, like all her children, will rest to enjoy the fruits of her labor.

Mary is not only Mother; she is also the prototype of the heavenly City, the New Jerusalem. Already in her the future of that City is revealed in glory. At the end of this age, when the census of those who inhabit that City is complete, Mary's full role as Mother and role-model will be manifest.

There is an illuminating dialogue in the Acts of the Apostles on the occasion when Paul is being flogged in Jerusalem. He asks the centurion, "It is lawful for you to scourge a man who is a Roman citizen?" (Acts 22:25).

> Then the commander came and said to [Paul], "Tell me, are you a Roman citizen?" "Yes," he answered. The commander replied, "I acquired this citizenship for a large sum of money." Paul said, "But I was born [a citizen]" (Acts 22:27-28).

One can catch in the words of the one a sense of awe, in the other a sense of self-assurance, being the citizen of no mean city. And so it often is for those who come from an important place. Not everyone is born in Nazareth; some with pride find their origins in the capital. Spiritually, of course, every worthy Jew claimed the capital as his or her home. It is this sense of prideful belonging that the Psalmist captures, even as, in unusual but inspired magnanimity, he envisions citizenship in Zion being extended to the Gentiles: Philistines, Egyptians and Babylonians.

> The Lord loves the city founded on holy mountains, loves the gates of Zion more than any dwelling in Jacob. Glorious things are said of you, O city of God! From Babylon and Egypt I count those who acknowledge the Lord. Philistia, Ethiopia, Tyre, of them it can be said: "This one was born there." But of Zion it must be said: "They were all born here." The Most High confirms this; the Lord notes in the register of the peoples: "This one was born here." So all sing in their festive dance: "Within you is my true home" (Ps 87:1-7).

The Church chooses this psalm as one of those to be prayed on the feasts of Mary, interpreting it to signify that in the life to come it will truly be recounted of each and every one of the Saints: "This one was born [in her]," namely in and from Mary. In that life each will personally say to the Mother of God, "All my fountains are in you."

The manner in which the psalm is used here helps us to understand the freedom exercised by the Church in her use of Israel's hymns, and her insight as well. Zion becomes the heavenly city. Zion is also understood as connoting Mary who is truly the Mother of all the inhabitants of that city as well as the model for the entire city's own future. In this way, the Church prays the Psalmist's words with eyes and heart opened and widened by the fullness of Revelation that came with Mary's Son. In Him even the past takes on not a different but a fuller meaning. As Vatican Council II teaches, quoting Augustine:

God, the inspirer and author of the books of both Testaments, so wisely disposed things that the New Testament would lie hidden in the Old and the Old would be made clear in the New. For although Christ established a new Covenant in His blood, the Books of the Old Testament are integrally assumed in the preaching of the Gospel, and acquire and show forth their full meaning in the New Testament (cf. Mt 5:17; Lk 24:27; Rom 16:25-26; 2 Cor 3:14-16) while it illumines and explains them *(Dei Verbum, 16).*

Christ Himself and His Mother have always been particular examples of what the Church is teaching here. For the Church sees that the Old Testament prepared for and, in various ways, anticipated the new Adam and His associate. Their coming was prophesied and prefigured. The New Testament writers understood this and were followed in this by the Fathers of the Church. The application of Psalm 87 to Our Lady is an example of a type of Patristic exegesis, the value of which has often been indicated in ecclesiastical documents.

[In respect to the exegesis of Scripture] from our present day point of view, the method of the Fathers presents certain undeniable limits. They did not know, and could not have known, about the resources of a philological, historical and anthropological-cultural order, nor the input of research, documentation and scientific elaboration that are available to modern exegesis; and therefore, a part of their work is to be considered timeworn. Nonetheless, their merits for a better understanding of the Sacred Books are incalculable. They are still true teachers for us and superior in many ways to the exegetes of the Middle Ages and the modern era due to "a sort of sweet intuition about heavenly things through an admirable peneration of spirit, whereby they go farther into the depths of the divine word" (Pius XII, *Divino Afflante).* The example of the Fathers can indeed teach modern exegesis a truly religious approach to the Sacred Scriptures as well as an interpretation that constantly adheres to the criterion of communion with the experience of the Church proceeding through history under the guidance of the Holy Spirit. When these two interpretative principles—religious and specifically Catholic—are neglected or forgotten, modern exegetical studies often result in being impoverished and distorted.

That exegesis in which spiritual life is blended with rational theological reflection always aims at the essentials, while being faithful to the entire sacred deposit of the faith. It is entirely centered on the mystery of Christ to whom all the individual truths are referred in a wonderful synthesis. . . . The Fathers seek to embrace the totality of the Christian mystery by following the basic movement of Revelation and of the economy of salvation that goes from God through Christ to the Church, sacrament of union with God and dispenser of divine grace, in order to return to God. Thanks to this insight, due to their lively sense of ecclesial communion, to their proximity to Christian origins and familiarity with Scripture, the Fathers look at the whole in its center and make this whole present in each of its parts, reconnecting each outer question with itself. Following the Fathers in their theological itinerary means, therefore, grasping more easily the essential nucleus of our faith and the *specificum* of our Christian identity.[52]

Like the Church Fathers, we must look at the "whole [of Revelation] in its center and make this whole present in each of its parts." Proximate to that center Who is Christ is His Mother through whom God became a human to sum up in Himself the whole of Revelation. In the life to come she remains beside Him, His Mother and Mother of all the living. What delight there shall be in seeing her, conversing with her, having her as Mother and friend. We must imagine periods with her like that between Augustine and his natural mother at Ostia. Indeed, the scene at Ostia with mother and child should be recognized as only a hint of what will occur in the life to come as the Mother of all speaks intimately with each of her own.

Dante describes the first sight of her.[53]

Vidi a lor giochi quivi e a lor canti ridere una bellezza che litizia era ne li occhi a tutti li altri santi;	*I saw a Beauty smile on the angelic games and songs, a Beauty that was joy to the eyes of all the other Saints.*
e s'io avessi in dir tanta divizia quanta ad imaginar, non ardirei lo minimo tentar di sua delizia.	*And if I had the power to speak such riches as is possible to imagine, I would not dare attempt to speak the least of her delights.*

---

[52] Congregation for Catholic Education, *Instruction on the Study of the Fathers of the Church in the Formation of Priests* (Nov. 1989), nos. 26-27, *TPS*, vol. 35, no. 3, pp. 175-176.

[53] Dante, *Paradise*, canto 31 and 32.

*Riguarda omai ne la faccia che a Christo
piu si somiglia, che la sua chiarezza
sola ti puo disporre a veder Christo.
Io vidi sopra lei tanta allegrezza
piover, portata ne le menti sante
create a trasvolar per quella altezza,
che quantunque io avea visto davante,
di tanta ammirazion non mi sospese,
ne me mostro de Dio tanta sembiante.*

Now look upon that face which is most similar to that of Christ; its clarity alone can dispose you to see the Christ. I saw such happiness rain upon her, joy carried in the holy minds created to traverse such heights, that whatever I had seen previously did not fill with such admiration nor show me so great a likeness to God.

Dante.

In the scene depicted by Italy's Virgil, Our Lady is surrounded by her children, the Saints of the Lord who both preceded and followed her in time. They exult in her glory, but she in turn glorifies them. Like her Creator and her Son, Mary delights in seeing glory shared, not grasped. And through her the Son she bore, the mysteries of His life, indeed the very mystery of the Trinity is magnified.

> *Hail Mary, Mother of God, World's Treasure;*
> *You are the dwelling that held Him Whom the universe cannot contain.*
> *In your virginal womb you have embraced the Immense and Incomprehensible.*
> *Through you, the Blessed Trinity is worshiped and glorified.*
> *Through you, the inestimable Cross is everywhere revered and adored.*
> *Through you, the heavens exult, the angels and archangels rejoice.*
> *Through you, the devils are scattered, the Tempter is driven from heaven.*
> *Through you, our fallen race is raised to heaven.*
> *Through you, joy of the universe, all have come to know the truth.*
> *Mother and Virgin, you are an ever-shining Light, and the gauge of true doctrine.*   (Mansi, *IV, 1251*)

She takes nothing from the glory of God, serving only to reflect His majesty. This Hopkins conveyed to us when he wrote:

> *Through her we may see him*
> *Made sweeter, not made dim,*
> *And her hand leaves his light*
> *Sifted to suit our sight.*[54]

What she does now and has always done for her God/Son, namely transmit His light without alteration, seeing Him made sweeter and not more dim, she will do forever for all who are her children in Him. Dante's vision too points this out. Nonetheless, the description given us by Alighieri is, for all its beauty, somewhat static. The Queen Mother sits surrounded by her heavenly family.

Much more dynamic a picture of Miriam of Nazareth, the new Eve, is presented in a sermon that was long attributed to Augustine. There Our Lady is compared to Miriam, the sister of Moses, who, after the crossing of the Red Sea, led the Hebrews in a song of joy.

> The prophetess Miriam, Aaron's sister, took a tambourine in her hand, while all the women went out after her with tambourines, dancing; and she led them in the refrain (Ex 15:20-21).

No sedate Queen is the Mother of God in this view. Calling her "our tambourine player" (*"tympanistria nostra"*), the homilist imagines her dancing with the abandon of her ancestor David (cf. 2 Sm 6:14), leading the procession of all Saints who sing with her, "My soul magnifies the Lord."[55]

The image is fitting. Her life in heaven now and in the world to come, like that of her children, will not be the repose of the tired, but the rest of the rejoicing and creative. Like the industrious citizens of the abuilding Carthage, *dux femina facti*,[56] so too a woman shall lead the occupations of the citizens of the heavenly City, even as she directs their attention to the King.

---

[54] G.M. Hopkins, "The Blessed Virgin Compared to the Air We Breathe," *Hopkins Reader*, edited by John Pick, Image Books (New York: Doubleday, 1966), pp. 72-73.
[55] Cf. Augustine, *Sermon 144: PL* 39, 2105.
[56] *Aeneid*, bk. I, 364.

St. Joseph

Missing from Dante's description is the husband of the Ever Virgin. His absence is not surprising since a proper estimation of the role and place of Joseph grew only gradually in the Church. The slowness of the development was due to the natural human tendency to recognize and reward the achievements of those who *act*. Thus, the Baptist, Peter, other Apostles, the martyrs and many others have normally been given some measure of their merited attention. In the life to come, however, what will distinguish one from another is proximity to God, to the Messiah and to His Mother. Such nearness is what constitutes true virtue and dignity.

Since this is the case, "St. Joseph is the model of those humble ones that Christianity raises up to great destinies; ... he is the proof that in order to be a good and genuine follower of Christ there is no need of great things—it is enough to have the common, simple and human virtues, but they need to be true and authentic."[57] By bonds of marriage and paternity no one is more intimate with Mary and her Son than the man whose role reflected that of the Eternal Father Himself. Reaffirming the teaching of Leo XIII, Pope John Paul II has written:

> It is from his marriage to Mary that Joseph derived his singular dignity and his rights in regard to Jesus. It is certain that the dignity of the Mother of God is so exalted that nothing could be more sublime; yet because Mary was united to Joseph by the bond of marriage, there can be no doubt but that Joseph *approached as no other person ever could* that eminent dignity whereby the Mother of God towers above all creatures. Since marriage is the highest degree of association and friendship, involving by its very nature a communion of goods, it follows that God, by giving Joseph to the Virgin, did not give him to her only as a companion for life, a witness of her virginity and protector of her honor: He also gave Joseph to Mary in order that he might share, through the marriage pact, in her sublime greatness.[58]

---

[57] Paul VI, quoted in *Guardian of the Redeemer, TPS*, vol. 35, no. 1 (1990), p. 16.

[58] John Paul II, *Guardian of the Redeemer, TPS*, vol. 35, no. 1 (1990), p. 15.

Augustine was among the very first who gave due recognition to the role of Joseph. Around the year 420 he wrote to defend the true nature of Joseph's marriage, as well as his right to be called the Child's father.

> It is not true that the conjugal bond is broken between those [spouses] who have been pleased by mutual consent to abstain from the use of bodily desire; rather the conjugal bond will be more firm by reason of the promises they have entered into between themselves, which promises must then be preserved more affectionately and harmoniously, not by the pleasurable joining of bodies but by the willed affections of their souls. . . . Because of their faithful marriage both deserve to be called the parents of Christ, not just she the Mother but also he Christ's father, just as he was the spouse of Christ's Mother in the spirit and not in the flesh. . . .
>
> Every good of marriage was fulfilled in these parents of Jesus: offspring, fidelity, sacramental sign. We recognize the offspring as the Lord Jesus Himself; fidelity because there was no adultery; the sacramental sign because there was no divorce.[59]

Like every good marriage, theirs was one of mutual support. This we can readily recognize in Joseph's concern and provident action for the Mother and then for the Child and Mother amid the difficulties and threats at the time of the Nativity. Pope John Paul II mentions another type of marital support, and one which at first sight is quite striking.

> Looking at the Gospel texts of both Matthew and Luke, one can also say that Joseph is the first *to share in the faith of the Mother of God*, and that in doing so he supports his spouse in the faith of the Divine Annunciation.[60]

The Holy Father's emphasis is clearly directed to the share that Joseph had in the faith of Mary. However, he adds what may be a remarkable new insight when he observes that Joseph *supported* the faith of Mary in the Annunciation. It is not usual to reflect on the fact that Mary's faith needed support. Completely free of sin as she always was, and responding in faith as she always did, we tend to presume implicitly that, with God's grace, she was totally sufficient unto herself, at least on the human level. The pope is saying that such was not the case. Like her Son

---

[59] Augustine, *De Nuptiis et Concupiscentia*, I, 12-13: *CSEL*, 42, pp. 224-225.
[60] John Paul II, *Guardian of the Redeemer*, *TPS*, vol. 35, no. 1 (1990), p. 7.

Who, in His agony, needed support (cf. Lk 22:43), so Mary needed support, and found it in her husband, the just Joseph.

Of all the many around Mary, Joseph's place is unique. Their place in heaven now and their relationship symbolize for us the companionship of heaven, a companionship enjoyed and shared with all the Elect in the midst of the new garden and the heavenly city. There is a lovely sermon from the twelfth century that speaks of the glory of heaven. Commenting on the text of Luke 24:35 ("Then the two recounted what had taken place on the way and how [Jesus] was made known to them in the breaking of the bread") the unknown author writes:

> We can refer this verse to that joy of blissful quiet when each one will sit under his own vine and own fig tree in the beauty of peace, in the tabernacles of trust, in sumptuous rest; when the plazas of Jerusalem will be strewn with gold, when Alleluia is sung through all its streets and when there has been fulfilled [the prophecy] about the children and young girls dressed in white robes and following the Lamb wherever He goes. Then we will talk about the things that happened to us on the way and how we knew the Lord in the breaking of bread; of how pleasantly He humiliated us here in this place of affliction so that He might be the delight of our hearts, He Who hides His secrets from the wise and prudent and reveals them to little ones. Then we will remember the dangers we encountered, the tribulations we suffered, and we will marvelously rejoice because all of them have passed away like a shadow, and in the splendors in which we will exist our bones will sprout forth joy.
>
> Then we will plant vines on the mount of Samaria, and we will hear the voice of joy and gladness, the voice of the bridegroom and of the bride. We will see the King of glory and the beauty of the Queen. Then the Virgin will rejoice in chorus, wearing the royal diadem on her head and showing to us the fruit of her most blessed womb. The Lord of majesty will be seen in our humanity. Then our hearts will perceive and abound and be marvelously enlarged because we shall see, eye to eye, countenance to countenance; we shall know face to face; dialogue mouth to mouth, as we say: To You, O Lord, power and dominion, to You honor and glory. Let every spirit praise You forever and ever. Amen.[61]

---

[61] "Sermon for Monday of Easter Week": PL 184, 981-982. The work is found among those attributed to St. Bernard, but it is not his. It is perhaps the work of Blessed Oglerius (Ogerius), a Cistercian monk, who died around 1214.

In that Kingdom Mary and Joseph, together with all the Saints, feast on God.

The Heavenly Banquet

During a pilgrimage—the description of which is largely a Catholic celebration of the glories of nature—Hilaire Belloc wrote exuberantly and with exaggeration:

> But Catholic men who live upon wine
> Are deep in the water and frank and fine;
> Wherever I travel I find it so,
> Benedicamus Domino.[62]

The intent in these verses is to praise those who revel in the gifts of nature such as wine, and who are consequently (according to Belloc) not shallow people, but rather "deep in the water" unlike the abstemious heretics he had unecumenically lambasted in the previous verse. For Belloc wine alleviated the rigors of pilgrimage. For his friend Chesterton, a tavern with great flagons awaits those who have successfully completed the pilgrimage of life.[63]

Now all but prohibitionists will admit that Belloc's views on the value of wine were correct. Wine is solace on the pilgrimage. Indeed, for the Catholic, all wine can serve as a reminder of the best of wines that has been changed by the wonder-worker of Cana into His own blood to sustain us on the journey. On the other hand, even some who "are deep in the water" would not follow Chesterton, except metaphorically. It has become a truism for some, including St. Thomas, that the Elect will not eat or drink in heaven.[64]

---

[62] Hilaire Belloc, *The Path to Rome,* Image Books (Garden City, N.Y.: Doubleday, 1956), p. 106

[63] G.K Chesterton, *Collected Works,* vol. XV, *Chesterton on Dickens* (San Francisco: Ignatius Press, 1989), p. 209.

[64] On St. Thomas' opinion, cf. *Summa Contra Gentiles,* bk. 4, ch. 83. For a modern application, cf. G. O'Collins, "Did Jesus Eat the Fish (Lk 24:42-43)?" *Gregorianum,* 69, 1 (1988), pp. 65ff who says that Jesus did not eat. The eating of the fish is a Lucan symbol to stress the reality of the Resurrection, etc. O'Collins says that to actually eat the fish would be play-acting on the part of Jesus since the Resurrected do not eat (p. 69).

It is clear to all, of course, that the Bible is filled with imagery that speaks of future eating and drinking. The God Who fed the hosts of Israel in the desert with the "bread of angels" (Ps 78:25; New Vulgate) is the same God who promised a day when "the poor will eat their fill" (Ps 22:27). The poor spoken of are the Lord's servants, those who from the recognition of their own lack look to Him for all their good. Addressing Himself to the rich and satisfied, He makes promises on behalf of the poor: "My servants shall eat, but you shall go hungry; my servants shall drink, but you shall be thirsty; my servants shall rejoice, but you shall be put to shame" (Is 65:13). It is a pledge never completely fulfilled in the times of the Old Testament. Therefore, at the beginning of the New, the Mother of Him Who is the Bread of God proclaims as accomplished what her Son would in fact achieve: "The hungry he has filled with good things; the rich he has sent away empty" (Lk 1:53).

Jesus Himself continued the imagery of the Old Testament. What awaits His triumphant followers is a banquet, indeed a wedding banquet (cf. Mt 22:2ff; 25:1ff). Already that banquet has begun. It is anticipated at Cana and at the other meals in which Jesus takes part; it is especially present at that Supper which He orders repeated in His memory, a meal that draws its efficacy from the past but creates the future by feeding its participants for eternal life. The Lord knows, however, that what has already begun will only be fully achieved in the life of the world to come. Through Isaiah it was foretold that the banquet would occur only when death will have been eaten up.

> On this mountain the Lord of hosts will provide for all peoples a feast of rich food and choice wines, juicy, rich food and pure, choice wines. On this mountain he will destroy the veil that veils all peoples, the web that is woven over all nations; he will destroy death forever (Is 25:6-7).

And so, having eaten with us here and feeding us now on His own flesh, Jesus holds out before us the vision of the banquet yet to come. To it He invites us with insistence. "Behold, I stand at the door and knock. If anyone hears my voice and opens the door, then I will enter his house and dine with him, and he with me" (Rv 3:20). It is a repetition of the invitation that He, eternal Wisdom, spoke long ago. "Come, eat of my food, and drink of the wine I have mixed!" (Prv 9:5). The food that will be served in the banquets of heavenly Jerusalem will be that which gives not temporary sustenance, but immortality. As it is pledged: "Whoever has ears ought to hear what the Spirit says to the churches. To the victor I will give the right to eat from the tree of life that is in the garden of God" (Rv 2:7).

Sustenance, of course, will not be the real purpose of the heavenly banquet. That feast is better compared to the dalliance of lovers over a meal, or the excuse that friends use to spend time together. Recognizing this, the Church applies to herself the mood and words of the bride in the Song of Songs: "He brings me into the banquet hall and his emblem over me is love" (Song 2:4). And she anticipates this even as she awaits hearing His words. "I have come to my garden, my sister, my bride; I gather my myrrh and my spices, I eat my honey and my sweetmeats, I drink my wine and my milk. Eat, friends; drink! Drink freely of love!" (Song 5:1). As she longs for the feasts of the land of the living, the Church knows that, in the meals of the life to come, there will be fulfilled the Lord's own instructions for the giving of a banquet, namely "the poor, the crippled, the lame, the blind" (Lk 14:13) will have special place.

It is relying on such lessons of the Bible that the Church prays on Wednesday of the First Week of Advent: "We beg You, O Lord Our God, to prepare our hearts by Your divine power so that, when Christ Your Son comes, we may be found worthy of the banquet of eternal life and may merit to receive the heavenly food as He waits on us."

The Bishop of Hippo, as robust as Chesterton in his view of the life to come, had no difficulty in taking the lessons of the Bible and its imagery literally. This was not because he thought such pleasures as food and drink were a necessity in the life to come or that, without them, one could not be completely happy. Such thinking, said Augustine, would be basely carnal.

> When it is said that other things will be taken away and that we will delight in God alone, how constrained becomes the soul that is accustomed to delight in many things. And the carnal soul, the soul addicted to the flesh, the soul bound up in the desires of the flesh . . . says to itself: "What will it be like for me where I shall not eat nor drink nor sleep with my wife? What

> joy will I have?" This joy of yours comes from sickness, not
> from health. . . . There are certain desires that belong to sick
> people. . . . When health comes the desire vanishes. . . . The
> words spoken are the words of weakness, not of strength. We
> will need nothing and therefore we shall be blessed. We shall
> be full, but filled with our God, and all the things that we desire
> so greatly here He Himself will be for us. Here you seek food:
> God will be your food. Here you seek the embraces of the flesh;
> however "to adhere to God is my good." Here you seek riches.
> How will you lack anything when you possess Him Who made
> all things?[65]

Having God, we shall need nothing. It is a lack of faith bordering on foolishness to think that the life to come would need
any delight other than God. Foolish also, however, to fear that,
"having Him I must have naught besides."[66] Although intent on
correcting one error, Augustine does not fall into the other. God
is all and all-sufficient: we will need nothing more. But what we
will not *need* may be ours at will to enjoy.

> Therefore the body in the future resurrection would have im-
> perfect happiness if it were not able to take food, imperfect hap-
> piness if it needed food.[67]

> They will not eat unless they wish, since they will have the ca-
> pacity not the necessity.[68]

They shall eat if they wish. In saying this, Augustine would
appear to be less consistent than Aquinas. St. Thomas eliminates
eating as well as sexual union from the life to come, giving as his
reason the fact that the purpose for which God created them will
have ceased. For him, eating exists to preserve life and sexual in-
tercourse to give life. In the life to come there will be no begetting
of children and the Elect will be immortal. Thus, eating, like sexual union, will have no purpose. Augustine agreed with such a
thesis in what concerns the purposes of eating and sexual union.
In our day, undoubtedly, we realize more adequately than either
of them the ability of sexual union to foster the other purposes of
the special friendship that is marriage. They would likely agree

---

[65] Augustine, *Sermon 255*, 7: *PL* 38, 1189-1190.

[66] Francis Thompson, *The Hound of Heaven*.

[67] Augustine, *Letter 102*, 6: *CSEL* 34, 2, p. 549. Cf. *Sermon 242 (147)*, 2: *PL* 38,
1139-1140, where he says the same of the Lord's Risen Body.

[68] Augustine, *City of God*, bk 13, ch. 22: *CCSL*, 48, p. 405.

with these insights, but respond that, in the life to come, the expression and even enrichment of love will have been perfected and be realized in ways deeper and fuller than sexual union. However, the same can be said of food. Thus, if one admits that the needs for which eating exists will have ended, why allow its continuance in the life to come, as Augustine clearly did?

In admitting the possibility of eating and drinking while excluding that of sexual union in the life to come, Augustine implies a distinction between the pleasures of this life that will not carry over into the life ahead and those that can and will endure. When one inquires as to the basis for such a distinction, one is left with no sure answer. Perhaps it is simply that he is willing to exclude only what the Lord Himself explicitly rejected. Other goods he holds out at least as possibilities.

In addition to the principle of following only an explicit statement of Jesus, Augustine may be applying again his use of the *via pulchritudinis;* even when usefulness has passed, some things will remain simply for the sake of beauty and to be enjoyed.[69] Would he be willing to admit that those that remain do so simply for the sake of enjoyment or pleasure? Aquinas says that such cannot be because pleasure is intended by God to accompany an activity that has a purpose beyond the pleasure itself. To seek the pleasure alone is a violation of the virtue of temperance, and such lack of virtue cannot exist among the Blessed.[70] For Thomas the virtue of temperance exists to moderate our appetites.[71] Now Augustine would surely have agreed with this, at least as it applies to our fallen condition. Nonetheless his thoughts on the possibility of eating in the life to come may also reflect what we have seen to be his definition of temperance. "Temperance," he writes, "is love giving itself integrally to that which is loved."[72] Surely, this is a more dynamic and less impeding definition of the virtue than the one usually considered. With such a definition it is possible that, for the resurrected whose appetites have been totally purified and perfected, some

---

[69] Cf., above, under Chapter V: "The Saints Who Are in the Land," p. 202, the first quote of Augustine under *via pulchritudinis,* found in note 3.
[70] Cf. Aquinas, *Summa Contra Gentiles,* bk. IV, ch. 83.
[71] Cf., for example, *Summa Theol.,* II, IIae, q. 141, a. 3, ad 1; q. 141, a. 4, 5, 7, etc.
[72] Augustine, *De Moribus Ecclesiae Catholicae: PL* 32, 1322.

pleasures may be enjoyed simply as pleasures. In the case of sexual union, however, its proper enjoyment is intended to come from the sense of personal union between husband and wife, which is why the Bible speaks of it as a "knowing." Such awareness in the future will be so profound and so real that apparently symbolic expression of it will be unnecessary. We will know each other more deeply than sexual union is capable of giving. The words of a dying wife may capture well what Augustine, in following Jesus on this issue, is implicitly teaching us.

> He is a priest;
> He cannot marry therefore, which is right;
> I think he would not marry if he could.
> Marriage on earth seems such a counterfeit,
> Mere imitation of the inimitable:
> In heaven we have the real and true and sure.
> 'Tis there they neither marry nor are given
> In marriage but are as the angels: right,
> Oh how right that is, how like Jesus Christ
> To say that! Marriage-making for the earth,
> With gold so much,—birth, power, repute so much,
> Or beauty, youth so much, in lack of these!
> Be as the angels rather, who, apart,
> Know themselves into one, are found at length
> Married, but marry never, no, nor give
> In marriage; they are man and wife at once.[73]

They are the words of an unhappy woman, spoken after she has been fatally wounded at the hands of her husband. Consequently they are not, in any way, the most likely words to speak correctly of marriage. Yet they do express truths or give insights to the same. In heaven all will be like the Angels who, "apart, know themselves into one, are found . . . married, but marry never." And the reason: marriage is "mere imitation of the inimitable." Even the pleasure of the marriage act will have been sublimated into this new type of knowledge that is Eucharist-like: intimate, fleshy and virginal.

Other reasons for the perdurance of eating and the disappearance of sexual union may be sought in the "sacramental" nature of food. Food, bread and wine, are sanctified by so inti-

---

[73] Robert Browning, "Pompilia," lines 1821-1836, *The Ring and the Book*, p. 375.

mate an association with the Risen Lord as to serve as the means by which He comes to us physically. Marriage, on the other hand, exists as a sacrament so as to symbolize the reality of the Eucharist. Thus, marriage participates in the dignity of the higher sacrament, the Sacrament that comes to us under the appearance of food. Perhaps it is not too far off the mark to speculate that ministering to the Body and Blood of the Lord in this way now is what entitles food to a share in the life to come that other goods of this earth cannot match. One might continue such speculation and say that some pleasures are so intimately bound up with things *needed* that there will be no place for them when exigency has ceased, or that food is a much more common part of human life than is even sexual activity and this fact alone may explain why it may remain while other things do not.

All this is speculation, of course. Supposition, though, is all one can do if one accepts Augustine's views that some bodily pleasures will continue to exist in the life to come while others will not. In any case, like Augustine, we should be slow to eliminate from the human future anything that is not certainly incompatible with that life or that the Lord Himself has not indicated as being excluded.

Let it be remembered, finally, that eating—if there be such in the life to come—will always be a reminder of Him Who feeds us with Himself. For the finest food of the new creation will be that which is our best food now. As an eleventh-century writer put it, "The citizens of both cities live on the same Bread."[74]

---

[74] *Rhyme on the Glory of Paradise: PL* 40, 921. The author of the little rhyme is unknown, but it was attributed to Peter Damian.

VII

TO GAZE ON THE BEAUTY OF THE LORD

Sunset and evening star,
And one clear call for me!
And may there be no moaning of the bar,
When I put out to sea,

But such a tide as moving seems asleep,
Too full for sound and foam,
When that which drew from out the boundless deep
Turns again home.

Twilight and evening bell,
And after that the dark!
And may there be no sadness of farewell,
When I embark;

For though from out our bourne of Time and Place
The flood may bear me far,
I hope to see my Pilot face to face
When I have crost the bar.[1]

THESE are words of hope, based on faith. They are also the final thoughts of that same man who penned the Job-like challenges of the *In Memoriam*. By his own instructions, this poem was to be placed at the end of all the editions of Tennyson's works, even though it was not chronologically the last. The pain of the *In Memoriam* had given way to, was subsumed by, serenity. *Crossing the Bar* expresses the conviction that, despite the collapse of all around us and the death of loved ones and our own impending demise, we do not navigate alone. The journey in exile is always being guided; the pilgrimage is not without its Pilot. The One Who leads, moreover, is not merely a Guide; He is Himself the End and the reward of the journey.

The Apocalyptic Promises

To give us comfort during the passage and assurance of the good things that await its completion, this Steersman, Who is

---

[1] Tennyson, "Crossing the Bar," *Tennyson: A Selected Edition,* edited by Christopher Ricks, Univ. of California Press, 1989, p. 665.

the Giver of gifts, has promised particular rewards to those who persevere in the struggle. Each promised favor is an encouragement to go on when the difficulties seem insurmountable.

1. "To the victor I will give the right to eat from the tree of life that is in the garden [paradise] of God" (Rv 2:7).

We have seen already the significance of this promise. It is partly metaphorical in the sense that the Elect will not actually derive their immortality from the fruit of a tree. On the other hand, it communicates a reality since the trees of the new Paradise will recall the original promise and its loss, as well as the Fruit of that Tree which endowed our race with immortal life.

2. "The victor shall not be harmed by the second death" (Rv 2:11).

There will no longer be any fear of losing what has been gained. The victory will be final. No threat, either external or from within the personalities of the Blessed, will pose any danger to what has been given and achieved. Indeed no such threats will exist at all. Hell in particular will be no object of fear for those who have been confirmed in good.

3. "To the victor I shall give some of the hidden manna; I shall also give a white amulet [stone] upon which is inscribed a new name, which no one knows except the one who receives it" (Rv 2:17).

It is possible that the reference to "hidden manna" is intended to evoke the memory of the prophet Jeremiah's hiding of the Ark of the Covenant at the time of the Exile. This Ark, which had contained the gold jar of manna (cf. Heb 9:4), was to remain concealed until the time of Israel's restoration (cf. 2 Mc 2:1-8). In that perspective the promise of the hidden manna would indicate the end of exile, the return home. Jesus Himself, however, had given a new meaning to the word and concept of manna when He spoke of the true manna that would be a bread of Flesh and not of wheat (cf. Jn 6). It is the Lord, under the appearance of bread, Who is the hidden manna and the reward for those who, in Him, win the victory. A Benedictine monk, Ambrose Autpert (died c. 784), has left a beautiful and extensive commentary on the Book of Revelation, and writes thus on the hidden manna:

Whoever now eats with faith the manna in the Sacrament will then eat the Reality by sight; what is hidden now will then be manifest.[2]

What Jesus means by the white stone with the new name that is known only to the recipient has puzzled commentators. The stone itself is probably the equivalent of an identification bracelet; it is white because that color, frequently used in the Book of Revelation, is a sign of holiness (cf. number 5 below). The name on the identification stone will be the full revelation of who and what its wearer truly is. Even Jesus is reported to have a "new name" that is known only to Himself (cf. 3:12 and 19:12). In fact, it is His own new name that the King of kings will give to those who are victorious (3:12). This conferral of a new name had readily been foretold through Isaiah (cf. 62:2 and 65:15), and the prophet indicated that the name would concern the marriage of God with His people and land (62:4-5). Thus, the name written on the stone will be an endearment, a diminutive used by the Bridegroom for His bride. It will be like the night He called them "friends" rather than servants (Jn 15:14-15). Friends and children, such is what we are now. But the ultimate name remains for now unknown, because "what we shall be has not yet been revealed. We do know that when it is revealed we shall be like him, for we shall see him as he is" (1 Jn 3:2). What we will be is engraved on the white stone, a name of love.

The notion of the secret name to be given each of the Elect is not unlike what later theology would call the "aureole," the "little crowns or halos" that the Saints would have in heaven. Thomas explains them this way:

> [The aureole] is a certain joy from works accomplished, which works have the nature of a special type of victory.[3] It is a type of privileged reward corresponding to a special victory.[4] Properly speaking, it exists in the soul because it is a joy owed to these deeds. Nevertheless, from the joy of this aureole there results a certain beauty in the body; by a kind of overflow it shines in the body.[5]

---

[2] Ambrose Autpert, *In Apoc.*, II: CCCM 27, p. 133.
[3] Aquinas, *Summa Theol.: Supplementum*, q. 96, 1 c.
[4] *Ibid.*, a. 11 c.
[5] *Ibid.*, q. 10 c.

Correctly understood the notion of the "aureole" is a metaphorical way of saying that the individual deeds of the Saints, those works that were especially remarkable examples of Christian virtue (e.g., martyrdom), leave their own permanent imprint; it tells us that the individual work has value. We have already seen that this is so for all the positive contributions to the coming Kingdom. Therefore, what the concept of the aureole tells us is that some deeds are much more significant than others, and are especially rewarded. In a sense the works become part of the very identity of the Saints, an aspect of their personality, a name unknown now by any but the one who receives it, but to be divulged later for the admiration and communal rejoicing of the entire society of the everlasting city.

4. "To the victor . . . I will give authority over the nations . . . just as I received authority from my Father" (Rv 2:26-27).

In one significant passage of the fifteenth chapter of First Corinthians, Paul writes, "Then comes the end, when he hands over the kingdom to his God and Father, when he has destroyed every sovereignty and every authority and power. . . . When everything is subjected to him, then the Son himself will also be subjected to the one who subjected everything to him, so that God may be all in all" (1 Cor 15:24-28). These verses can be and have been interpreted so as to make it appear that the Father demands back from the Son the lordship over the universe that has been His since the first Easter: it is as though the Father parceled out authority for a while but will ultimately demand it back. Such views are foolish, of course. Indeed, were such an interpretation true, the text of Revelation 2:26-28 would contradict it, since here Jesus is not returning authority to the Father but rather sharing it with the Saints, the members of His Body.

What Paul is trying to emphasize, of course, is that the Father is the Source of all. Even in the mystery of the Trinity, the Son proceeds from Him. The Father remains always the Origin and Font of all. The Word receives from Him, is begotten of Him, and that reception of being is reflected in all the prayer and work of the Word Incarnate. Thus when Paul speaks of Him being subjected to that Father, he is only recognizing the truth that the Father is indeed all in all. Like the Son, however, Who is His equal and without Whom He would not be Father nor exist, He does not grasp at power. He bestows all that is His on the Son, and the Son in turn shares with the Elect. Indeed, Jesus makes what is His belong to them, not by nature but by grace.

When the visionary of the Book of Revelation recounts the Lord's promise to give the Elect authority *over the nations,* he is expressing metaphorically a principle of Catholic doctrine, and of Catholic social doctrine particularly: the state exists for the person, not vice versa. Even the collectivity, the community, is meant to enrich the individual members. Having authority "over the nations" thus means that the individual will never again be subject to the anonymity of structures or situations of injustice and sin, or be a victim of social conditions. In the community of fully responsible freedom, the person will be supreme. The Lord teaches this same doctrine in Revelation 3:20 when He promises: "I will give the victor the right to sit with me on my throne, as I myself first won the victory and sit with my Father on his throne."

This fourth promise concludes with the words, "And to him I will give the morning star" (Rv 2:28). The morning star is Jesus Himself, as is revealed later in the same Book of the Bible where the Lord declares, "I am . . . the bright morning star" (Rv 22:16). A fine commentary on the Book of Revelation explains it this way.

> The faithful Christian, therefore, will not only be favored with sharing in Christ's juridical activities, but will be blessed with the possession of Christ himself. St. Peter gives the identical consoling message: "Attend to the word of prophecy until the day (the parousia) dawns and the morning star rises in your hearts" (2 Peter 1:19). Nor should we regard the expression as foreign and strange since each year on the holiest of feasts we personally make a joyous, hopeful plea using the same words: "May the Morning Star behold its flame—that Morning Star who knows no setting, who rose from hell and gently shines on man" (second edition of the Exsultet in the Easter Vigil liturgy). Participation in Christ's Easter glory would be a specification of the gift of the "Morning Star."[6]

---

[6] William G. Heidt, O.S.B., *The Book of The Apocalypse,* New Testament Reading Guide (Collegeville, Minnesota: Liturgical Press, 1962), p. 36.

Like anyone in love trying to find new gifts to shower on the chosen, as if all that has already been promised is insufficient, the Lord continues.

5. "The victor will thus be dressed in white, and I will never erase his name from the book of life but will acknowledge his name in the presence of my Father and of his angels" (Rv 3:5).

Being dressed in white is a sign of holiness. White is also the traditional color of glorification as we can see from the Gospel accounts of the Transfiguration and the Resurrection of the Lord. Thus, the Saints, themselves resurrected, will radiate goodness.

The Book of Life is a common Biblical metaphor. It is the register in which the census of God's own people is kept. We have seen it above when speaking of the Mother of all those therein recorded. Those who are not inscribed there are destined for the second death, and thus the pledge here is a renewed avowal, in different simile, of the second promise.

The next words are likewise a repetition, not of what has been previously said in the Book of Revelation but of what the Lord spoke to His disciples during His visible ministry on earth. "Everyone who acknowledges me before others I will acknowledge before my heavenly Father" (Mt 10:32). Peter heard those words and initially failed the test. Instead of acknowledgment, he denied that he knew Jesus. Later, however, the Rock affirmed his Master in striking words: "There is no salvation through anyone else, nor is there any other name under heaven given to the human race by which we are to be saved" (Acts 4:12), and sealed the affirmation by his death. Such acknowledgment is a form of praise, and so the Lord promises to praise His servants in turn. It is proper enough to look for praise as long as that desire is correctly founded and is unstained by flattery and ambition. Undoubtedly we spend much of life's play looking for the acclaim of those on stage with us, but the applause of only One is really needed. If He acknowledges our performance other critical reaction is of little account. Jesus here promises His faithful followers a "good press."

6. "The victor I will make into a pillar in the temple of my God, and he will never leave it. On him I will inscribe the name

of my God and the name of the city of my God, the new Jerusalem, which comes down out of heaven from my God, as well as my new name" (Rv 3:12).

The Lord God revealed Himself to Moses as "I am" and as the "God of Abraham, Isaac, and Jacob" (cf. Ex 3:14-15). For us that same God is also—but much more profoundly—"the God and Father of Our Lord Jesus Christ." This title is, for the Christian, both an identification and a prayer.

> . . . that with one accord you may with one voice glorify the God and Father of our Lord Jesus Christ (Rom 15:6).

> Blessed be the God and Father of our Lord Jesus Christ, the Father of compassion and God of all encouragement (2 Cor 1:3).

> Blessed be the God and Father of our Lord Jesus Christ, who has blessed us in Christ with every spiritual blessing in the heavens (Eph 1:3).

> Blessed be the God and Father of our Lord Jesus Christ, who in his great mercy gave us a new birth to a living hope through the resurrection of Jesus Christ from the dead (1 Pt 1:3).

In the verse of the Book of Revelation, Jesus emphasizes the relationship between Himself and the Father. It is the temple of "*my* God," the name of *my* God, the city of *my* God that descends from *my* God; four times the possessive of identification appears in one verse. The Father is the God of Jesus Christ, and what the Father has given to Jesus, the Nazarene gives to His beloved. These gifts include permanent residence in the courts of God as well as the right to be stamped with the name of God. Like quality paper that is bonded, so the sealing of the Elect signifies that they will belong completely to the Father, as Jesus Himself does. In addition, they will have the name of the heavenly Jerusalem, the City of the Great King (cf. Mt 5:35), engraved on them for they will be permanent citizens of that city. They will, finally, be marked with the name of Jesus as belonging to Him. The idea of being marked as a sign of belonging to God is found, as are so many of the references in the Book of Revelation, in the prophet Isaiah.

> One shall say, "I am the Lord's," another shall be named after Jacob, and this one shall write on his hand, "The Lord's," and Israel shall be his surname (Is 44:5).

When Jesus promises that His chosen ones will be marked with His name, He is responding to the plea of the Bride, "Set me as a seal on your heart, as a seal on your arm; for stern as death is love" (Song 8:6). She will be sealed, stamped in His heart and on His arm; His name will be grafted on her. At last, with full assurance and no danger of further loss, she can exclaim, "My lover belongs to me and I to him" (Song 2:16).

7. "Behold, I stand at the door and knock. If anyone hears my voice and opens the door, then I will enter his house and dine with him, and he with me" (Rv 3:20).

What may be considered the last of the promises is also heavily reminiscent of the Song of Songs. There we hear the Bride say, "I was sleeping, but my heart kept vigil; I heard my lover knocking: 'Open to me, my sister, my beloved, my dove, my perfect one!" (Song 5:2). What awaits the one who opens is that feast of love where delight does not cease owing to satiety.

To be noted is the fact that in the third, fourth, sixth and seventh promises, Jesus pledges to give Himself. Like every lover, his gifts—real as they are—are tokens of what He truly longs to give, the gift of self, and to have that gift accepted. Those who read His promises and those who have already begun to share in them know well that they are not just words: the Bread of life Who gives Himself daily does not stint in self-bestowal.

Reflecting on the divine assurances given in the Book of Revelation, one is reminded again of what Isaiah predicted, "Your eyes will see a king in a splendor, they will look upon a vast land" (Is 33:17). The land that stretches afar will be the restored universe; the sight of the King in His beauty will be what makes the land an everlasting Springtime for love. Only when that Springtime of love flowers will all the prophecies be fulfilled that spoke in various accents of the King and His beauty.

> The scepter shall never depart from Judah, or the mace from between his legs, while tribute is brought to him, and he receives the peoples' homage. He tethers his donkey to the vine, his purebred ass to the choicest stem. In wine he washes his garments, his robe in the blood of grapes. His eyes are darker than wine, and his teeth are whiter than milk (Gn 49:10-12).

The wait for that One to Whom the obedience of the nation belongs was long. Ezekiel was one who kept the hope alive. Recalling the prophecy of Genesis, he said of the land: "Twisted, twisted, twisted will I leave it; it shall not be the same until he comes who has the claim against the city; and to him I will hand it over" (Ez 21:32).

The Hidden Face

As the longing to see the King in His beauty increased, so too did another longing develop in a parallel fashion in Israel, the desire to see the face of God Himself.

Peter Kreeft, in a beautiful section of his work on heaven, writes of the resurrection body as being *all face:*

> The face is me. It is where the body comes to a point, comes to its expression. Perhaps you have noticed the amazing change in the face of a friend who has suddenly fallen in love (with a human being or with God), or who has fallen out of love, or into depression or despair or dishonesty. . . . The face is a window.
>
> We are *responsible* for our face, as we are not responsible for our legs, or our height.
>
> Contrast the face of a saint with that of a gross sinner. Notice especially the eyes. Contrast eyes tempered with love and suffering with eyes that have refused these lessons. Environmental tools providentially wielded by the divine sculptor have chiseled fine lines on His masterpieces, the saints. Yet it is impossible to put it into a verbal formula. You just *see* it.[7]

What is quoted suffices to let us realize that if all this be true of the face of any person, how much more must be said of the divine Face. To see that Face became a desire, impatient through passion, that surfaced over and over again in holy Scripture. That desire is not without its ambivalent aspects, however. There is a current of thought in the holy books that reminds us that the sight of God is a fearsome thing. Jacob-Israel voices that realization when, having wrestled with the Almighty and won, he acknowledges that his daring was tolerated. "Jacob named the place Peniel, 'Because I have seen God face to face,' he said, 'yet my life has been spared' " (Gn 32:31). More circumspect, the gentle Moses fell to the ground and covered his own face when God

---

[7] Kreeft, *Every Thing You Wanted To Know About Heaven*, pp. 100-101.

first came to him. "God said, . . . 'I am the God of your father, . . . the God of Abraham, the God of Isaac, the God of Jacob.' Moses hid his face, for he was afraid to look at God" (Ex 3:6). Later, more familiar now and more daring, he needed to be taught that some desires cannot be fulfilled here.

> Then Moses said, "Do let me see your glory!" He answered, "I will make all my beauty pass before you, and in your presence I will pronounce my name, 'Lord'; I who show favors to whom I will, I who grant mercy to whom I will. But my face you cannot see, for no man sees me and still lives" (Ex 33:18-20).

That lesson was learned well by the people Moses led from captivity. The faithful among them and their descendants never sought to make a likeness of Him Who was the God of their fathers, the Lord Who spoke to Moses. Nonetheless the sight of the countenance of this Faceless One was also recognized as being a blessing:

> If my people, upon whom my name has been pronounced, humble themselves and pray, and seek my presence and turn from their evil ways, I will hear them from heaven and pardon their sins and revive their land (2 Chr 7:14).

> The Lord is just and loves just deeds; the upright shall see his face (Ps 11:7).

In fact the sight of God's face came to be recognized as a form of blessing; the one who saw would be enriched.

> The Lord let his face shine upon you, and be gracious to you! The Lord look upon you kindly and give you peace! (Nm 6:25-26).

Awareness that the face of God itself was a benediction led both to the desire to see and to the injunction to search for that face. St. Peter Chrysologus, reflecting on the desire to see the face of God, wrote:

> Love is incapable of not seeing what it loves. That is why all the Saints considered everything they had merited as little if they could not see the Lord. . . . That is why Moses dared to say, "If I have found favor with You, show me Your face." That is why Elijah said, "Show me Your face." Even the Gentiles fashioned images so that they might discern with their eyes what they worshiped in their errors.[8]

---

[8] Peter Chrysologus, *Sermon 147: CCSL* 34 B, pp. 912-913.

And so Israel began to pray in expressions that became an injunction to search for the face of the Lord: "Look to the Lord and his strength; seek his face always" (1 Chr 16:11; *NIV*). The faithful Jew turned the injunction into a prayer of longing, so well expressed in Psalm 27.

> "Come," says my heart, "seek God's face"; your face, Lord, do I seek! (Ps 27:8).

It is easy to understand how that desire to see His face took its place in the marriage imagery that portrayed the relationship of the Lord God and Israel. Anxiously, longingly, lovingly, the Bride craves the face of her Beloved.

> O my dove in the clefts of the rock, in the secret recesses of the cliff, let me see you [your face], let me hear your voice, for your voice is sweet and you are lovely (Song 2:14).

What was desired was granted and withdrawn, sought again, found and again apparently lost. The Spouse of Israel Who invited the search for His face was also a God Who hid Himself. In this way the theme of the "hidden God" finds repeated formulations in the Bible. The Psalmist has the wicked say: "God has forgotten; he covers his face and never sees" (Ps 10:11; *NIV*).

> How long, Lord? Will you utterly forget me? How long will you hide your face from me? (Ps 13:1).

> Do not hide your face from me; do not repel your servant in anger. You are my help; do not cast me off; do not forsake me, God my savior! (Ps 27:9).

Such "hiding" on God's part is not merely the coyness of a lover who withdraws himself so as to increase the desire of the beloved. That surely is part of the divine intent, but there is a more common reason: the unworthiness of God's unfaithful Bride. Nevertheless, God's love is stronger than Israel's infidelity. He promises to return, to reveal Himself anew. Through His prophet, God declares, "In an outburst of wrath, for a moment I hid my face from you; but with enduring love I take pity on you" (Is 54:8).

At last, in the fullness of time, if only for a brief space of years, God does reveal His face. He comes into His own, being born in human likeness, and shows us the human face of God.

Jesus of Nazareth is what God is and looks like as a human. Cognizant of that truth, Richard Crashaw said of Our Lady that, in Bethlehem, when she saw her child:

> Tis heaven, 'tis heaven she sees, heaven's God there lies;
> She can see heaven and ne'er lift up her eyes.
> This new guest to her eyes new laws hath given:
> T'was once look up, 'tis now look down to heaven.

During His sojourn among us, there were those who even saw that face with some of its heavenly glory. "He was transfigured before them; his face shone like the sun and his clothes became white as light" (Mt 17:12). Such glory was fleeting in those years, for He had come to show us a face marked by our buffeting so that "there was in him no stately bearing to make us look at him, nor appearance that would attract us to him" (Is 53:2).

> He advanced a little and fell prostrate [with his face to the ground] in prayer, saying, "My Father, if it is possible, let this cup pass from me: yet, not as I will, but as you will" (Mt 26:39).

> When [Jesus] said this, one of the temple guards standing there struck Jesus [in the face] and said, "Is this the way you answer the high priest?" (Jn 18:22).

> [The soldiers] came to him and said, "Hail, King of the Jews!" And they struck him repeatedly [in the face] (Jn 19:3).

Pointing to that marred face which could have drawn pity from the hardened but not the heartless, Pilate proclaimed, "Behold the man!" (Jn 19:5). That same face, resurrected now in the fullness of glorified beauty, is what awaits the predestined as their joy and fulfillment.

The Person of God the Word, revealed to human eyes through His face, is all that any human has ever truly needed. Seen through that face is everything that makes for human beatitude. This His Church ceaselessly proclaims to be the case.

> The Church, while she helps the world and receives much from it, tends toward this one thing: that the Kingdom of God come and that the salvation of the whole human race be established. Indeed every good thing that the People of God during the time of its earthly pilgrimage is able to offer to the human family flows from the fact that the Church is the "universal sacrament of salvation," simultaneously manifesting and working the mystery of God's love toward humankind.

The Word of God, through Whom all things were made, Himself became flesh so that, as perfect Man, He might save all and recapitulate all things. The Lord is the goal of human history, the point in which the desires of history and civilization converge, the center of the human race, the joy of all hearts and the fullness of all their desires. He it is Whom the Father raised from the dead, exalted and placed at His right hand, establishing Him as judge of the living and the dead. Made alive and unified by His Spirit, we make our pilgrimage toward the fulfillment of human history that is in full harmony with His loving plan: "To restore all things, which are in heaven and on earth, in Christ" (Eph 1:10).

The Lord Himself says: "Behold I come quickly, and My reward is with Me, to render to each according to his works. I am the alpha and the omega, the first and last, the beginning and the end" (Rv 22:12-13) (*Gaudium et Spes*, 45).

A speech given by Pope Paul VI during his pastoral visit to the Philippines mirrors the words of *Gaudium et Spes*, even while elaborating on the centrality of the human face of God for our race.

Christ is the center of history and of the whole world. He knows and loves us and stands by us as our friend and companion throughout life. He is the man of sorrows and of hope. He is the One Who is to come one day to be our judge and, we hope, to be the eternal fullness of our existence, our happiness.

I can never speak enough about Christ. He is the light and the truth. Indeed, He is the way, the truth, and the life. He is the bread and the source of living water to satisfy our hunger and our thirst. He is our shepherd, our leader, our ideal, our consoler, and our brother.

Like us, and even more than us, He has experienced lowliness, poverty, and humiliation; He has worked with the sweat of his brow; He has known misfortune and remained patient. . . .

Jesus Christ . . . is the beginning and the end, the alpha and the omega. He is the King of the new world, the hidden Key to human history and our part in it. He is the Mediator, that is, the bridge, between heaven and earth. Above all, He is the Son of Man, more perfect than any human, because He is also the Son of God, eternal and infinite. He is the Son of Mary, His earthly Mother, most blessed among all women.[9]

---

[9] Paul VI, *Homily in Manila, Nov. 29, 1970*, Second Reading of the *Roman Breviary* for Thirteenth Sunday of Ordinary Time.

The Council and the pope are providing a commentary on what St. John tells us at the opening of his version of the Good News. Reflecting on the beginning of everything and on what was before the beginning, he proclaimed Christ as the ultimate explanation of all we know. "All things came to be through him, and without him nothing came to be" (Jn 1:3). Paul too teaches the same truth.

> For us there is one God, the Father, from whom all things are and for whom we exist, and one Lord Jesus Christ, through whom all things are and through whom we exist (1 Cor 8:6).

Through Him *all* was created. Indeed, Jesus is not only the medium of creation; He is, as the Father's own Idea, God's own knowledge of Himself and His power, the Model according to which all things were fashioned. For that very reason, the universe, created through Him and in His image, will be re-created through Him and modeled after Him. It is as a reaffirmation of this profound mystery that the Council and the pope can make such apparently extravagant claims for Nazareth's first-century carpenter and rabbi.

As the "eternal fullness of our existence" and the "fullness of all our desires," Jesus the Christ is also the Light that brightens our darkness even now as He proclaimed Himself to be then (cf. Jn 8:12). It is true that the face that was seen in Galilee and Judea can now be gazed upon by us no more. He has become, in that sense and then only partly, the hidden God. Commenting on Psalm 18:12 ("He made darkness the cover about him"), Augustine, anticipating the "dark night" theology of John the Cross, wrote:

> He established the obscurity of the sacraments and the hidden hope in the hearts of believers where He Himself might hide while not deserting them. Darkness is also His covering in that we still walk by faith and not by sight, while we hope for what we do not see and wait for it with patience.[10]

Though we cannot see Him now, we love Him and follow Him in and through the Eucharist, the Sacrament of His Presence in His Church, fortified by the conviction that whoever does follow Him does not walk in darkness. Indeed it is the firm assur-

---

[10] Augustine, *Ennarr. in Ps. 17*, 12: CCSL 38, p. 96.

ance of those who have come to know Him this way that only in Him can humans understand themselves.

> Really only in the mystery of the Incarnate Word is the mystery of the human race truly clarified. Adam, the first man, was a type of the future, namely of Christ the Lord. Christ, the last Adam, in the very revelation of the mystery of the Father and His love, fully manifests mankind to itself and makes clear to our race its highest calling (*Gaudium et Spes,* 22).

It is only by following Christ that our race can realize all its own potentialities. These possibilities will never be fully realized here: only the life to come will bring the Elect, in Christ and under His leadership, to a perfection that, despite all efforts, will always elude us until all the just see His face. In this life, which for so many—and so often—seems to be like the darkness of night, there is for those who know Him the realization that this night can shine like day, as the *Exsultet* sings. And the light He presently gives is but a portion of what is to come in that City where the sun will appear not to exist since "the Lamb will be its light."

He, the Church's Spouse and Lord, came and dwelt among us. Although He is gone now from sight, the Church awaits Him, reminding herself of His graciousness even as she longs.

> My lover is radiant and ruddy; he stands out among thousands. His head is pure gold; his locks are palm fronds, black as the raven. His eyes are like doves beside running waters, his teeth would seem bathed in milk, and are set like jewels (Song 5:10-12).

For the Bride, no words were or are adequate. Nonetheless as she waits for Him, the Church never tires of prompting our imaginations to dwell upon Him, although she knows that, like the disciples on the road to Emmaus, our eyes and our imaginations are presently obstructed. We long, our hearts burn within us, but we cannot yet see.

> "Their eyes were held lest they recognize Him." The human soul, aware of its own infirmity, trembles before the ineffable glory of such pleasantness. Thus Elijah covered his face, Eliphaz shook, and even Moses did not dare to look on the Lord (Ex 3:6). Job said, "If He came to me, I would not see Him" (Jb 9:11). "Their eyes were held." Oh, if they had known the Lord, how greatly would they have rejoiced! How greatly would we

ourselves rejoice if we could see Him in His own appearance! Who would not approach, indeed run, to hold His feet? But "Joseph" is still speaking to His brothers through the interpreter: He still hides from us His sweet face. Why? We are mortals, and we dwell in exile and we are not able to grasp the joyous happiness of perfect vision because of the magnitude of the glory. For who is able to breathe amid the delight of the overflowing jubilation that will be given to us in the homeland, when even that drop of sweetness that is shown to us on the way, away from our homeland on pilgrimage, inebriates the whole mind and stretches the whole breadth of the heart with new delights? And so their eyes were held because the Lord came dressed as a pilgrim. And since we see Him daily on the altar under the appearance of bread and wine He dwells with us in pilgrim's dress.[11]

The purpose of all such writing is, of course, to express or incite longing; to have each of the faithful pray with the Church herself, "Come, Lord Jesus," so that all He is for us individually and for our race may be brought to fulfillment. That prayer will be answered. The One Who fulfills all prophecy, all desire and all human need will come again and live with His own.

Companionship with Jesus

The word "Paradise" occurs three times in the New Testament (cf. 2 Cor 12:4 and Rv 2:7). The most familiar is found in that promise which encompasses all those others we have already reflected on. It was made to a criminal, the condemned and dying rebel. "Amen, I say to you, today you will be with me in Paradise" (Lk 23:43). In a sense, each of the saved will hear those words as they die. For the most fortunate, the Lord Christ, as Viaticum, will come to meet them at those last hours and then accompany them through death. Catholic piety rightly hopes and prays that all the departing will have been anointed, fortified by the Apostolic Blessing and Plenary Indulgence at the hour of death, consoled by the presence of Mary and Joseph, and thus not "put out to sea" alone. The Church desires, above all, that Christ, in the memorial of His own death, will be their food and companion, as He was for the Good Thief.

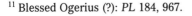

[11] Blessed Ogerius (?): *PL* 184, 967.

How difficult to imagine the experience of the resurrected in that restored universe in the presence of its King Whom they shall then see with the eyes of the reanimated and spiritual body! The wonder of seeing Christ then can perhaps be best compared with what Adam experienced as he stirred in Eden after the sleep during which Eve had been formed. He opens his eyes to discover this new phenomenon at his side, and is enraptured by a beauty unlike any he has previously witnessed in what had been his world of vegetation and animals.

> Watching her, Adam forgot his hunger, and the soreness of his side. For she was more beautiful than the gazelle to look upon. When she moved, the sunshine touched a sheen on her skin, glancing over her heel and thigh, and the hollow of her back: but it stayed in her hair. . . .

> But she was looking at Adam. . . . She put out a hand and touched him; touched his bearded cheek and laughed; then her own; and glanced down to compare their faces in the water. . . . When she leaned down, the daybright tresses slid in a cascade over the slenderness of her shoulder, against her mouth; and she tossed her head to fling them back.[12]

The encounter is intensified when he recognizes that she is intelligent like himself, one who hears and can speak, who can share. Adam may then have been aware for the first time of a need previously unarticulated. He had not been lonely, but he was alone of his kind. He was now fulfilled with her companionship. We have all encountered analogous situations, but never one the same. How much greater will be the wonder, awe and delight of those who, at trumpet's sound, arise to the New Adam in His new world! They shall say with the Psalmist, "When I awake, I will be satisfied with seeing you" (Ps 17:14; *New Vulgate*). There is no way to picture Him adequately, nor describe the joy that He will bring to His own. The author of the Book of Revelation throws out descriptive phrases that tumble over themselves in an attempt to leave the reader with an impression of this Son of Man Who is the eternal God. Jesus is the faithful witness, the firstborn from the dead, the ruler of the kings of the earth, the Alpha and Omega, He Who is and was and is to come, who was dead and has come to life and holds the keys of death and hell.

---

[12] David Bolt, *Adam*, pp. 62-63.

He is the holy and true, the Amen, the Lamb who was slain but lives, the Rider on the white horse who is Faithful and True, the King of kings and Lord of lords, the Root, the Offspring of David, the Morning Star. His face is like "the sun at its brightest" (1:16).

The fairest of the children of men will know all, see through each awaking person completely; He will be judge. Yet, the saved who look upon Him, aware of past sins, will, again like Adam and Eve in the first Paradise, feel no shame. For those predestined from the foundation of the world, both at the particular judgment and at the last judgment and entrance into resurrected life, there will be no place then for shame, just gratitude.

Conversation with Jesus

The beautiful *Jesu, dulcis memoria,* from the twelfth century and long ascribed, probably erroneously, to St. Bernard, captures some idea of what companionship with Christ will be in heaven. Formerly used in the Breviary for the feast of the Holy Name of Jesus, part of the hymn is now used at Lauds for the Feast of the Sacred Heart.[13]

Iesu, spes paenitentibus,
quam pius es petentibus,
quam bonus te quaerentibus;
sed quid invenientibus?

Nec lingua valet dicere,
Nec littera exprimere;
Expertus potest credere,
Quid sit Jesum diligere.

Sis, Jesu, nostrum gaudium
Qui es futurus praemium:
Sit nostra in te gloria,
Per cuncta semper saecula.

Jesus, hope of the penitent, how kind you are to those who ask, how good to those who seek You; what will You be to those who find You?

No tongue is able to say, nor words express what that will be like; only one who has experienced it is able to believe what it is to love Jesus.

Jesus, be now our joy as in the future You will be our reward. May our glory be in You for all ages.

Citing the Song of Songs 5:16 ("His conversation is sweetness itself"; *Jerusalem Bible),* Blaise Arminjon in his outstanding meditation writes:

---

[13] The text of the *Jesu, dulcis memoria* is taken from M. Britt, O.S.B., *The Hymns of the Roman Breviary* (New York: Benziger Bros., 1955), p. 91.

"How beautiful you are . . . how delightful!", she had exclaimed at the first encounter (1:16). And together with her, the psalmist: "Your promise, how sweet to my palate! Sweeter than honey to my mouth" (Ps 119:103). The reason is that the beauty of the one she loves, even though she thinks she has seen it at times, even if she attempts to describe it in her song, is essentially a hidden one. "Truly, God is hidden with you" (Is 45:15). On the other hand, his discourses, spoken in her inner life, are like his perfumes: something that she experiences; this Word, in particular, that speaks to her secret heart, so sweetly and tenderly at times. Yes, "his conversation is sweetness itself" and "there has never been anybody who has spoken like him" (Jn 7:46).[14]

Each of the Elect will experience for himself the truth of those words: never has anybody spoken like Him. In a life without secrets each conversation will nonetheless be intensely personal; where love is fully communal, it will be nevertheless more intimate. And the Master Who has so often seemed the silent companion of the journey will share the secrets of His own heart fully.

Coheirs with Christ

The Saints, in seeing Him and conversing with Him, will be ever more personally aware that Jesus the Lord is the one Who has made their everlasting life what it will be. Indeed, it will be His coming, the great Parousia, that will have transformed their bodies so as to make them like His own.

> From [heaven] we also await a savior, the Lord Jesus Christ. He will change our lowly body to conform with his glorified body by the power that enables him also to bring all things into subjection to himself (Phil 3:20-21).

That resurrection and conformity of bodies is only the beginning. The Blessed are to be given title to what is Jesus' own. They will be, as Paul reminds us, coheirs with the Firstborn from the dead.

> If [we are] children, then [we are] heirs, heirs of God and joint heirs with Christ, if only we suffer with him so that we may also be glorified with him (Rom 8:17).

---

[14] Blaise Arminjon, *The Cantata of Love*, p. 265.

To inherit what the Father gives and to enter into joint custody of the Kingdom is the endowment prepared by Christ for His chosen ones. Then, when they will have reached the full measure of the stature of Christ (cf. Eph 4:13), the Saints will fully realize the depth of the love from which nothing was able to separate them.

Candido Pozo tries to highlight what it means to be coheirs with Christ, as well as the everlasting importance of His humanity, by emphasizing the role that the risen Lord will play for the Elect in their vision of God. According to Pozo, the humanity of Christ, viewed with human eyes, will disseminate the divine splendor of the Person Whose nature it is. Beholding this splendor, the Saints will experience the invitation to know Christ totally, intimately, fully. But a knowledge such as that can only be had in a vision of the Word Himself Whose humanity the eyes of the Blessed behold. Through the humanity that He took from us to make us coheirs with Him, those who dwell in the homeland will be drawn to know the Person Who, in turn, can only be adequately known as the Begotten of the Father and co-Breather of the Spirit. In this way, living intimately with their risen Brother, the Saints inherit with His humanity a personal experience of the Father and the Spirit. Thus it will come about that the very Humanity of Christ does not represent merely an accidental joy that is added to the fully sufficient vision of God. Rather, seeing the humanity of Christ will be the "point of departure" as it were for the Beatific Vision. This opinion, which we believe to be correct, brings to light the significance of creation and of matter since, even in the life to come, it will be the material humanity of the Lord that will lead the Saints to His Person and to the knowledge of His Father and Spirit.

It might be objected that the Constitution *Benedictus Deus* excludes any creature from being the objective means of the Beatific Vision. There is to be no "intermediary" between the face-to-face, intuitive and immediate knowledge of God, not even an idea or concept in our mind. God will be known in Himself, no longer mediated to His children. Pozo's view, however, in no way denies this truth. In it, the Humanity of Christ is not a *means by which* or *in which* one knows God. The humanity of the Lord is rather the *starting point*. In the Sacred Humanity there is present to the Blessed what may be described as an enigma that finds its only solution in the *immediate* vision of God. Furthermore, to say that the essence of God and the other two divine Persons are seen in the Word contains nothing contrary to the Constitution *Benedictus Deus,* which only excludes a creature being an objective intermediary. The Word is a divine Person and not a creature, and thus His role in making the Father and Spirit known in the life to come will be but a continuation of what He has done since creation itself.[15]

Satisfaction of Desires

Psalm 107:9 praises God for the fact that He satisfies the thirsty and fills the hungry with good things. All that moisture betokened in a land where the early and late rains denoted life itself to the people can be understood even by those who, in lands of abundant water, experience the occasional summer of drought. Without water, the earth thirsts, the animals thirst, we thirst. In the Holy Land, one could watch the caking of soil as well as the desiccation of animals and humans because of the lack of water. This daily awareness led readily to the appreciation that our race itself thirsts, metaphorically, for more than natural water. Our very desires and human wants are a thirst. In response to such needs, God, who compared Himself to the gentle waters of Siloam (cf. Is 8:6, called "Shiloah" there), answered by watering His people with His own presence, inviting them to refreshment.

Owing to the value of pure water, it is not surprising that polluted waters were recognized as a curse and a plague, as Pharaoh saw without learning (cf. Ex 7:14-24) and as, in one of those many repetitions of history forced by our inability to learn, the enemies of the King of kings will discover at the end time (cf. Rv 16:4-5). The Fountain of life has never willed such misery for any of His creation, and so repeatedly He invited a parched people, "All you who are thirsty, come to the water! You who have no money, come, receive grain and eat; come, without paying and without cost, drink wine and milk! (Is 55:1). To decline that

---

[15] Cf. Pozo, *Teología del Más Allá,* notes 101 and 108 on pp. 161 and 162.

invitation was to suffer thirst, to become dry as dust, a punishment like the fate of the Tempter himself who was condemned to lick the dust of the earth (cf. Gn 3:14).

> Two evils have my people done: they have forsaken me, the source of living waters; they have dug themselves cisterns, broken cisterns, that hold no water (Jer 2:13).

> O hope of Israel, O Lord! all who forsake you shall be in disgrace; the rebels in the land shall be put to shame; they have forsaken the source of living waters, the Lord (Jer 17:13).

Anyone who has ever suffered great thirst understands well the imagery involved in such lines. Even God knows it, for the Lord of rains and waters put Himself in a condition to know what it was to long for the comfort of water. "Aware that everything was now finished, in order that the scripture might be fulfilled, Jesus said, 'I thirst' " (Jn 19:28). For the Crucified there was the elementary, physical need for water. Preachers, however, have rightly seen much more implied in those words. Jesus' thirst was a desire for us, for our salvation, for our love. He wanted us, He Who had promised that "I will come back again and take you to myself, so that where I am you also may be" (Jn 14:3). When He cries from the Cross "I thirst," it is as if the very Source of living Water had itself dried up, begging to be refreshed by the shallows that draw from Him as fountain.

Moved by compassion, Jesus endured and expressed His own thirst to satisfy ours. It was not the first time, of course, that He had attempted to convey the same lesson. The Fountain of life, seated weary and thirsty in the heat of a day, petitioned a woman of Samaria for water, using His dryness to slake hers.

> Jesus answered and said to her, "If you knew the gift of God and who is saying to you, 'Give me a drink,' you would have asked him and he would have given you living water" (Jn 4:10).

Without Him we are empty cisterns. And His own gentle recalling of that fact to the Samaritan was itself one of the many subtle ways in which He led her and us to the recognition of Who He is. He is Israel's God Who gives water and all that water signifies: life, refreshment, satisfaction of desires, relaxation. And what He said to that one woman, type of all who are not fully aware of their own many thirsts and who think to satisfy them with what is not capable of quenching, He offered to all.

> On the last and greatest day of the feast, Jesus stood up and exclaimed, "Let anyone who thirsts come to me and drink. Whoever believes in me, as scripture says: 'Rivers of living water will flow from within him' " (Jn 7:37-38).

There are always some whose need for the refreshment of those waters is more pronounced. Then too the extent of the need may vary according to one's lot in life or the vicissitudes of the hour. Frequently enough, the apparently sterile, the eunuch, will in a particular way long for the water that moistens roots, produces fruit, reinvigorates. Gerald Manley Hopkins set forth the cry of such as those in a beautiful poem. Working from the text of Jeremiah (12:1ff) where the Prophet, beset on all sides and apparently a failure, presents his complaint to God, the poet presents his own case to the Lord. He laments the fact that while the works of others are crowned with success his own seem doomed to failure and disappointment. He reminds his Savior that he has dedicated his life and work to Him, but that it all seems to no purpose. It is almost as if God, Who is his friend, were his enemy. Even the lesser creatures of the Lord are more successful in achieving their purposes.

> . . . *birds build—but not I build; no, but strain,*
> *Time's eunuch, and not breed one work that wakes.*
> *Mine, O thou lord of life, send my roots rain.*
>
> (A Hopkins Reader, p. 82)

Time's eunuch! Such was God Himself for a term, and so, in His human feelings, it must have felt to Him during the course of His ministry and during that last day and night before His death. All for nothing, not one work that wakes. In like fashion so many of His followers, not only those who have made themselves eunuchs for the Kingdom of heaven but all who live to follow Him, have, at times, experienced that sense of being deprived of what He alone can give—and deprived by Him. "Wert thou my enemy, O thou my friend!" The words are not said in anger, however; they are merely a complaint that ends for all the faithful in prayer: Lord of life, send my roots rain! And when it comes, it never seems sufficient; we yearn for more. Such is the testimony of all those who drink deeply of Him at the Eucharist and in prayer. It is Water so limpid that we want to need more. And more indeed is to come. Every river and stream of the renewed heaven and earth, delightful and refreshing in themselves, runoffs from the "river of life-giving water, sparkling like crystal, flowing from the throne of God and of the Lamb" (Rv 22:1), will but reflect the Fountain of life-giving waters, God Himself in His Paradise. There he will not only "lead them to springs of life-giving water" (Rv 7:17) but also give them to drink: "To the thirsty I will give a gift from the spring of life-giving water" (Rv 21:6). And what they will drink is their fill of Him, for opening their mouths He Himself will fill them (cf. Ps 81:10).

The Spirit

As John the Evangelist makes clear, the water with which Jesus intended to slake the thirst of those willing to come to the waters and drink freely was the Holy Spirit of God.

> He said this in reference to the Spirit that those who came to believe in him were to receive. There was, of course, no Spirit yet, because Jesus had not yet been glorified (Jn 7:39).

St. Cyril of Jerusalem sought to give an explanation of why Jesus compared the Spirit to water.

> "The water that I will give will become in him a fountain of living water." . . . Why is it that the grace of the Spirit is described by the word "water"? It is because all things are made of water; because water is that which makes vegetation and animal life; because water comes down from heaven as rain. It falls in one way and one form but begets multiform effects: it exists in one way in the palm tree, another in the vine, and in all kinds of ways in all things. Not changing itself, the rain descends with various effects. Accommodating itself to what receives it, it effects for each thing what is suitable for it.
>
> In the same way the Holy Spirit, although He is one and of one form and is indivisible, proportions grace to each person as He wills. . . . Although the Spirit is always one and the same, He effects many powerful things, by the will of God and in the name of Christ.[16]

The same idea, with different imagery, is expressed by St. Basil the Great.

> Simple in His Being, He is manifold in His powerful deeds; wholly present to each person, wholly present everywhere. Incapable of change, He is divided; unable to be diminished, He is shared. He is like the image of the sun's rays, which is present

---

[16] Cyril of Jerusalem, *Cat. 16: de Spiritu Sancto*, I, 11: *PG* 33, 932-933.

to each person as though to that one alone and which enlightens the land and sea and air. So the Holy Spirit is present to each who is capable of receiving Him, as if for that person alone, and while remaining intact pours forth grace sufficient for all.[17]

It is this Spirit flowing from Christ that is bracing coolness for the parched and consolation for the afflicted.

Consolator optime	*O Best of Consolers,*
Dulcis hospes animae,	*Dear Guest of the soul,*
Dulce refrigerium.	*You are pleasant refreshment.*
In labore requies,	*You are Rest in labor,*
In aestu temperies,	*Moderation in the heat,*
In fletu solatium.	*Solace in tears.*

The Refreshment promised and given by the Risen Jesus is, as the Creed confesses, the "Lord and Giver of Life." As such this delightful Guest of the soul is, as so often symbolized in the Bible, a great and mighty wind, a power, a kindling fire. Already in Ezekiel the Spirit of the living God was discerned to be what would give life to the dead bones of a people in exile.

The hand of the Lord came upon me, and he led me out in the spirit of the Lord and set me in the center of the plain, which was now filled with bones. He made me walk among them in every direction so that I saw how many they were on the surface of the plain. How dry they were! He asked me: Son of man, can these bones come to life? "Lord God," I answered, "you alone know that." Then he said to me: Prophesy over these bones, and say to them: Dry bones, hear the word of the Lord! Thus says the Lord God to these bones: See! I will bring spirit into you, that you may come to life. I will put sinews upon you, make flesh grow over you, cover you with skin, and put spirit in you so that you may come to life and know that I am the Lord. I prophesied as I had been told, and even as I was prophesying I heard a noise; it was a rattling as the bones came together, bone joining bone. I saw the sinews and the flesh come upon them, and the skin cover them, but there was no spirit in them. Then he said to me: Prophesy to the spirit, prophesy, son of man, and say to the spirit: Thus says the Lord God: From the four winds come, O spirit, and breathe into these slain that they may come to life. I prophesied as he told me, and the spirit came into them; they came alive and stood upright, a vast army. Then

---

[17] Basil, *On the Holy Spirit,* IX, 22-23; *Sources Chrétiennes,* vol. 17, trans. by Benoît Pruche, O.P., pp. 146-147.

he said to me: Son of man, these bones are the whole house of Israel. They have been saying, "Our bones are dried up, our hope is lost, and we are cut off." Therefore, prophesy and say to them: Thus says the Lord God: O my people, I will open your graves and have you rise from them, and bring you back to the land of Israel. Then you shall know that I am the Lord, when I open your graves and have you rise from them, O my people! I will put my spirit in you that you may live, and I will settle you upon your land; thus you shall know that I am the Lord. I have promised, and I will do it, says the Lord (Ez 37-14).

We have already reflected on the work of the Holy Spirit in preparing the world to come.[18] He is the One Who will give life to these mortal bodies, breathed anew into the clay to which our bodies are destined to return. "If the Spirit of the one who raised Jesus from the dead dwells in you, the one who raised Christ from the dead will give life to your mortal bodies also, through his Spirit that dwells in you" (Rom 8:11).

It is this same Spirit, within us now, Who gives us the ability to approach the Father of Jesus as our own, making us bold enough to address Him as "Abba."

> You did not receive a spirit of slavery to fall back into fear, but you received a spirit of adoption, through which we cry, *Abba*, "Father!" (Rom 8:15).

Continuing to fulfill the same role, it will be *in* the Spirit of Christ that the Blessed will possess the Father, Who Himself loves them and gives them life.

Beyond the Face of Jesus: The Father

The face of Christ is itself the Image of Another, as the New Testament writers strive to teach us in a variety of ways.

> The god of this age has blinded the minds of the unbelievers, so that they may not see the light of the gospel of the glory of Christ, who is the image of God (2 Cor 4:4).

> He is the image of the invisible God, the firstborn of all creation (Col 1:15).

> In times past, God spoke in partial and various ways to our ancestors through the prophets; in these last days, he spoke to us through a son, whom he made heir of all things and through

---

[18] Cf. above in Chapter VI: "City of Compact Unity," p. 260, the quotation from *Gaudium et Spes*, 39.

whom he created the universe, who is the refulgence of his glory, the very imprint of his being, and who sustains all things by his mighty word. When he had accomplished purification from sins, he took his seat at the right hand of the Majesty on high (Heb 1:1-3).

The radiance of God's glory and the exact representation of His being, such is what Jesus of Nazareth is. As a consequence, He points to what He represents, to the One Whose image He is. It was Jesus Himself, of course, Who, during His public ministry, reminded us that there was another Face. "See that you do not despise one of these little ones, for I say to you that their angels in heaven always look upon the face of my heavenly Father" (Mt 18:10). It is to the Face beyond the face of Christ that the Church refers when she prays to the Father, asking Him to look with benign countenance on the Body and Blood of His Son, the holy Bread of life eternal and the chalice of endless salvation.[19]

Commenting on one of the psalms, Augustine observes:

[The psalm says] "You will hide them in the secret of Your face." What kind of a place is this? It does not say: "You will hide them in Your heaven"; it does not say, "You will hide them in Paradise"; it does not say, "You will hide them in the bosom of Abraham." For in many faithful ways the future places of the Saints are set forth in the holy Scriptures. But all that which is other than God is worthless. He Who keeps us safe in the place of this life will Himself be our place after this life.[20]

To hide in the face of the Father is to find one's own *place* there. As we know, when the men and women of the Old Testament prayed, "Show us Your face," they invoked a God Who, as pure Spirit, was recognized as having no face at all. Nevertheless, He Himself wants to be seen, and His glory, which shines on the human face of the Incarnate Word, will not be all of the face of God that will be seen. The Father Himself will be known and experienced. Jesus prayed that we might come to know the glory of the Father's own face. This He did in a particular way the night before He died. "Father, they are your gift to me. I wish that where I am they also may be with me, that they may see my glory

---

[19] The *Unde et memores* prayer of the Roman Canon continues as *"Supra quae propitio ac sereno vultu respicere digneris . . ."* ("Deign to look upon these gifts with a pleased and gracious face").

[20] Augustine, *Ennarr. in Ps 30, II s. III,* 8: CCSL 38, p. 218.

that you gave me, because you loved me before the foundation of the world—that they [may] know you, the only true God" (Jn 17:24 and 3).

Pointing always beyond Himself to another face, Jesus conducts His followers to the realization that it is for His Father, the source of life, that our poor race thirsts. It is from that paternity that the life-giving Spirit is sent by Christ.

> For the benefit of the human race the Word has been made dispenser of the grace of the Father, and for the race He has accomplished the great "economies," showing God to the race and presenting the race to God. He preserved the invisibility of the Father lest we esteem God less and so that we might have something to strive for. At the same time He made God visible through the multiple "economies" lest, totally deprived of God, the race might completely cease to exist. The glory of God is the existence of the race; the life of mankind is the vision of God. If the revelation of God gives life to all beings that live on earth, how much more will the manifestation of the Father through the Word give life to those who see God![21]

Speaking of this Father Who has life in Himself and gives it to the Son Who in turn shares it with us (cf. Jn 5:26), Augustine preached:

> He Himself is eternal life in which we will live when He takes us to Himself; and that eternal life, which He is, exists in Himself, and where He is we will be, namely in Him.[22]

And commenting on John 17:21-23 where in such sublime words Jesus reminds the disciples of the Father's love, the Doctor of Charity said:

> Jesus says, "You have loved them, as you have loved Me," which is saying nothing else than "You have loved them because You have loved Me." He Who loves the Son will love the members of the Son, nor is there any other cause for loving the members than that He loves the Son. However, He loves the Son according to His divinity, because He begot the Son as His equal. He loves Him also inasmuch as He is man because the same only-begotten Word was made flesh and, because of the Word, the flesh of the Word is dear to the Father. Moreover He loves us because we are the members of the one He loves, and

---

[21] Irenaeus, *Adversus Haereses*, bk. IV, 20, 7, *Sources Chrétiennes*, no. 100, pp. 646-649.

[22] Augustine, *In Iohannis Evangelium*, 70, 1: CCSL 36, p. 502.

in order that we might be members He loved us before we existed.[23]

The love of this Father—a gentle but firm, tender and deliberate love—is evident already in the Old Testament. When Isaiah spoke of Him as coming with power, he immediately added: "Like a shepherd he feeds his flock; in his arms he gathers the lambs, carrying them in his bosom, and leading the ewes with care" (Is 40:11). And Hosea speaks for Him saying: "When Israel was a child I loved him. . . . It was I who taught Ephraim to walk, who took them in my arms. . . . I drew them with human cords, with bands of love" (Hos 11:1, 3-4). Receiving little but ingratitude for such love, He asks plaintively, "O my people, what have I done to you, or how have I wearied you? Answer me! (Mi 6:3). Such love came to be fully and astoundingly manifested when he gave of His own, out of love, even to death on the cross.

The Father's Love in Predestination

It is Paternal love, furthermore, that has predestined the Saints to the joys that will be theirs in the life to come. St. Paul makes this strikingly clear by proclaiming:

> We know that all things work for good for those who love God, who are called according to his purpose. For those he foreknew he also predestined to be conformed to the image of his Son. . . . And those he predestined he also called; and those he called he also justified; and those he justified he also glorified (Rom 8:28-30).

> For by grace you have been saved through faith, and this is not from you; it is the gift of God; it is not from works, so no one may boast. For we are his handiwork, created in Christ Jesus for the good works that God has prepared in advance, that we should live in them (Eph 2:8-10).

The mystery of predestination has often been portrayed as a doctrine of gloom and even of terror. The realization that God has predestined the just by gratuitously saving them and preparing ahead of time the good works that would be theirs—together with the fact that He knows what each person does and will do

---

[23] Augustine, *In Iohannis Evangelium*, 110, 5: CCSL 36, p. 626.

and what is to be the outcome of the life of each—all this has led some to think that the doctrine denies free will, or to say that it is useless to strive to do good because everything is already decided. Augustine, the Doctor of Grace, repudiated such notions. Preaching on John 12:37-43 where the Evangelist records that some of the Jews did not believe in Jesus and that this occurred to fulfill the word of Isaiah the prophet, Augustine tackles this most difficult theme, one to which controversy would bring him back many times in his later life.

> To treat this question with any competence, to examine and shake the dust off its tortured paths in a way that is worthy, is, I think, something beyond my ability, beyond the time that remains and beyond your capacity. Nevertheless, because of your expectations, we are not free to pass on to other things unless we say something. So accept what we are capable of saying; and where we are not adequate to your expectation, demand the growth from Him Who sent us to plant and water since, as the Apostle says, "The one who plants is nothing, nor the one who waters, but rather God Who gives the growth" (1 Cor 3:7). Thus, there are some people who mutter to themselves and, when they are able, sometimes speak aloud and contend in turbulent debate, saying, "What did the Jews do or what fault was theirs if it was necessary that the word of Isaiah the prophet be fulfilled . . ."?
>
> To such people we reply that the Lord Who knows future realities predicted the unfaithfulness of the Jews through the prophet. Nevertheless He predicted it; He did not make it happen. For God does not compel anyone to sin because of the fact that He already knows a person's future sins. He knows *their* sins ahead of time, not *His* sins; not the sins of another but their sins. Therefore if those sins that He knew beforehand to be theirs were in fact not theirs then indeed He did not know them; but, because His foreknowledge cannot be deceived, it is certain that they whom God knew would be sinners did themselves sin and not another. Therefore the Jews committed a sin that He, to Whom sin is displeasing, did not compel them to commit. He, to Whom nothing is hidden, predicted that it would happen. Therefore, if they had willed to do good instead of evil, there would have been nothing to keep them from doing it. What they were going to do was foreseen by Him Who knows what each will do and Who knows what each will receive for his or her work.[24]

---

[24] Augustine, *In Iohannis Evangelium*, 53, 4: CCSL 36, pp. 453-454.

God in no way, he is saying, predetermines anyone to evil or to damnation. He gives everyone more than what is truly sufficient help to be saved but leaves each the freedom to refuse what is offered. If it is not refused—as it ultimately is not on the part of the predestined—then it efficaciously produces in them good works, *gratia victrix* (victorious grace) as Augustine called it.[25] Such was the teaching of Augustine and such has always been the teaching of the Church of Christ. On the other hand, the Father, Who wills to save all, has predestined the Elect. Having predestined, He calls, graces and justifies, preparing for them the good works that He will reward as their own. And all this He does gratuitously, although in His largesse He gives His chosen the right to merit even more. This predestination is a work of love on His part and it is accomplished by love. As Augustine taught in so many places, God draws His own to Himself by delighting them *(delectatio* is a favorite word in the Augustinian vocabulary) with His beauty and by His truth that He lets them experience inwardly.

> There is a certain manifestation of God of which the unholy are completely unaware; for them there is no manifestation of God the Father and the Holy Spirit. For them there can be a manifestation of the Son, but only according to the flesh.[26]

It is by interior manifestation producing delight that the Father draws His children (cf. Jn 6:44). The impression one obtains from reading carefully Augustine's many writings on predestination is that God predestines the Elect and then achieves what He has determined by *alluring them.* And it is, I think, an accurate picture, both of what Augustine means and of what is the reality. Predestination is a work of love from beginning to end: love offered freely and with nothing in the beloved to entice the divine Lover; love in its execution, which sees an expectant Father awaiting the sinful creature, a Father Who invisibly and mightily entices the wandering child to return and the justified to persevere; love in the everlasting embrace when He welcomes His own into the life to come as He gives the order, "Quickly,

---

[25] On the intricate question of the nature of sufficient and efficacious grace, one can still confer with great profit Jacques Maritain's *Existence and the Existent,* pp. 99-112, and Charles Journet's *The Meaning of Grace,* pp. 17-50.

[26] Augustine, *In Iohannis Evangelium,* 76, 2: CCSL 36, p. 518.

bring the finest robe and put it on them. Put rings on their fingers and sandals on their feet. . . . Let us celebrate with a feast" (cf. Lk 15:22-23). At that point the Father will begin the Son's wedding banquet (cf. Mt 22:1) in this Kingdom of God and His Christ (Eph 5:5). Journey done, the Promise will have been reached.

The Book of Joshua tells us what happened when the Jews arrived at the promised land and ate their first meal in the new land: "On that same day after the Passover on which they ate of the produce of the land, the manna ceased. No longer was there manna for the Israelites who that year ate of the yield of the land of Canaan" (Jos 5:12). So shall it be with those who are saved. Those who have fed on the Hidden Manna here, either sacramentally or in desire, will feed on that way no longer. They will have entered into the homeland. The Father will give them to feast on the Son, to Whom He has drawn them in the Spirit from all time (cf. Jn 6:44). Thus, it is through the Son and in the Spirit that we shall have life from the Father, feast with Him, be satisfied by Him and enjoy all the wonders that are normally expressed—in a type of theological shorthand—by the phrase Beatific Vision.

The Beatific Vision

In the introduction to his chief work, *The Phenomenon of Man*, Teilhard de Chardin wrote as Foreword an essay on the importance of sight.

> *Seeing.* We might say that the whole of life lies in that verb—if not in end, at least in essence. Fuller being is closer union; such is the kernel and conclusion of this book. But let us emphasize the point: union can only increase through an increase in consciousness, that is to say in vision. And that, doubtless, is why the history of the living world can be summarised as the elaboration of ever more perfect eyes within a cosmos in which there is always something more to be seen. After all, do we not judge the perfection of an animal, or the supremacy of a thinking being, by the penetration and synthetic power of their gaze? To try to see more and better is not a matter of whim or curiosity or self-indulgence. *To see or to perish* is the very condition

laid upon everything that makes up the universe, by reason of the mysterious gift of existence. And this, in superior measure, is man's condition.[27]

The history of the living world is summarized as the elaboration of ever more perfect eyes. That statement I believe to be true, as well as its corollary: we must see or perish.

There are, of course, different ways of seeing. As is obvious, sight is more than ocular vision. The Teacher struck the Pharisees with that truth.

> Jesus said, "I came into this world for judgment, so that those who do not see might see, and those who do see might become blind." Some of the Pharisees who were with him heard this and said to him, "Surely we are not also blind, are we?" Jesus said to them, "If you were blind, you would have no sin; but now you are saying, 'We see,' so your sin remains" (Jn 9:39-41).

So much of life depends on how we see it. To fail to see is to perish. God's Revelation gives sight we would not otherwise have had; it strengthens what sin has weakened in our race's vision. That Revelation informs us that the goal of our lives is sight, a vision that will answer all questions, fill the seer with light and indeed be the source of life. The race is called to see and ultimately to see God Himself. This, in part, is what is meant by the term Beatific Vision.

Matthias Scheeben called Aquinas' study of the Beatific Vision (namely of that sight of God which makes us beatific, happy) "incomparably clear and profound."[28] Some of the highlights of St. Thomas' teaching follow:

> [In this vision] it is necessary that a created intellect see the divine essence by means of the divine essence itself. . . . Therefore we shall see God face to face because we shall see Him immediately—seeing Him in that manner by which He sees Himself.[29]

Silvester of Ferrara, in his commentary on the *Summa Contra Gentiles*, rightly observes that to see God through His own essence and to see Him immediately amount to saying the same thing. He notes as well that when we speak of "face to face" we

---

[27] Teilhard de Chardin, *The Phenomenon of Man*, p. 31.

[28] Scheeben, *The Mysteries of Christianity*, p. 660, note 16.

[29] Aquinas, *Summa Contra Gentiles*, III, q. 51.

are, of course, using analogy, since properly speaking God as Spirit has no face.[30] Aquinas continues:

> Moreover it is necessary for so noble a vision that the created intellect be elevated by some influence of the divine goodness. . . . In order that the divine essence may become the intelligible species for a created intellect—which is what is required so that the divine substance may be seen—it is necessary for the created intellect to be elevated for this purpose by a higher disposition. . . . Furthermore, an increase by means of an intensification of [the created intellects'] natural powers is not sufficient: because this vision is not of the same nature as the vision of the natural created intellect. . . . It is necessary therefore that there be an increase of the intellective power through the acquisition of some new disposition. . . . This disposition by which the created intellect is raised to an intellectual vision of the divine substance is fittingly called the *light of glory*: . . . This is the light of which the psalm speaks when it says "In your light we see the light" (Ps 36:10).[31]

There is much profound thought here. What Thomas is saying, in part, is that, for those who see God immediately, there will be nothing intervening between the human intellect and God Himself. In this life, we know things intellectually by means of or through the ideas we form of them. Not so with the Beatific Vision. No human idea could express God adequately, and so the Blessed shall know Him intuitively and directly, with no intervening concept or idea. Since such a type of knowing is not natural to the human person, God will give the Saints a special power for knowing in this fashion. This power Thomas calls "the light of glory." It is, in other words (and he is still speaking analogously, using images to convey his meaning), a gift that will make the human mind capable of perceiving the divinity directly.

> Moreover it is possible that there be various degrees of participation in this light so that one person may be more illumined by it than another. Therefore it is possible that one who sees God sees Him more perfectly than another, even though each sees His substance. . . . Some people are greater in virtue, some less, and virtue is the road to happiness. Thus it is necessary that there be diversity in the vision of God, that some see the divine substance more perfectly, others less perfectly.[32]

---

[30] Cf. Silvester, *Commentary on Contra Gentiles*, III, 51, *Opera Omnia*, p. 143.
[31] Aquinas, *Summa Contra Gentiles*, III, q. 53.
[32] *Ibid.*, q. 58.

This vision is the reward of the pure of heart, according to the promise of Jesus, "Blessed are the clean of heart, for they will see God" (Mt 5:8). The sight will constitute perfect happiness. Of that vision it is said in Scripture: "We shall be like him" (1 Jn 3:2), for we "shall know fully as [we are] fully known" (1 Cor 13:12). Commenting on that, the priest Hippolytus wrote:

> . . . taught by the living God, you will have an immortal and incorruptible body, together with your soul. You will be born into the heavenly Kingdom because, while living on earth, you knew the King of Heaven. You will be sharers with God and coheirs with Christ, not enslaved to any evil desires or inclinations, or subject to any sickness. For you will have been made God. Whatever evil things you put up with, being human, these you endured because you were human; those things that follow upon being God, those God has promised to you, because you will have been deified,[33] and made immortal. This is what is meant when it is said, "Know yourself," i.e., know the God Who created you, for knowledge of oneself is what happens to the one who is known by Him Who called us.[34]

It is evident that in all this talk of "knowing" God, the word "know" is being used in its biblical sense of intimate and total union. Indeed, the knowledge spoken of is like the sexual union of man and wife, which is never meant to be merely a carnal knowing, but a full personal knowledge of heart, mind and affections brought about by dwelling together. So it is when the Saints will know as they are known. One is speaking of a total personal union with God, in which He imparts Himself and all His attributes so that they become the property of His Elect by participation.

Some think that the Beatific Vision absorbs those who inherit everlasting life so completely that nothing else will be necessary or even possible. Such a view is a misunderstanding of God's goodness. St. Thomas has a statement in his comment on the article of the Creed, "Creator of heaven and earth," that is the equivalent of a principle. I believe it is correct and pertinent to the refutation of the notion that sees the vision of God as absorbing the Elect.

---

[33] Reading *Theopoiethes* with the *PG* footnote, rather than the *etheopoiethes* of the text.

[34] Hippolytus, *Refutation of All Heresies*, bk. 10, 34: *PG* 16, 3, 2454.

> . . . all things are arranged according to various levels of beauty and excellence, and the nearer one draws to God, so much the more beautiful and excellent are these things.[35]

There is an illustrative passage in the Book of the prophet Zechariah that may be used to support Thomas' observation. It reads:

> The Lord shall save the tents of Judah first, that the glory of the house of David and the glory of the inhabitants of Jerusalem may not be exalted over Judah. On that day, the Lord will shield the inhabitants of Jerusalem, and the weakling among them shall be like David on that day, and the house of David godlike, like an angel of the Lord before them (Zec 12:7-8).

The passage was written after the Babylonian captivity and after the family of David had ceased having any public role in the affairs of the people. Nonetheless the prophet predicts a future greatness for that shepherd clan: "the house of David [will be] godlike." In fact the Eternal Shepherd would come among us from that family. Even so, the greatness of the Davidic family and of Jerusalem would not make insignificant the glory of the most feeble of Judah. On the contrary, as the glory of David and Jerusalem became greater in the last days, God would see to it that the lowly would become proportionately great in glory. And so it is with those who will delight in the vision of God. His glory will make the Saints lustrous; His beauty will magnify the loveliness of His creation; the sight of Him face to face will only make every other face more attractive, not less. Like any person wildly in love who sees everything in new lights and tones, so will it be with those who drink in God. His beauty will not absorb; it will enchant and, in its very fascination, enrich the pleasure to be drawn from everyone and everything else.

Augustine once thought that the vision of God about which we are speaking would be purely intellectual, i.e., that the citizens of the world to come would not see Him with bodily eyes.

> The invisible and incorruptible God "Who alone is immortal and dwells in inaccessible light, Whom no one has seen nor is capable of seeing" (1 Tm 6:16), is therefore not able to be seen by anyone in the manner by which we see bodily things while

---

[35] Aquinas, *The Sermon-Conferences on the Apostles' Creed*, trans. by Nicholas Ayo, pp. 36-37.

we ourselves are in the body.[36] Both now and in the future life the vision of God is the office of the inner man.[37]

Always one to rethink his own positions, the Bishop of Hippo Regius did not rest content with this opinion and ultimately modified his view. In the *City of God* he writes:

> The capacity of those eyes [of the resurrected body] will be very powerful, not in order that they may see more keenly . . . but so that they may see incorporeal realities. . . . Therefore it is very believable that we will see the earthly bodies of the new heaven and the new earth in such a way that we shall see God, with the bodies we will then have, most clearly as He is present everywhere and governing the corporeal universe. . . . Therefore God will be seen by those eyes. . . .[38]

Having carefully chronicled the evolution of Augustine's thought on this matter, Eugene Portalie made the following judgment.

> All that [i.e., the remarks above from the *City of God*] is very vague, just as are the two imaginary suppositions to justify the sight of a spiritual being by a material organ. The first is the hypothesis of such a transformation that the glorified eye would no longer be a bodily eye, but a spiritualized eye, that is, because it would no longer be an eye. The second imagines that God is seen simultaneously in creatures and in Himself. . . . According to the *Retractations*, this is his last word on the subject. Posterity has not understood him. Philosphers like Nourrisson have accused him of abandoning the clear distinction he had established with Plato between the sensible and the intelligible. His earlier opinion has prevailed in the schools and in the Church.[39]

Great student that he was (even yet, I think, Portalie's work on Augustine is unsurpassed in the field of anything of comparable size and purpose), one need not follow the French Jesuit in this instance. It is undoubtedly true that Augustine moved away from the Platonic distinction between the sensible and the intel-

---

[36] Augustine, *Letter 92*, 3: CSEL, 34, 2, p. 438.

[37] *Ibid.*, p. 439.

[38] Augustine, *City of God*, bk. 22, ch. 29: CSEL 40, 2, pp. 661 and 663. Ambrose Autpert, *In Apocalypsin*, X: CCCM, vol. 27 A, pp. 841-851, treats this question, quoting Augustine extensively in all his development. He ends by saying we can't be sure whether we see God with bodily eyes. Later theology was more apodictic.

[39] Portalie, pp. 303-304.

ligible. However, he had moved so far in so many directions
beyond the early Platonic cast to his thought (and all that movement was in terms of a greater noetic realism and a more profound and more fully Biblical view of the importance of matter,
material creation, and the body) that his change of mind in this
case as well should not surprise us. And to admit that he abandoned Plato's distinction should not, without proof, be sufficient
to insinuate that he was wrong in so doing. Father Portalie's remark that later theology did not follow Augustine in this matter
is also true. Subsequent theologians, including St. Thomas, continued to speak of the Vision as had the early Augustine: as being
a purely intellectual perception.

In defense of the North African, it must be said that Father
Portalie's reference to the "two suppositions," however, are very
wide of the mark. The "spiritual" eye, for Augustine, is still a real
eye; it is the eye that is concordant with a "spiritual" body,
which, for Augustine and all Catholic teaching, is not to be opposed to "material," but rather to the material self as existing in
a fallen world. It is not true, moreover, to say that, like theologians, the Church herself has chosen the earlier Augustine over
the later. She has no official teaching on this matter at all, as long
as one does not say that the senses, in any way, mediate the Vision of God to the Elect. As for seeing God in Himself *and* in His
creatures, we have already indicated that we think such will be
the case and that Augustine is completely correct. God will be
known immediately in Himself and reflected gloriously in everyone and everything else. As one of Augustine's disciples wrote:

> Brethren, we will enjoy God in that eternal and perfect
> beatitude in a threefold way: seeing Him in all creatures, hav-
> ing Him in our very selves, and, what is ineffably more pleasant
> and blessed than these two things, knowing the Blessed Trinity
> in itself and contemplating that Glory with the clean eye of the
> heart and without any obscurity.[40]

Augustine's mature position, moreover, is a wonderful reminder to us that the Vision of God will satisfy and give exquisite
delight not merely to human souls, but to the senses as well. It is
also a teaching that helps resolve the old Scholastic discussion

---

[40] St. Bernard, *In Festivitate Omnium Sanctorum; Sermo 4, Opera Omnia*, vol.
V, p. 357.

about whether the essential happiness of the life to come would be found in the intellect or the will. In effect, it will be found in the whole person, intellect, will and senses.

When we were considering above the mystery of predestination, we cited Augustine's words about the inner manifestations that the good God makes of Himself to those who belong to Him. Such disclosures are consequents of what we know in theology as the grace of inhabitation, that gift through which God dwells in those who enjoy His favor. Truths such as this are a reminder that already the Saints are being prepared for what will be theirs in the life to come. As the present universe transformed—and not something completely new—will be theirs, so, in a like way, will it be with the sight of God. The immediate experience of God will be the fulfillment of faith, the flowering of what they already possess, though obscurely.

> When the soul is imbued with the beginning of faith that works through love, it strives, by right living, to arrive at vision where the ineffable beauty—the vision of which is total happiness—is known to the Saints, the perfect in heart. . . . That which is first and that which is last is this: to begin in faith, to end in vision.[41]

This is essentially what St. Thomas was saying in his remarks on the "light of glory." The Saints will be graced, raised above their natural powers, to be able to experience directly what is already known in faith. The fact that the Beatific Vision will complete and perfect faith is consistent with the teaching that *already* in some sense we live the life to come.

> If then you were raised with Christ, seek what is above, where Christ is seated at the right hand of God. Think of what is above, not of what is on earth. For you have died, and your life is hidden with Christ in God. When Christ your life appears, then you too will appear with him in glory (Col 3:1-4).

The same doctrine is put succinctly in Philippians 3:20 where Paul writes: "Our citizenship is in heaven" (cf. Eph 2:19). There is surely much obscurity in such texts, but they indicate that, because of our union with the risen Lord, there is some real sense in which we already dwell with Him where He is, namely

---

[41] Augustine, *Enchiridion*, I, 5: CCSL 46, p. 50.

in the life to come. Vague as it may seem at times, we are—by an obscure anticipation—*experiencing* what God has prepared for those who love Him. Augustine strongly affirms this when he preaches for the Feast of the Ascension of the Lord.

> Since He ascended but did not depart from us, so we are already there with Him even though what He promised to our body has not yet happened to us. . . . He, although He is there, is also with us; and we, although we are here, are also there with him. . . . This is said because of unity, that is because He is our Head and we are His Body.[42]

Such an apparently mythical outlook is grounded on the truth of our bond with Christ in His Church and in His Eucharistic Flesh. We may say that what is being taught is, at the minimum, that we truly live where our affections are, as anyone who is in love but physically separated from the beloved realizes. There is more even than this, however, in the case of the faithful Christian. Union with Christ, especially Eucharistic union, works magnetically to pull us out of the present age into what lies before us. Those who belong to Him live truly with a "foot in two worlds."

For the moment the present world appears to be what is substantial, the one to come ethereal, the sight of a beloved face something real, the thought of the vision of God nebulous. In fact, however, what C.S. Lewis remarked about the solidity of the new creation will also be true of God. And much more profoundly so! In the life to come, the experience of God will not be something vague. He will not be lacking in definition as He so often is for most of us now. Then He will be concrete with a solidity that will amount to tangibility. God will be the most "palpable" of all the realities in the land of the living. Such indeed is what He is: Being itself, that which is most real and also most personal. In thinking such thoughts, one sees again the inadequacy of the analogous terminology of Beatific Vision. The Vision is not something to look at, or merely a Person seen. It is a living with Someone, a precious and totally intimate awareness, a loving, fully personal relationship.

---

[42] Augustine, *Sermon on the Ascension: PLS*, 2, 494-495.

The Trinity

The relationship of the Saints with God, presently and as resurrected in the future, is a reality rooted in the Relations that constitute His existence, and from which the universe draws its being. For the Father, Son and Spirit are God Who, in His Being, Knowing and Loving is perfectly One while being uniquely differentiated. What the Blessed will experience, the One they will know and love, is so rich in being that He is integral diversity, a Trinity. Augustine writes of this the greatest of the mysteries.

> Consider the case of two men. If this is the father, that is the son. The fact that he is a man is true in relation to himself; that he is a father is true in relation to a son. The fact that the son is a man is true in respect to himself; the fact that he is a son is in relation to a father. "Father" is a word said about relation to another, and "son" about relation to another. However these are two men. But God the Father is Father in relation to another, namely the Son. God the Son is son in relation to another, namely the Father. However, as those were two men, these are not two gods. Why is this not so? Because the first case was one thing, this something else because this is divine. There is something ineffable that cannot be expressed by words, namely that there is number and there is not number. See if there does not appear to be a number: Father and Son and Holy Spirit, the Trinity. If three, then three what? Number fails. Thus God does not withdraw from number nor is He comprehended by number. Because there are three, there is number as it were; if you ask "Three what?" number does not exist. . . .
>
> When you begin to think, you begin to number; when you have counted, you are not able to say what you have counted. The Father is Father; the Son is Son; the Holy Spirit is Holy Spirit. What are these three, Father and Son and Holy Spirit? Are they three gods? No. Are they three almighties? No. Are there three creators of the world? No. But is not the Father almighty? Clearly He is almighty. Is not the Son almighty? Clearly the Son is almighty. Is not the Holy Spirit almighty? Indeed He is almighty. Therefore are there not three almighties? No, because there is only one almighty.
>
> Number insinuates itself only in respect to what they are to each other, not in what they are to themselves. Because God the Father in respect to Himself is God—as are the Son and Holy Spirit—there are not three gods; that He is almighty in respect to Himself, together with the Son and Holy Spirit, does not make three almighties. Because He is Father not in respect to

Himself, together with the Son and Holy Spirit, does not make three almighties. Because He is Father not in respect to Himself but to the Son, nor Son in respect to Himself but rather to the Father, nor Spirit in respect to Himself, but rather because He is said to be the Spirit of the Father and the Son, there is not anything I can call three except Father and Son and Holy Spirit, the One God, the One Almighty.[43]

We have seen previously the remark of Teilhard de Chardin to the effect that "unity differentiates." Perhaps only a Christian could arrive at such a conception, and do so because of the revelation of the mystery of Divinity's inner life. God is one with a simplicity in unity that nothing in creation can even approximate. Nevertheless that most simple and unmixed of unities is so wondrously rich in being that it must be, by intrinsic necessity, self-relational in such a way that it is perfectly differentiated. Knowing Him everlastingly as Father, Son and Spirit, the Elect will be fascinated by the richness of His being in a way matched only by His beauty. Seeing, they will understand but not comprehend, be satisfied but be unceasingly enticed. The intuitive, immediate vision of God will give the Saints a knowledge of Him that will enchant and entice. They will never comprehend, but they will, I think, experience a strong trace of the familiar. In fact, they may marvel that He is so simple—with the simplicity found beneath the apparent complexities of His creation. The Trinity will quite simply, without being fully comprehended, "make sense." It may sound disrespectful to say, but the very "ordinariness" of God may be the most compelling thing about Him. He just is. How could one ever hope to put into words the love that such Presence will draw forth from the Blessed!

I love You, O Lord, not with a doubting but with a sure consciousness. You have wounded my heart with Your word, and from that moment I loved You. Moreover both heaven and earth and all things that are in them cry out to me on every side that I should love You, and they do not cease to say the same to all, so that there is no excuse for any not to love you. Yet, in a higher way, "You will have mercy on whom You will have mercy," and "You will show pity to whom You will show pity" (Rom 9:15), otherwise heaven and earth speak Your praises to deaf ears.

What then is it that I love when I love You? Neither the beauty of the body nor the graceful order of time, nor the

[43] Augustine, *In Iohannis Evangelium*, 39, 4: CCSL 36, pp. 346-347.

brightness of light, so agreeable to these eyes, nor the sweet melodies of all kinds of songs, nor the fragrant scents of flowers, ointments, or spices, nor manna and honey, nor limbs agreeable to carnal embraces—none of these things do I love when I love my God. And yet when I love Him, it is true that I love a certain light and a certain voice and a certain fragrance and a certain food and a certain embrace; but they are the type that I love in my inner self, where my soul is flooded with the light that no place can contain, the sounds that no time can carry away, the scent that no current can disperse, the relish that no eating can diminish, and the embrace that no satiety can break. It is this that I love when I love my God.[44]

If that is what we love when we love our God now, with this limited and inconsistent love to which we are fated because of sin, what can be said of the life to come when nothing shall impede the perfect love of the Saints? Even then, we suspect, they shall search for analogies to put into words of praise what it is they love when they love their God. And, like Augustine, they shall find images of that Lover in what He has created and re-created for them, a universe that will then reflect Him with total clarity. They shall especially look at His greatest creation, the humanity He made for Himself. The imagination, purified and honed like all the powers of sense, will be stronger and more vivid. With both the abandon and the acuity of a poet it will be at the service of a love constantly outdoing itself in praising its Joy. In the new creation the Saints will see Him reflected, even as they understand, without the obscurity of faith, the secrets of the Incarnation. For the Divine Word will be known both in Himself and in His sacred humanity, which certain fact is further confirmation of what Augustine says when speaking of our eyes beholding Him in His creatures.

In knowing the Blessed Trinity, infinitely differentiated Unity, the Blessed shall become like Him. Their unity with the Trinity, in and through the humanity of the Word, will be such a familiarity of shared life and love that the best of earthly marriages is only a pale reflection of it. They will be one, but, in that very unity, be more themselves, more distinct, more perfectly individualized. Augustine captured that unity by saying that then "there will be one Christ loving Himself."

---

[44] Augustine, *Confessions*, bk. 10, ch. 6, trans. J.M. Lelen (New York: Catholic Book Publishing Co., 1952), pp. 234-235.

They shall sing for joy! Exultant, wordlessly and with abandon. We have from that keen observer of life a description of people at harvest, singing without words as they work.

> "Sing in jubilation!" For this is what it means to sing well for God: to sing in jubilation. What does it mean to sing in jubilation? It is to realize that one is not able to put into words what is sung in the heart. For those who sing, whether at the harvest or in the vineyard or in some other fervent work, although they will have begun to exult joyfully with the words of a song, soon turn away from the lyrics—as if, filled with so much joy, they can't express it with words—and continue with just the sound of jubilation.[45]

The above is the reading for the feast of St. Cecilia (November 22), the patroness of music. And what Augustine is speaking of we ourselves have experienced. Expanded with happiness we hum, forgetting the words of the song while we let the lilt of the music carry us along in joy. It is like certain operatic pieces (think of those of a Mozart or Verdi) where the lyrics are sheer silliness, but the music sublime. One abandons the words and simply sounds the melody. So shall it be in heaven. Bursting with joy, they shall simply resound in jubilation. Those who have sowed in tears will truly reap rejoicing. Only then shall the injunction of St. Paul be completely obeyed: "[Speak to] one another in psalms and hymns and spiritual songs, singing and playing to the Lord in your hearts" (Eph 5:19).

> God Himself will be the end of all our desires; He will be seen without end; He will be loved without satiety; He will be praised without tiring.[46]

Such lyricism will be part of the prayer of the Elect. Prayer in the life to come, of course, will be different in some ways, like everything else. There will be nothing to distract one from God since He will be always present to each. Therefore, the discipline involved in prayer now will not exist then. It is only here that we must purify the emotions, the imagination, feelings, and the senses in order to pray well. The dark nights belong to this world, not the next. In the future, the prayer of the Saints will not be hindered but helped by all that their senses convey to them.

---

[45] Augustine, *Ennarr. in Ps.* 31, Sermon 1, 8: *CCSL* 38, p. 254.
[46] Augustine, *City of God*, bk. 32, ch. 30: *CSEL* 40, 2, p. 666.

Augustine had already told his congregation about the prayer of this life: "If one does not cease living well, then one always praises God. . . . If you never fall away from a good life, then your tongue is not silent because your life cries out."[47] That will be so much more true in the world to come. Then, unlike the now of this world where it is not possible, everything will be prayer— even the delights that the senses will take in, in the restored creation.

> "Sing to the Lord a new song." The praise in singing is the very singer. Do you want to sing praise to God? Then let yourselves be what you sing! You are His praise, if you live well.[48]

In the land of the living, of course, all will live well, and the very living will be song and prayer. Nevertheless one can surmise that even in the life to come there will be periods of communal prayer, the unanimous acclamation of all those who will reside in God's own land.

> "The voice of the turtledove is heard in our land." I can no longer ignore that for a second time He, Who is from heaven, speaks of the earth: indeed He speaks of it as honorably and amiably as if He were from the earth. The Bridegroom is He Who, when He sent the flowers to appear in the land, added "*our*," and now He says, "The voice of the dove is heard in *our* land." Does God, therefore, have no purpose when He uses so unusual (lest I say unworthy) a mode of speaking? I think that you will nowhere find Him speaking this way of heaven, nowhere else this way of earth. Therefore notice with what sweetness it is that the God of heaven says, "in *our* land." "Listen, all you who dwell on earth and all you sons of men: the Lord has done wonderful things for us." He has done much for the earth and much for the bride whom He has been pleased to acquire for Himself from the earth. . . . He has made Himself as one of us. I should not say "as," but rather He has made Himself one of us. It is a little thing to be equal with men: He is a man. Therefore He claims our land as His own, but as His homeland, not as a possession. . . . As Son of Man He inherits the earth, as Lord He rules it, as Creator He administers it, as Spouse He communicates with it. By saying "In *our* land," He renounces proprietary rights but not society with it.[49]

---

[47] Augustine, *Ennarr. in Ps. 148*, 2: CCSL 40, p. 2166.

[48] Augustine, *Sermon 34*, 6: CCSL 41, p. 426.

[49] St. Bernard, *Super Cantica Canticorum: Sermo 59*, 1-2, *Opera Omnia*, vol. 2, pp. 135-136.

Bernard, faithful follower of Augustine that he was, here summarizes many of the themes that we mentioned in the Introduction. God creates, He loves what He has created, He became a human taking that material creation to Himself, becoming "one flesh" with it. This love He continues bodily in the Eucharist. But it is, as yet, a love not fully consummated. What was meant to take place in Eden is kept now for Paradise. Then in the Garden made new, with the trees of life and knowledge, with the wonders of every material and spiritual work He has ever produced, the universe's Gardener, the great Artist-Carpenter, will forever take His bride to Himself. And theirs will be the transformed, material and spiritual universe to delight in. Such is the Christian hope. It is for this we pray. In the words of Augustine's most learned disciple and ablest interpreter as he invokes the Eucharistic Christ, Who Himself taught us to pray: Thy Kingdom come, we plead:

Bone pastor, panis vere,
Iesu, nostri miserere:
Tu nos pasce, nos tuere:
Tu nos bona fac videre
In terra viventium.
Tu, qui cuncta scis et vales:
Qui nos pascis hic mortales:
Tuos ibi commensales,
Coheredes et sodales
Fac sanctorum civium.

Jesus, Good Shepherd and True Bread, have mercy on us. May You feed and protect us: May You lead us to see good things in the land of the living. You, Who know and can do all things; You Who feed us mortals now, make us banquet as coheirs and friends with You and the Saints of the Holy City.

BIBLIOGRAPHY

Bibles

The New American Bible, with revised New Testament and revised Psalms. New York: Catholic Book Pub. Co., 1992.

The New International Version. Grand Rapids, Mich.: Zondervan Bible Publishers, 1973, 1978, 1984.

The New Jerusalem Bible, Henry Wansbrough, general editor. Garden City, N.Y.: Doubleday and Co., Inc., 1985.

The New Oxford Annotated Bible with the Apocrypha. Edited by Herbert G. May and Bruce M. Metzger. New York: Oxford Univ. Press, 1977.

Nova Vulgata Bibliorum Sacrorum (New Vulgate). Rome: Libreria Editrice Vaticana, second edition, 1986.

Other Works

Aldwinckle, Russell. *Death in the Secular City,* Grand Rapids, Michigan: Eerdmans Pub. Co., 1974.

Anselm, St. *Opera Omnia,* edited by F.S. Schmitt, Edinburgh: Thomas Nelson and Sons, 1946.

Arminjon, Blaise. *The Cantata of Love.* San Francisco: Ignatius Press, 1988.

Aquinas, St. Thomas. *Super Epistolas S. Pauli Lectura.* Rome: Marietti, 1953.

———. *Super Evangelium S. Matthaei Lectura.* Rome: Marietti, 1951.

———. *Compendium of Theology,* translated by Cyril Vollert, S.J. St. Louis, Mo.: B. Herder Book Co., 1955.

339

————. *Summa Contra Gentiles,* Book Three, *Opera Omnia* (Leonine edition). Rome.

————. *Summa Theologica,* Leonine ed. Rome, 1888-1906.

————. *The Sermon-Conferences of St. Thomas Aquinas on the Apostles' Creed.* Translated from the Leonine and edited by Nicholas Ayo, C.S.C. Notre Dame, Indiana: University of Notre Dame Press, 1988. (The Latin text of the not-yet published Leonine edition of the *Collationes Super Credo in Deum* is included here.)

Balducci, Corrado. *The Devil.* Trans. by Jordan Aumann, O.P. New York: Alba House, 1990.

Barth, Karl. *Church Dogmatics.* Edinburgh: T. and T. Clark, 1963.

Bernard, St. *Opera Omnia.* J. Leclercq, C. Talbot, H. Rochais (editors). Rome: Ed. Cistercienses, 1957-1977.

Bolt, David. *Adam.* New York: John Day Co., 1960.

Boros, Ladislaus, S.J. *The Mystery of Death.* New York: Herder and Herder, 1965.

Bovone, Ratzinger, et al. *Mysterium Filii Dei: Dichiarazione e Commenti.* Vatican City: Libreria Editrice Vaticana, 1989.

Brown, Peter. *The Body and Society.* New York: Columbia Univ. Press, 1988.

CCCM (Corpus Christianorum Continuatio Mediaevalis). Turnhout, Belgium, 1953-.

CCSL (Corpus Christianorum Series Latina). Turnhout, Belgium, 1953-.

Communio: International Catholic Review, a quarterly. Notre Dame, Ind.

Cooper, John W. *Body, Soul and Life Everlasting.* Grand Rapids, Michigan: William B. Eerdmans Publ. Co., 1989.

Cornelis, H., O.P. et al. *The Resurrection of the Body.* Notre Dame, Indiana: Fides Publishers, Inc., 1964.

CSEL (Corpus Scriptorum Ecclesiasticorum Latinorum). Vienna 1865-.

Cullman, Oscar. "Immortality of the Soul Or Resurrection of the Dead" in *Immortality and Resurrection*. Krister Stendahl, editor. New York: Macmillan Co., 1965.

Crouzel, Henri. *Origen: The Life and Thought of the First Great Theologian*. New York: Harper and Row, 1989 [French, 1985].

Dante Alighieri. *The Divine Comedy*, 3 vol. Translated by Dorothy L. Sayers and Barbara Reynolds. Penguin Classics.

DeLubac, Henri. *Catholicism: Christ and the Common Destiny of Man*. San Francisco: Ignatius Press, 1988.

Dickens, Charles. *Christmas Stories*, The Oxford Illustrated Dickens. New York: Oxford Univ. Press, 1987.

Dillard, Annie. *Pilgrim at Tinker Creek*. New York: Harper and Row, 1988.

Dykmans, Marc, S.J. *Les Sermons De Jean XXII Sur la Vision Béatifique*, vol. 34 of *Miscellanea Historiae Pontificiae*. Rome: Gregorian Univ. Press, 1973.

Fortmann, Edmund J. *Life Everlasting*. New York: Alba House, 1986.

Funk, Franciscus Xaverius. *Patres Apostolici*, 2 vols. Tubingen: 1901.

Garrigou-Lagrange, R. *Life Everlasting*. St. Louis, Mo.: B. Herder Book Co., 1952.

Guardini, Romano. *Prayers From Theology*. New York: Herder and Herder, 1966.

Hawking, Stephen W. *A Brief History of Time*. New York: Bantam Book, 1988.

Hayes, Zachary. *Visions of a Future*. Wilmington, Delaware: Michael Glazier, Inc., 1989.

John Paul II. *Insegnamenti di Giovanni Paolo II*. Rome: Libreria Editrice Vaticana.

Journet, Charles. *The Meaning of Grace*. New York: P.J. Kennedy and Sons, 1960.

Kelly, J.N.D. *Early Christian Doctrines*. New York: Harper and Row, 1960.

Kilmer, Joyce. *Anthology of Catholic Poets*. New York: Image Books, Doubleday, 1955.

Konig, Adrio. *The Eclipse of Christ in Eschatology*. Grand Rapids, Michigan: William Eerdmans Pub. Co., 1989.

Kreeft, Peter. *Heaven*. San Francisco: Ignatius Press, 1989.

————. *Every Thing You Ever Wanted To Know About Heaven But Never Dreamed of Asking*. San Francisco: Ignatius Press, 1990.

Lewis, C.S. *The Great Divorce*. New York: Macmillan Publishing Co., Inc., 1946.

————. *Present Concerns* (ed. Walter Hooper). New York: Harcourt Brace Jovanovich, 1986.

Maritain, Jacques. *Existence and the Existent*. New York: Image Books, Doubleday and Co., 1957.

Martinez, Luis M. *The Sanctifier*. Boston: St. Paul Editions, 1982.

McCool, Gerald A. (editor). *A Rahner Reader*. New York: The Seabury Press, 1975.

McDannell, Colleen and Lang, Bernhard. *Heaven: A History*. New Haven and London: Yale University Press, 1988.

Meier, John P. *Matthew*. Wilmington, Delaware: Michael Glazier, Inc., 1980.

Mersch, Emile. *The Theology of the Mystical Body*. St. Louis, Mo: B. Herder Book Co., 1958.

Moltmann, Jurgen. *Theology of Hope*. New York: Harper and Row, 1967.

————. *Religion, Revolution and the Future*. New York: Charles Scribner's Sons, 1969.

Muggeridge, Malcolm. *Confessions of a Twentieth-Century Pilgrim*. San Francisco: Harper and Row, 1988.

Murphy, Marie. *New Images of The Last Things*. New York: Paulist Press, 1988. (A Study of the Theology of Rahner.)

Mysterium Salutis (Spanish edition). Madrid: Ediciones Cristiandad.

Newman, John Henry. *Parochial and Plain Sermons.* San Francisco: Ignatius Press, 1987.

Nicolas, Jean-Hervé. *Synthèse dogmatique.* Paris: Beauchesne, 1986.

O'Connor, Flannery. *The Complete Stories.* New York: Farrar, Straus and Giroux, 1972.

O'Hagan, Angelo P. *Material Re-Creation in the Apostolic Fathers.* Berlin: Academie Verlag, 1968.

Pascal, Blaise. *Pensées.* Trans. by A.J. Krailsheimer. New York: Penguin Books, 1981.

Pelikan, Jaroslav, *The Shape of Death.* Westport, Conn.: Greenwood Press, Westport, Conn., 1961.

Phan, Peter C. *Eternity in Time.* New Jersey: Susquehanna Univ. Press, 1989.

Pieper, Josef. *Death and Immortality.* New York: Herder and Herder, 1969.

PG (Patrologia Graeca). Migne, Paris. 1857-1866.

PL (Patrologia Latina). Migne, Paris. 1878-1890.

PLS (Patrologiae Cursus Completus, Series Latina). Paris, 1957-

Plato. *The Phaedo. Great Discourses of Plato.* Translated by W. H. D. Rouse. New York: Mentor Books, 1956.

Portalie, Eugene, S.J. *A Guide to the Thought of St. Augustine.* Chicago: Henry Regnery Co., 1960.

Pozo, Candido, S.J. *Teología del Más Allá.* Madrid: Biblioteca de Autores Cristianos, 1968.

Rahner, Karl. *Foundations of Christian Faith.* New York: Seabury Press, 1978.

———. *On the Theology of Death.* New York: Herder and Herder, 1963.

———. *Spirit in the World.* New York: Herder and Herder, 1968.

————. *Theological Investigations,* I. Baltimore, Md.: Helicon Press, Baltimore, 1963.

————. *Theological Investigations,* X. New York: Herder and Herder, 1973.

Ratzinger, Josef. *Dogma and Preaching.* Franciscan Herald Press, 1985.

————. *Eschatology: Death and Eternal Life.* Washington, D.C.: Catholic Univ. of America Press, 1988.

Robillard, Edmond, O.P. *Reincarnation: Illusion or Reality?* New York: Alba House, 1982.

Scheeben, M.J. *The Mysteries of Christianity.* Trans. by Cyril Vollert, S.J. St. Louis, Mo.: B. Herder Book Co., 1964.

Schillebeeckx, Edward. *Jesus.* New York: Crossroad Book, The Seabury Press, 1979.

Sorensen, Clifford Gerrit. *The Elucidarium of Honorius Augustodunensis* (a translatioin and annotation). Salt Lake City: Brigham Young University, 1979.

Tennyson, Alfred Lord. *Idylls of the King and A Selection of Poems.* New York: A Signet Classic, New American Library, 1961.

Teilhard de Chardin. *Hymn of the Universe.* Trans. by Simon Bartholomew. New York: Harper and Row, 1965.

————. *The Divine Milieu.* New York: Harper Torchbooks, Harper and Row, 1960.

————. *The Phenomenon of Man.* Trans. by Bernard Wall. New York: Harper and Brothers Pub., 1959.

————. *The Future of Man.* Trans. by Norman Denny. New York: Harper and Row, 1964.

————. *Christianity and Evolution.* Trans. by René Hague. New York: Harcourt, Brace, Jovanovich, 1969.

TPS (The Pope Speaks). A Quarterly of Papal Documents. Huntington, In.: Our Sunday Visitor Inc.

Trapé, Agostino. *Saint Augustine: Man, Pastor, Mystic.* New York: Catholic Book Publishing Co., 1986.

Troisfontaines, Roger, S.J. *I Do Not Die.* New York: Desclée Company, 1963.

Tugwell, Simon, O.P. *Human Immortality and the Redemption of Death.* Springfield, Illinois: Templegate Publishers, 1990.

Vatican Council II. *Constitutiones, Decreta, Declarationes.* Vatican City, 1966.

———. *Acta Synodalia,* 26 vol. Vatican City, 1970-1980.

Von Balthasar, Hans Urs. *Dare We Hope That All Men Be Saved?* San Francisco: Ignatius Press, 1988.

———. *The Christian State of Life.* San Francisco: Ignatius Press, 1983.

———. *Origen: Spirit and Fire.* Translated by Robert J. Daly, S.J. Washington, D.C.: Catholic University of America Press, 1984.

Vonier, Anscar, O.S.B. *The Life of the World To Come.* London: Burns Oates and Washbourne, Ltd., 1926.

———. *Death and Judgment.* New York: The Macmillan Co., 1931.

Vorgrimler, Herbert. *Commentary on the Documents of Vatican II.* New York: Herder and Herder, 5 volumes, 1969.

Winklhofer, Alois. *The Coming of His Kingdom.* New York: Herder and Herder, 1966.

Wojtyla, Karol (Pope John Paul II). *The Sign of Contradiction.* New York: Seabury Press, 1979.

———. *Collected Poems.* Translated by Jerzy Peterkiewicz. New York: Random House, 1982.

Williams, Oscar (editor). *Major British Poets.* New York: Mentor Books, 1963.

William Wordsworth: The Complete Poems, 2 volumes. John O. Hayden, editor. London and New York: Penguin Classics, 1989.

———. *The Prelude: A Parallel Text.* J.C. Maxwell, editor. London and New York: Penguin Classics, 1988.

INDEX